THE COMPLEAT TEACHER'S ALMANACK

BY DANA NEWMANN

MJF BOOKS
NEW YORK

Published by MJF Books
Fine Communications
Two Lincoln Square
60 West 66th Street
New York, NY 10023

Compleat Teacher's Almanack
ISBN 1-56731-214-4

Manufactured in the United States of America on acid-free paper

MJF Books and the MJF colophon are trademarks of Fine Creative Media, Inc.

10 9 8 7 6 5 4 3 2 1

This book is dedicated to three teachers, who made all the difference in my life:

To Mrs. Croft who read the entire 'Jungle Book' aloud to her sixth grade class — giving me the single most important educational experience of my elementary school years.

To Miss Edna Reichmuth, art teacher, whose high standards and personal attentions influenced me for the rest of my life.

To Miss Rita Newton, Asst. Professor of Education, Mills College, who showed us that originality, spirit, grace — and a certain eccentricity — must be present for extraordinary learning to take place.

I remain indebted to each of you.

D.N.

About the Author

A graduate of Mills College in Oakland, California, Dana Newmann has been an elementary teacher for more than 15 years. She has taught in California and New Mexico and for the U.S. Army Dependents Group in Hanau, Germany.

Mrs. Newmann has authored a variety of practical aids for teachers including *The New Teacher's Almanack* (The Center, 1980) and *The Early Childhood Teacher's Almanack* (The Center, 1984).

She presently lives in Santa Fe, New Mexico, where for the past six years she has worked for Project Crossroads, a nonprofit educational resource organization. Mrs. Newmann heads the elementary school program and conducts workshops for teachers throughout the state and the Southwest.

a word of introduction

This is the third edition of `The Teacher's Almanack´ and the third decade of elementary teachers it has served. The Compleat Almanack covers all 12 months, reflecting the expanded school year of many school districts today. Each month has creative original reproducible pages for classroom fun and your convenience. The basic format remains similar to that of `Poor Richard's Almanack´ of the 18th century: practical unusual ideas and information, as well as edifying historical tales and quotations. This third edition also includes information and activities to expand the environmental awareness of your students, cooperative games, and peacemaker stories to be used with these burgeoning global citizens of the 21st century!

I have again included the addresses of businesses and organizations which offer free and inexpensive learning materials; kids LOVE writing letters and receiving information/materials in response.

I have personally contacted every one of the sources noted in this book, but a WORD of CAUTION: it is only realistic to recognize that with time some of these addresses may change, some offers may be discontinued. Please point this out to your class in advance. (Any thwarted letter-writer can contact one of the always-forthcoming sources: state, national parks, Chambers of Commerce, foreign embassies, the U.S. Supt. of Documents.)

One reader kindly told me that she describes 'The Teacher's Almanack' as "the only how-to book any elementary teacher ever needs to buy." ..... I hope you'll find this Compleat Teacher's Almanack stimulating and inspiring, always there for you with a fresh idea or a new way of looking at things!

So: here's to the 90s — and to each of us who is part of the world's most important profession, this grand endeavor — TEACHING!

Dana Newmann

Contents

DECEMBER • 103

Calendar of important dates—holidays, events and famous birthdays; etymology of December; stimulating quotations for classroom use; and historical background, unique displays, information sources, and activities related to:

JANUARY • 143

Calendar of important dates—holidays, events, and famous birthdays; etymology of January; stimulating quotations for classroom use; and historical background, unique displays, information sources, and activities related to:

FEBRUARY • 177

Calendar of important dates—holidays, events, and famous birthdays; etymology of
February; stimulating quotations for the classroom use; and historical background,
unique displays, information sources, and activities related to:

MARCH • 209

Calendar of important dates—holidays, events, and famous birthdays; etymology of
March; stimulating quotations for classroom use; and historical background, unique
displays, information sources, and activities related to:

APRIL • 237

Calendar of important dates—holidays, events, and famous birthdays; etymology of April; stimulating quotations for classroom use; and historical background, unique displays, information sources, and activities related to:

MAY • 277

Calendar of important dates—holidays, events, and famous birthdays; etymology of May; stimulating quotations for classroom use; and historical background, unique displays, information sources, and activities related to:

JUNE • 307

Calendar of important dates—holidays, events, and famous birthdays; etymology of
June; stimulating quotations for classroom use; and historical background, unique
displays, information sources, and activities related to:

JULY • 329

Calendar of important dates—holidays, events, and famous birthdays; etymology of
July; stimulating quotations for classroom use; and historical background, unique
displays, information sources, and activities related to:

AUGUST • 351

Calendar of important dates—holidays, events, and famous birthdays; etymology of
August; stimulating quotations for classroom use; and historical background, unique
displays, information sources, and activities related to:

THE COMPLEAT
TEACHER'S
ALMANACK

AXIMS,

PHORISMS, AND

UOTES RELATING

TO TEACHING

Treat people as if they were what they ought to be and you help them to become what they are capable of being.

—Johann Wolfgang Goethe (1749–1832)

Children have more need to models than of critics.

—Joseph Joubert

All who have meditated on the art of governing mankind have been convinced that the fate of empires depends on the education of youth.

—Aristotle (384–322 B.C.)

Love values the effort, not the prize.

—Chinese proverb

One of the most important things a teacher can do is to send a pupil home in the afternoon liking himself just a little better than when he came in the morning.

—Dr. Ernest Melby

There is nothing in the intellect that has not been in the senses before.

—Aristotle

1

One must ask children and birds how cherries and strawberries taste.

—Johann Wolfgang Goethe

The opposite of order is not chaos. The opposite of authority is not anarchy.

—Frank Barron

. . . It is in fact nothing short of a miracle that the modern methods of instruction have not yet entirely strangled the holy curiosity of inquiry; for this delicate little plant, aside from stimulation, stands mainly in need of freedom; without this it goes to wrack and ruin without fail.

—Albert Einstein

The secret of education is respecting the pupil.

—Ralph Waldo Emerson (1803–1882)

The hated child fears nothing.

—Japanese proverb

We should abolish the required curriculum. Children want to learn about the world and grow into it; adults want to help them. Let their work together grow out of what the children need and want and what the adults have to give.

—John Holt

Do not train boys to learning by force and harshness, but lead them by what amuses them, so that they may better discover the bent of their mind.

—from *The Republic* by Plato

I would rather learn from one bird how to sing
Than teach ten thousands stars how not to dance.

—e.e. cummings

If the pupil is good, the master is praised.

—Yiddish proverb

Adults can't be bothered with what is childhood's best way of learning—through first-hand experience and through their own personal exploration. We seem more and more determined to get children who will sit, who will be quiet, who will produce . . . conform . . . give up childhood and become little adults.

—Dr. James L. Hymes,
University of Maryland

Where interest lags, memory lags too.

—Johann Wolfgang Goethe

As the twig is bent the tree inclines.

—Virgil (70–19 B.C.)

Learning is like rowing against the stream: if one does not advance, one falls right back.

—Vietnamese proverb

Where is the Life we have lost in Living?
Where is the Wisdom we have lost in Knowledge?
Where is the Knowledge we have lost in Information?

—T. S. Eliot,
The Rock

Everything is going so fast and the technology demands similarity and sameness; human beings, however, require difference. This is the source of the central pathology of our civilization.

—Tony Romeo

Everyman is worth just so much as the things are worth about which he busies himself.

—Marcus Aurelius (121–180)

Commandment Number One in any civilized society is this: Let people be different.

—David Grayson

Mushrooms scramble up in a night, but diamonds, you know, lie a long while ripening in the bed.

—Charles Lamb

Don't be apprehensive if some of your attempts seem risky. This is appropriate, since so much of life involves taking risks—for you as well as the children. That's how we grow.

—Anonymous

Jean Piaget has said that anything is only understood to the extent that it is reinvented and that every time we teach a child something we rob him of the chance to discover it.

One must learn by doing the thing; for though you think you know it, you have no certainty until you try.

—Sophocles

To gain tranquility: Be not disturbed at trifles or at accidents common or unavoidable.

—Victorian advice

The Wisdom of Nations lies in their Proverbs which are brief and pithy. Collect and learn them. You have much in little; they save time speaking; and upon occasion may be the fullest and safest answers.

Poor Richard's Almanack

Edifying quotations appear throughout *The Compleat Teacher's Almanack.* Any of these which are appropriate for your students can be clearly printed on large rectangles of paper or card stock and posted about the room. Frequent changes will be especially effective in keeping the children's attention and interest.

A Very Short History of the Calendar

Thirty dayes hath November
April, June, and September,
February hath xxviii alone,
And all the rest have xxxi.

—Richard Grafton, 1562

Early man kept track of time by counting the suns and darknesses, by tying knots in ropes, by making notches on sticks, and, eventually, by noticing the changes in the positions of the sun, moon, and stars.

Most of the holidays are in some way related to divisions of time—especially to the seasons. Primitive man celebrated the beginning of each of the four seasons; those early holidays exist today in differing forms throughout the world.

The Babylonians made the first calendar and based it on the moon, counting 12 lunar months to a year. An extra month was added about every 4 years to keep the seasons straight. The Greek, Semitic, and Egyptian peoples adopted the Babylonian calendar. Later, the Egyptians created a calendar that more nearly matched the seasons. This lunar calendar is used today by the Muslims and the Jews.

Therefore, the exact dates of the Jewish holidays vary from year to year. The Jewish calendar reckons from the year 3761 B.C., which is traditionally given as the date of the Creation. (Although most of the world now operates on a Gregorian calendar, which is a solar one, the lunar calendar is still of some contemporary significance. Your Jewish students celebrate holidays based on it.) The Jewish holidays include Rosh Hashana, Yom Kippur, Sukkoth, Hanukkah, Purim, Pesach, and Shabuoth. Each is noted in this book as it occurs during the school year.

In 46 B.C. Julius Caesar ordered a new calendar developed. This Roman calendar made use of the Egyptian year and encompassed 365¼ days, every fourth year having 366 days. There were 12 months in this calendar; Augustus and Julius Ceasar each named one for himself, each taking a day from February, making August and July months having 31 days. (A complete historical description precedes each month as it is covered in the almanack.)

In 1582, Pope Gregory XIII requested that the error in the old calendar be corrected; the resulting leap year system is still in use today. The Gregorian calendar also made January first New Year's Day.

English-speaking countries began using the Gregorian calendar in 1752 and moved the calendar up 11 days. China adopted this calendar in 1912, as Russia did in 1914, and it is the standard in use throughout the world today.

Calendars for the Classroom

Lower Grades

Stretch white oilcloth over a 2-foot-square piece of lightweight wood. Screw 35 hooks into the board through the oilcloth: five rows of seven across. Each month, use rubber cement to affix cutout paper letters in an appropriate color to the oilcloth at the top of the calendar. Keep 31 tagboard cards (each with a hole at the top to fit over a hook and each bearing a large, clear number) at the side of the calendar. Place the calendar upright in the chalk tray of the chalkboard, and each morning, hang the card, bearing that day's date, on the appropriate hook.

Middle and Upper Grades

Make a big bright pocket calendar from felt. The detachable pockets with (lightly) glued-on numerals can hold classroom reminders, children's letters to the teacher, what-to-do-in-your-free-time ideas, or riddles of the day. Attach pockets (and felt letters that spell out the name of the month) to felt backing via velcro strips. Have a student rearrange these letters and pockets to suit each new calendar month.

When presenting background information on each holiday, be careful to distinguish clearly between historical and legendary material. Make certain the children do, also. It may be pointed out to the class that holidays are observed for specific reasons: to preserve a tradition, to mark a patriotic or religious event. (Can the children think of any other reasons?)

The use of holiday themes should not dominate a teaching program to the exclusion of other meaningful themes, of course.

Be discriminating in your choice of the projects suggested here. Next year you can always try those projects which you were unable to fit into this year's schedule.

Allow the children to interpret these projects. In fact, different approaches to the same project should be encouraged whenever practical. Many times the children's variations will afford learning experiences that are especially fruitful.

SEPTEMBER

The Crow Indians called September "When the Leaves Turn Yellow." The Pawnee word for this month means "Harvest." The Yuman's name for September was *Xipa:* "Cholla Cactus Ripens When It Rains; It's Raining This Month."

Calendar of Important Dates

- Rosh Hashana, movable Jewish New Year's celebration, occurring in September or October.
- National Better Breakfast Month.
- Labor Day, the first Monday of September.
- Grandparents Day is the first Sunday after Labor Day.
- Hispanic Heritage Week begins with the second Sunday in September.
- National Dog Week, begins with the Sunday of the last full week of the month.

1   Anna Comstock, biologist, artist, and nature study pioneer, was born in 1854.

   World War II began with Germany's invasion of Poland in 1939.

2   England and her colonies adopted Gregorian calendar in 1752.

   U.S. Treasury Department was established by Congress in 1789.

3   On this day in 1895, the first professional football game was played, in Latrobe, Pennsylvania.

The U.S. *Viking II* satellite landed on the planet Mars, 1976.

4   In 518 B.C., Pindar, the greatest Greek choral lyrist, was born.

George Eastman patented the first roll-film camera and registered the brand name Kodak on this day in 1888.

5   Louis XIV, king of France, was born on this day in 1638.

In 1774, the first Continental Congress opened in Philadelphia.

John Cage, American concrete poet and composer was born in 1912.

The first color videotape recording was made on this day in 1958.

6   The first Pacific Coast colonists left New York City, 1810.

Jane Addams, pioneer social worker, was born, 1860.

7   This is the anniversary of the birth of Queen Elizabeth I of England, 1533.

8   Richard the Lionhearted, king of England, soldier, politician, lyric poet, was born in 1157.

First permanent settlement of Europeans on the North American continent: St. Augustine, Florida, was established by Spaniard Don Pedro Menendez de Aviles in 1565.

The Pledge of Allegiance was adopted in 1892.

On this day in 1974, President Gerald Ford granted former President Richard Nixon "a full, free and absolute pardon for any crimes he may have committed when he was in Office."

9   On this day in 1776, the term "United States" became official when the Second Continental Congress ruled that the words "United Colonies" would be altered for future use to the "United States."

Leo Tolstoy, great Russian writer, was born in Yasnaya Polyana in 1828.

California Admission Day commemorates the 31st state's entrance into the Union in 1850.

Mary Hunter Austin, who worked to protect deserts around the world, was born on this day in 1868.

11   On this day in 1609, Henry Hudson discovered Manhattan Island.

First artificial heart valve implant was made in 1952.

12   Elizabeth Barrett, poet, married Robert Browning, poet, against her father's will on this day in 1846.

Jesse Owens, U.S. athlete who won four gold medals at the 1936 Olympics, in Berlin, was born in 1918.

13   First National Election was authorized by U.S. Congress "to be held the first Wednesday in January next, 1789."

First U.S. auto fatality, H. H. Bliss, died in New York City in 1899.

Roald Dahl, author of such children's books as *James and the Giant Peach,* was born in 1916.

Robert Indiana, American painter, was born in 1928.

14   Alexander von Humboldt, scientist and one of the originators of the idea of modern geography, was born on this day in 1769.

Fulton tested his steamboat on the Hudson River in 1807.

Francis Scott Key wrote *The Star Spangled Banner* in 1814.

Theodore Roosevelt became our 26th president on this day in 1901 when he succeeded President William McKinley who had died of a gunshot wound he had received on September 6, 1901.

Kate Millett, American feminist, was born in 1934.

15   William Howard Taft, 27th U.S. president, was born in Cincinnati, Ohio, in 1857.

On this day in 1935, the Nazis in Germany enacted the Nuremberg Laws depriving all Jews of their citizenship, reviving ghettos, and proclaiming the swastika as the national emblem. A pogrom of violent racial and religious prosecution began.

16   On this day in 1620, the Pilgrims sailed on the *Mayflower* from Plymouth, England, to the New World.

The town of Shawmut, Massachusetts, changed its name to Boston on this day in 1630.

Cherokee Strip Day marks the opening of Oklahoma Territory to 100,000 settlers, who rushed into the strip to claim shares in the 6,000,000 acres between Oklahoma and Kansas in 1893.

First non-Indian woman to be so honored, H. M. Converse, was chosen the chief of the Six Nations Tribe on this day in 1891.

On this day in 1974, the Federal Bureau of Investigation was found guilty of perjury in the trials at Wounded Knee.

17   By presidential proclamation, Constitution Week, which includes this day, commemorates the Constitutional Convention's adoptions of the U.S. Constitution (subject to ratification by the states) in 1787.

This is Citizenship Day, which also marks the adoption of the Constitution.

18   On this day in 1634, Anne Hutchinson, one of the founders of Rhode Island, arrived in Boston.

The cornerstone of the Capitol in Washington, D.C., was laid by George Washington in 1793.

Greta Garbo, silent screen star, was born in 1905.

19   On this day in 1863, Abraham Lincoln delivered his Gettysburg Address.

Vice President Chester A. Arthur succeeded President James A. Garfield as our 21st president who died after being wounded (by a disappointed office-seeker) in a Baltimore & Ohio railroad station.

Fannie Farmer, famous American cook, was born in 1910.

First time Mickey Mouse was seen in Disney's *Steamboat Willie,* the first animated sound cartoon, in New York City in 1928.

20 Alexander the Great, military leader and world conqueror, was born on this day in 356 B.C.

Portuguese explorer Ferdinand Magellan, with five ships and 270 men, set sail under the Spanish flag on the first voyage around the world in 1519.

21 The U.S. Post Office was established in 1789.

On this day in 1792, France abolished the monarchy, replacing it with the First Republic.

President Lincoln issued the Emancipation Proclamation in 1862.*

22 On this day in 1777, Tracy Richardson, a young girl, rode her favorite horse, Fearnaught, to General George Washington's camp and warned them of the approaching British troops.

President Ford escaped 2 California assassination attempts, 1975.

23 Autumnal equinox: fall begins on or about this day.

The Lewis and Clark expedition, after 2 years, 4 months, and 10 days, completed its exploration of the West and arrived back in St. Louis, Missouri, in 1806.

On this day in 1932, Ray Charles, American singer and musician, was born, as was another American musician, singer Bruce Springsteen, in 1945.

24 F. Scott Fitzgerald, author, was born in 1896 in St. Paul, Minnesota.

First U.S. National Monument designated: Devil's Tower, Wyoming.

25 On this day in 1513, Balboa discovered the Pacific Ocean.

First American newspaper, *Publik Occurrences,* was published (on an irregular basis) in Boston, 1690.

---

*The Library of Congress (Archive of Folk Culture, Washington, DC 20540) offers *An Inventory of the Bibliographies & Other Reference & Finding Aids Prepared by the Archive of Folk Culture,* which includes "Slave Narratives," 1981.

In 1789, Congress submitted 12 constitutional amendments to the states for ratification. Ten were ratified and became the Bill of Rights.

William Faulkner, writer, was born on this day in 1897 in New Albany, Mississippi.

26   American Indian Day. (In many states, this is celebrated on the fourth Friday in September.)

John Chapman, widely known as Johnny Appleseed, was born in 1774. He spent his life planting trees and promoting wildlife conservation.

On this day in 1888, in St. Louis, Missouri, the poet-playwright T. S. Eliot was born.

In 1919, after making 40 speeches on behalf of the Treaty of Versailles, President Wilson collapsed in his private train enroute to Wichita, Kansas. He was taken back to the White House where he suffered the stroke that incapacitated him for months and from which he never recovered.

30   On this day in 1927, Babe Ruth hit his 60th homerun of the season for the New York Yankees.

Elie Wiesel, Jewish writer and Nobel Peace Prize winner in 1985, was born, in 1928.

After 3 futile phone conversations with Mississippi Governor Barnett directing him to comply with a federal court order to admit black student James Meredith to the University of Mississippi, President John Kennedy sent National Guard troops to Oxford, Mississippi, to restore order. A violent riot broke out as U.S. marshals escorted Meredith on campus. This happened in 1962.

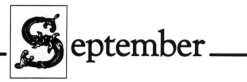

September

The early Roman calendar began with March; therefore, September was its seventh month. *Septem* = seven in Latin.

September Quotations

I quote others only the better to express myself.

—Michael Ey quem de Montaigne

Labor Day: There are three rules for happiness in Industry; these three rules are: A self-selected task, a self-created plan for doing that task, and freedom to use the plan.

—Anonymous

Only work which is a product of inner compulsion can have spiritual meaning.

—Walter Gropius

A man's work is nothing but this slow trek to rediscover, through the detours of art, those two or three great and simple images in whose presence his heart first stopped.

—Albert Camus

4   Actually I'm not all that interested in the subject of photography. Once the picture is in the box, I'm not all that interested in what happens next. Hunters, after all, usually aren't cooks.

—Henri Cartier-Bresson

5   After about an hour or so in the woods looking for mushrooms, Dad said, "Well, we can always go and buy some real ones."

Computers are always right, but life isn't about being right.

—John Cage

6   We are impatient with the schools which lay all stress on reading and writing, suspecting them to rest upon the assumption that the ordinary experience of life is worth little, and that all knowledge and interest must be brought to the children through the medium of books. Such an assumption fails to give the child any clue to the life about him, or any power to usefully or intelligently connect himself with it.

—Jane Addams (1902)

13   Voters quickly forget what a man says.

—Richard M. Nixon

It makes no difference who you vote for—the two parties are really one party representing 4% of the people.

—Gore Vidal

Bad officials are elected by good citizens who don't vote.

—George Jean Nathan

17   As soon as any man says of the affairs of state, "What does it matter to me?" the state may be given up as lost.

—Jean-Jacques Rosseau

A silent majority and government by the people is incompatible.

—Tom Hayden

21 As I would not be a slave, so I would not be a master. This expresses my idea of democracy.

—Abraham Lincoln

23 However high a tree, its leaves must still fall to the ground.

—Chinese proverb

Ten junks arrive in port, but still the dog only has its tail.

—Malay proverb

26 The savage American was conquered and subdued at the expense of the instinctive and intuitive sympathy of the human soul. The fight was too brutal.

—D. H. Lawrence

When asked by an anthropologist what the Indians called America before the white man came, an Indian answered simply, "Ours."

—Vine Deloria, Jr.

30 Americans are free . . . to disagree with the law, but not to disobey it. . . . Show that you are men of patriotism and integrity. . . . It lies in your courage to accept those laws with which you disagree as well as those with which you agree.

—John F. Kennedy,
to the people of Mississippi

September Events

Rosh Hashana

This is the 10-day period which the Jews call their high holy days as they are the most important days of the Jewish calendar. During this time, Jewish people all over the world celebrate their new year. Rosh Hashana falls at a different time each year as it is reckoned by the 5,000-year-old Jewish calendar.

According to Jewish tradition, in Heaven there is a Book of Life in which is written the fate of each person for the upcoming year. This is why many Jewish New Year's cards have a message such as, "May you be inscribed in the Book of Life for a good new year!"

During these 10 days, Jews try to make up for any wrongs they may have done. Yom Kippur is the tenth and holiest day of this period. It is a Day of Atonement and is spent in prayer and fasting.

Traditionally, slices of apple dipped in honey are served on Rosh Hashana in anticipation of sweetness for the year ahead.

Better Breakfast Month

Good nutrition must become an integral part of classroom learning every week. It is true that many people don't eat breakfast and it is simply being realistic to admit that, as a teacher, you are not in a position to monitor your students' eating patterns. But you can help the children become aware, and more conscious of, the importance of good nutrition.

A Breakfast Survey: Make copies of "The Breakfast Survey" form. Explain to the class that they are each to respond to this questionnaire by filling in the first column after each question with their own personal answers. Next, they are to take this survey out of their classroom and use it to interview three other people, family or friends, NOT classmates. And, finally, they are to bring the completed survey back to class where each of them will make a graph based on the four persons' responses on their survey.

Once these graphs are completed (with *your* help when necessary), they can be compared and the students may discuss what these graphs imply about their breakfast-eating patterns, the nutrition involved, and areas of good nutrition which they may be missing (i.e., each meal needs grain, vegetable, fruit, dairy—eggs, cheese, yogurt— and milk.) A big classroom Breakfast Graph (with *your* survey input too) could become a fine bulletin board display.

What are the 11 vitamins, their functions, sources and histories? You need wonder no longer. Write for a free vitamin chart to

Merck Sharp & Dohme
West Point, PA 19486

Labor Day [first Monday in September] ━━━━━━━━━━━━━━

Etymology: The first Monday in September is observed as "Labor's holiday" in the United States. The word "labor" comes from the Latin *laborare*, which means "to be tired." This is the day on which the workers of America are honored.

Name _____

the Breakfast Survey

	you	#1	#2	#3

1. Do you usually eat breakfast?

2. Does your breakfast have a grain in it?
   (cereal, bread)

3. Does it have milk, meat, or a dairy product?
   (eggs, yogurt, cheese)

4. Does it have fruit in it?

5. What did you have for breakfast TODAY?
   (Put a check in the square if it had: a grain, a dairy product & a fruit.)

6. Why do you think it's important to eat a good breakfast everyday?

_____
_____
_____
_____
_____

7. What is your very favorite breakfast menu? _____

_____
_____
_____
_____

Two interesting sources of labor-related educational materials are

> Communications Workers of America
> Education Department, Suite 823
> 1925 K St., NW
> Washington, DC 20006

which offers Learning About Work, a kit for discussion in the schools, two 70-slide presentations featuring over 30 different occupations, & a 28-page slide-by-slide guide, and

> The American Labor Education Center
> 1835 Kilbourne Place, NW
> Washington, DC 20010

which also has back issues of the magazine *American Labor* at a nominal charge and will send you subject guides to these if you contact the Center. Older students would find these useful for research assignments.

Grandparents' Day (first Sunday after Labor Day)

Elicit from the children a long list of ways their lives have been enriched as a consequence of having and knowing their grandparents. Talk about the ways that older people can make special contributions which younger people may not be able to make—and why. Let the children's areas of interest and their curiosity, dictate the slant of this talk (retirement communities, rest homes, wisdom, illness, patience, impatience).

Provide the materials for each child to make some special cards to send to grandparents or any much older friend. These could say, "Thank you for being my Grandpa! I love you." Or "I'm sure glad you're my Grandma!! XXOX!!" (See February valentine suggestions for card design ideas.)

U.S. Treasury Department (established, 1789) [2]*

Alexander Hamilton was the first secretary of the treasury. Today the Department of Treasury has two main functions. First, the secretary of the treasury acts as a financial advisor to the president; second, the department is responsible for tax collection, making coins and currency, and law enforcement by the U.S. Secret Service. This includes the physical protection of the president and the suppression of counterfeiting and forgery.

You can receive free information about this government department, for example, *Counterfeiting and Forgery* and *The Secret Service Story,* by writing

> Department of Treasury
> U.S. Secret Service
> 1800 G St., NW, Room 805
> Washington, DC 20223

---

*Number in brackets refers to day of month to which activity relates.

First Roll-Film Camera (patented, 1888) [4]

In 1884 George Eastman invented a machine that made photographic paper in long rolls. This made photography inexpensive and popularized the "Brownie" box camera.

The first actual photograph had been taken in 1824 by Joseph Niepce in France.

Write to the address that follows and request a list of the Kodak Customer Service Pamphlets, for example, "A-A-5, How to Make and Use a Pinhole Camera," or "AC-2, Kodak Self-Teaching Guide to Picture-Taking." Catalogs listing Kodak video programs and 16mm film slide show programs are also interesting.

Eastman Kodak Co.
Photo Information, Dept. 841
Rochester, NY 14650

Mystery Photos is a game that stimulates creative thinking and logic!

To prepare the Mystery Photo cards, go through back issues of, for example, *National Geographic, Scientific American,* and *Quest* magazines. Choose a large collection of photographs of subjects that are curious, intriguing, or emotion charged, and then carefully mount each on a colorful piece of matboard (such scraps are free from a frame shop).

To play this game, children sit so they can each clearly see the teacher who holds up a Mystery Photo card and challenges them to solve this mystery, for example, "What has happened right before this photo was taken? How can you tell?" Each solution must be substantiated by the child noting a detail, such as facial expression in a photograph. "How does this person feel and how can you tell?" "What is this person thinking?" "How does this picture make you feel?" "What time of year (day) is it?"

A simple, direct answer may be printed on the back of each card. The teacher does not give an answer, but rather after everyone with a solution has offered it, the teacher reverses the card and allows students to learn for themselves the definitive answer to this mystery card. . . . if there is one.

Occasionally show a Mystery Photo (e.g., aerial photo, enlargement of cellular structure) upside down or sideways, just to add a little extra intrigue to the game!

California Admitted to the Union (1850) [9]

California is our 31st state.

Etymology: California gets its name from the sixteenth-century fairy tale, *Las Sergas de Esplandian.* The heroine of this Spanish romance, Calafia, ruled over a fabled treasure island, California, and this name was probably applied to lower California soon after its discovery by the Spanish in 1533!

National Hispanic Week [second Sunday in September]

It isn't possible, in five school days, to deal in depth with America's Hispanic heritage. But this week can afford the beginning of a year-long awareness of the many heritages of America's people.

A classroom chart, compiled by the students and based on the one accompanying this activity, can be started this week. Additions to the chart can be made throughout the year. These could emphasize the ethnic origins of class members or of groups of people who interest the individual children and have contributed to making our country "the Great Melting Pot."

The children make the illustrations for this chart, and it can remain posted, as it develops, all year.

Here are some ways in which the people of America have influenced each other:

A. Foods we get from
   1. Native Americans—corn, squash, beans, chile, turkey
   2. Spaniards—fruit trees, spices, sugar, grains
   3. Mexicans—chocolate, tomatoes, peas, potatoes

B. Clothing we get from
   1. Native Americans—turquoise and shell bead necklaces, moccasins, leather fringe
   2. Spaniards—laces, full skirts, cowboy-style clothing
   3. Mexicans—woven serapes, rebozos, huipiles

C. Tools we get from
   1. Native Americans—pottery, baskets, hanging loom, irrigation canal system
   2. Spaniards—guns, the wheel, workhorses
   3. Mexicans—wooden ranching and farming tools

D. Architecture we get from
   1. Native Americans—adobe building bricks, vaulted horno (oven), apartment multi-dwelling buildings
   2. Spaniards—arches, ironwork on doors, windows, carved support posts, chimney construction, patios, tiles
   3. Mexicans—viga roof beams, latilla cross-lattice ceilings

E. Words we get from
   1. Native Americans—caribou, hickory, bayou, moccasins, skunk, opposum, moose, hominy, chipmunk, toboggan, raccoon, squaw, wigwam, totem, tomahawk
   2. Spaniards-Mexicans (Spanish)—patio, taco, canyon, bronco, mosquito, burro, buffalo, breeze, cockroach, siesta, tornado, vigilante, sombrero, pronto, tamale, Fritos, key, alligator

Students could also trace on a world map the routes of the Spanish people to the New World, by way of Florida, New Mexico, California, and Arizona.

Many teachers (grades 4–8) will find this catalog valuable. It offers a wealth of social studies enrichment materials, including Hispanic-related posters, sound filmstrips, books, and a video cassette, *The Ballad of Gregorio Cortez,* suitable for older students. Write, requesting the current catalog.

> Social Studies School Service
> 10200 Jefferson Blvd., Rm 16
> P.O. Box 802
> Culver City, CA 90232-0802

Birth of Jesse Owens (1913) [12] ─────────────────────

One of America's greatest track and field athletes, he set a record by running the 100-yard dash in 10 seconds—when he was still in junior high school!

As a member of the U.S. team during the 1936 Olympics in Berlin, Owens won 4 gold medals and broke 4 records! This great achievement provoked a worldwide controversy. Adolf Hitler, leader of the Nazi party in Germany, had been preaching a Nazi master race theory to the world: he claimed that blue-eyed blonds were genetically superior in all ways to dark-haired and dark-skinned people! Jesse Owens surpassed every one of the other athletes, of all skin and hair types, in four separate divisions of the Olympic games, and Hitler had to sit there and see this achievement. Rather than acknowledge these Olympic victories by Owens, a black man, Hitler walked out of the German stadium.

Jesse Owens achieved more than his four gold medals that day. His was victory over racism, and he continues to be an inspiration to all young athletes today.

Constitution Week [includes September 17, Citizenship Day] ─────────────

What was it like for the men who drew up our U.S. Constitution? During the time when our Constitution was being given its final form, there was a tense atmosphere among these delegates, and one of absolute secrecy!

The delegates met in Philadelphia behind locked doors. They each swore never to divulge what took place within those rooms. No outsiders were admitted—and this included the press!

The Constitutional Convention was called for May 14, but it wasn't until September 12, with the proceedings still secret, that the Constitution was adopted when 39 delegates signed— and 16 refused to sign.

When the Constitution was at last made public and offered to the states for ratification, only three states (Georgia, Delaware, and New Jersey) did so unanimously. Businessmen and landowners generally favored the document, but it drew strong criticism from great numbers of people. John Adams, himself, admitted that he felt our Constitution "was extorted from the grinding necessity of a reluctant people."

The Veterans of Foreign Wars offer an excellent pack of educational materials on patriotic subjects, including the U.S. Constitution, our Declaration of Independence, the U.S. flag, the Bill of Rights, the Pledge of Allegiance, and others. Single copies are free to teachers and school librarians.

> National Headquarters VFW of the USA
> Broadway at 34th St.
> Kansas City, MO 64111

First Voyage Round the World (began 1519) [20] ─────────────────

Etymology: Fernão de Magalhaes, a Portuguese navigator, and his five ships, set sail on this day in 1519. The long, hard journey was filled with bad luck. Water supplies ran low, food was infested with insects, and on the very day that Magellan, as we call him, was to discover a passage, one of his ships turned and fled back to Europe.

Magellan kept going. At last, sailing west, he entered a huge calm body of water. After months of bad seas, Magellan's men were very happy to be on calm seas at last. Magellan called the ocean El Pacífico, the peaceful one!

It wasn't until the 1800s that seamen learned that the Pacific Ocean covers one-third of the earth—it is bigger than all the land on the planet put together. The edges of this ocean are often quiet and calm, but much of it is filled with storms and huge waves. By the time this was learned, everyone had grown accustomed to calling these often wild stormy seas the Pacific Ocean.

Autumnal Equinox [22, 23]

Etymology: In the Middle Ages, seven hundred years ago, the farmers spoke Latin and they had no calendars. The year was divided into periods for their work with the earth: planting time, tilling time, harvest time. One of their expressions, seed time, passed into the French language as *seison* and later came into English as the word "season."

With the beginning of this new season, fall, discuss with the children the meaning of "equinox": equal night and day, 12 hours of night and 12 hours of day. The sun rises directly in the east and sets directly in the west; at the equator, the sun is directly overhead at 12 o'clock noon. Discuss the cause of ensuing shorter days, the process and importance of hibernation, migration, and the possible reasons that this season is sometimes called "Indian Summer." Talk together about deciduous and nondeciduous trees.

Fall Bulletin Boards

General Suggestions: Remember that a bulletin board is a learning device to reward and encourage outstanding work; it is not a decoration. Try the incorporation of eye-catching titles, lead phrases, unusual textures, photographs, and actual objects. Place (written) materials at children's eye level. Ask yourself occasionally if the displays reflect *current* interests of the children.

Mix and Match Fall Trees and Leaves

As an ongoing bulletin board display, have the children collect various fall leaves and press them between paper towel sheets under books until leaves are dry and flat. Pin these leaves at random over display area. On a sheet of brightly colored paper, print "We have these kind of trees in our town: oak, pine, maple, beech, poplar, elm, birch, willow. Now can you name all the leaves that you see here? . . . . Be **care**-ful . . . not all these trees have leaves up on this board! HINT: Seven trees have leaves here! Good luck!"

Encourage the children to use this display in their free time. After a day or two, ask them to try to identify the leaves by name; let a well-informed child act as the expert.

On the following day, pin a magazine photo (from *Natural History* or a nursery catalog) of each of the trees with a leaf/leaves on the board and change the sign to read: "NOW try matching each leaf to the tree from which it fell. Can you do it? Give it a try!"

> List those trees which your students often see in their city.

Such a bulletin board display can be reinforced by the use of one of these activities:

Nature Collection Math and Language Arts

Provide the children with a collection of identical or similar fall items (e.g., various sizes of acorns, sheep wool, seed pods, bark samples, feathers, small dried gourds). These can be stored and transported on a tray or in a shallow box.

These nature objects can be used by students for math study. For example, the children can arrange the objects into major groups of things that have qualities in common (e.g., those that are parts of plants and those that are parts of animals) into sets. Within these two sets, some objects share qualities, for example, colors, in common: brown = one subset and yellow and white = two additional subsets. Simple computation can also be shown with these natural items.

Language Arts activities include progression of size—placing items from smallest to largest; color intensity—darkest to lightest; textural identification—smooth, rough, soft, firm; and weight—heaviest to lightest.

> Any classification that children devise and can substantiate should be accepted.

Fall Reading for Young Children

Send Away Word Game: The teacher prints a fall word on the board while the class watches, for example, "leaf," and erases it almost at once. Teacher asks, "What word did I send away?" Class responds and teacher replies, "That's right, it was 'leaf.'" Other fall words include tree, bird, fly, sing, nut, red, yellow, brown, fall, cool, wind, blow, fox. Encourage children who always respond correctly to tell the class "just how they do it, how they always read and remember the words so quickly and so well." This may help peers who do not find this game easy to play—at first.

Variation: Have a student come up and, with the help of a card on which you've printed a word, write a fall word on board and then send it away; or print all of the fall words, with a few longer ones, for example, squirrel, hibernate, autumn, on board, and ask a child to come up and send away any word he or she knows. Keep these game sessions short and brisk.

Student-Generated Fall Bulletin Board.   Discuss briefly with the class the function of bulletin board displays: to engage, to educate, to entertain the viewer, but not simply to decorate a room. Then ask for volunteers who would like to design and create their own classroom bulletin board. Emphasize that all the materials—everything they find they need—will be supplied; two to four students should work well together.

Ask these students to choose a fall science topic, for example, camouflage, autumn equinox, equal day and night, endangered species, or a topic of their own choice. Then encourage creativity.

Fall Science

Touch and Know is a game that helps young children learn to discriminate between similar objects; note details.

Players are blindfolded, perhaps five at a time, and each is given a (slightly dissimilar, but of the same type) fall object—for example, a pine cone or a feather—to examine with their hands and fingers. After several minutes, you collect the objects and place them in a pile. Players remove their blindfolds. Each child tries to identify the very objects he or she held during the game.

Have the players try to explain how they finally "knew" which object was theirs. Continue game with five other players and five new objects.

> It's a Fact: Birds do not migrate in the fall in order to escape from the cold to a warmer climate. They migrate in order to eat, because their food supply disappears as the weather grows colder.

Natural Dyes

Natural dye sources include

Red: Bermuda onion skins, cherries

Pink: sassafras tea (sold in health food stores)

Yellow: onion skins, grass, leaves of pear or willow trees, petals of the marigold

Orange: sassafras roots, bark

Blue: chestnuts, red cabbage

Green: rhubard leaves, Morning Glory blossoms

    (Caution: Rhubarb leaves are poisonous if eaten.)

Purple: blackberries, elderberries

Brown: tea leaves, (unpolished) walnut shells

Black: Black Walnut leaves

(Rusty nails added to a dye will make the dye darker.)

Cut the plant desired into small pieces and place these in a pan. Add a little water (use distilled water that has no minerals in it) and boil for 5 to 20 minutes, depending on the color intensity wanted. Strain the dye through a piece of dampened cheesecloth and pour contents into a glass jar. Add a tablespoon (15 ml) vinegar to each batch of dye except that made of onion skins. Vinegar sets the color.

Children will enjoy experimenting with other plants and substances to invent their own natural dyes. Each student may produce his or her own dye chart with samples of the same yarn, fabric, or paper dyed different colors and the dye source identified next to each sample. Kids can also experiment with decorative paper dyeing by folding into a small square a piece of rice paper or newsprint and dipping the corners into dye and then refolding it in a new way and dipping it into another color of dye.

Fall Art: Leaf Prints

Fall leaves can be used to make several kinds of prints. Place leaf, vein side up, on a piece of cardboard. Lay a sheet of thin paper over leaf. Hold leaf in place as you gently but firmly rub a crayon over leaf, producing print.

Use a brayer (a print-making roller of medium hard rubber) to spread a small amount of water-base ink on a nonporous surface (Formica, glass). Next, roll this ink on the vein side of a large leaf. Lay sheet of thin paper over leaf and gently hold leaf in place as you rub the paper covering it. This rubbing may be done with your fingers, the bowl of a spoon, or another (clean) brayer. A leaf print will appear.

A multicolored autumn picture print can be obtained by older students. You will need 4 brayers, 3 (nonporous) mixing surfaces, a sheet of cardboard, large pieces of thin paper, different types and sizes of fall leaves, and 3 colors of water-base inks—red, yellow-orange, and tan—as well as cleanup materials. Apply a small amount of each ink to glass or plastic surface. Roll a brayer in one ink and apply to parts of several leaves; then arrange these on cardboard surface. Repeat this process with each of the other 2 inks. You may overlap ink colors on any single leaf if you like. Once all 5 to 10 leaves are inked and arranged (without overlapping) on the cardboard, carefully lay a large sheet of white or colored paper on top of the leaf composition. Firmly run roller over paper's surface, being careful not to move leaves. These leaf pictures can be exquisite!

Fall Games _____

Science in general emerged from a competitive culture. Most scientists are still inspired by competition or at least supported by those who are. But when you come to apply the methods of science to the special study of human behavior, the competitive spirit commits suicide. It discovers the extraordinary fact that in order to survive, we must, in the last analysis, not compete.

—B. F. Skinner, *Walden Two*

Here's a game that fosters cooperation. Play it outdoors on a pleasant fall day.

The Animal Sizes Game: Divide students into three groups of ten each. Give each child a small slip of paper on which a common animal's name is printed. The players in each group are not allowed to make a sound. By simply pantomiming their animals, the children are to arrange themselves in order from the smallest to the tallest. Once these formations (appear to) have been achieved, discuss briefly how the players were able to work together without even talking.

Variation: Again each player in each group is given the name of an animal, but this time one that makes a distinctive sound. Children arrange themselves from smallest to largest. (For an added twist, have older players wear blindfolds!??)

The Incredible Journey: This is a group activity that helps to build group spirit. (Make sure young children understand the meaning of "incredible" and "journey.") This game can be played indoors in a limited area or outside with children traveling all over the school yard. Students may play in a single line follow-the-leader fashion or spread out, responding to a leader's descriptions.

This is a journey being taken by the group. Every player pantomimes actions necessary to overcome each successive challenge; for example, "Leader" (child with creative mind) calls out, "We're walking through the forest. It's fall and the moose are migrating! Watch out! Here they come! Now we're on the bank of a swift-moving river. Wade in, but watch out for the current. . . . Look out, it's pulling us toward that waterfall!" . . . and so on. Various children may take turns adding new incredible situations. Encourage players to show lots of details in their miming. Enjoy one another's inventiveness!

The Comforter

National Dog Week [begins with the Sunday of the last full week in September]

The Animal Protection Institute of America offers brochures on dog (and cat) care and first aid for pets as well as pamphlets on whales, the harp seal, wolves, and endangered species and a children's reading list. Write, requesting the current price list of publications, to

> Animal Protection Institute of America
> 2831 Fruitridge Rd.
> P.O. Box 22505
> Sacramento, CA 95822

Dog Riddles:

1. When is a yellow dog most often going to enter a brick house? (When the door's open)
2. What is taller sitting down than standing up? (A dog)
3. When is a dog's tail not a dog's tail? (When it's a-waggin' [a wagon])

American Indian Day [26]

The American Indians are not a single people with a single way of life. This basic fact makes it difficult to teach about Native Americans in generalized terms. Each American Indian group has its own singular way of life. The Bureau of Indian Affairs recognizes 308 Indian tribes, pueblos, and groups (plus 197 Native Alaskan communities). About 250 Indian languages exist today. In 1990, there were 281 federally recognized Indian reservations in the United States.

Help the children to see beyond the usual stereotype of the American Indian dressed in feathers, riding a pinto, hunting buffalo, and living in a tepee. Start by exhibiting a U.S. map that shows the different Indian groups (for a nominal fee from the U.S. Government Printing Office), and supplement this with good slides, photographs, documented quotations, and authentic recordings. A good source of these is

U.S. Department of the Interior
Bureau of Indian Affairs (Code 130, room 4627-N)
Washington, DC 20240

Also write, requesting *American Indians Today, Answers to Your Questions,* to

Council for Indian Education
517 Rimrock Rd.
Box 31215
Billings, MT 59107

Ask, too, about their current list of books and prices.

Native American-Inspired Art Projects

Sand painting is an impressive ceremonial art. These designs, made with colored powders, are profoundly sacred and are a part of formal healing ceremonies which can be executed only by Navajo medicine men. There are a 1,000 different sand painting designs, and one medicine man may know several hundred sacred patterns. Each is directed toward the cure of a specific illness. Each detail of a painting must be executed perfectly and in a specific sequence; the slightest variation or deviation would be considered unseemly and could have serious negative consequences.

The ground, or a large skin, is smoothed, and a neutral background color is sifted onto it. The medicine man holds each colored powder in his clenched fist and builds up designs by letting the trickles of colored sand escape down the second joint of his first finger. The thumb is used to stop the sand flow. The medicine man refers to no drawing but the one he carries in his mind.

When the design is finished, the patient sits on it in order to come into direct contact with the spirits. When the ritual is completed, the sand painting is destroyed from the center out, following the order in which it was made. The powders, now contaminated by the illness they have absorbed, are carefully gathered up and removed to the north side of the medicine lodge.

> The students should understand that the sand paintings made in the classroom are simply decorative variations of a serious ceremonial art.

Young children can paint with slightly thickened poster paint directly onto squares of sandpaper, or they can use crayons on sandpaper. These drawings can then be pressed on the reverse side with a warm iron to allow the colors to bleed into one another.

Older children can dye fine builder's sand or sieved sand from a lake or river. (Sand from a seashore must be washed several times in large amounts of water and then spread out on newspapers to dry.) Mix the sand with the coloring agent in small baby food jars.

A speedy way is to half-fill baby food jars with sand. Add a few drops of food coloring. Put on jar lid and shake jar. If color is too dark, add more sand. Lay down newspapers. Draw a simple design on a piece of smooth board or tagboard. Place board on the newspapers. Start at top and apply thin coat of white glue in a small area. Cover with sand. Shake off excess and return to its jar at once. Use that color of sand everywhere else it is needed and then take a new color. Start at top of board or tagboard and repeat process until entire area is filled.

September Activities

I have observed that a Letter is never more acceptable than when received upon a rainy Day.

—Charles Lamb, September 9, 1826

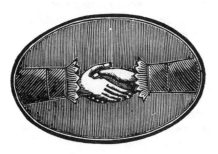

Pen-Pal Projects

This is a good time to initiate pen-pal projects. Bulletin board displays of pictures, appropriate stamps, maps, and photos can stimulate student interest in long-distance correspondence.

A permanent classroom chart might be displayed which recommends the following:

1. When writing pen-pal letters, remember to answer promptly. You'll feel most like writing on the day you receive the letter from your pen pal.
2. Write legibly. You have to keep in mind that your penmanship will be unfamiliar to your pen pal.
3. Tell all about yourself. Tell about your family, friends, school, home, hobbies, pets, favorite books, sports. Be careful not to sound as if you're boasting, be sincere about what you write; be polite.
4. Don't use slang. Kids from other places often may not be familiar with slang you use at your school.
5. Avoid controversial subjects. Don't talk about things that might make your pen pal uncomfortable, for example, comparisons of religions, political views.
6. Think about things you'd like to exchange—photos, buttons, slides, drawings, sea shells, tapes, friendship bracelets.
7. Learn your pen-pal's birthday. Be sure to send him or her a card or small gift.

You might pass out sheets of leading question suggestions to help the students with these first letters.

Here's a method you can use for becoming pen pals with another class in a different (exotic) state. Go to your (state) library reference room where the U.S. phone books are kept. Choose a phone book from a state or states that will interest your students. Look in the Yellow Pages under

Schools, Elementary, Academic, and then copy down the names and addresses of two or three (public or private) elementary schools. Next, write a brief letter addressed to the principal of the school,* stating how your class has written some stories and poems which you (have photocopied and) are enclosing in booklet form. Request that these be given to a similar grade-level class that might enjoy reading them and be interested in corresponding further with your students. Usually, that's all it takes, but don't mention anything to your class until you have a positive response (occasionally a principal will not pass on your letter, and, if this happens, simply write to a second school). Once correspondence has begun (be sure to ask and answer lots of good questions), you can exchange postcards, tapes, rocks, pressed plants, coins, stamps, local folk stories, recipes, and newspapers. Ask that the teachers also enclose printed notes telling what the children in their school are doing, saying, planning. If answers are quickly and faithfully prepared, this activity can lead to exceptional social studies enrichment and student bonding.

I Know My Home Address: This is a reproducible page for young children. Now is a fine time to have youngsters each memorize their home address and phone number (and the local emergency number, just to be extra safe).

A *Getting-to-Know-You Questionnaire* (for older students): Make copies of the questionnaire, one for each of your students. Ask them to fill them out completely (as homework for the night). Explain how their answers will help you know each of them better and will give you ideas about what you will all study this year!

Surprise them the next morning by bringing in a large newsprint copy of the questionnaire which <u>you</u> have filled out. Post it at their eye level for free-time reading!

September Talking-Head Puppets

For each puppet, you will need a flip-top hardpack cigarette box,† felt, paper, (spray) paint, yarn, scissors, markers, cloth (lace, cotton), string, rubber band, a metal or plastic ring, a cork or scrap of foamcore, glue (or a hot glue gun), and a long dowel or straight stick.

Have each child choose the character of his or her puppet and design facial features accordingly. The cigarette box has two holes made in it, top and bottom, and a rubber band knotted, inserted and knotted again.

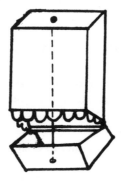

---

*Or you may address the envelope to fourth-grade class interested in being pen pals with a class in (e.g., San Francisco: substitute your own grade and city).
†Now this is an unusual example of recycling/reusing packaging!

Name _____

I Know my Home Address!

Draw a picture of YOU here:

1. The street I live on is called: _____
_____

2. The number of my house is _____ If you live
in an apartment, put its number here: _____

3. My town is called: _____

4. My whole address is: _____
_____

5. Now draw a picture of your house on your street . . . in your
town! **2**

6. This is my phone number: _____

7. If I need HELP I can call: _____

Name _____

© 1991 by The Center for Applied Research in Education

Birthday _____

Birthplace _____

Here's a Getting-to-Know-You Questionnaire!

Fill in the blanks so I can know more about you—and what you'd like to learn more about this year!

1. A movie-or video-I really liked was: _____

   I liked it because: _____

2. The best book I ever read was: _____

3. An animal I'd like to know more about is: _____

4. My favorite snack is: _____

5. I'd like to learn how to: _____

6. Somebody I really admire is: _____

7. To me a really great time is: _____

8. My fantasy is: _____

   _____

9. One thing I can't stand people to do is: _____

   _____

10. My biggest worry is: _____

11. I really love: _____

12. Not many people know this about me: _____

    _____

13. One mistake grown-ups make with kids is: _____

14. Three things that always make me MAD: _____

    _____

15. I guess I'll know I'm grown-up when: _____

_____

Box may be spray or poster painted. Eyes are circles of felt and nose can be a small cork, button, or triangle of foamcore glued in place. Teeth, hair, moustache, beard, freckles, eyebrows, lashes—any, or none, of these may be added to give the puppet personality.

A long stick is firmly glued to back of puppet's head. A metal or plastic ring is tied to one end of a long piece of string. The other end of string is tied to the outside base of knotted rubber band. The stick is held in one hand as the ring is pulled by the other, allowing the puppet to open and close its mouth as it talks.

If appropriate, two felt arms can be glued inside two small slits in cloth which in turn is glued to neck (stick) of puppet. The children will need very little practice before their talking heads begin performing!

How to Help This Be Your Best School Year EVER!

To show your new students how you appreciate them as unique individuals—and to help them bond with you right from the first day—try using some of these suggestions throughout this school year.

At appropriate moments, share details of your life with your class, e.g., speak of your family, your parents, **your** childhood, funny things you remember, an embarrassing or problem situation you experienced as a child. Bring in photographs of your younger self and examples of your hobbies, collections, or artwork. Tell them about your very favorite teacher when YOU were a child and then ask them to tell you what they believe makes a wonderful teacher (*and* a less than wonderful one).

Eventually, you might have fun composing your personal autobiography and printing up copies for interested students to read. Do invite their (written) comments, or examples of their life histories.

Show your respect for them by asking your students' input and advice concerning the daily schedule, plans, or proposed field trips. Let them rank choices for field trips. Encourage them to suggest topics for upcoming units, films, library book selections, and then DO something with this information *right away*!

Over a weekend, have interested students experiment with creating their own worksheets or review tests. (Provide them with examples of various worksheet/test formats, i.e., Mix and Match, Fill in the Blanks, Auditory instruction: "Put an X in the box on line 1," written instruction: e.g., crossword puzzles or "Cross out the word that doesn't belong.") Then use parts of these tests in class. The authors and other students will enjoy them.

Later in the year, you could ask students on Fridays to write you a short message about how this week went, what wasn't done that they'd like to have had happen, their ideas, concerns—a personal message that will never be mentioned, except to the writer, privately.

To give your students special recognition, try one, or several, of these:

(1) Keep on hand some little boxes of raisins, or bags of sunflower seeds to occasionally share with after-school helpers or to reward extra efforts.

(2) Give a student your home phone number and ask him or her to call you sometime this weekend for a little personal chat.

(3) Tape record a really personal message for a different student of your class each week.

(4) From a card and party shop, buy some self-sticking labels—the kind with peel-off backs and pretty flower borders. Print a personal message in the middle of each label, e.g., This entitles you to 10 minutes of free time whenever you'd like it!, or Special Award for Great Improvement in _____ this Week, or Outstanding Thinker, etc. Young children will enjoy wearing these badges. Be sure they understand what each sticker means.

(5) Older students may enjoy the occasional use of Student Appreciation coupons which acknowledge special efforts with small special privileges. Encourage weekly use of these ballots and share results together.

(6) When a child needs a special pick-me-up or recognition of improvement or personal effort, hide a special note in his/her desk, book or lunchbox where s/he is sure to find it unexpectedly—and soon! It might say, "When you read this, you can choose the game we play outside today!" or "You really have been working hard this week, so you get to have a little rest break for the next 15 minutes. Draw, read, or think whatever you like!"

Lastly, have fun together! Ask your class to help you plan a small surprise birthday party for your boss (their principal) or for a fellow teacher at their grade level. Encourage them to prepare the refreshments, flower arrangement and to serve the guests.

Each month, invite several children to come to your home on one Saturday night for dinner. Have them agree upon a favorite main course (often, it's pizza or spaghetti) and dessert. (Make certain every child gets the chance to come for dinner once during this year). Let the children help by setting the table, washing the salad greens or just let them relax, talk, look around while you prepare the meal for your guests. This once a month event will give you very special insights into your students, and will strengthen the rapport and affection you have, with and for, each other.

If you are happy, you can always learn to dance.

—Balinese proverb

OCTOBER

The Omaha Indians called October "When the Dear Rut." The Crow Indians refer to this month as "When the Leaves Fall." To the Pawnee Indian tribe, October, like September, is "Harvest," and the Eskimos call October "Water Freezing, Snowing."

Calendar of Important Dates

- National Newspaper Week, first or second Sunday of October.
- Fire Prevention Week, always held during the week of October 8 in memory of the Chicago Fire of 1871, which destroyed 17,430 buildings and cost $196,000,000—an amount that today would be near to a billion dollars.
- National Forest Products Week, by presidential proclamation, beginning on the third Sunday of October.

1 James Earl Carter, Jr., 39th U.S. president, was born in Plains, Georgia, in 1924.

Roger Maris hit his 61st home run of the season for the New York Yankees, a major league baseball record, 1961.

First-ever communications satellite, launched by the United States in 1960.

2 King Richard III was born at Fotheringhay, England, 1452.

Mohandas Gandhi, pacificist leader for India's independence, was born in 1869.

First black U.S. Supreme Court justice, Thurgood Marshall, was sworn in, 1967.

3   Child Health Day.*

First woman senator, Rebecca L. Felton of Georgia, was appointed to a brief term in the U.S. Senate on this day in 1922.

U.S. Navy Commander Walter Schirra, Jr., orbited the earth almost six times in the Project Mercury Capsule, 1962.

4   Rutherford B. Hayes, our 19th president, was born in Delaware, Ohio, in 1822.

Space Age began as the USSR orbited the first artificial satellite, *Sputnik,* 1957.

5   Chester A. Arthur, 21st U.S. president, was born in Fairfield, Vermont, 1830.

6   First public showing of his motion pictures by Thomas A. Edison in West Orange, New Jersey, 1889.

7   Denmark's King Christian X defied the Nazi occupiers of his country by attending a service in a synagogue in Copenhagen where he said, "If the Jews are to wear the Star of David, then we shall all wear it. You are all Danes. You are all my people."

8   First and only World Series "perfect baseball game" was pitched by Don Larsen of the New York Yankees in 1956 in a game against the Brooklyn Dodgers (final score: 2–0).

9   Leif Erickson Day commemorates landing of the Viking explorer on the North American mainland in about 1000 A.D.

10 Limited nuclear test ban treaty went into effect, 1963.

11 Parson Weems, born October 11, 1759, is remembered for the stories he made up, and people believed as truth, the most familiar of which is the story about George Washington cutting down the cherry tree with his little hatchet!

Pulaski Memorial Day, authorized by President Truman in 1946 to honor the Polish nobleman, Casimir Pulaski, who died on this day in 1779 while fighting for American independence during the Battle of Savannah, in Georgia.

---

*World Food Day is October 16. An excellent K–3 or 4–7 curriculum is produced by Church World Service/Office on Global Education with the Center for Teaching International Relations, University of Denver. Write requesting these materials: National Committee for World Food Day, 1001 22nd Street, NW, Washington, DC 20437.

Eleanor Roosevelt, U.S. diplomat, humanitarian, and first lady, was born in New York City in 1884.

12 Sighting of the New World (San Salvador, one of the eastern Bahama Islands) by Christopher Columbus on this day in 1492. Columbus Day is now observed on the second Monday of the month.

13 Molly Pitcher, heroine of the Revolutionary War, was born in Carlisle, Pennsylvania, 1754.

14 William the Conqueror, at the Battle of Hastings, conquered England for the Normans in 1066.

William Penn, founder of Pennsylvania, was born in London, 1644.

On this day in 1912, Theodore Roosevelt was shot in Milwaukee during the U.S. presidential campaign. He recovered to be elected.

Dwight D. Eisenhower, 34th U.S. president, was born in Denison, Texas, in 1890.

First live television broadcast from a spaceship in orbit: U.S. *Apollo 7,* 1968.

15 Poetry Day.

16 Queen Marie Antoinette of France was guillotined, 1793.

Noah Webster was born on this date in 1758. He created the first American edition of the dictionary.

Oscar Wilde, writer, was born in Dublin, Ireland, 1854.

On this day in 1859, Abolitionist John Brown raided Harper's Ferry, Virginia, and seized the hotel, arsenal, firehouse, and 30 citizens. His objective was to free the nation's blacks and establish them in a black republic.

Quotation of the Day: I pity the poor in bondage that have none to help them; that is why I am here, not to gratify any personal animosity, revenge or vindictive spirit.

—John Brown, at Harper's Ferry, 1859

17 A. S. Neill, educator-reformer, creator of Summerhill, an innovative British elementary school that continues to operate, was born in England, 1883.

On this day in 1933, Albert Einstein came to America as a refugee from Nazi Germany.

18 Alaska Day marks transfer of Alaskan Territory from Russia to the United States, 1867.

U.S. and Soviet satellites reached the planet Venus on this day in 1967.

U.S. Department of Health, Education, and Welfare (now the Department of Health and Human Services) stopped all use of cyclamates in foods, 1969.

19 Yorktown Day marks the surrender of Lord Cornwallis at Yorktown, Virginia, which ended the Revolutionary War in 1781.

20 On this day in 1967, Roger Patterson photographed what he alleged to be a female Sasquatch or Bigfoot, near Bluff Creek, California. This remains the clearest Bigfoot photo to date.

25 Pablo Picasso, Spanish artistic genius, was born in 1881 and lived to 1973.

26 The Erie Canal between Hudson River and Lake Erie was opened in New York State, 1825.

27 Theodore Roosevelt, 26th U.S. president, was born in New York City in 1858.

Sylvia Plath, poet and author, was born on this day in 1932.

28 On this day in 1260, Chartres Cathedral was completed in Paris.

Captain James Cook, explorer, was born in Marton Village, England, 1728.

King James III was crowned king of England, 1760.

On this day in 1886, the Statue of Liberty, a gift from the people of France, was unveiled to the American public.

29 Sir Walter Raleigh, charged with participating in a plot to oust King James I, was executed in London, 1618.

In 1929, the stock market crashed on this date and so began the worst depression in U.S. history.

On this day in 1969 the U.S. Supreme Court ordered immediate school integration.

30 John Adams, 2nd U.S. president, was born in Quincy (Braintree), Massachusetts, in 1735.

31 Halloween.

National UNICEF Day observed on behalf of United Nations Children's Fund (U.S. Committee for UNICEF, 331 E. 38th St., New York, NY 10016).

Nevada was admitted into the Union as the 36th state, 1864.

In the early Roman calendar, October was the eighth month. *Octo* = eight in Latin.

October Quotations

§   If you want to see what children can do, you must stop giving them things.

—Norman Douglas

§   Newspapers are the world's mirrors.

—James Ellis

§   Congress shall make no law abridging the freedom of speech or of the press.

—The U.S. Constitution

§   Our liberty depends on freedom of the press, and that cannot be limited without being lost.

—Thomas Jefferson

§   Eternal vigilance is the price of liberty.

—Oliver Wendell Holmes

3   With a good heredity, nature deals you a fine hand at cards; and with a good environment, you can learn to play the hand well.

—Walter C. Alvarez, M.D.

Nature requires 5
Custom allows 7
Idleness takes 9
and Wickedness, 11.

—Hours in bed, *Mother Goose*

4   Space travel is utter bilge.

—Sir Richard Vander Riet Wooley, 1956

I knew there was something in the nature of homesickness called nostalgia, but I found that there is also a homesickness for the earth. I don't know what it should be called, but it does exist. There is nothing more splendid . . . than Mother Earth on which one can stand, work, and breathe the wind off the steppes.

—Major Gherman Titov,
Soviet cosmonaut

10   All wars are civil wars, because all men are brothers . . . Each one owes infinitely more to the human race than to the particular country in which he was born.

—François Fenelon

More and more, the choice for the world's people is between becoming world warriors or world citizens.

—Norman Cousins

12   Truth is the nursing mother of genius.

—Margaret Fuller

15   Poetry comes with anger, hunger and dismay; it does not often visit groups of citizens sitting down to be literary together, and would appall them if it did.

—Christopher Morley

Even when poetry has meaning, as it usually has, it may be unadvisable to draw it out . . . . Perfect understanding will sometimes almost extinguish pleasure.

—A. E. Housman

Poetry is what Milton saw when he went blind.

—Don Marquis

16   Experience is the name everyone gives to their mistakes.

—Oscar Wilde

17   One thing I have learned in a long life: that all our science, measured against reality, is primitive and childlike—and yet it is the most precious thing we have.

—Albert Einstein

The World War after the next one will be fought with rocks.

—Albert Einstein

I live in that solitude which is painful in youth, but delicious in the years of maturity.

—Albert Einstein

Education Week—Happy is he who knows the reason for things.

—Virgil

The goal of education must be to develop a society in which people can live more comfortably with change than with rigidity. In the coming world the capacity to face the new appropriately is more important than the ability to know and repeat the old.

Better courses, better curricula, better coverage, better teaching machines, will never resolve the dilemma in a basic way. Only persons, acting like persons in their relationships with their students, can even begin to make a dent on this most urgent problem of modern education.

—Carl R. Rogers

Since we cannot know all there is to know about anything, we ought to know a little bit about everything.

—Blaise Pascal

"Why," said the Dodo, "the best way to explain it is to do it."

—Lewis Carroll,
Alice in Wonderland

24   We, the peoples of the United Nations, determined to save succeeding generations from the scourge of war, which twice in our lifetime has brought untold sorrow to mankind, and to reaffirm faith in fundamental human rights, in the dignity and worth of the human person, in the equal parts of men and women and of nations large

and small . . . and for these ends to practice tolerance and live together in peace with one another as good neighbors . . . have resolved to combine our efforts to accomplish these aims.

—Preamble to the Charter
of the United Nations

30 Yesterday, the greatest question was decided which ever was debated in America; and a greater perhaps never was, nor will be decided among men. A resolution was passed without one dissenting colony, that these United Colonies are, and of right ought to be, free, and independent States.

—John Adams in a letter
to Mrs. Adams, July 3, 1776

You are apprehensive of monarchy; I, of aristocracy. I would, therefore, have given more power to the President and less to the Senate.

—John Adams to Thomas Jefferson

October Events

National Newspaper Week [begins first or second Sunday] ————————

Students of all ages love to see their words and drawings presented in a format that their friends and families can read and enjoy. Producing a class newspaper is a terrific way to do this. It is a bonding activity that reinforces such basic skills as organizing, summarizing, lettering, measuring, and estimating.

Very young children will have fun going through a local newspaper, listing all the various elements: headlines, photographs, news stories, comics, sports, want ads, and so on. Next, each child may make a small picture of his or her favorite part of the newspaper. This drawing will be done using a black marker. Finally, each child will tell you a little about this drawing, and you will faithfully record these comments. The first edition of their classroom newspaper will be created by grouping together their art and quotations (i.e., headlines, front page stories, news, sports, comics, classified) and Xeroxing these to be folded by them and put in their lunchboxes to share at home that night.

Further issues might appear at Thanksgiving and other holiday times and could become compilations of their direct quotations, their descriptions of what is going on in school, and their small art pieces.

Classroom Newspapers for Older Students. After briefly discussing the various newspaper staff members & their duties, and after visiting a newspaper office, if at all possible, have the students each select a staff position they would like to explore. Certainly, if several want to be "the editor," discuss the role of assistant editors, that is, sports, human interest, business, entertainment. Once the managing editor is selected, let him or her lead the remainder of the organizational discussion during which the class should decide what they want their newspaper to include, for example, editorials, classified, letters to the editor, comics, advice column, political commentary, amusements (brain teasers), book of the week, science column, crossword puzzles, amazing facts, and news flashes (classroom announcements, reminders).

Job delegations may be editors, reporters, layout, advertising, photographer, political cartoonists, illustrators, copiers, collators (and staplers). Additional suggestions should help the editors to coordinate the reporting and write-ups and still meet a publication deadline. Perhaps this last can be decided at another meeting, along with a name for their newspaper.

Encourage them to look at local papers to see how important good layout can be. Have them each collect a variety of newspaper lettering and examples of various graphic techniques (montage, cross-hatching, computer-drawn illustrations). Older students can experiment with rub-on lettering (from an art store) and collage pasteups for graphic variations.

On the day that they hand out their finished publication, set aside 15 minutes for quiet—and enthusiastic—reading. Elicit positive comments about every aspect of the paper. Praise this product of cooperation.

Before work begins on the next edition, have the editor-in-chief (perhaps a new one for this new edition—have the students decide this) lead the class in a critical examination of the first issue—what do we want to keep, change, vary, introduce into our new edition? This entire activity emphasizes the value of democracy in a very concrete way.

*Mohandas (Mahatma) Gandhi [2]** —————————————————————————

A pacifist, Gandhi believed in the use of nonviolence to achieve political ends. He led India to freedom from British rule through a nonviolent revolution.

Of him Albert Einstein said, "The moral influence which Gandhi has exercised upon thinking people may be far more durable than would appear likely in our present age, with its exaggeration of brute force. We are fortunate and grateful that fate has bestowed on us so luminious a contemporary, a beacon to a generation to come."

———————————

*Number in brackets refers to day of month to which activity relates.

Two sources of peace education materials are

> The Peace Resource Center
> Pyle Center, Box 1183
> Wilmington College
> Wilmington, OH 45177

> The Institute for Peace & Justice
> 4144 Lindell Blvd., Suite 122
> St. Louis, MO 63108

Unique Peacemaker card games, that feature both historic (Gandhi, Winnemucca, Einstein, Tolstoy, etc.) and contemporary figures of both sexes as well as many nationalities and races, are available from the following address:

> Project Crossroads: Peacemaker Cards
> 3878 Old Santa Fe Trail
> Santa Fe, NM 87505

These cards can be used to play nine different games for which instructions are included. Three card sets are available: Nobel Peace Prize Winners, Women Peacemakers, and a 52-card pack, Peacemakers of the World. Card sets cost $11.95, including postage. Specify the set(s) you wish.

Child Health Day [3]

You may write the U.S. Committee for UNICEF requesting their free materials, for example, "Reaching the Children," "A Development Education Kit," and "Ethiopia, Information Kit and Guide" to learn about the state of child health in the world and what you and your class can do to help.

> U.S. Committee for UNICEF
> 331 East 38th St.
> New York, NY 10016

Fire Prevention Week [includes October 8]

The Great Chicago Fire began on October 8, 1871 when allegedly Mrs. O'Leary's cow kicked over a lantern in the barn on her property at 137 DeKoven Street. The fire swept over 21,000 acres, burned 17,000 buildings, and killed hundreds, leaving 98,000 people without homes.

Hot Tips That Can Save Your Life. Every year more than 65,000 people in America are killed or injured in fires because many of us don't know what to do in such an emergency. You can help your students become aware of these life-saving procedures:

1. Most fire deaths happen at night while people are sleeping. We lose our sense of smell when we are asleep and even in heavy smoke often will not waken if we don't hear a loud noise! This is why smoke detectors should be installed near every room where someone sleeps.

2. Draw a floor plan of your house. With bright green, mark every possible way you can get out of each room. Now take this drawing home, and at some quiet moment, talk with your parent (family) about these escape routes. Ask them to suggest a place outside your home well away from the building where you can all meet if there ever was a fire. Make sure every one of you knows and agrees on this place to meet.

3. Once you have your map drawn showing your escape ways, practice using it.

4. Also make sure you and your family all know the local emergency number (or the phone number for your fire department).

5. Always sleep with your bedroom door closed. A closed door slows down the spread of a fire, heat, and smoke. If you ever have to escape from a fire, try to always close the doors behind you as you go!

6. What exactly should you do if you are ever in a fire? Let's practice right now. The smoke detector goes off and wakes you up. The second you hear it, roll out of bed onto the floor and crawl on your hands and knees to the door. (The air near the floor is cleaner and safer to breathe!) Touch the door to see if it is hot. If it is cool, open it a crack and check for smoke. If there isn't any, crawl along your escape route. Keep your head down and crawl fast. *Don't* stop to get anything: not clothes or jewelry—nothing! Keep your head down and crawl to safety!

   If your bedroom door feels hot when you touch it, don't get excited. Keep calm. Don't open the door, but just climb out the window or use another way of leaving your bedroom. If you can't leave the room or apartment, roll up (wet) towels or clothes and stuff them along any cracks around your door to seal out the smoke. Open your window at the top and the bottom and then crouch low near the window and breathe the fresh air. If you have a phone in your room, call the fire department; give them your address and tell them exactly where you are in the building.

7. Once you are safely out of the building, go right to the place where you agreed to meet in case of such an emergency and take a head count. You should never go back into the building once you are out!

8. If you are ever in a fire, *NEVER* hide under the bed or in your closet. Crawl out to safety, or, if you can't do this, crouch by an open window until the firefighters rescue you. Never hide! You *want* to be found and *rescued!*

9. If your clothes ever catch on fire, *DO NOT RUN!* Drop to the ground and roll over and over to put out the fire.

10. Now that you and your family have a home fire escape plan and can protect yourselves in case of fire, why not tell your neighbors about it so they can be protected too!

Write, asking for any Smokey the Bear Fire Prevention Week information that may be currently available:

U.S. Forest Service
Fire and Aviation Management
P. O. Box 96090
Washington, DC 20090-6090

A Save-Our-Trees Bulletin Board

Specifically, you can order the large "What We Get from Trees" chart (#FS279) which has fascinating information but is not very interesting visually. Then you can divide this chart into 12 pieces, 1 for each group of products obtained from a tree (e.g., logs and their products, mill wastes, resins, gums, stumps, sap, cordwood and their products, and so on). Divide the class into 12 groups of two to three persons each. Ask each group to find a way to illustrate (drawings, magazine photos, actual objects, containers) each of the products on their section of the chart. Have a volunteer using tempera, paint a tall tree, the height of a classroom bulletin board, and once it is dry, carefully cut it out. This tree is pinned to the center of the bulletin board, and each category of products is neatly attached to its branches.

Columbus Day [12]

When Columbus set sail, he was not worried that his ships might fall off the edge of the world. He had read many times *Imago Mundi,* which summarized the geographical knowledge of that time and which included many demonstrations that the earth was round. What Columbus did fear was "monsters of the deep" that could destroy his ships and eat his crew members. He was also afraid that his men might run out of fresh water before they could reach the Canary Islands again.

Have students make paintings and drawings that show how the earth, sky, sea, and space might have looked if Columbus had sailed to "the edge of the world." These drawings might also include sea dragons, monsters, and fantastic marine life.

AN ASTROLABE

Early mariners, such as Columbus, had only the crudest navigational instruments. Gauging their longitude (distances east and west of Greenwich) often was left to dead reckoning, while their latitude (distance north or south of the equator) was measured by using an instrument called an astrolabe. Here's how to make a simple one:

Provide each student with a rectangular piece of corrugated cardboard that can be easily held in the hands (dimensions are unimportant), and a string plumb line. On one side of the board, draw the line C–D at right angles to the side A–B. Fasten a piece of string with a weight at one end to the board at point C.

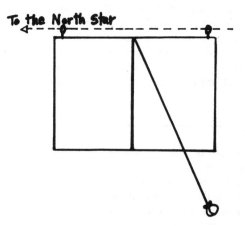

Fix a small screw eye in each end of side A–B to serve as sights. Add glue to base of eye. Acquaint students with the North Star and where it will be seen in the sky in the evenings. Ask them to each hold their astrolabe so they can see the North Star through the two sights. When they are exactly on it, they will press the plumb line tightly against the board and hold it there as the board is lowered and the string position is marked at the bottom of the board. Next, a line is drawn from C to the point. Finally the angle between C–D and C–G is measured with a protractor. The latitude of the place from which the sight was taken will be equal to the number of degrees in this angle.

It's a Fact: Columbus made four trips to the New World, and during each of these journeys, he struggled between two opposite attitudes—the two opposing strains that also appear in his name: Christ bearer (Christopher) and Colonizer (Columbus). He raised crosses everywhere he landed, and, at the same time, he saw the native peoples as goods, kidnapping them by the hundreds and sending them to Spain as slaves!

Creative Writing Idea

On his fourth and final journey to America, Columbus brought along his 13-year-old son, Fernando. They sailed from Cádiz, Spain, on May 9, 1502 with 4 ships. Young Fernando braved storms in which 2 ships were lost, mutinies, murderous natives, hunger (supplies ran out by May 13, 1503), and the deteriorating health of the captain, his father, Columbus, who often was close to insanity. Two and a half years later (November 7, 1504), Fernando, his father, and the remaining crew made it back home to Spain.

Ask the students to imagine that they each took part in this adventure. Have them write in narrative form a journal entry (or a letter to be sent back to Spain) including their observations and experiences. They might write in the voice of Fernando, Columbus, a crew member, a captive Native American, or even as a seagull wheeling over one of those Spanish vessels!

Corrected papers with colorful accompanying drawings will make a bulletin board display that many will enjoy reading. It can be titled "Come Read Voices from the PAST!" or "16th Century Adventure" or "We Were All Part of Columbus' Last Voyage!"

Poetry Day [15]

> No one spoke,
> The host, the guest,
> The white chrysanthemums.
> —Ryota

William Carlos Williams wrote poems that can be enjoyed, read, and understood by all ages of children. Obtain copies of the following poems written by Williams and share them with your class:

"This Is Just to Say"

"The Red Wheelbarrow"

"Between Walls"

"The Locust Tree in Flower"

Other works of poetry which students will enjoy include *The Serpent,* by Theodore Roethke, *The White Horse,* by D. H. Lawrence, *The Velvet Shoes,* by Einor Wylie.

Older students may be interested in learning about how a poet gets published. They can obtain "The Poet's Guide to Getting Published" by writing to:

> The American Poetry Association
> 250 A Potrero St.
> P.O. Box 1803 IN 89
> Santa Cruz, CA 95061-1803

If I keep a green bough in my heart,
The singing bird will find it.

—Chinese proverb

Birth of Noah Webster [16]

Here are two dictionary games to play with your class in celebration of the birth of this great lexicographer!

Cooperative Guide Word Game: This game is introduced only when children thoroughly understand the meaning and use of the term "guide words." Explain to your class that this is a game in which you will work together as a team so that everybody wins. If you all together succeed in scoring a certain number of points,* every player will win a little prize, for example, a small bag of corn nuts or peanuts or a card game period. If you score less than the agreed-upon number of points, you can play the game again and try harder! (A grand total of three to five games might earn "an educational video this afternoon.")

The Game: Two guide words from the dictionary page (student edition for grades 3–4) are written on the chalkboard. Each student thinks of words that fall between the guide words and therefore should be found on the given dictionary page. One or two students should stand at the board and list the words. Decide beforehand, as a class, if common variants should be listed as separate words. At the end of a given period of time, the students compare their list of words with those listed on the actual given dictionary page. One point is scored for each correct word

---

*You can ascertain the winning number of points by counting the number of common entry words (not including abbreviations, prefixes, suffixes, or foreign words) that appear on the dictionary page. Give each word entry a 5-point value and then add them all up. Subtract 10 from the total. The resultant number equals the total points your class should amass in order to win the proffered prize (e.g., *Dictionary* page 1059: guide words, "Papist" and "Parade"; total word entries, 15; $15 \times 5 = 75$ minus $10 = 65$. This is the winning number of points possible for page 1059.) You may, of course, modify this game and the point total to suit your particular group of students.

on the list. For each incorrect word, one which could not be found between the two guide words in two or three dictionaries, 2 points are subtracted.

This game can also be played with students each writing a list at their own desk and then combining the words with one another by having them written on the chalkboard at the end of the game. Competitive versions are not suggested as they promote a sense of individual failure and aren't really fair to those students who have difficulty with the written word.

Another variation: Hand out papers, at the top of which appear two guide words, each paper different from all the others. Using two guide words, individual children write down one word that would come on the page, one word before the page, and one word after the page. Example: Guide words: missile, myth; entries: mistake (on page), mark (before page) name (after page). Correct spelling earns 2 extra points. Older students could be asked to write as many entries for each of three pages concerned (on, before, after) as they can in 15 minutes. Papers are then exchanged and students correct one another's work, adding up scores: 5 points for each correct entry, 2 points for each correctly spelled word, and minus 1 point for incorrect entries. Papers are returned & students check scores for accuracy.

Etymology: The word "dictionary" comes from the Middle Latin word *dictionarium* which comes from the Latin *dicto* meaning "speaking" or "saying." The Indo-European root for diction and dictionary is *deik*, "to point out or show." Both good diction and a good dictionary point out, show, and make things more clear.

Edison Lamp Day [21]

Thomas Edison did not actually invent the lightbulb. He perfected one in 1879—50 years after Humphrey Davey produced an arc light and years after Joseph Swan made a crude lightbulb. What Edison did was spend years in research and experimentation in order to greatly improve the lightbulb by discovering a superior filament.

Older students may be interested in reading "Sylvania Presents: Light and Man" and "Saving Lighting Energy" available free from:

> GTE Lighting Products
> Sylvania Lighting Center
> Danvers, MA 01923

In science the credit goes to the (one) who convinces the world, not to the one to whom the idea first occurs.

—Sir William Osler
1849-1919

National Forest Products Week [beginning the third Sunday in October]

Project Learning Tree

The American Forest Institute and the Western Regional Environmental Education Council have collaborated to develop a project that elementary and secondary teachers could use in helping students understand their interdependence with the total forest community and develop the knowledge, skills, and commitment all citizens need if society is to use resource lands wisely for the long-term benefit of all. Based in Boulder, Colorado, this project is now available in more than 20 states (from Maine and Rhode Island to Florida, New Mexico, and California). Project Learning Tree has a helpful periodic publication, *The Branch,* and inservice workshops at which the *K–6 Supplementary Activity Guide,* an outstanding resource book, is provided at no cost to teachers. Write Project Learning Tree and request sample pages from the guide; get on their mailing list:

> Project Learning Tree
> Salina Star Route
> Boulder, CO 80302

The Forest Service (U.S. Department of Agriculture, P.O. Box 96090, Washington, DC 20090-6090) offers free materials to help you teach about forest conservation. Write, requesting their catalog (FS-28) and "Suggestions for Incorporating Forestry into the School Curriculum" (FS-62). These materials are more staid in tone than those offered by Project Learning Tree, but order them and use the most lively of the ideas suggested. Also available are "How a Tree Grows" (FS-32), "Making Paper from Trees" (FS-2) and a chart you'll need to review orally with children—"How a Tree Grows" (FS-8).

A third source of forest products information is:

> Hammermill Papers
> P. O. Box 10050
> Erie, PA 16533

This company offers "From Forest Tree to Fine Papers," which students could reinterpret graphically for a smashing wall chart, and "How to Make Paper by Hand," a classroom project for the study of papermaking, which comes with a little screen & 5 sheets of Hammermill ledger paper for use with this project.

Etymology: "Tree" is an ancient word. It comes from Middle English *tres* or *trew,* which sprang from the Anglo Saxon *treow.* The Indo-European root, *derew,* a tree, gives us many other words also: tray (from Anglo Saxon *treg,* a wooden board), trough (from Anglo Saxon *trog,* a wooden object), and the Indo-European *dru-wid,* "oak-wise, very wise," which became the Old Irish word *drui,* the Druids, a Celtic religious order of priests, poets, and soothsayers. All this variety and history from the noble "tree."

The word "field" goes back to the Anglo-Saxon *feld,* which meant a place where trees had been cut down (obviously, felled). American pioneers created an equivalent to it with the use of the word "clearing."

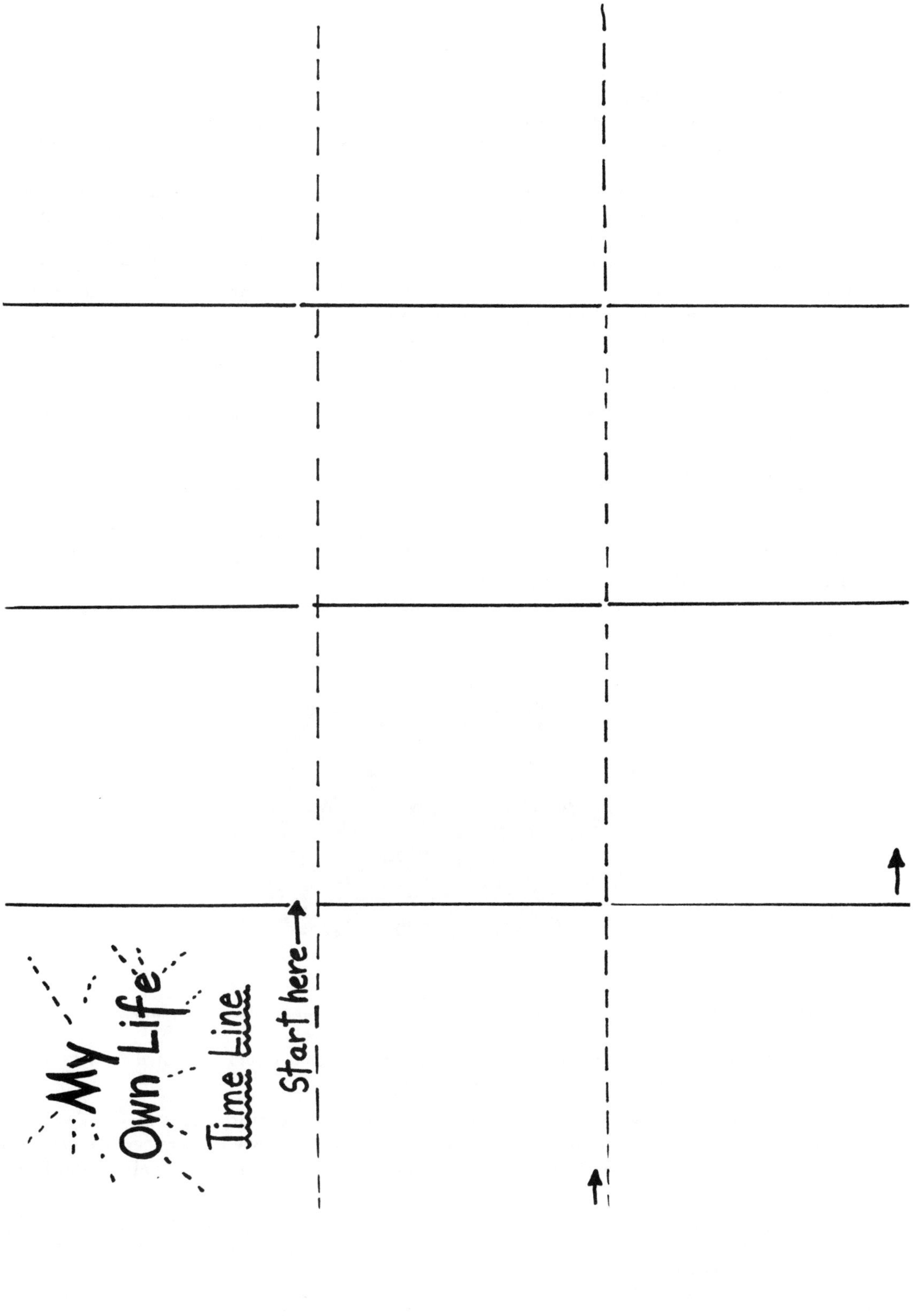

My
Own Life

Time Line

Start here →

Family Trees. Family trees trace the roots of one's family, how it has branched out over the years, and how children are the young, green leaves on these branches. Very young students will enjoy tracing their own lives back to their beginnings. The reproducible page, "My Own Life Time Line," may be introduced in this way:

Begin by saying, "A time line is a long line of pictures that shows what has happened over the years. Think about your life. Now turn your paper longwise and draw a picture of the biggest or best thing that happened to you in each of your years. Use a pencil to draw each year in the right place on your paper." (Here you may want to demonstrate with a blank sheet going from babyhood to 1 year on to 2 years, then 3 years, and so on. This is for those children who learn best by seeing, not by listening to instructions.)

"Next, color in each of your pictures. When all your pictures are colored, cut along the ——— (draw this line on board), tape the three strips together into one long strip. You've made a Time Line of Your Life—up until right now!"

These personal time lines could make a bulletin board display that everyone will "read."

United Nations Day [24]

The United Nations is an international organization formed on January 2, 1942 by the nations opposed to the fascist coalition of Germany, Japan, and Italy and their satellites. The members were committed to promote world peace and security under a permanent charter drawn up in San Francisco in 1945, and since 1946, they have had their headquarters in New York City.

Halloween [31]

Halloween is an ancient celebration, a combination of a Druid autumnal festival and a Christian feast day and dates from the seventh century.*

Etymology: There was a great deal of violence in 14th century England. Charles II organized civic watches to help protect the citizens. Each of these civic officers carried a lantern at night, and soon jokes were being made about "Jack of the Lantern." Eventually, a shortened

---

*Tactfully inquire to learn if any of your students do not celebrate Halloween for religious reasons. You will show your caring and respect for such students when you provide alternative assignments for them whenever Halloween-oriented activities are proposed.

form of the expression became popular and then began to be used to describe a child's lantern made of a hollowed-out turnip or gourd. Now linked with Halloween, this imaginary watchman has become a holiday institution.

During medieval times "Soulers" roamed the streets of English towns, praying, singing hymns, and asking for alms. In return for the money, the Soulers were to pray for the donor's relatives who might be in Purgatory. "Trick or treating" is an outgrowth of these Soulers' parades.

"Bonfire" was probably coined during the reign of Henry VIII during the time when he was rebelling against the Church. In his frustration and anger, Henry burned all the religious relics he could find in England. Many of these were "the bones of saints" and so in this practice originated the term "bonfire."

Halloween Language Arts (for young children)

Mystery Sounds Guessing Game. Listening skills can be reinforced by having the group listen to "mystery sounds." Provide a large basket of objects, each of which produces a characteristic sound (rocks, two squares of sandpaper, a comb, a large salt shaker, a hammer and board, telephone for dialing, egg-beater, etc.). Position a big cardboard box on a table at front of the class; box should have its open side away from the class, facing the front wall. Place a (pair of) sound-producing objects within the box and call a volunteer to come up to the table. Ask the class to listen to the mystery sound and try to identify its source. First, child with correct answer is asked to think of words to describe the sound (raspy, crunching, whining), and he or she gets to produce the next mysterious sound. Praise attentiveness, don't let the class see the object as it is placed in the box, and stop play while children are still enjoying it! A basket of such objects may be placed out for them to experiment with during free time. Change objects from time to time and encourage *them* to contribute things to this mystery sounds basket!

Halloween Bulletin Board

My Scary House. Very young children will benefit from being able to talk openly about personal fears. This activity helps youngsters deal with some anxieties.

Begin by discussing as a group in a circle "any things in the world that seem scary to you." Talk about scary times each of us has known. Include yourself in this discussion. Point out how fear is very helpful in that it keeps us from getting into dangerous situations. Then talk about scary things that are not real and why they can make anybody—kids or grownups—feel threatened and afraid. Now give each child a big piece of paper and have them each draw the outline of a *big* old house. Explain that they are to cut out (magazine or hand-drawn) pictures of things that make them feel afraid and then paste these inside their Scary House. Once these papers are completed, encourage the children to talk about their houses and how it feels to put those scarey things all in one place. Exhibit these collage pieces (including one of your own) at child-eye level so they may be examined and considered throughout the day.

For Older Students. Open-ended stories can provide excellent creative writing motivation. Here are two eerie Halloween story self-starters. Pass out paper to each student. Then read one of these open-ended stories aloud to the group. Get the group involved in the story and then stop at its end with a real flourish, instructing each of them to finish the story in the same style.

The Scops Eared Owl

Open-Ended Story 1. Just as I was turning to see where the voice came from, I heard the door behind me slam shut! I ran to it and tried to push it open but, of course, it was locked. Now we had to go on; we could not turn back . . . . Chris and Megan called softly to me and I groped my way toward them in the dark. "I think we can still make it if we just stick together and don't panic," Megan cautioned. "Here, let's use my belt to keep us together. We can each hold onto part of it as we walk along and even if we can't see, we can at least know where . . . ." The belt flew out of my hands as Megan's voice fell away beneath us! I fumbled in the dark for a second and then said, "Darn it! Why didn't I think of this before? Right then and there I produced . . .

Open-Ended Story 2. The hunchbacked figure beckoned to us to follow him, and we entered the castle, our teeth chattering. The hunchback turned and looked at us. He laughed softly and said, "Don't fall behind. People have gotten lost in these hallways and starved to death before they were found . . . hee-hee-hee!" He led us into a huge room where a whole tree was blazing in the fireplace. I noticed some golden eyes glowing in the far-off corner. "Don't be worried, my dear," our host assured me, "that is just Fiona and she's not one bit hungry. She ate an entire piglet just this morning." At the sound of the hunchback's voice, Fiona growled sweetly. "I will be back shortly with some hot chocolate. You warm yourselves by the fire until I return." He turned sharply, and with narrowed eyes, warned us: "But do not attempt to leave this room, my dears" . . . .

Some students may enjoy reading their endings aloud for the rest of the class to appreciate. Corrected papers could become the basis of a Halloween bulletin board.

The following lists can be used in different ways. They can be duplicated and cut crosswise into 25 strips. These are put into a large sack and drawn out by the students, who then use each slip as the basis for a creative writing assignment. Or you might supply three sacks, one for people, one for places, and one for things. The lists are copied and cut apart into 25 slips for each category. The children draw one of these slips from each sack and write a story based on the three slips drawn, or you can suggest that they trade some of their slips with friends to secure a story outline that especially interests them.

PEOPLE	PLACES	THINGS
Witchdoctor	Darkest Africa	A voodoo charm
Dracula	A castle in Transylvania	Hovering bats
Ghost	A haunted house	Rattling chains

PEOPLE	PLACES	THINGS
Vampire	A Gothic castle in ruins	Mists from the swamps
Werewolf	A graveyard	A smell of blood
Mummy	The tombs of Egypt	A smell of mold
Zombies	The cellar	Vulture and a bodyguard
Hunchback	A belfry	Deformed features
Frankenstein	A mad scientist's laboratory	Struck by lightening
Abominable Snowman	The Himalayas	A fur-covered body
Dr. Jekyll and Mr. Hyde	An English doctor's office	A cup of strange green liquid
Ghoul	A crypt	A moldy coffin
Ogre	A damp, stinking moat	Green scaly arms
Minotaur	A desert island	A labyrinth
Banshee	The windy plains	A scream that curdles your blood
Sorcerer	A castle dungeon	A crystal ball
Warlock	An altar with a fire burning	A cup of blood
Witch	A dark, windy hillside	A savage black cat

Halloween Riddles

1. Why does every friendship need the letter "R"? (Because without it, our friends would be "fiends.")
2. If you worked in a mortuary, what would you call your free time? (Coffin breaks)
3. What kind of people go to Heaven? (Dead people)
4. What holiday do vampires celebrate to show their gratitude for all the good food they've had this year? (Fangsgiving)
5. What is a vampire's favorite fruit? (Neck-tarines)
6. What does Frankenstein do on Mother's Day? (He sends a dozen roses to the Electric Company.)
7. What kind of boats do vampires like best? (Blood vessels)
8. What would you have if you crossed a Frankenstein with a Werewolf? (An electric fur coat or a pinball machine that bites!)
9. What should a person do if they're afraid of dying in bed? (Run to the *LIVING* room)
10. What's the best way to get into a locked cemetery at midnight? (Use a skeleton key)
11. What has a head like a black cat, feet like a black cat, a tail like a black cat, but *isn't* a black cat? (A black kitten)
12. What would you get if you crossed a mummy with a vampire? (Either a flying Band Aid or a gift-wrapped bat)
13. Why is the letter "E" like death? (Because it's always at the end of life)
14. What would Dracula hate to have for breakfast? (Stakes at sunrise; they're sure to give him heartburn.)
15. Why does Frankenstein love good riddles? (Because they keep him in stitches)
16. What's the difference between a cat and a comma? (One has its claws at the end of its paws and the other its pause at the end of its clause!)

Halloween Reading ━━━━━━━━━━━━━━━━━━━━━━━━━━━━━━━━━━━━

Many young students love to read "Choose Your Own Adventure" books. Here is an example of such an adventure written by a third grader. You could print out the eight pages and duplicate them to use as Halloween classroom reading.

> The
> Mystery of
> the Haunted
> House
> by
> Paul Channel

Page 1

It is summertime again, vacation time. You go to your uncle's house. He takes you on a tour around the city. There are many old buildings, but the oldest of all is on Main Street. The address is 880. He says that it is haunted, but you don't believe him.

    Choice: Do you go inside? (turn to page 2)
    Or: Do you stay there? (go to page 3)

Page 2

You say, "I will go inside." He says, "I want to watch you." You start up the stone steps of the old haunted house. You open the door and step inside and suddenly a sharp arrow streaks across in front of you! But it misses you.

    Choice: Do you go up the staircase? (turn to page 4)
    Or: Do you go through the swinging doors? (go to page 5)

Page 3

You stay there. Then you decide to go home, have an ice cream, and go to bed.

THE END

Page 4

You go up the stairs. You lean against the railing and it breaks. You fall and that's the end of you.

THE END

Page 5

You go through the swinging doors. You walk through the room.
  Choice: Do you go into the closet? (go on to page 6)
  Or: Do you go into a passageway under the house? (go to page 7)

Page 6

You go into the closet. You fall through a trapdoor and break your leg. The walls are too smooth to climb. There is no other way up.

THE END

Page 7

You go into a passageway under the house. You make your way along and it leads to a trapdoor that takes you back to where you started from. You meet a policeman at the top and he says to you, "You were lucky to get out of there. Don't ever go in there again!" You go home and have some ice cream.

THE END

Some children will want to write (or dictate to you) their own "Choose Your Own Adventure" stories. Encourage the children to share their books with each other.

Halloween Math for Young Students

Hunt the Black Cat. Number 90 tiny black cats* from one to nine (or higher). During a recess, hide these cats throughout the classroom. At a signal have the children hunt for cats. Allow 5–10 minutes for this. Then have the children return to their desks and have each add up all the numbers on the cats they found. Let the child with the highest number come up to the chalkboard and write numbers of each child's total cats in a long column on the board. Discuss how to reach a grand total. Have children attempt to find their sum. Then they find their total as a group.

The Human Skeleton. Have some math fun with "The Human Skeleton," a reproducible page.

Halloween Science

Make a classroom collection of odd found bones, cleaned chicken bones, pictures of bones (from biology and physiology textbooks), and discarded hospital X rays. Once you have these, here are some activities you can do. (The bones and list can form the basis of a fascinating Learning Center.)

---

*Have an artistic child (or you) draw 10 cats on a sheet of paper. Xerox this 9 or 10 times. Write a number (1–9) in each cat. Cut the cats apart in rectangular pieces of paper.

Name_____

The Human Skeleton: Answer the Math questions below.*

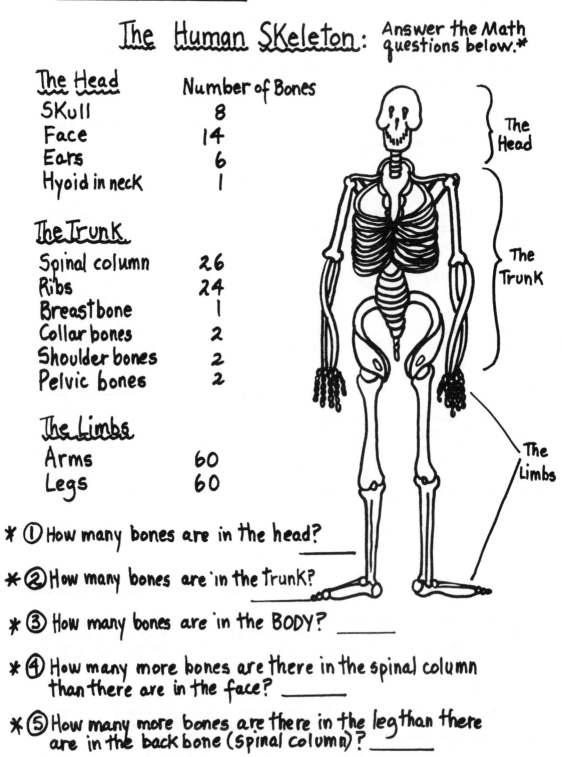

The Head	Number of Bones
Skull	8
Face	14
Ears	6
Hyoid in neck	1

The Trunk	
Spinal column	26
Ribs	24
Breastbone	1
Collar bones	2
Shoulder bones	2
Pelvic bones	2

The Limbs	
Arms	60
Legs	60

The Head

The Trunk

The Limbs

* ① How many bones are in the head? _____

* ② How many bones are in the trunk? _____

* ③ How many bones are in the BODY? _____

* ④ How many more bones are there in the spinal column than there are in the face? _____

* ⑤ How many more bones are there in the leg than there are in the back bone (spinal column)? _____

1. Sort the bones into those that are similar looking and those that seem to have served similar purposes.
2. Compare chicken bones with pictures of human bones.
3. Use airplane glue to assemble bones into a mythological creature or a dinosaur.
4. Try to find some bones that were meant to fit together.
5. Use several of the bones to measure, weigh, and compare in a chart.
6. Choose 1 bone and study it thoroughly. Now let it inspire a drawing of an entire imaginary skeleton!
7. Compare a bird bone with that of a mammal. Find 3 ways that they are alike and 3 ways in which they are different.
8. Use fine sand and a measuring cup to compare various skull capacities.
9. Think of the skull as a container beautifully suited for protection and strength. Find some examples (at home and bring to class) of manufactured containers specifically designed for strength and protection. Compare these with the skulls. Find similarities and differences.
10. Use popsicle sticks (matboard), glue, fine felt-tipped pens, thin telephone wire, the pointed end of a compass for drilling holes, sandpaper, scissors, matknife, string and straight pins to construct a model of the human skeleton.

    Use these materials to make jumping jack skeletons of other creatures:

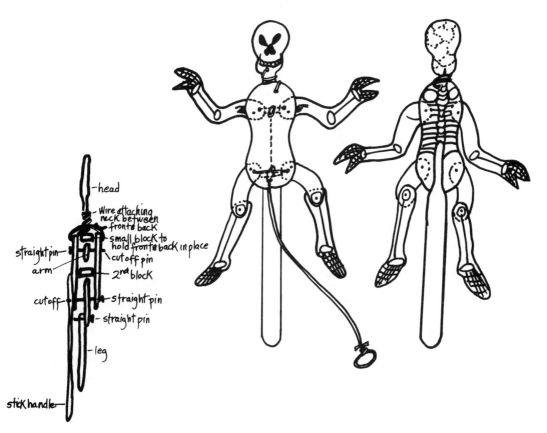

Masks

Make copies of the "Mask" pattern. Each child receives a copy of the pattern and cuts it out. The children place the pattern in the middle of colored construction paper of their choice and then trace around the pattern. The mask is cut out, and hole reinforcers are glued to the back side of each hole area.

Once glue is dry, use the hole punch to punch out paper in middle of each reinforcer. Yarn lengths (or small lengths of elastic) are tied to either side of mask, and then the mask is decorated by child, using markers to draw designs, glued-on feathers, or stars and sprinkles of glitter over lines of glue. Voilà! A mask is born!

Variation: Pieces of 8″ × 16″ colored construction paper are provided. Child traces around pattern placed in center of paper. Then child adds funny ears, moustache, and silly hair to the mask outline.

Finally mask is colored and cut out as described earlier.

Bat Mask: You will need a very lightweight paper plate, posterboard bat pattern, glue, scissors, black and red construction paper, small paper punch, yellow poster paint, brush, stapler, string, and a pencil.

Gently press plate to child's face and mark where his or her eyes are. Cut out eye holes. Have child paint plate yellow. While paint is drying, child draws or traces bat, cuts it out, and then cuts out 2 tiny red triangles for bat eyes and glues these in place. Bat is positioned on dry plate just beneath eyeholes and is then stapled in place. Two small holes, one on either side of mask, are punched and threaded with strings. Now all you need is a Polaroid of your class in their bat faces!

1. Make a painting as if your paper were the mouth of a cave. You are inside the cave where it is dark, and you look out into the light. Cobwebs or icicles or dripping moss hang down from the cave walls. What do you see out there? People, animals, a river, trees, cars, or . . . ? Paint your view from inside your cave.

MASK

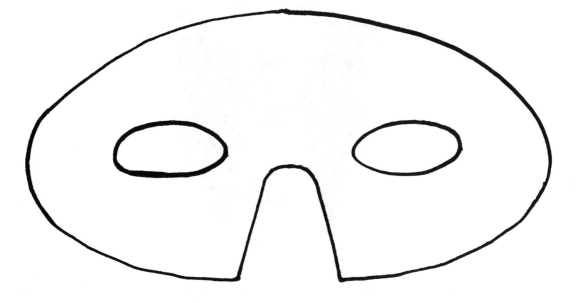

2. **Refer** to the list of spooky characters (Halloween Language Arts) and choose one to use in a handmade comic book. Show your character having adventures on October 31. This can be a co-op comic with several kids contributing to one story. Talk it over and see what you all want to do.

3. **Design** a mask that is decorated with things that can be threatening. Don't identify them until your mask is finished. Then share it with your class. Consider including scary things that aren't usually thought of as having a specific shape, for example, loneliness, rejection, loss of friends.

Halloween Puppets _____

A Peanut Puppet: You will need a popsicle stick, white glue, bit of fur, a big thin needle, thread, lightweight green, black, or red fabric scraps, black felt-tipped pen, poster paint, brush, five or 6 large peanuts in the shell, scissors, string, and a small piece of posterboard.

Thread the needle with a double thread and knot. Carefully sew the peanuts together loosely, as shown. Be careful not to break any of the peanut shells. Choose a round peanut (or cut out a small circle of posterboard) for the puppet head. Glue on cutout ear shapes, fur for hair, and paint according to the character of puppet, for example, Dracula, Batman, a skeleton, Frankenstein.

Once paint is dry, carefully attach puppet head to body. Now cut out a cape if you like, and with a running stitch, gather it to form stand-up collar. Knot sewing thread, and using white glue at neckline, attach cape to puppet's back. Finally, attach main guide string to top of puppet's head (with knotted sewing thread and 2 stitches) and then cut this string to a handy length (6 to 10 inches), and tie it to one end of popsicle stick. Once glue is dry, your peanut puppet is ready to dance, cavort, or menace—just as the puppeteer commands!

Ghost Puppet: You will need a 15-inch square of the lightest weight fabric, a small ball of cotton or fiberfill, string, 2 pebbles, thread, nylon string, and 4 small metal or plastic rings.

Place small ball of cotton in center of cloth and gather up fabric around it, tying it off to become ghost's head. Using this technique, tie one small pebble in a corner of the fabric and a second pebble in the opposing corner to form the ghost's hands. Now use the nylon thread and tie a length around the neck and another around each hand to form a 3-string marionette. Finally, tie a metal ring midway along each of the 3 strings and then join the strings together at the top with a final ring.

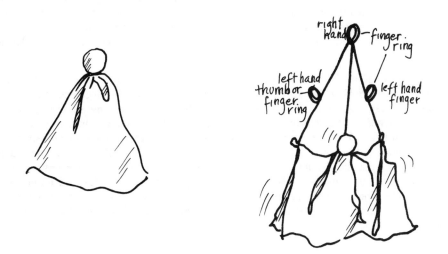

Child puts a finger in each ring while guiding puppet with the top ring. These tiny ghosts are very effective when flying along in a half-light. (Thank you, Maria!)

Encourage the children to create little dramas in which the peanut puppets and floating ghosts interact!

The Ternate Bat

Halloween Games

Witch's Shadows. This game for young children helps them to learn to pay attention. The witch walks around the room and finally touches a child on the shoulder, saying "Come along, dearie." The child follows the witch closely. Once 4 to 6 children have been chosen in this way and they form a long shadow behind the witch, she turns suddenly and claps her hands in the air! At this signal, everyone runs back to their seats, and the first child correctly seated becomes the new witch and the game continues. Of course, this game can *also* be *Warlock's Shadows* . . . .

Spider and the Flies: Two goals are marked with jump ropes at about 40 feet apart. Halfway between the goals, a 6 to 10 foot circle is drawn; it should be large enough to hold all the players when they are standing close together. A Head Fly is designated. One player, who is the spider, crouches in the middle of the circle and all the other players, the Flies, stand along the goal lines. The Flies advance and, walking, skipping, or running, move around close to the circumference of the circle. All travel in the same direction (following the movement of Head Fly). At any time the Spider may give chase to the field, tagging as many as possible before the Flies reach one of the goals. If tagged, a Fly becomes a Spider and joins the first Spider in his circle. The original Spider always gives the chasing signal, so other Spiders may not leave the circle until the signal is given. The last Fly caught becomes the Spider for the next game.

Halloween Party

Children, in committees, are encouraged to do the majority of the planning. A time schedule is set up as a guide for these committees, for example, at 2:15, recess: children will be dressing in their costumes in the restroom (supervision may be needed); at 2:30, everyone is in his seat; at 2:35, short games, a story; at 2:55, on the dot, refreshments (soft, "spooky" music may be played as a calming device); at 3:10, napkins discarded, everyone seated; at 3:15, dismissal. Clean up committee remains (to wash paint off windows).

Decorations. The classroom windows have been painted with Halloween motifs using a combination of kitchen cleanser mixed with poster paint. The cleanser facilitates window-washing on Friday afternoon. Torn tissue paper ghosts may have been lightly glued atop these paintings. Small scraggly tree branches have been suspended from light fixtures; brightly colored child made shapes (bats, owls, witches, moon) twirl on threads tied to these branches. The children can draw a large graveyard scene on the chalkboard, using only yellow and white chalks. This drawing might be done during free time on the day of the party.

Entertainment. Games should be kept fast-paced, quickly rewarding, and controlled. This helps to prevent younger children from becoming overly excited.

During the recess prior to the party, you will hide unshelled peanuts all around the room. A few of the peanuts are tied with orange and black yarn. When the children come back into the room, they each get a plastic sandwich bag and are told to look for the nuts around the room and to go and collect them. Mention that the orange and black ones are special. These are rewarded with "Casper the Ghost" comic books or "Spiderman" or "Sesame Street" which can often be purchased secondhand at thrift stores or garage sales.

Refreshments. Children can vote on the choice of food prior to their party. It need not be elaborate, because an abundance of sweets will probably be consumed that evening. Treat suggestions include hot or cold apple juice, cupcakes in which foil-wrapped fortunes and tiny prizes have been baked, caramel apples, and doughnuts with icing faces.

Two notes to the teacher: (1) Try to keep the day of the party as calming in mood, and as organized in method, as you can. (2) Bring an extra mask or two (or a bedsheet) for "that one child who couldn't have a costume this year."

Nevada Admitted to the Union (1864) [31]

Nevada is our 36th state.

Etymology: *Nevada* gets its name from a Spanish word which means "snow covered." The Spanish conquistadores first called the mountain range bordering this state the *Sierra Nevada* ("snow-clad mountains"). Nevada was named after these mountains.

October Activities

Class Pumpkins

If you are able to contact a farm produce market, you can often purchase tiny pumpkins for each youngster in your class. Then, spoon in hand, each child can carve his or her own jack o'lantern. You may slice off the tops of pumpkins with a knife, but usually the handle of the spoon can be used by each child to open the top. Newspapers are spread on each desk so that the seeds can be saved (recipe follows) and as an aid to clean up.

As the pumpkins are scooped out, discuss the layers of the shell, the way in which the pumpkin grew from a blossom, and the importance of water to the growth of pumpkins. Basic geometric shapes can be drawn on the front board so children can use them as guides when cutting features in their pumpkins. Remember to tell children to bore a small hole with a pencil in the lid of each jack o'lantern as an escape route for the candle's smoke.

Toasted Pumpkin Seeds

Thoroughly wash and clean the seeds. Drain them well on paper towels. Sprinkle the bottom of a cookie sheet with a solid layer of salt. Arrange the seeds in a single layer on the salt. Place the cookie sheet in a moderately low oven (300° F) for 40 to 45 minutes, or until the seeds are lightly browned. Allow to cool in pan.

Flower Bulbs

Now is the time to plant bulbs indoors. Hyacinth should bloom by Christmas; daffodils, tulips, and mauve crocus are also usually successful. (Yellow crocus will not bloom indoors.) Plant bulbs in special fiber purchased at a nursery or in a bulb jar (which need not be set in a dark place until roots appear and so allows class to watch bulb's growth).

Look-Ahead Chart: A Seasonal Note

Looking ahead to other holidays, you may find it useful to discuss the accompanying form with other teachers. Compare their ideas with your own. This can help you clarify your sense of the holidays and how you can most effectively integrate holiday themes into classroom learning situations.

HOLIDAY	MEANING OF HOLIDAY	HOW CHILDREN SEE IT	HOW SENSITIVE, CONCERNED TEACHERS MAY BEST PROVIDE MEANINGFUL HOLIDAY EXPERIENCE	
			In the Classroom	Suggestions to the Parents
HALLOWEEN				
THANKSGIVING				
HANUKKAH				
CHRISTMAS				

October Field Trip Suggestions

This is a great month to arrange for your class to visit a local newspaper and see the newsroom, layout area, and printing presses.

Other appropriate trips include visits to a local nursery that specializes in native plants or hybrid varieties of flowers; a hospital to tour the X-ray room, kitchen, and outpatient ward; a fire station; a pumpkin farm; a veterinarian's office (choose one who enjoys young visitors); and a cemetery that has very old gravestones for making rubbings!

Classroom visitors could include a nutritionist, a forest ranger, or a poet who understands the tastes of a young audience.

NOVEMBER

The Crow Indians call this month "When the First Snow Falls"; the Omaha Indians named it "When the Deer Shed Antlers." It is "Shamans Get Busy, Caribou Cohabit" to the Eskimos of the Aleutian Islands.

Calendar of Important Dates

- American Education Week, the week in November prior to Thanksgiving (N.E.A., 1201 Sixteenth St., NW, Washington, DC 20036).
- National Stamp Collecting Week, third Monday in November.
- Thanksgiving, the fourth Thursday of November; first celebrated by the Pilgrims in 1761.
- National Children's Book Week, dates vary (Children's Book Council, 175 Fifth Avenue, New York, NY 10010).
- Cat Week, first Sunday of November (American Feline Society, 41 Union Square, New York, NY 10003).
- Election Day the first Tuesday after the first Monday in November.

1 First weather observations made by U.S. Weather Bureau, 1870.

First barbed wire manufactured, 1873.

2   Day of the Dead: Mexican holiday for cheerfully but respectfully remembering deceased loved ones.

James Polk, 11th U.S. president, was born in Mary County, Tennessee, 1795.

Warren G. Harding, 29th U.S. president, was born in Corsica, Ohio, 1865.

North and South Dakota were admitted to the Union as 39th and 40th states, 1889.

Authors Day originated by Nellie McPherson in 1928.

First test explosion of H-bomb was held at Eniwetok, Marshall Islands, 1952.

3   First space dog, Laika, carried by Soviet spaceship *Sputnik II* was launched on this day in 1957.

First presidential election in which citizens of the District of Columbia were allowed to vote, 1964.

4   Will Rogers Day marks the birth of this cowboy humorist, in Oolagah, Oklahoma, 1879.

5   Eugene V. Debs, Socialist leader, was born in Terre Haute, Indiana, 1855.

Ida Tarbell, investigative journalist, was born in Erie County, Pennsylvania, in 1857.

First U.S. patent for an automobile was issued to George B. Seldon of Rochester, New York, 1895.

6   James Naismith, inventor of basketball, was born in Ontario, Canada, 1861.

7   On this day in 1781, the last woman was burned by the Spanish Inquisition.

Marie Curie, scientist and winner of two Nobel Prizes, was born in Warsaw, Poland, 1867.

First woman elected to the U.S. House of Representatives: Jeannette Rankin of Montana, 1916.

Revolution Day in USSR, commemorating the revolution which overthrew the czarist government, 1917.

Museum of Modern Art opened in New York City, 1929.

President Franklin D. Roosevelt was elected to a fourth term of office, 1944.

8   The Louvre, great Paris museum, whose construction began in 1204, was opened, 1793.

Hermann Rorschach, creator of psychological ink-blot tests, was born, 1884.

Montana was admitted to the Union as the 41st state, 1889.

9   The Puritans reached Cape Cod and began to explore the coast, 1620.

Moses Montefiore became England's first Jewish knight, 1837.

Anne Sexton, relentlessly honest poet, was born in Newton, Massachusetts, 1928.

Carl Sagan, popular scientist/environmentalist, born, 1934.

10 Birthdate of Mohammed, founder of Islam, 570.

Birthdate of Martin Luther, German religious reformer who began the Protestant Reformation, 1484.

The Mayflower Compact was signed on this day in 1620.

11 Veteran's Day honors all those who have served in the U.S. Armed Forces and honors the memory of those who died in wars (National Headquarters, VFW, Broadway at 34th St., Kansas City, MO 64111).

On this day Feodor Dostoevsky, great Russian writer, was born, 1821.

Washington was admitted to the United States as the 42nd state, 1889.

Kurt Vonnegut, Jr., American writer, was born, 1922.

12 Elizabeth Cady Stanton Day marks the birth of this feminist in Johnstown, New York, 1815.

13 Robert Louis Stevenson, creator of *Treasure Island,* was born in 1850.

14 Favorite Authors Day.

Claude Monet, French artist, was born in 1840.

On this day in 1889, Nellie Bly (Elizabeth Cochrane), reporter for the *New York World,* set off to outdo the feat of Jules Verne's hero in *Around the World in Eighty Days.* She did it in 72 days!

15 Georgia O'Keeffe, artist, was born in Sun Prairie, Wisconsin, 1887.

Marianne Moore, poet, was born in Kirkwood, Missouri, 1887.

W. C. Handy, American composer and "Father of the Blues" was born in 1883.

16 Oklahoma Statehood Day commemorates Oklahoma's admission to the Union as the 46th state, 1907.

17 Queen Elizabeth I succeeded to the throne of England in 1558.

First session of U.S. Congress, Washington, DC, 1790.

> Quotation of the Day: "In all my years of public life, I have never obstructed justice . . . Your President is no crook!"
> —President Richard Nixon, November 17, 1973

(Less than a year later, on August 9, 1974, President Nixon, threatened with impeachment, resigned his presidency.)

18 Antarctica discovered by U.S. Navy Captain Nathaniel Palmer, 1820.

Louis Daguerre, French inventor, who created photographs on copper plates; born, 1789.

U.S. adoption of Standard Time, 1883.

19 On this day in 1620, the *Mayflower* arrived off Cape Cod, Massachusetts.

James A. Garfield, 20th U.S. president, was born in Orange, Ohio, 1831. Abraham Lincoln delivered his Gettysburg Address, 1863.

Indira Gandhi, daughter of Nehru, and leader of India, was assassinated; she was born on this date in 1917.

20 First child, Peregrine White, a girl, was born to the Pilgrims in the New World, aboard the *Mayflower* off Cape Cod, 1620.

Senator Robert F. Kennedy was born on this day in Brookline, Massachusetts, 1925.

On this day in 1967, the population of the United States reached 200 million.

21 The Puritans put ashore at Plymouth on November 21, 1620.

North Carolina was admitted to the Union as the 12th state, 1789.

On this day in 1864, President Lincoln sent a letter of condolence to Mrs. Bixby, whose five sons were killed in the Civil War: "I pray that our Heavenly Father may assuage the anguish of your bereavement and leave you only the cherished memory of the loved and lost and the solemn pride that must be yours to have laid so costly a sacrifice upon the altar of freedom."

22   First volcanic eruption recorded in the United States: Mt. Lassen, California, 1842.

George Eliot, pen name of Mary Ann Evans, great Victorian novelist, was born on this date in 1857.

Benjamin Britten, leading British composer of the mid-twentieth century, was born, 1913.

John Fitzgerald Kennedy, our 37th president, was assassinated as he rode in a motorcade through the streets of Dallas, 1963.

On this date in 1971, Elgin Long became the first person to have flown over both the North and South poles.

23   Abigail Adams, wife and mother of U.S. presidents, was born in Weymouth, Massachusetts, in 1744.

Franklin Pierce, 14th U.S. president, was born in Hillsboro, New Hampshire, 1804.

On this day in 1938, German Jews were fined 20% of all their property to finance Hitler's government.

First fossil bones were discovered in the Antarctic, 1969.

24   Zachary Taylor, 12th U.S. president, was born in Orange County, Virginia, in 1784.

Carlo Lorenzini (nee Carlo Collodi), creator of storybook character *Pinocchio,* was born in Italy on this day in 1826.

Scott Joplin, American composer of ragtime, was born in 1868.

Women from 21 states of the Union convened in Cleveland in 1869 to organize the American Woman Suffrage Association. The chairperson was vigorous women's rights leader, Lucy Stone; the main speaker was Julia Ward Howe.

On this day in 1963, Lee Harvey Oswald, alleged assassin of President Kennedy, was murdered by Jack Ruby.

25   Indian Heritage Day.

On this day in history, Andrew Carnegie, U.S. industrialist and philanthropist, was born in 1835.

Robert Ripley, creator of *Believe It or Not,* a compendium of factual oddities of our world, was born in 1893.

Joe DiMaggio, baseball great, was born in 1914.

26   John Harvard, founder of Harvard University, in 1636, was born on this date in 1607.

On this day in 1864, Charles Dodgson sent an early Christmas gift to 12-year-old Alice Liddell. It was a handwritten story he had created for her, called "Alice's Adventures Underground." Today we know the story as *The Adventures of Alice in Wonderland* and Dodgson by his pen name, Lewis Carroll.

28   On this day in 1520, Ferdinand Magellan entered the Pacific Ocean on his way around the world, the first European to sail the Pacific from the east.

First sky-writing demonstration, New York City, 1922, by Captain Cyril Turner of the Royal Air Force, who wrote HELLO USA!

29   Ohio was admitted to the Union, as the 17th state, 1802.

Louisa May Alcott, author of *Little Women* and many other novels about young people during the Civil War years, was born in 1832.

Nellie Tayloe Ross, the first woman ever elected governor of a U.S. state (Missouri in 1924), was born on this day in 1876, as was C. S. Lewis, author of *The Lion, the Witch and the Wardrobe* fantasy, the first of seven Narnian tales, in 1898.

On this day in 1922, Lord Carnavon of England and his American assistant, Howard Carter, discovered the tomb of King Tutankhamen in Egypt.

30 On this day, Jonathan Swift, author of *Gulliver's Travels,* was born in 1667.

Mark Twain (Samuel Langhorne Clemens), author of *Tom Sawyer* and *Huckleberry Finn,* was born in 1835.

Winston Churchill, prime minister of Great Britain during World War II, was born on this date in 1874.

> Quotation of the Day: I have never accepted what many people have kindly said, namely, that I inspired the nation. It was the nation and the race that had the lion's heart. I had the luck to be called upon to give the roar.
>
> —Sir Winston Churchill on his 80th birthday

Born in 1912, Gordon Parks, black journalistic photographer.

Shirley Chisolm, the first black woman elected to Congress, born in 1924.

In 1954, on this day, in Sylacauga, Alabama, a woman was struck by a falling meteorite!

November

In the early Roman calendar, November was the ninth month. *Novem* = nine in Latin.

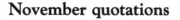

November quotations

§ Unless you plow your fields, you will have nothing to eat, and unless you read some books, your descendants will be ignorant.

—Chinese proverb

℘   Three days away from study makes for plain conversation.

—Chinese proverb

℘   What's money to a cat?

—Japanese proverb

℘   To all ye Pilgrims: Inasmuch as the great Father has given us this year an abundant harvest of Indian corn, wheat, peas, beans, squashes, and garden vegetables and has made the forests to abound with game and the sea with fish and clams . . . (on) November 29th (we shall) render Thanksgiving to Almighty God for all His blessings.

—William Bradford

2   I am a man of limited talents from a small town. I don't seem to grasp that I am President.

—Warren G. Harding

We are going to have to find ways of organizing ourselves cooperatively, sanely, scientifically, harmonically, and in regenerative spontaneity with the rest of humanity around earth . . . . We are not going to be able to operate our spaceship earth successfully nor for much longer unless we see it as a whole spaceship and our fate as common. It has to be everybody or nobody.

—Buckminster Fuller

5   While there is a lower class, I am in it; while there is a criminal element, I am of it; while there is a soul in prison, I am not free.

—Eugene Debs

7   The workers have nothing to lose in this revolution but their chains. They have a world to gain. Workers of the world, unite!

—*The Communist Manifesto*

From each according to his abilities, to each according to his needs.

—Karl Marx

Since we are destined to live out our lives in the prison of our minds, our one duty is to furnish it well.

—Peter Ustinov

Good example is one half a sermon.

—Anonymous

Now 'tis the spring and weeds are shallow-rooted;
Suffer them now and they'll o'er grow the garden.

—Shakespeare

It is not enough to be busy. So are the ants. The question is: What are we busy about?

—Henry David Thoreau

Intelligence grows in the happy mind.

—Chinese proverb

11   That which we die for lives as wholly as that which we live for dies.

—e.e. cummings

We are what we pretend to be so we should be careful about what we pretend to be.

—Kurt Vonnegut, Jr.

12 (It's odd) To think that all in me of which my father would have felt a proper pride had I been a man, is deeply mortifying to him because I am a woman.

I am weary of seeing our laboring classes wretchedly housed, fed, and clothed, while thousands of dollars are wasted every year over unsightly statues. If these great men must have their outdoor memorials, let them be in the form of handsome blocks of buildings for the poor.

—Elizabeth Cady Stanton

30 Personally I am always ready to learn, although I do not always like being taught.

—Winston Churchill

November Events

National Children's Book Week

To celebrate this week, help your class make some of these handmade books!

Handsize Books: Cut paper* into 3″ × 7″ strips. Use colored paper for cover and assemble into 10-strip stacks. These are carefully folded in half crosswise and 3 holes are meticulously punched in the middle of the fold, using a large, sharp maptack or needle. Each child is provided with a needle threaded with waxed (carpet) thread. Be sure to thread all these needles—one for each child—the night before class and have them all ready when this activity begins.

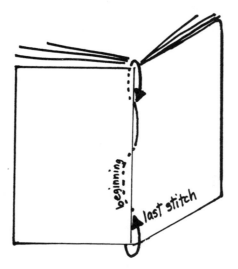

*Paper strips are free from printshops. These are many times high-quality paper, edges of large sheets, and wonderful when recycled by children into handmade books!

Each child will carefully sew the spine of his or her book in this manner. Finally, ends of thread are firmly knotted on the outside of book spine. Have the children plan out on scratch paper exactly how each page of their book will be used. This helps prevent mistakes & erasures in these charming hand-sized books.

Scratch and Sniff Sticker Books: These stickers (available at party shops) can be used throughout a child-written (dictated) tale, incorporated as part of the illustrations, or the stickers can be cut up into small pieces (for economy's sake) and used as scented highlights within the stories. Kids love writing stories that will involve six or seven scents!

One-Color Books: Help young children create entire books based on their favorite colors, for example, the cover and pages are red and the youngsters search magazines for, and make drawings of, everything they like (or can think of) that is RED. Encourage them to come up with clever cover titles & illustrations.

Hidden Pocket Books: Older students enjoy devising stories that incorporate hidden messages or tiny objects in sometimes (hard-to-find) pockets within the context of a book's story or illustrations. These books require a storyboard layout before actual book is created. Many students' creativity blossoms with this project! Let them personally share these books with a group of first or second graders.

Books with Movable Parts: Bring in several pop-up books and let interested students study them and then execute their own variations, perhaps on a large scale!

Book Reports: It's always a challenging prospect to come up with uncommon ways for students to acknowledge and celebrate books they've finished reading. Here are a few suggestions you may find helpful:

1. Have each child create a rebus for the book's title, author, and theme. These puzzle pages can be posted as a bulletin board display with the title:

2. When a student reads a how-to book, he or she might give a demonstration (cooking, craft, etc.) as if it were a TV presentation.

3. A student could choose to illustrate a book by making a filmstrip of it to be shown to the class on an overhead projector. Here's how: Provide long (4″ × 24″ or 36″) pieces

of acetate (sold at art stores). Child divides strip into 12 frames. Then the book's story is divided into ten sections. The first space on acetate contains title, author, and date of publication; the following ten sections illustrate the story; and the final frame should be a clever ending statement. Have the student experiment with felt-tipped pens, watercolors, tempera, colored pencil on frosted acetate, and so on to achieve results that please the artist.

4. Older students can pretend to ghostwrite a novel for a favorite author using the author's voice, tone, style, and subject matter as much as possible. This can be very challenging.

5. After reading a biography or a fictionalized story about a child living in America before 1900, the student is asked to answer a questionnaire, requiring that he or she compare aspects of the book character's life with his or her own. See the reproducible worksheet "Comparing _____ with You & Your Life." The resultant reports should lead students to be both introspective and empathetic. These reports can make fascinating reading.

As this is Children's Book Week, here are the addresses of several unusual sources of books which you may appreciate. Write, requesting a current catalog.

Zephyr Press
430 S. Essex Lane
Tucson, AZ 85711

Zephyr Press has very creative, engaging books for children/teachers, including books on cooperative learning, and a newsletter.

Greenhaven Press
P. O. Box 289009
San Diego, CA 92128-9009

Greenhaven's publications offer excellent social studies themes, emphasizing opposing viewpoints (grades 5 and up).

Chandler Press
P. O. Box 268
Maynard, MA 01754

Chandler Press offers unique little books from the period of 1825–1900 (20 titles, $2.50, minimum order of 12). (Go in with a friend on an order.)

Name _____

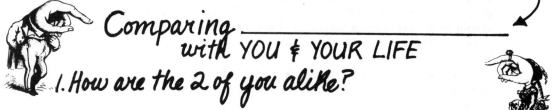

Use complete sentences to answer the questions below. Fill in the book character's name here.

Comparing _____
with YOU & YOUR LIFE

1. How are the 2 of you alike?

2. How is your life very different from theirs?

3. Would you have liked to live back then? (Tell why (not.))

4. Why would it have been fun to have known them?

5. What do you think you would have enjoyed doing together?

6. How were children long ago different from kids today?

7. How were parents different?

8. What - if anything - do you think you have given up "in exchange for the modern conveniences you have?

Cat Week [beginning with first Sunday in November]

Bulletin board suggestion: Use the basic Halloween mask idea, cited earlier, to quickly construct six or seven different sizes and colors of cats (spotted, long-haired, striped, etc.). Have students help make these. Staple them to the bulletin board.

The cats will be used on a bulletin board entitled: *This Is Cat Week. I Bet You Didn't Know These Things About Us!*

Use the cats to point up the written areas of display. Answers are discovered by lifting up balloons which are stapled or glued to background paper on which answers are written. Make certain students can reach the balloons.

How long have cats been around? "Fossils of cats have been found which are 2 million years old!"

Who had the first pet cats? "About 5,000 years ago wildcats were first tamed. The Egyptians had pet cats 4,000 years ago, but probably there were no pet cats in Europe until after 1000 A.D."

How can cats see in the dark? "In the dark the pupils in my eyes open very wide. This lets in lots of light so I'm able to see more at night than you can."

Why does a mother cat hide her babies? "Newborn kittens are helpless. Their eyes are not strong. We hide our kittens to keep them safe and to keep bright light from hurting their eyes."

City life is hard on a cat. How is it making the cat family change? "City cats are growing darker in color than cats that live outside cities. Scientists say this change is genetic*—it's evolution† at work! Cats show changes faster than people do because there are about 15 generations of cats during 1 human generation. Scientists think that city cats are getting darker because they need to keep away from many enemies (dogs, other cats, people) and darker fur helps them keep out of sight more easily."

"When did cats win a war? (Ha! I bet I got you on this one!) In 600 B.C., the Persians were trying to take the Egyptian city of Memphis. But the city walls were too thick and high and the Persians couldn't get in. In those days the Egyptians felt that cats were like gods. The Persians didn't believe this at all. So the Persians rounded up a lot of cats and began throwing them over the walls of Memphis. The Egyptians were in a panic! They couldn't stand to see their gods hurt, and although they were stronger than the Persians, the Egyptians gave up their city in order to save the cats."

First Weather Observation Made by U.S. Weather Bureau (1870) [1] ――――――

Over a century ago Congress established the Weather Bureau "to record the climate of the United States." Through the years, a group of dedicated, unpaid observers has provided climate and weather records for over 25,000 locations in America. They use instruments furnished and maintained by the National Weather Service and often continue this daily recording for 30 to 40 even 50 years!

―――――――

*(je-ne-tik) involved with the beginning of something.
†(ev-o-lu-shun) the growth or development of an animal and its family over many many long years.

It's a Fact: Mr. Edward G. Stoll of Arapahoe, Nebraska, took weather observations for 76 straight years!

Perhaps someone in your class would like to be a volunteer weather observer. If so, contact your local National Weather Service or write

> The Association of American Weather Observers
> P.O. Box 455
> Belvidere, IL 61008

A Bottle Barometer: For a simple but reliable weather forecaster, fill a glass bottle with a tapered neck half full of water. Invert a smaller bottle into the first bottle's neck. This smaller bottle should fit quite snugly into the neck of the larger bottle, and its mouth should come about an inch above the surface of the water.

Now, as the weather changes from warm to cool, differences in atmospheric pressure will make the water rise and fall inside the smaller bottle. After observing this barometer for a week or so, students will be quite able to forecast simple weather changes!

North and South Dakota Admitted to the Union (1889) [2]

North and South Dakota are our 39th and 40th states, respectively.

Etymology: The Dakotas are a group of the Siouan tribe of Native Americans who originally populated that area of the continent where these two states are located.

Montana Admitted to the Union (1889) [8]

Montana is our 41st state.

Etymology: the word *montana* is a Latin noun meaning "a mountainous area."

Elizabeth Cady Stanton Day [8] ————————————————

Born on this day in 1815, Elizabeth Cady was an intelligent young woman, but in those days college degrees were not given to women. So she studied law with her father, who was a judge. Because she was a woman, she could not get a license to practice law.

While in her father's office, she learned of the many laws and discriminations there were against women. In 1848 with her friend Lucretia Mott, she held a women's rights convention in Seneca Falls, New York. This was the beginning of our modern Women's Rights Movement.

Elizabeth Cady Stanton had great charm, wisdom, humor, and courage. She was the mother of seven children, and she successfully ran a large, loving household. All her life she worked for the emancipation of women. Today we honor her nearly 200 years after her birth.

Washington Admitted to the Union (1889) [11]

Washington is our 42nd state.

Etymology: This state with its name honors the Father of Our Country, our first president, George Washington.

Favorite Author's Day [14] ————————————————

Take the class to the library and let them look through the books until each has found a favorite (contemporary) author.* Make a list of these authors. Have them each compose a letter to their favorite writer, making sure to use correct letter form. Interesting comments about the author's work, questions, a drawing, or a photo could be included.

You can secure the addresses of writers by finding the author in *Current Biography* (addresses follow each article) or by locating the publisher of the author's work and addressing the letter to the author in care of his or her publisher.

National Stamp Collecting Week [second week in November] ————————

Students interested in stamp collecting may write, requesting a catalog and information, to

United States Postal Service
Philatelic Sales Division
Box 997
Washington, DC 20265-9997

————————————

*Arrange with the children's librarian to make this visit—and to have a selection of appropriate books ready for interested students to look through.

Oklahoma Admitted to the Union (1907) [16]

Oklahoma is our 46th state.

Etymology: The name Oklahoma is derived from the Choctaw Indian words, *okla* meaning "people" and *humma* or *homma* meaning "red." So Oklahoma means the red people, the Native Americans.

Lincoln's Delivery of the Gettysburg Address (1863) [19] ⎯⎯⎯⎯⎯⎯⎯⎯

> It's a Fact: Lincoln was invited to speak at Gettysburg almost as an afterthought. The president of Harvard College, Edward Everett, was the keynote speaker. Lincoln was contacted unofficially in October and began writing his speech on November 8. Two draft copies in his handwriting exist today so we know that he did not "scribble it down on the back of an envelope while riding on the train to Gettysburg" as some stories have related.

Lincoln's speech was not received with much enthusiasm that day in 1863, and it is ironic that over 100 years later it is read with such admiration and respect.

North Carolina Admitted to the Union (1789) [21]

North Carolina is our 12th state.

Etymology: In 1629, King Charles I of England granted Carolana (Carolina) to Sir Robert Heath, who was unable to establish a colony there. The first North Carolinans (c.1653) were farmers moving south from Virginia in search of good land. *Carolina* means "of Charles," or the period of his reign. The name "Charles" comes from Old High German *Karl* meaning "a full-grown man" and is related to the Anglo-Saxon word *churl,* originally meaning "a peasant" and which now means "surly, unruly, and hard to control"!

First Recorded U.S. Volcanic Eruption (1842) [22] ⎯⎯⎯⎯⎯⎯⎯⎯

Kids love the threat and thrill of volcanoes. Here are some easy ones to create in the classroom.

A Child-Sized Volcano: You will need a large piece of slate or flagstone (or 8″ × 8″ piece of cardboard), modeling clay, a long plastic tube with a rubber bulb at the end, and talcum powder or cornstarch.

Child uses slate as base on which to model clay into a realistic-looking gray and brown volcanic crater with red and yellow lava streaking down the sides. Crater will be 5 to 6″ at base and 3″ across at the summit. Insert the tube at the base of crater's cavity. Fill bulb (rubber ball with hole in it) with talcum or cornstarch. Child squeezes bulb to make a volcanic eruption; repeated eruptions will give the effect of lava moving down the mountain.

Erupting Volcano Flipbooks: Have each child draw a volcanic peak on a piece of inner tube, carefully cut it out, and, using airplane glue, adhere it to a small wooden block. Place this under a flat heavy weight. Cut cardstock (end pieces of heavy paper are often free from printshops) into 4″ × 7″ strips. Now press rubber stamp onto ink pad. Make a volcano print at about the same place on each of the 6 to 8 cardstock pieces which are laid out horizontally. Use felt-tipped pens to show the (6 to 8) successive steps of an erupting volcano: (1) add grass, trees; (2) show a bit of smoke; (3) sparks, flames; (4) belching smoke, lava, and so on. Arrange illustrations, beginning with no. 1 on the top and the last one in sequence on the bottom. Place strips in a stairstep fashion so that each successive strip is ¼″ beyond the previous one. Staple along back edge of final strip (cut edges even) and duct-tape this entire end to secure it. Child will flip through the little book to see "a simulated volcanic eruption taking place."

Indian Heritage Day [25]

Etymology: Heritage means the culture and tradition handed down to us by our ancestors. Heritage comes from the Latin word *hereditas,* which also gives us the word "heredity," the passing on from parent to child of certain resemblances or characteristics.

The first humans to enter North America made up the first mass exodus in history. Some 25,000 or even perhaps 35,000 years ago these people walked the 55 miles across a land mass then uniting Siberia with Alaska and by doing so, they became the first "Americans!"

With time, these people spread from Alaska to Tierra del Fuego, from California to Maine. Eleven thousand years ago, their cultures were diverse enough as to already be identifiable as separate tribes. The 1980 Census stated that 1½ million Native Americans now reside in this country.

To learn more about these peoples, and their unique heritage, you may write to

> Navajo Curriculum Center, #34
> RRDS-Box 217
> Chinle, AZ 86503

and request materials, price list, and catalog, Navajo readers, and reference materials. Or

> The University of Arizona Press
> 1615 E. Speedway
> Tucson, AZ 85719

to obtain the Sun Tracks catalog of excellent literature, for example, *Between Sacred Mountains.* An inexpensive Indian cookbook is available from

> Whisler World Wide
> 3405 Kelly's Ferry Rd.
> Chattanooga, TN 37419
> Request current price.

The deer, the horse, the great eagle, these are our brothers. The earth is our mother. All things are connected like the blood which unites one family. Whatever befalls the earth, befalls the sons of the earth.

Man did not weave the web of life. He is merely a strand in it. Whatever he does to the web, he does to himself.

—Chief Noah Seathl, 1854

(Look in the index of this book for appropriate environmental games and projects (see Environmental, Ecological, Conservation). Try to help each of your students really understand the web of life of which we are all a (small) part.

The Native American Blindfold Game: This game was used long ago to test a brave's ability to sense direction correctly, even when blindfolded.

Stand with the group in a flat open area. Have one student, the target, stand 25 feet away from the group. Then blindfold another child, and gently spin this student around a few times and aim him or her toward the player who is standing away from the group. The blindfolded student must try to reach the target player who does not move from his or her spot.

Once everyone who wishes to (including *you,* if you're game) has had a try, ask the players to share their success secrets with the group ("I listened for sounds made by other players, or the wind in a nearby tree; I detected ground variations, warmth of sun," etc.). Briefly discuss exactly how these variables would relate to a Native American tracking a wild animal or finding his way home in the dark.

AMERICAN INDIAN RIDDLES*

1. What animal is stronger than all others? (The skunk) —Comanche

2. Four stampers, two lookers, two man-killers, and a fly-swatter: who is he? (The bull) —Yucatán (Mexican)

3. What was born standing up and runs lying down? (A canoe)

4. I'm little, pale, and delicate, yet I can make the strongest man cry. Who am I? (An onion) —Aztec

5. What do you get into by three roads and out of by one? (A shirt) —Plains Indians

6. What is a mirror with a house made of pine boughs? (An eye and eyelashes)

7. What is completely white-haired and yet grows green plumes? (A green onion)

Thanksgiving [fourth Thursday of the month]

Etymology: Widespread travel was restricted until the days of the Roman Empire. Then it became quite common in large cities to see a sailor or merchant wearing odd clothes and speaking a curious strain of Latin. Such a foreigner was called a *peregrinus* (stranger). This word entered the English language as "pilgrim."

The Spanish explorers discovered many new plants and animals here in the New World. Among these was a big bird domesticated and raised by the Pueblo Indians of the Southwest. When this bird was brought to Europe in about 1519, it created a sensation. Nothing like it had ever been seen there before, and many people thought it so curious that they felt it must have come from Turkey—a land of mystery to Europeans at that time. So the bird became known as a "turkey" from its supposed land of origin.

William Bradford, first governor of the Plymouth Colony, searched for a title for his group, a band of radicals who had left church and state to make their homes in the New World.

---

*From Carl Withers and Sula Benet, *Riddles of Many Lands* (New York: Abelard Shuman, 1956).

Bradford happened upon the reference to pilgrims in the Bible—Hebrews 11:13—and he used this word to describe this small band of strangers who, for conscience sake, had come here as pilgrims in 1621.

The first Thanksgiving was proclaimed to be November 26, 1789, by President George Washington at the request of Congress, which asked him to recommend "a day of public thanksgiving and prayer to be observed by acknowledging with grateful hearts the many and signal favors of Almighty God, especially by affording them an opportunity peaceably to establish a form of government for their safety and happiness."

Many of our impressions about the Pilgrims are stereotyped and even incorrect. See how many misconceptions these facts will dispel:

1. Plymouth Colony existed for just 72 years, from 1620 to 1692, when it merged with the Massachusetts Bay Colony.

2. Half of the original 100 *Mayflower* passengers died the first winter they were here.

3. The Pilgrims were able to establish a colony here in the New World, after all other groups failed, largely because of a lucky accident: after the Pilgrims landed, they sent out a scouting party which discovered a 10-bushel store of seed corn that had been hidden by the Indians for use in spring planting. The corn was buried under sand in a place that is today called Corn Hill. This corn* eventually saved the colony from starvation during the long New England winter.

4. For the first ten years, the Pilgrims did *not* have spinning wheels, candle-dipping, horn books, or diamond-paned windows.

5. Bright colors, not somber grays, were typical Pilgrim clothing! Household inventories and Plymouth Colony court records list bright colored clothing more often than black or gray.

6. The average household consisted of 9 or 10 people. The main room of a cabin was crowded and untidy, as it was filled with tools, drying plants, and stacks of hides. Little real furniture was available.

---

*Today maize or "Indian" corn provides more people with more calories than any other plant.

Thanksgiving Language Arts: I Am Thankful Lists. Give each child a 4″ × 8″ lined sheet of paper. Ask the kids to write their names at the top of these papers and follow with "I am thankful in 19____ for:" Then they complete this sentence on each line with the description of something for which they feel grateful, such as "We can afford to buy our groceries," "Grandma and Grandpa write me letters," "We don't have much homework tonight."

These lists will give insights into your students' thoughts and feelings and may also indicate personal spelling words they need to practice.

Thanksgiving Crossword Puzzle

Ask young children to think of a noun (or verb) that begins with "T" (and each of the successive letters in the word THANKSGIVING.) They draw a small descriptive picture next to each number and add as many boxes for each letter in the word as needed. The worksheet "Thanksgiving Crossword Puzzle" shows an example drawn by a 7-year-old.

[**Answers:**   1. Turtle, 2. Heart, 3. Apple, 4. Nut, 5. Kitten, 6. Sun, 7. Grabbing, 8. Ice cream cone, 9. Vinegar, 10. Icicle, 11. Nuts, 12. Garage]

Once these puzzles are prepared (you may check them for spelling errors), they may be exchanged with classmates, and the kids can have the fun of trying to complete a friend's Thanksgiving puzzle.

Creative Writing Ideas: Have the students write a (short) description of a "perfect" Thanksgiving dinner to which "you may invite anyone in the whole world." Once this has been carefully considered, ask them to explain why each guest was selected and then list the various foods you would eat (this could be done in the form of an actual menu from appetizers through desserts).

Young children can create very thoughtful and touching blessings at this time of year. These don't need to be long and they may—or may not—be shared aloud, as the individual child wishes. Here is one by a third grader:

> Thank you for the food.
> Thank you for God.
> And dreams.
>
>   Amen

Such blessings may also be inspired by hearing and talking about Native American poems of thankfulness. Children can then create nature poems written in the voice of an early American Indian.

> Oh, God, will you let me wash my body?
> Let me eat good venison.
> Help my tribe be good.
> In ten suns my tribe leaves for the hills.
>
>   Benjie Viljoen, fourth grade

Name _____

THANKSGIVING CROSSWORD PUZZLE

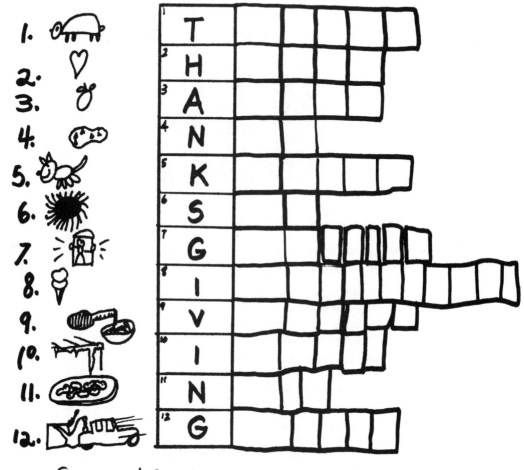

Crossword Puzzle by a 7-year-old

I thank thee, my God, for the House.
I think thee, God, for my house.
It shelters us from rain and snow.
We can sleep in it,
Eat in it,
Play in it,
Pray in it.
We can do many things in a house.

                                        Mike G., fourth grade

Thanksgiving Reading ————————————————————————

This is a Tewa prayer for well-being. The skyloom described in it refers to small desert rains that resemble a loom hung in the sky:

> Oh our Mother the Earth, Oh our Father the Sky,
> Your children are we, and with tired backs
> We bring you the gifts that you love.
> Then weave for us a garment of brightness;
>
> May the warp be the white light of morning,
> May the weft be the red light of evening,
> May the fringes be the falling rain,
> May the border be the standing rainbow.
>
> Thus weave for us a garment of brightness
> That we may walk fittingly where the birds sing,
> That we may walk fittingly where the grass is green,
> Of our Mother the Earth, Oh our Father the sky.

This translation is from *Songs of the Tewa* by Herbert J. Spinden and is used with permission of the Palace of the Governors Print Shop in Santa Fe, New Mexico. The Print Shop offers handprinted ritual songs of the Apache, Hopi, Navajo, Tewa, and Zuni ($3.00 each). Also offered are *Remedies and Advice from the Old West;* paragraphs of nineteenth-century wit and wisdom ($1.50); handbills from the nineteenth-century ($0.25 ea.); *Tales of the Mountain Men,* a classic collection of authentic stories ($7.95); and the very special *Historic Book Arts Projects,* * a

————————————

*Checks for the *Historic Book Arts Projects Packet* should be made payable to The Palace Print Shop, P. O. Box 2087, Santa Fe, NM 87504-2087. (Please include $1.50 for the mailing of each order.)

revised edition of a 1984 issue. This is a unique educational portfolio featuring more than 30 projects in the book arts, especially designed for young people, along with actual samples of children's work and a blueprint for building your own wooden press. It was the winner of the Museum Publications 1989 Award of Merit ($15.00). Another award winner is *The Bicycle and the Bronco,* a nineteenth-century poem by Jack Crawford, Indian scout, concerning the coming of the Industrial Revolution to the Old West ($5.00).

THANKSGIVING RIDDLES

1. What 3 things do people seem to think it is more blessed to give than to receive? (Pills, advice . . . and punches)
2. On Thanksgiving, what is the one kind of jam you cannot eat? (A traffic jam)
3. How do all cooks act mean on Thanksgiving? (They beat the eggs and whip the cream.)
4. What's the best key to a really good Thanksgiving dinner? (A big tur-key)
5. On Thanksgiving is it safe to write your Congressperson on an empty stomach? (It's safe, but wouldn't it be better to write him on a piece of paper?)
6. What is usually eaten for breakfast except on Thanksgiving when you drink it? (Toast)
7. What's the best thing to put into a Thanksgiving pie? (Your teeth)
8. What increases the more you share it? (Happiness)

Thanksgiving Math ─────────────────────────

Following is a reproducible math page, "A Math Sheet for Thanksgiving," based entirely on historic figures and measurements. Young students might tackle it in small groups, or perhaps as a class, while older students should enjoy the information in this combination social studies–mathematics activity.

[**Answers:** 1. Two months and 5 days, 2. About 2 months, 3. 49, 4. 7, 5. (Will vary), 6. 145, 7. 72 years, 8. (Will vary according to the year), 9. (Will vary), 10. (Will vary)]

A Few Thanksgiving Recipes ─────────────────────────

Cooking presents an excellent opportunity to learn by the actual handling of materials and by watching math in action.

If possible, separate your class into groups of 4 children, each group at a separate table or area of the room and each with its own large plastic or stainless steel bowl, set of measuring cups, spoons, more than adequate quantities of each required ingredient, a clearly printed, worded copy of the recipe, & big stirring spoons, one for each child at the table. You may also cover the table top and area beneath table with large clean lengths of (newsprint) paper; these, plus a bowl of warm soapy water and sponges should facilitate cleanup!

Name _____

a Math Sheet for Thanksgiving.......

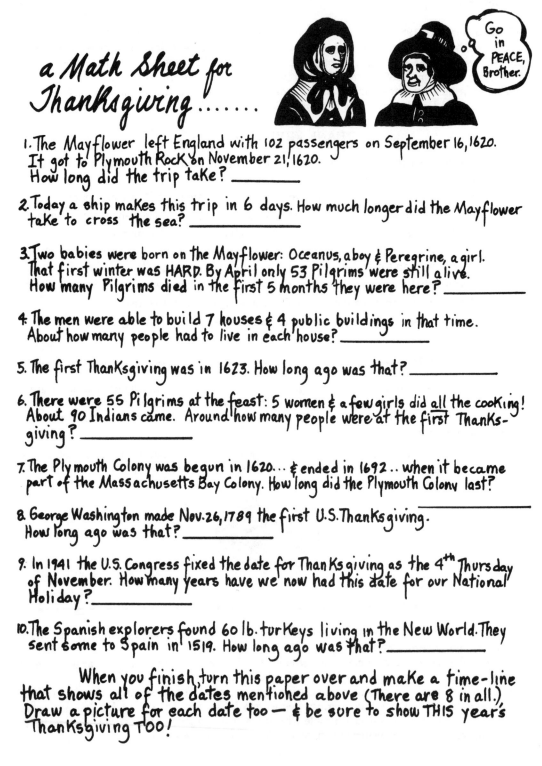

Go in PEACE, Brother.

1. The Mayflower left England with 102 passengers on September 16, 1620. It got to Plymouth Rock on November 21, 1620. How long did the trip take? _____

2. Today a ship makes this trip in 6 days. How much longer did the Mayflower take to cross the sea? _____

3. Two babies were born on the Mayflower: Oceanus, a boy & Peregrine, a girl. That first winter was HARD. By April only 53 Pilgrims were still alive. How many Pilgrims died in the first 5 months they were here? _____

4. The men were able to build 7 houses & 4 public buildings in that time. About how many people had to live in each house? _____

5. The first Thanksgiving was in 1623. How long ago was that? _____

6. There were 55 Pilgrims at the feast: 5 women & a few girls did all the cooking! About 90 Indians came. Around how many people were at the first Thanksgiving? _____

7. The Plymouth Colony was begun in 1620... & ended in 1692.. when it became part of the Massachusetts Bay Colony. How long did the Plymouth Colony last? _____

8. George Washington made Nov. 26, 1789 the first U.S. Thanksgiving. How long ago was that? _____

9. In 1941 the U.S. Congress fixed the date for Thanksgiving as the 4th Thursday of November. How many years have we now had this date for our National Holiday? _____

10. The Spanish explorers found 60 lb. turkeys living in the New World. They sent some to Spain in 1519. How long ago was that? _____

When you finish, turn this paper over and make a time-line that shows all of the dates mentioned above (There are 8 in all.) Draw a picture for each date too — & be sure to show THIS year's Thanksgiving TOO!

Here is a recipe that younger children as a group can help prepare. Then they might each take home a small jar of this relish to contribute to their family's holiday meal.

Cranberry-Orange Relish

The night before class, sterilize 30 small jars (which your group has collected to be recycled in this way) with boiling water. Also sterilize the accompanying lids. Sometimes heavy plastic wrap, held onto the jar with thick rubber bands, may take the place of a lid. You be the judge.

2 bags of whole cranberries, prepared
    according to package directions
	3 packages unflavored gelatin
	     sugar to taste

6 seedless oranges and their juice	4½ cups hot water

Add hot water to gelatin, and stir until dissolved. Add cooked cranberries. Peel oranges, removing all pith. Cut oranges into tiny pieces, collecting all juice. Add oranges and juice to gelatin mixture. Ladle into jars. When relish has cooled, cover each jar with a lid or with heavy plastic wrap. Provide a strong brown paper bag for each child to use to carry this relish home. Add a note saying that this relish must be refrigerated until Thanksgiving dinner.

Yield: 30 small jars.

Stove-Top Cornbread

Grease a 10″ heavy black skillet. Sift together:

¾ cup unbleached white flour	3 tsp. baking powder
3 Tbsp. sugar	¾ tsp. salt

Add ¾ cup Indian corn meal. In a second bowl, beat 1 large egg; beat 3 Tbsp. bacon drippings and ¾ cup milk into egg.

Pour the liquid mixture into the dry mixture. Give it a few rapid strokes with a wooden spoon. Pour batter into greased skillet. Cover with a tight-fitting lid. Place skillet over low heat on hot plate and cook for 20–30 minutes, until a toothpick inserted in the middle of bread comes out clean. Serve hot with butter.

Yield: 16 pieces.

Succotash

6	cups cooked fresh, canned, or frozen corn	¾	tsp. paprika
			butter
6	cups cooked fresh, canned or frozen lima beans	3	tsp. salt
			parsley, chopped

Combine all ingredients. Heat in double boiler. (Green string beans can be included. If they are added, change proportions to 4 cups corn, 4 cups lima beans, 4 cups finely shredded cooked green string beans.)

Yield: 30 servings.

Indian Pudding

Scald 4 cups of milk. Pour slowly over ⅓ cup corn meal. Cook in a double boiler for 15 minutes. Stir in 1 cup dark molasses and cook 5 minutes. Remove from heat and stir in

¼	cup softened butter	1	tsp. salt
1	tsp. freshly grated ginger	1	well-beaten egg
½	tsp. cinnamon	(½	cup raisins, if you like)
2	tsp. grated lemon peel (optional)		

Pour batter into a well-greased baking dish. Pour 1 cup milk over the batter. Bake the pudding in a 325° F oven for 1½ hours. Serve pudding hot with vanilla ice cream or whipped cream.

Yield: 15 small servings.

Want to know more about corn? Send for free materials and recipes to

Corn Refiners Assoc., Inc.
1100 Connecticut Ave., NW
Washington, DC 20036

Thanksgiving Social Studies

Young children often like to play Pilgrims and Indians, or the First Thanksgiving at this time of year. You can provide them with striking feather headdresses to forever replace those colored construction paper ones! Here's how:

Real Feather Headdress*

In September begin collecting poultry feathers from a poultry farm. Each headdress requires 6 to 10 feathers, a piece of 6″ × 12″ heavy cloth or felt, and the use of a stapler. Fold cloth in half lengthwise; do this twice so that the cloth is 1½″ wide. Now slide each feather into the fold and staple it to back layer of cloth, leaving top cloth smooth. Repeat with each feather. Tie finished headband around child's head.

Students enjoy duplicating this colonial home recipe. For it you will need a tall jar, spring-water (filtered or bottled water will do), fine white ashes, a bowl, fine sieve, and newspaper.

Pilgrim Soap and Scouring Powder

Fill jar half full with water. Carefully pour in ashes until jar becomes full, with water going above the ashes. Let stand one week. Pour off liquid into bowl. Spread the wet ashes out on paper to dry. Then sift these dry ashes. The liquid was used as detergent and the ash became the Pilgrim's scouring powder!

Experiment with these cleaning agents. How well do they work on dirty dishes, soiled cloth, with hot or cold water?

Today and Long Ago _____

"Today and Long Ago" is a reproducible worksheet for children in grades 4 through 6. This activity gives children practice in following written directions, as well as understanding and clarifying the concepts of "contemporary" (today) versus "historic" (long ago).

Students are asked to fill in the chart by giving historic equivalents for the modern-day conveniences cited.

---

*Help youngsters understand why it is traditional for many Native Americans to wear feathers on their heads; ask for the children's ideas before sharing the traditional religious reasons: to be close to their totem animal, or bird brothers, and to have some of the bird's strength, beauty, and energy.

Name _____

Today and Long Ago

People of long ago had many of the same problems we have—but they had to use different things to help *them*selves.

Try thinking of some modern things that you are glad we have today . . . . Then try filling in the list below. You can draw pictures too, if you want. The first one has been done for you.

NOW we use: **THEN** people used:

1. a car . . . .   *horse & buggy or their feet!*

2. electric lights . . . .

3. a refrigerator . . . .

4. a washing machine . . . .

5. a doorbell . . . .

6. an electric blanket . . . .

7. the telephone . . . .

8. an electric mixer . . . .

9. a tape recorder . . . .

10. a hair dryer . . . .

11. a sewing machine . . . .

12. plastic wrap . . . .

13. a flashlight . . . .

14. a digital watch . . . .

15. TV or a VCR . . . .

16. a vacuum cleaner . . . .

17. a gas station . . . .

18. the Sunday newspaper . . . .

[**Answers:** (In some cases, more than one correct answer is possible): 2. oil lamps or torches; 3. cold cellar or dried foods; 4. a rock in the river, wash tub; 5. a wooden knocker; 6. bed-warming pan or hot rock; 7. a loud yell; 8. a wooden spoon or a strong arm; 9. handing down stories from "father to son" or storytellers; 10. the wind and the sun; 11. thread and needle; 12. a layer of hot wax or a clean cloth; 13. lantern; 14. an hourglass or sundial; 15. plays, group singing, a husking bee, square dancing; 16. a broom and cornmeal; 17. feed store, inn, barn; 18. town crier, a handbill, a peddler, a "busybody"]

It's a Fact: In addition to the Smiths, Aldens, Bradfords, and Standishes, some of America's first settlers were named the Gunniesackes, the Narrowcarts, the Stuffchins, Bunnyduckes, Inchbalds, Foulfoots, and the Klinkhearts!

November Activities

Reporting on Students' Work

Ask each student to give thought to their answers while filling out the reproducible questionnaire. You fill in the first blank with the name of any subject you wish surveyed. Students have the option to sign their name to the letter at the top of the page.

Collect the pages; read their answers carefully, and then speak privately with any students whose responses indicate that a personal conversation is appropriate.

You may want to devote a Language Arts period to discussing their responses as a group and any changes or modifications of class time that may be needed. The children will be happy to see how you have really heard their ideas and opinions.

Save these papers for the upcoming parent conferences and discuss each briefly at that time with the parent(s), if this is appropriate.

> The student thinks of his exams, the farmer of haytime, and the thief of prison all in the same way.
>
> —Chinese proverb

Name _____

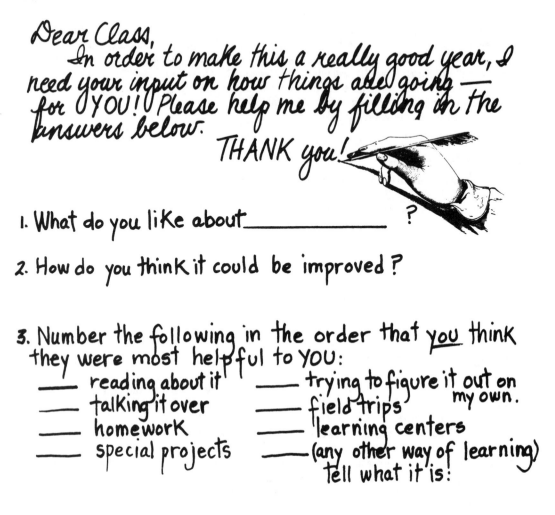

Dear Class,
    In order to make this a really good year, I need your input on how things are going — for YOU! Please help me by filling in the answers below.
                    THANK you!

1. What do you like about_____ ?

2. How do you think it could be improved ?

3. Number the following in the order that you think they were most helpful to YOU:
   ____ reading about it   ____ trying to figure it out on my own.
   ____ talking it over   ____ field trips
   ____ homework   ____ learning centers
   ____ special projects   ____ (any other way of learning) tell what it is:

4. Write anything you'd like to say about school and how it could be changed maybe to make it better for you:

                                        Thanks!

Student Travel Kits ─────────────────────────────

At this time of year, students often leave school for a few days "to spend Thanksgiving with their grandparents." Whenever a child leaves town on a trip, send a small travel kit with him or her. These kits show your involvement with and concern for the child, even when he or she is not in class.

Use a large clear plastic Zip-Loc™ bag to hold the *Trip Book,* a good sharp pencil with eraser, markers or a small box of crayons, small white glue, small pair of blunt-nosed scissors, which may be returned to you following trip. You may also want to add a few pages of puzzles or mazes if it's to be a long drive or plane flight. Use the samples on the next page to make a master *My Trip Book** and then copy in quantity and have students collate and staple pages together. Store *Trip Books* somewhere close at hand so they may be quickly given to any child who is (unexpectedly) off for a quick trip!

Fall Art Projects ─────────────────────────────

Scrimshaw: New England whalers returned home only when every barrel on board ship was filled with whale oil, and this usually took around three years. In between whale sightings, sailors carved tiny detailed pictures into whale teeth; these pictures were called scrimshaw.

Etymology: The Old English word *scrimshank* meaning "to avoid regular work," "to fool around," may be the basis for our modern-day "scrimshaw."

You will need a clean empty white opaque plastic bleach or liquid soap bottle, a big needle or sharp-pointed nail, soot,[†] large shears, and reproductions of early American scrimshaw pieces.

Have each child use the shears to cut out a flat piece of white plastic (to resemble the shape of a whale tooth, or a box-lid, or small picture frame). Let the students study pictures of scrimshaw work, and then, on scratch paper, plan out their own design or picture. These drawings are next transferred to the plastic pieces. Each drawing is then engraved by scratching it onto the plastic with a needle or nail. Cross-hatching will give a shadowy effect. Next, using a finger, child lightly rubs soot into all the scratches and then gently wipes off excess with a tissue. Some children may want to add age to "their piece of ivory"; this can be done by carefully applying a little yellow (brown) watercolor or food coloring along frontal edges of the plastic (and rubbing this in with one's finger) to give a warmth to the surface of each of these scrimshaw pieces.

To display these modern-day scrimshaw works, cover a bulletin board with brown (wrapping) paper. Use double-stick tape adhered to the back of each scrimshaw piece to mount various ones at random across the bulletin board. Now ask for some volunteers who feel like being creative; ask them to help complete the display in this way: using a variety of brightly

---

*The format for this original book was created by artist and dear friend Gail Rieke.
[†]Collected from inside a fireplace or by inverting a saucer over a lighted candle.

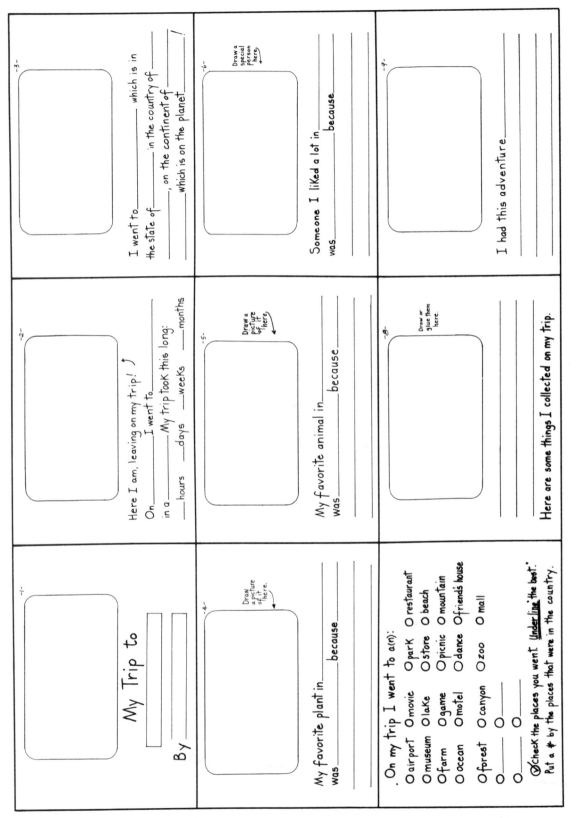

-1-

My Trip to _____

By _____

-2-

Here I am, leaving on my trip! ♪

On _____ I went to _____

in a _____ My trip took this long:

____ hours ____ days ____ weeks ____ months

-3-

I went to _____ which is in

the state of _____ in the country of _____,

on the continent of _____,

which is on the planet _____ !

-4-

Draw a picture of it here. →

My favorite plant in _____

was _____ because _____

-5-

Draw a picture of it here, →

My favorite animal in _____

was _____ because _____

-6-

Draw a special person here →

Someone I liked a lot in _____

was _____ because _____

-8-

Draw or glue them here.

Here are some things I collected on my trip.

-9-

I had this adventure _____

On my trip I went to a(n):

○ airport ○ movie ○ park ○ restaurant
○ museum ○ lake ○ store ○ beach
○ farm ○ game ○ picnic ○ mountain
○ ocean ○ motel ○ dance ○ friend's house

○ forest ○ canyon ○ zoo ○ mall
○ _____ ○ _____
○ _____ ○ _____

✓Check the places you went. Underline the best.
Put a ★ by the places that were in the country.

colored paper, cut out lots of hands. These may be traced from your own hands, or they can be different kinds of hands (long-fingered, hairy-backed, with a tattoo, plump, with nails polished). Make these hands doing things: pointing, cupped as if holding a scrimshaw, widespread fingers as if in surprise, and so on.

Then, using double-stick tape or straight pins, attach a variety of hands to the display; have the hands interacting with the scrimshaw pieces,* for example, appearing to hold a piece, pointing at a neatly drawn title or subtitle, such as, Come See Our Modern-Day Scrimshaw! You may want to include the etymology of scrimshaw somewhere on this bulletin board as well.

Three November Finger Puppets

You will need felt and cloth scraps, scissors, cotton yarn, white glue, needle and thread, sequins, little buttons, tiny plastic movable eyes, little feathers, and ric-rac bits.

1. Child decides what identity his or her puppet is to have. Next felt of an appropriate color is cut into 2 arch shapes that will fit easily and completely over child's finger. Two arms with hands (wings, legs with paws) are cut out and inserted between arch shapes, and glued in place. Yarn (or fake fur) hair (or ears) are inserted between arch shapes and glued in place. The 2 arches are carefully glued[†] or stitched together. Finally, facial features and clothing details are glued in place.

2. Child designs finger puppet animal or person on paper, showing either a profile (good for animals, birds, or people) or a frontal view. Now this drawing, scaled to fit child's finger, is transferred to felt. Head, arms, body are cut out as one piece; a second identical felt or fake fur is also cut out. These two pieces are carefully sewn together, leaving finger hole open. Feathers, yarn, and fur details are then glued in place.

---

*Sometimes allow the hand to bend out away from the board, or curl some fingers under to give the hands added dimension.

†Never soak felt with glue as this causes cloth to become stiff and brittle.

3. Cut a rectangle of felt that can be wrapped sleevelike around child's finger. Glue or slipstich overlapping ends in place. Make a small rolled tube of felt and tack down across back to form arms. Cut 2 keyhole shapes (head and neck) and glue or stitch edges together, leaving bottom of neck open. Once glue is dry, gently stuff head with cotton. Insert neck into top of body and glue or stitch in place. Facial features, hair, beard, hands, and clothing details are now added to give these little guys individual character.

November Field Trip Suggestions _____

This is a fine time of year to arrange to visit a working blacksmith, a weather station, or a book bindery.

Call your Department of Environmental Management and Engineering (see Yellow Pages) and inquire if a class trip (or class visit by one of their employees) might be arranged. Students may be able to see demonstrations of how water and air are analyzed for pollutants and how experiments are conducted to detect hazardous wastes.

Other November visitor ideas: a stamp collector with a few "special" stamps from his or her collection, a children's book author to talk about "how you get ideas for a book and how you get your book published," a meteorologist, or a bird-fancier!

DECEMBER

The Pawnee Indians called December *Kaata*, meaning Darkness. The Seminoles called it "Big Winter." The Yuman tribes referred to it as "The Month We Do Nothing." The Eskimos called December "Horns Drop: Time of Departure" (for seals and caribou) and "They Shine" (referring to the morning and evening stars).

Calendar of Important Dates

§ Hanukkah (movable) Jewish Festival of Lights, may occur in November or December.

1 Woody Allen, American filmmaker was born, 1935.

   On this day in 1955, Mrs. Rosa Parks, a black seamstress of Montgomery, Alabama, was arrested because she refused to give up her front section bus seat to a white man; this was the beginning of the Montgomery bus boycott.

2 On this day in 1804, at the Cathedral of Notre Dame, Napoleon Bonaparte crowned himself emperor of France. Just as Pope Pius VII raised the jeweled crown to place it on Napoleon's head, Bonaparte snatched it from his hands and placed it on his head, himself!

   On this day in 1823, President James Monroe presented The Monroe Doctrine to the world.

Quotation of the Day: We should consider any attempt on their (the European powers') part to extend their system (of government) to any portion of this hemisphere as dangerous to our peace and safety.

—James Monroe

On this day in 1859, Georges Seurat, French pointillist painter, was born.

And in 1859, John Brown was hanged in the public square at Charleston, Virginia, for his raid on Harper's Ferry in October. The old man was very calm before and during his ordeal and, while being driven to the gallows, looked at the passing view and said, "This is a beautiful country."

First self-sustaining nuclear reaction was achieved at the University of Chicago, 1942.

3   Illinois was admitted to the Union as our 21st state, 1818.

First human heart transplant, by Dr. Christian Barnard in Capetown, South Africa, on Louis Washkansky who lived for 18 days following the operation.

4   First "Thanksgiving Day" in America, Berkeley Plantation, 1619.

5   Martin Van Buren, 8th U.S. president, was born in 1782, the first native-born U.S. president.

6   St. Nicholas' Day.

Marie Curie, physicist/chemist, discovered radium & polonium with her husband in 1867; later they shared the Nobel Prize for chemistry and physics.

7   Birthdate of Mary, Queen of Scots, 1542.

Delaware became the first state to join the Union in 1787.

10 United Nations Human Rights Day marks the adoption of the United Nations Declaration of Human Rights, 1948.

Quotation of the Day: All human beings are born free and equal in dignity and rights. . . . Everyone has the right to freedom of thought. . . . Everyone has the right to freedom of opinion and expression.

—United Nations Declaration of Human Rights

Mississippi was admitted as the 20th U.S. state in 1817.

First distribution of Nobel Prizes, 1901, on the anniversary of the death of Alfred Nobel (1896). The Peace Prize is awarded in Oslo and the other Nobel Prizes are awarded in Stockholm. In 1964, civil rights leader Martin Luther King, Jr., became the 12th American and third black American to win the award.

Quotation of the Day: I accept this award today with an abiding faith in America and an audacious faith in the future of mankind.

—Martin Luther King, Jr.

11 First aurora borealis was recorded on this day in 1719.

Indiana was admitted to the Union as our 19th state, 1816.

Alexander Solzhenitsyn, Russian writer and another winner of the Nobel Peace Prize, was born in 1918.

First U.S. monument to an insect was dedicated in Alabama in 1918, to the boll weevil!

On this day in 1930, the Bank of the United States was declared insolvent; 400,000 depositors lost their life savings.

In 1946, UNICEF (United Nations International Children's Emergency Fund) was established.

12 Feast of Our Lady of Guadalupe, Mexico's patron saint. This is Mexico's most joyous day of celebration.

Pennsylvania was admitted as the 2nd state of the Union, 1787.

Margaret Chase Smith, Republican senator from Maine, who stood up against the anticommunist hysteria of fellow Senator Joseph McCarthy, was born in 1897.

13 On this day in 1642, New Zealand was discovered and named by Abel Tasman of the Netherlands.

14 Alabama became the 22nd state to join the Union, 1819.

15 Nero, Roman Emperor, was born in Antium, 37 A.D.

Bill of Rights Day marks ratification of first 10 amendments to the U.S. Constitution.

> Quotation of the Day: Congress shall make no law respecting an establishment of religion, or prohibiting the free exercise thereof; or abridging the freedom of speech, or of the press; or the right of the people peaceably to assemble, and to petition the Government for a redress of grievances.
>
> —First Amendment

On this day in 1890, Sitting Bull, chief of the Sioux Indians, was shot and killed in South Dakota following a dispute with federal troops.

16 Ludwig von Beethoven, musical genius who brought the symphony to its highest perfection, was born, 1770, in Bonn, Germany.

Jane Austen, writer, was born on this day in Steventon, England, 1775.

Anthropologist Margaret Mead, was born in Philadelphia, 1901.

On this day in 1916, Gregory Rasputin, "The Mad Monk," who maintained a great influence over the czar and czarina of Russia, was lured to the palace of a Petrograd noble, murdered by poison & gunshot wounds, and then thrown beneath the ice of a nearby canal.

Arthur C. Clarke, science fiction writer, was born on this day in Somerset, England, 1917.

The Safe Drinking Water Act became law in 1974.

17 Poet John Greenleaf Whittier was born, in Haverhill, Massachusetts, 1807.

Wright Brothers Day marks the first successful airplane flight in history, Kitty Hawk, North Carolina.

> Quotation of the Day: The first flights with the power machine were made on December 17, 1903. Only five persons besides ourselves were present. . . . Although a general invitation had been extended to the people living within five or six miles, not many were willing to face the rigors

of a cold December wind in order to see, as they no doubt thought, another flying machine not fly.

—The Wright Brothers

Frances Hamerstrom, wildlife biologist who helped save the greater prairie chicken from extinction, was born in 1907.

18   New Jersey became the third state to join the Union, 1787.

The 13th Constitutional Amendment was ratified in 1865, abolishing slavery in the United States.

First commercial power plant in the United States began supplying electricity to Shippingport, Pennsylvania, in 1957.

19   In 1154, Henry II was crowned king of England, beginning the British-ruling House of Plantagenet.

First issue of Benjamin Franklin's *Poor Richard's Almanack* was published in 1732.

Corrugated paper was patented in America on this day in 1871.

In 1963, the United States launched the 19th *Explorer* satellite.

20   The conscientious objectors to the Revolutionary War were released from prison on this day in 1780.

First state to secede from the Union—South Carolina—voted unanimously to do so at a special convention in Charleston, 1860.

Georgia became the first state to enact an antilynching law in 1893.

The Union of Soviet Socialist Republics was formed by 14 Communist states in Moscow, 1922.

21   Winter solstice, the beginning of winter, falls on December 21 or 22.

Forefathers' Day: Commemorates the first time that the Pilgrims set foot on American soil, Plymouth, Massachusetts, 1620.

22   International Arbor Day

On this day in 1440, Bluebeard was executed.

In 1894, Dreyfus was unjustly found guilty of treason.

On this day in 1938, a Coelacath, a fish thought extinct for 65 million years, was caught off the coast of South Africa.

> Quotation of the Day: We buried Abraham Lincoln and John Kennedy, but we did not bury their dreams or their visions.
>
> —President Lyndon B. Johnson,
> ending the nation's month of official
> mourning, 1963

23 First transistor is invented by John Bardeen, Walter Brattain, and William Shockley, 1947.

On this day in 1986, the aircraft *Voyager,* piloted by Jeanna Yeagar and Dick Rutan, completed the first round-the-world flight without stopping or refueling.

24 In 1968, 3 U.S. astronauts made 10 circuits around the moon.

25 Christmas Day

On this day:

In 800, Charlemagne was crowned Holy Roman Emperor & king of the Franks.

In 1066, the first monarch of Great Britain to be crowned in Westminister Abbey, William the Conqueror, after killing Harold took his throne on Christmas Day.

The first performance of *Silent Night* was heard in the village church in Aberndorf, Austria in 1818 (it had been written the night before by the village schoolteacher); & finally,

Clara Barton, compassionate nurse and founder of the American Red Cross, was born in 1821.

26 Kwanza, a black American holiday based on traditional African harvest festivals, is celebrated from December 26–January 1.

27 Johannes Kepler, father of modern astronomy, was born in 1571.

Louis Pasteur, who established the process of pasteurization of milk, was born in 1822.

28 Iowa was admitted to the Union as the 29th state, 1846.

Woodrow Wilson, 28th U.S. president, was born on this day in Staunton, Virginia in 1856.

In 1789, chewing gum was first patented in the United States.

Earl "Fatha" Hines, American musician-composer, was born in 1905.

29 Andrew Jackson, 17th U.S. president, was born on this day in Raleigh, North Carolina, 1845.

30 On this day in 1853, U.S. negotiator James Gadsden signed an agreement with Mexico for the United States to purchase 45,000 square miles of land south of the Gila River (the southern portion of Arizona and New Mexico) for $10 million.

31 Henri Matisse, French painter, was born in 1869.

Ellis Island, in New York Harbor, became the receiving station of all immigrants entering the United States on the Atlantic Coast. (From 1892 through 1954, 16 million immigrants entered the United States through Ellis Island.)

The end of World War II was officially announced by President Harry S Truman, 1946.
NEW YEAR'S EVE!!

December

This is the tenth month in the Roman calendar. *Decem* = ten in Latin.

December Events and Activities

Hanukkah (a movable holiday in November or December)

"Hanukkah" means dedication and is the Jewish Festival of Lights or of Dedication. It was begun two thousand years ago in 165 B.C. by Judas Maccebeus to honor the rededication of the temple in Jerusalem which 3 years earlier had been desecrated by a Syrian conqueror.

Hanukkah lasts 8 days, and at sundown of each day candles are lighted—one of the first day, two on the second, and so on until the eighth evening. It is a happy holiday, and special songs are sung each evening.

A Hanukkah dreidel is a toy top with four sides. It is designed to help children learn about this holiday. Each of three sides has a Hebrew letter & each of these is the first letter of one of the words in the Hebrew sentence "A great miracle happened there": *Nes gadol (godol) haya (ha-ya) sham (shawm)*. The fourth side has the letter *nun* for nothing.

One way to play with the dreidel is to give each player five peanuts in the shell. Put a pile of them in the middle as the kitty. You spin the dreidel & if the letter *nun* (noon) appears, you get nothing; if *gimmel* appears, you take all; if *hay* appears, you get half the kitty; and if *shin* turns up, you must put one peanut from your pile into the kitty.

Your students may enjoy preparing a small Hanukkah repast. It would be fun to invite your parent helper, room mother or the principal to come to help you enjoy the festivities. The candies can be made well in advance. The cakes can be baked that morning, or the day before, and a batch of the potato latkes, fried in an electric skillet, can be kept heated on a warming tray, while additional latkes are fried up right there on demand. Forks (plastic), plates (paper), and napkins will also be needed.

Katowes Cake

Katowes is an old riddle-puzzle game that must be answered in numbers totaling 44. The measurements for the ingredients of this cake total 44—the number of candles lighted during Hanukkah.

16	Tbs. (1 cup) flour	3	eggs
1	tsp. baking powder	16	Tbs. orange juice
1	tsp. grated orange peel	7	tsp. confectioners sugar (optional) (butter for oiling pan)

Stir flour, baking powder, and orange peel until well mixed. Set aside. In a large bowl of a mixer, beat eggs 10 minutes, or until very thick and lemon-colored. Gradually beat in sugar until very thick and light. Fold in flour mixture, about a third at a time. Gently fold in orange juice. Turn this into a very-well-oiled 9″ fluted (bundt) tube pan. Bake in preheated 325° oven 50 minutes or until toothpick (inserted halfway between edge of pan and tube) comes out clean. Cool in pan. Invert onto rack. Remove pan and sprinkle cake with sifted confectioners sugar.

Yield: 12 servings.

Note: Cake shrinks as it cools.

Potato Latkes (Pancakes)

10	eggs, beaten well	1¼	tsp. pepper
15	Tbs. flour		Oil
15	cups grated, drained potatoes		Parsley sprigs
1	Tbs. salt	20	Tbs. grated onions

(accompaniments: apple sauce, sour cream)

In a large bowl, mix potatoes, onion, eggs, flour, salt, and pepper. In large electric skillet, heat enough oil to coat bottom of pan. Drop batter by ¼ cupfuls into oil. With back of spoon, spread evenly to 3″ pancakes. Cook over medium-high heat until golden brown and crisp, turning once. Drain on paper towels, place on warm platter and garnish with parsley. Serve at once with desired accompaniments.

Yield: 30 to 40 latkes.

A Maze for the Children

Make copies of the "Maccabee Maze" worksheet for the students and let them try to find the holy oil. (Tell them to always go from START toward the oil, NEVER from the oil backward to the entrance!)

Nursing Home Visit _____

You might consider taking your class to visit a nursing home during the holiday season. If you do, here are a few suggestions:

1. First go and check out the facility, yourself. Is it really an appropriate place for your class to visit? Ask the administrators what small gifts or food your class might bring. Discuss the idea of the class singing carols or giving a puppet show or a short play. If your group were to come, see if you might visit with some of the patients on a more personal level in the reception room.
2. Check with your principal and get his or her okay.
3. Then present the idea to the class and get their thoughts.
4. Notify the parents via a memo and get their input. Children should understand in advance the types of elderly people they'll be meeting (e.g., bed-ridden, blind, deaf, in wheel chairs, sedated).
5. Help the kids write a follow-up letter to the nursing home patients and staff.

Illinois Admitted to the Union (1818) [3]

Illinois is our 21st state.

Etymology: The name "Illinois" is the French form of *Iliniwen,* meaning "men," the name of a group of Algonquian Indians who lived in this region of the New World when the first Europeans arrived.

Delaware Admitted to the Union (1787) [7]

In 1610, Captain Samuel Argall of Virginia named the large bay adjacent to this area in honor of Lord De La Warr, a Virginia governor. The name Delaware has survived to this day. The state is one of the original 13.

Mississippi Admitted to the Union (1817) [10]

Mississippi is our 20th state.

Etymology: The name, taken from the river which forms the boundary of this state, may be Choctaw meaning "beyond age" or Illinoian, meaning "great water" or "father of all waters."

First Distribution of Nobel Prizes (1901) _____

The money for the Nobel Peace Prize comes from a bequest of $9,200,000 left by Alfred Nobel at his death in 1896. The inventor-philanthropist founded his huge fortune on the sale of dynamite and other explosives. He accidentally discovered how to make dynamite by mixing nitroglycerine with inert substances. By the end of the 19th century every major nation was buying the death-dealing smokeless powder produced in Nobel's factories.

Name _____

A Maccabee Maze

Over 2000 years ago the Jewish Temple in Jerusalem was attacked & ruined. Later some Jews called Maccabees went back into the temple to try & find the holy oil. They needed enough oil to burn for 7 days—but all they could find was ONE jar of oil—just enough for 1 day! What could they do? . . .

Then a great thing happened!! This one jar of oil burned & burned . . . & burned: it lasted 7 DAYS!

Hanukkah is the Jewish Festival of Lights: it honors that miracle of light which happened back in 165 B.C.

Help the Maccabees find the holy oil in their temple in Jerusalem!

START HERE ↓ **ONLY**

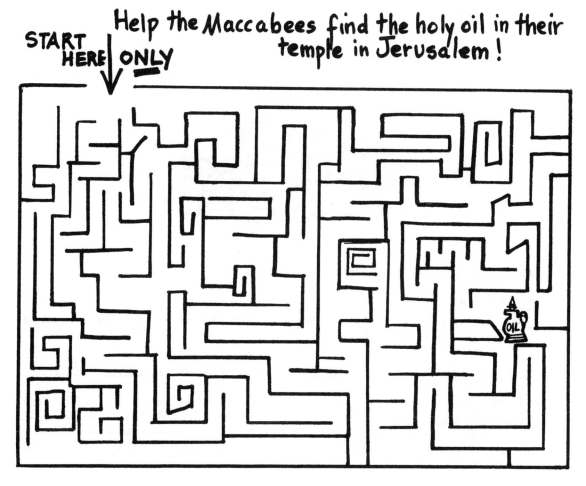

Nobel prizes are awarded for outstanding work done in the fields of physical science, chemistry, literature, and in medical science or physiology.

Acceptance of his responsibility for making his fortune from substances that people could (and did) use for killing each other is said to have been behind his establishment of the Peace Prize.

Indiana Admitted to the Union (1816) [11]

Indiana is our 19th state.

Etymology: The word "Indiana" means "land of the Indians."

Pennsylvania Admitted to the Union (1787) [12]

Pennsylvania is our 2nd state.

Etymology: The word "Pennsylvania" means "Penn's woods" and was named for its founder, English Quaker William Penn.

Alabama Admitted to the Union (1819) [14]

Alabama is our 22nd state.

Etymology: The word "Alabama" comes from the Choctaw Indian language and means (roughly) "the thicket clearers."

Formation of Union of Soviet Socialist Republics (1922) [20]

The USSR is the largest country in the world. Comprised today of 15 republics, with Russia as the biggest, the Soviet Union is 2½ times the size of the United States. Politically, we have been allies, enemies, and "estranged." Here is a game which can quickly teach children—4th through 6th grades—comparative facts about their country and the USSR. (The format of this game can be used to teach/review facts in any subject area and students love it!)

*Zip Around.** The goal of this game is to help students compare and learn facts about the United States and the Soviet Union. Each student is given a card; assure them that this is not

---

*This game was developed by Julie Wheeler of Portland, Oregon. It is part of a Soviet Studies for the Elementary Grades unit, an excellent collection of practical ways to teach about the USSR (puzzles, games, mimeos, etc.). It's available for $6.00 from Ms. Wheeler at 6600 S.W. Barnes Road, Portland, OR 97225.

a test and that it doesn't require them to answer the question on their card! Ask them if there are any numbers or words on their card that they cannot pronounce. Give them any needed pronunciations.

One student begins by asking the question on the bottom of his or her card. (The first time that the game is played, no one will try to go fast. Use this as a dry run to familiarize students with the game's structure. Successive games will be timed.) The student whose card has the answer to this question reads it out (no raised hands are needed to signal the response) and then reads the question on his or her card. In this way, all the questions are asked and answered, eventually coming back to the player who started the game.

Collect and shuffle the cards so that students will now receive different cards and learn different facts. Time the students and then see if they can beat their own record. Shuffle the cards and try again. (Two students may read from one card if you like, and you may pair a strong reader with a weak reader to offer peer assistance.)

Zip Around playing cards are $7'' \times 8''$ posterboard with the following printed clearly on each of 22 cards. Leave a big space between the statement and the question.

Washington, DC, is the capital of the USA.
Who is the leader of the USSR?

Mikhail Gorbachev is the leader of the USSR.
How many time zones are there in the Soviet Union?

There are 11 time zones in the Soviet Union.
How many people live in the USSR?

273 million people live in the USSR.
The Soviet Union lies on what two continents?

The Soviet Union is in Europe and Asia; this is sometimes called Eurasia.
How many time zones are in the USA?

There are four time zones in the US, not counting Alaska and Hawaii.
How big is the USA in square miles?

The US has 3 million 620 thousand square miles of land.
What are some big rivers in the Soviet Union?

The Amur, Volga, Ural, and Dneiper rivers are in the USSR.
What language is spoken in the USA?

English is the main language spoken in the USA.
How many republics are there in the USSR?

There are 15 republics in the Soviet Union.
What are some big rivers in the USA?

The Missouri, the Mississippi, and the Columbia are big rivers in the USA.
How many people live in the United States?
234,000,000 people live in the USA.
How big is the USSR?
The Soviet Union is 2 ½ times bigger than America in land size.
What are some important mountains in the US?
The Appalachian Mountains and the Rocky Mountains are in the USA.
What are some mountain ranges in the USSR?
The Ural Mountains and the Caucasus Mountains are in the Soviet Union.
On what continent is the United States of America?
The United States is on the continent of North America.
What is the money used in the USSR?
Rubles and kopeks are Soviet money. 100 kopeks = 1 ruble.
What language is spoken in the USSR?
Russian is the main language of the Soviet Union, but many other languages are spoken there.
How many states are there in the USA?
There are 50 states in the USA.
What is the capital of the USSR?
The capital of the USSR is Moscow.
What is the money used in the United States?
U.S. money is called dollars and cents. 100 cents = 1 dollar.
What is the name of the U.S. president?
George Bush is the president of the United States.
What is the capital of the United States? (The answer to this questions signals the end of the game.)

Winter Solstice [21, 22]

This is the day of winter solstice when the sun is farthest from the equator and its apparent northward motion along the horizon ends. In Latin, *sol* = "sun" and *sisto* = "to stand still."

Winter Science

Discuss nondeciduous trees and make a collection of cone and needle samples. From these, the children can learn to identify the seven most common genera (arborvitae, pine, hemlock, yew, fir, spruce, juniper). Emphasize the difference between the shapes of the trees. Use pictures from a seed or nursery catalog to illustrate a mix-match quiz or a bulletin board display. Remind the children that the shape of the needles begins with the same letter as the name of the tree: the fir has flat needles, the spruce has square needles.

Talk about cold and its relativity. Discuss how snow, sleet, hail, and rain are formed.

It's a Fact: When Wilson Bentley photographed more than 5,000 snowflakes, he discovered that each presents a beautiful hexagonal pattern and no two are alike.

Winter Language Arts

Have the children honor this day by writing "Winter Tales" to explain certain phenomena of the season. For example,

ᵹ How We First Got Icicles

ᵹ Why the World Grows Cold in Winter

ᵹ How Snowflakes are Made

ᵹ Why Winter Nights are Long

The children might each write a winter story with a friend, both contributing ideas to the tale as it progresses.

SOME WINTER RIDDLES

1. What has a sheet and cannot fold it? (Ice)
2. Why are icy sidewalks like music? (If you don't C sharp you'll soon B flat!)
3. How is snow different from Sunday? (Snow can fall on any day of the week.)
4. When you look around on a cold winter's night, what do you see on every hand? (A mitten or glove)
5. What can you see in the winter that you can never see on a hot summer's day? (Your breath)
6. When is a boat like a pile of snow? (When it's adrift)
7. What lives in winter, dies in summer, and grows with its root upward? (An icicle)
8. Why is sun bad for an icicle? (Because it turns it into an eavesdropper)

Christmas [25]

Germany is generally credited as being the country of the Christmas tree's origin. Some feel St. Winifred created the first tree; others say that Martin Luther, one Christmas Eve, envisioned a candle-lit tree as he gazed at the starry heavens. The first authenticated mention of decorated trees occurs in an Alsatian manuscript (1604).

Although there were no Christmas trees in colonial America, people visited one another's homes to deliver greetings personally. Christmas dinner was usually served around four o'clock.

In Virginia, the food was plentiful and varied. On the other hand, the Pilgrims thought it irreverent to make merry on December 25. New Englanders worked on this day as on any other. It is recorded that the German soldiers in the British army decorated evergreens to celebrate Christmas in 1776 at Trenton, New Jersey.

The Christmas tree was introduced to America by the Germans—the immigrants of Lancaster, Pennsylvania, in 1821. There was gift-giving among the English and German settlers. Gifts were usually foods: fruitcakes, hams, turkeys, dried fruit. Handmade gifts, furniture, and jewelry were also sometimes exchanged.

Dutch immigrants brought the traditions of Christmas stockings (they actually left shoes by the fireplace on Christmas Eve) and Santa Claus to the United States. The Dutch had a traditional St. Nicholas, but it wasn't until the poem *T'was the Night Before Christmas* became popular—after 1822—that Santa Claus became an American tradition.

In 1841, decorated trees became popular here and abroad when Queen Victoria had a tree decorated for her children at Windsor Castle at the suggestion of her husband Prince Albert.

In pagan times, bonfires were built to keep the waning sun alive during winter solstice. Christmas tree lights, fireplace fires, and candles may be descendants of those primitive blazes.

The word "holly" comes not from "holy" but from "holm oak," the leaves of which holly resembles. The Christmas wreath commemorates Christ's crown of thorns. Pre-Christian legends held that witches despised holly and that they would stay away from any house where it was hung as a wreath on the door.

A pre-Christian custom dictated that Roman enemies were to reconcile with one another if ever they met under mistletoe!

Why do we have turkey at this time of year? Because James I hated boar's head. His taste for turkey at Yuletide became popularized when, in 1603, he became the king of England.

Over 5,000 years ago, Mexican Indians made strings of popcorn for religious ceremonies. Even today, you may see strings of popcorn decorating statues in remote villages in Mexico. The Native American Indians taught the Pilgrims how to plant and cook corn. Ever since the seventeenth century, popcorn has been a part of our Christmas celebrations.

Etymology: The "nog" in eggnog is short for *noggin*, a small mug carved from a cylinder of birch. Old English taverns used to serve drinks at the table in noggins. Nog was also the name of a strong ale. The first eggnogs were made of milk curdles in ale or dry sack (the English name for Spanish dry sherry wine) flavored with spices.

Did you ever wonder why Santa named his reindeer as he did? Perhaps this may help make things clearer: *Dasher* comes from the Old Norse word for "rush"; *Dancer* is from Old High German "danson," which means "to extend"; *Prancer* is either Old Norse or Old French, from words meaning "to advance." *Vixen* is a very old word we get from the Anglo Saxon *fuxen*, which comes from earlier Indo-Europeans roots meaning "female fox" and "bad-tempered." *Comet* is from the Greek *kometes*, meaning "hair of the head" and referring to the comet's tail. *"Cupido"* is Latin for Cupid and means "desire and passion"; it is derived from an earlier Indo-European root meaning "to boil, smoke, or be disturbed." *Donner* is German for "thunder." And *Blitzen* is from the German *blitz*, lightning!

An Ornamental Bulletin Board

Here's an easy and attractive holiday bulletin board display that will preserve classmade ornaments until they are to be taken home as special gifts to each child's family. Bright green felt or paper strips are carefully stapled or adhered to the board with double-sided tape. Ornaments are pinned beneath the "branches."

How did we get these holiday traditions?* Older students can research and illustrate a bulletin board that answers this question. Origins of the Christmas tree, candles, lights, holly, mistletoe, fires, crèche scene, presents, Santa Claus, reindeer, sleigh, stockings hung by the fireplace, poinsettia, plum pudding, popcorn, eggnog, Yule log, bells, and Christmas cards can all be researched and simplified drawings made to accompany each tradition. Illustrations and written information should be kept quite large in scale to facilitate viewing. Students should experiment with placement of information until they are satisfied with the overall composition of the display. Give them assistance if it is required.

*The origins of many of these traditions are mentioned in this chapter.

Room Environment—Wall Decorators _____

A continuous narrative mural can be used as a runner above the chalkboard: "Winter Celebrations from 3000 B.C. to the Present." This could include Egyptians decorating their homes with palm branches, symbols of life triumphing over death; Romans hanging little Bacchus figures on pine trees during a Saturnalian revel; Scandinavian myth of a service tree springing from the blood-soaked earth where two lovers were violently murdered; the Druids worshipping oak trees and evergreens; the French knight who found a huge tree covered with burning candles and topped by the Christ Child; and so on.

Christmas Customs Around the World. Probably not all of these countries could be included in one mural. Perhaps you could use traditions from countries that represent the ethnic backgrounds of your students.

Belgium	Children leave carrot-filled (wooden) shoes out on St. Nicholas Eve. The carrots are for the saint's white horse.
China	Christmas trees were called the Trees of Life, and in some sections of this vast country "Old Christmas Father" brought gifts.
Czechoslovakia	St. Mikulas comes down from Heaven on a golden rope and wanders the earth looking for good children. An angel in robes follows him and so does his servant, Peter, who has become through time a red-tongued devil. On Christmas Eve the family sits around the tree and fortunes are told.
Denmark	Julenisse, a Yule gnome, lives in the attic all year long, with a cat. He is tiny, jolly, white-bearded and well loved. Rice pudding is left out for him on Christmas Eve. At 12 o'clock he comes down from the attic bringing gifts. Evergreens decorate the house, windows; rye and wheat decorate the barn and gates.
England	The British have Christmas trees, caroling, mistletoe, holly, and a big Christmas dinner. Gifts are found by the fireplace. Old English customs go back more than a thousand years, for example, mummers dress in strange clothes and act out old stories and legends.
France	The family goes to church on Christmas Eve and then has a big dinner before going to bed. Père Noël brings children gifts on Christmas Eve. He is white-bearded and wears white robes, carries a gold staff and comes down the chimney.
Germany	Christmas fairs have been held "by the well in the marketplace" ever since the days of the Crusades. Christmas trees are known to have been used in Strasbourg, Alsace, in 1605 and lighted ones were used by 1740. On Christmas Eve, gifts are exchanged. Back in 1603, people costumed as angels and devils came and asked children if they'd been good. While the children knelt in prayer, the parents put gifts on the table behind them and these gifts were said to have come from Heaven.
Greece	St. Basil brings gifts to the children of Greece, and he is said to arrive in a ship.
Holland	St. Nicholas and his servant Peter bring gifts to the children. St. Nicholas rides a horse and wears a red bishop's robes and a long white beard. Peter carries switches and toys and gifts. Children leave carrot-filled shoes out on St. Nicholas Eve. As in Belgium, the carrots are for the saint's white horse.

Italy	The crêche scene, *il presepio,* is the center of the celebration. Christmas Eve is spent at church and on Christmas Day there is a big dinner. Gifts are delivered on January 6 by a kindly old witch, La Befana, and lumps of coal are left for bad children. Kids have hung up their socks the night before.
Mexico	From December 6 to Christmas Eve, *Las Posadas,* are enacted. These show the quest of Mary and Joseph for a place to rest, and friends gather each night in the patio of a different home to sing *las posadas,* asking for admittance. Children carry the crêche scene. Later they are blindfolded and try to break a hanging gift-filled *piñata.* On January 6, the Day of the Three Kings, the children put their shoes on balconies or window sills to be filled with presents from the kings. Later that day there is another party, piñata, and play, and at night there is a cake made in the shape of a crown. Baked inside is a little doll of Baby Jesus, and it means good luck for the child who finds it in his piece of cake.
Norway	The animals are given special treats and people say: "Here's something to let you know that it is the Yuletide, my friend!" Wheat sheaves for the birds are tied to posts and houses. The Journey of the Queen of Lights is acted out from house to house. Star Boys go with her, bringing light to dark Norway.
Old Russia	Gifts were brought by Grandfather Frost (Dedush Ka Moroz). They were placed under a tree decorated with gilded walnuts and gay ornaments made by the family. The Christmas Eve feast began when the first star appeared.
Panama	Children write letters to Baby Jesus c/o St. Peter (El Niño Jesus, c/o San Pedro) promising good behavior and closing with love and kisses to Mary and Joseph.
Poland	When the first star appears, the gift-giving and feasting begin on Christmas Eve. Straw is put under the tablecloth to remind the family that Christ was born in a manger. Villagers dress up as animals and go caroling; in return they receive food and drink.
Puerto Rico	Children leave a gift for the Wisemen's camels on January 6 (often a basket of flowers). They find their presents the next morning.
Spain	As the first star on Christmas Eve appears, lamps are lit in the windows. After breakfast the next morning, the family dances around the *nacimiento* (manger scene), singing carols. Every year, the Magi pass through Spain on their way to Bethlehem, and they leave gifts for good children who have put their shoes out on the window sills the night of January 5.
Sweden	Little straw goats were the earliest Christmas gifts to Swedish children, and these are still important decorations today.

On December 13, a pretty young girl in a white gown wearing a crown of candles brings the family coffee and cakes. She is St. Lucia, Queen of Light. On Christmas Eve, an old bearded gnome, Jultomte, gives the children gifts wrapped in many layers of paper and held together with sealing wax.

Syria   On January 6, the camel brings gifts to the children who have put out bowls of water and food for him. An old legend says that the camel was the youngest of the animals ridden by the Magi, and finally he fell to the ground from weariness. The Christ Child later blessed him for his great efforts. In Syria each year candles burn to guide the Child home from over the Judean hills.

Yugoslavia   (This country is made up of six republics and so customs differ greatly within it.) Children write letters to Jesus and the angels, who bring them gifts on Christmas morning. Most of Yugoslavia burns a Christmas log, which must be a young oak that falls to the earth just as the sun rises on Christmas morning. It is ceremoniously carried home and placed in the fire next to the crèche scene. Corn and wine are sprinkled on the log, and everyone wishes for a good harvest. A young man strikes the log with an iron rod until the sparks of good fortune fly upward.

ROOM ENVIRONMENT—WINDOWS

For stained glass windows, have children paint windows with a mixture of equal parts of Bon Ami (comet cleanser), Alabastine (whiting), and dry tempera paint. Pour in enough water to make a creamy paste. Apply to window with small brushes, clean cloths, or little pieces of sponge. (Remove paint with a damp sponge over the Christmas holidays.)

ROOM DECORATIONS

Two little hanging decorations may be suspended from overhead light fixtures or thumbtacked by string to ceiling.

For (1) the stars and angels decoration, you will need scissors, pencil, glue, needle,* thread, glitter, and colored (metallic) paper. Use the canopy pattern to trace the canopy onto colored paper. Gently fold along each dotted line and glue flange to the opposing edge. Allow to dry. Using the patterns given, the children can cut out three stars from (metallic) paper, three

---

*Have needles threaded, each with a long, knotted thread, before class starts so they are ready for the children to use.

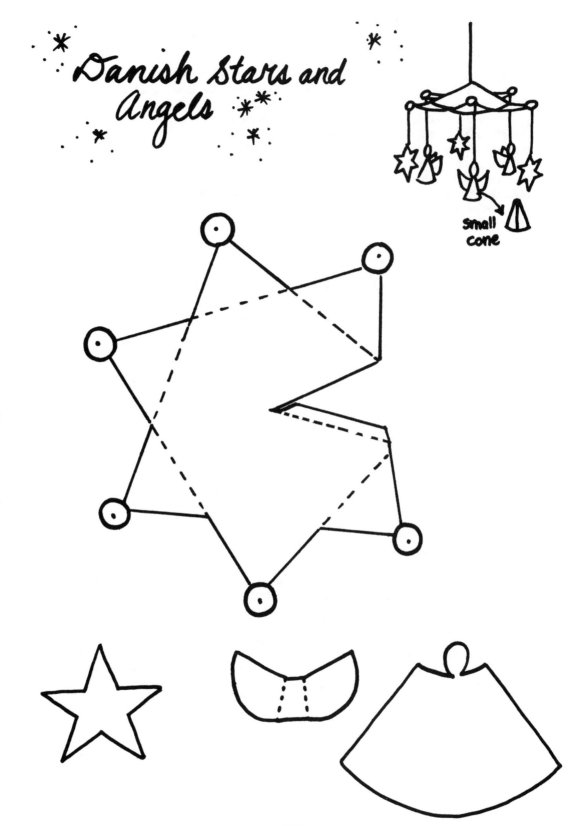

Danish Stars and Angels

small cone

121

angel skirts, and three angel wings. Fold the skirts to make little cones and glue in place. Allow to dry. Fold the wings back along the dotted lines and glue firmly to back of the angel skirt. Glitter may be added to bottom edge of the skirt or wing tips.

Now the child pokes a needle down through center (black dot) of a canopy point. Knot at end of thread anchors it to canopy and thread end is glued to back of angel's head. A drop of glue may also be dabbed on knot at canopy point. Repeat this process to make and suspend 2 other angels and 3 stars until this little hanging decoration is complete.

For (2) the crescent moon & star decoration, you will need a pencil, scissors, colored posterboard, glue (glitter), needle,* and thread. Cut out a crescent moon pattern as shown in the illustration and use it to trace two moons on yellow, white, or orange posterboard. Cut out and cut the slits as indicated. Insert one crescent into the other.

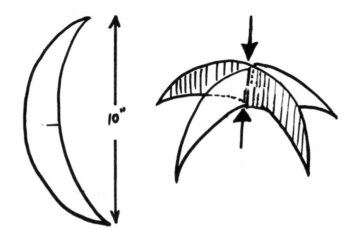

Cut out at least four hand-drawn stars from posterboard (& add glue & glitter to edges or surfaces if you want). Poke threaded needle through end of crescent & pull thread through until knot is anchored in moon; poke needle through a star point & pull thread through, tying end of thread to anchor it to star. Repeat with other stars and crescent points until decoration is completed. You can string several stars, going from tiny to big, from a moon point for a fine effect.

For a beautiful *pinecone wreath,* you'll need a circular wire base (sold at many flower shops), a hot glue gun or dark brown acoustical tile cement (sold at hardware stores), lots of pine cones, dried pods, small branches of dried berries, and Baby's Breath.

Children push the cones and pods tightly into the spaces between the outer and middle wire circles and then push cones into the spaces between the inner and middle circles. Hot glue or tile cement is generously applied to middle area and cones and pods are pressed into cement to fill all spaces. Let cement dry for 24 hours. Accent some parts of wreath by inserting sprigs of berries or Baby's Breath. Add a cheery big bow to complete your classroom wreath.

---

*Have needles threaded, each with a long, knotted thread, before class starts so they are ready for the children to use.

Language Arts

Here is a list of Christmastime subjects. (This list may be used for reference when students design cards, murals, ornaments, decorations.) It may also be used as the basis of holiday or free-time language lessons and enrichment. For example, children might be given copies of (selections from) the lists and asked to alphabetize them, to use as many as they can in a holiday story, to categorize words in any manner that is reasonable to each of them, to pick out names of things that were never alive, and so on.

manger	angel	wise man	snowman
sled	shepherd	star	camel
snowbird	lantern	wreath	crèche
Three Kings	caroler	Santa Claus	fir tree
choir	boot	ornament	helper
snow	sheep	reindeer	candle
Bethlehem	Joseph	tinsel	toy soldier
icicle	Mary	mistletoe	holly
teddy bear	drum	Christmas tree	candy cane
poinsettia	elf	North Pole	stained glass
doll	fireplace	snowflake	window
sleigh bell	castle	popcorn	stocking

Poetry Writing

The word WINTER or HANUKKAH or DECEMBER can be substituted for the word CHRISTMAS in the following activity.

Encourage each child to put down a very thoughtful personal response to complete each sentence on the worksheet. These poems will make good bulletin board reading, and parents often appreciate such poems when these are folded inside a green piece of paper to become a child's greeting card to his or her parents.

Name _____

✳A Christmas Poem ✿✿

Christmas is a time for _____

_____

Christmas is filled with _____

_____

Christmas smells like _____ and _____

_____ and _____

Christmas feels _____

It makes ME feel _____

Christmas is a time of _____

And _____

And _____

Christmas looks like _____ and _____

_____

To me Christmas will always be _____

_____

_____

_____

_____

Older students are challenged by the idea of writing a holiday poem (in blank verse) in the shape of a holiday symbol. Have each student choose a motif (e.g., a star, snowman, or X-mas stocking) and then try to visualize this object and write down the various sensory perceptions they identify with it—its texture, scent, taste, temperature, aesthetic qualities, how it might sound, and why it has special meaning for the writer. Once jotted down, these phrases can be organized into a pleasing cadence and corrected for spelling and punctuation.

Finally, the students make a large outline of their chosen symbol in pencil on a big sheet of white paper. Their poem is printed very lightly so that each line ends at the edge of their pencil outline. Finally, the poem is inked in and the pencil guidelines erased.

Christmas Reading

This is a perfect time of year to calm and soothe your classes by reading aloud to them (excerpts) from some good holiday books such as *The Christmas Mouse* by E. Wenning, *A Child's Christmas in Wales* by Dylan Thomas, *Journey of the Magi* by T. S. Eliot, *Carol for the Children* by Ogden Nash, and *Christmas in Cornwall* by Rosalind Wade.

CHRISTMAS RIDDLES

1. I'm filled every morning and emptied at night except once a year when I'm filled at night and then emptied in the morning. What am I? (A stocking)

2. Why does Santa Claus go down the chimney? (Because it always soots him)

3. Why is a cloud like Santa Claus? (They both hold the rein, dear!)

Christmas Ornament Math

You will need a compass, pencil, (metallic gold or silver) thin paper, scissors, white glue, a knitting needle (or a pencil with lead broken off), thin cardboard (or 2 buttons), a needle, and heavy thread.

Students will need to be familiar with the following concepts: a circle, diameter, inch, half, eighth, quarter, perimeter, and compass.

Student uses the compass to make 12 circles, each 4″ in diameter. The 1″ circles are then made in the middle of each of the larger circles. Circles are cut out, folded in half, once, twice, and a third time (making eighths). Have the child cut each crease up to the 1″ circle's perimeter. The knitting needle is used to roll each of these sections into a cone and a bit of glue will hold each cone's shape. This process is repeated with all 12 circles. Now use the compass to draw a ⅛″ cardboard circle and cut it out (or you may use a button); string this on heavy thread and then thread on the 12 stars. Top these with the second cardboard circle or button. The child pulls the string tight and ties a knot to hold ornament together, leaving enough thread to make a loop for hanging.

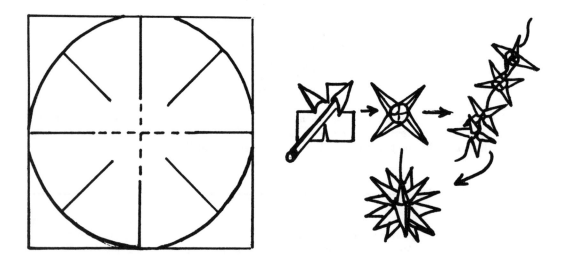

Christmas Cooking

Making Gingerbread People

Each child writes his or her name on a slip of paper and receives a piece of waxed paper for his or her desk top and a bit of flour. Using a large knife, cut dough, which has been made the night before, into appropriate number of pieces. Once hands are washed and sleeves pushed up, each child gets a lump of the chilled dough. Child rolls out dough & cuts out cookies as described here.

Gingerbread Dough

Mix thoroughly   Sift together

⅓   cup soft margarine   7   cups flour
1   cup brown sugar   ½ tsp. each of salt, cloves, cinnamon,
1–1½ cups dark molasses   allspice, fresh, grated ginger
Stir in ½ cup of cold water.

Combine sifted mixture with sugar and margarine. Add 2 tsp. soda stirred into
1 Tbs. cold water and form into ball. Chill dough. Roll out ⅓″ thick and form into
cookies. Decorate and place on lightly oiled baking sheets. Bake at 350°F for 15 to
18 minutes (longer baking will make brittle cookies).

Yield: 30–45 cookies.

Christmas Science — Botany

American Holly. This grows naturally from Massachusetts to Florida. In some places it
reaches a height of 50 feet. At nurseries, holly berries are sown and covered with mulch, and in
the spring of the second year, the seeds germinate. Holly is evergreen, shedding its leaves every
third year.

Mistletoe. This is a parasitic air plant growing on a host tree and manufacturing its own
food. The roots of an air plant anchor it to the host tree; specialized rootlets of mistletoe delve
into the tissues of the host, drawing a water and mineral supply from it.

Christmas Trees. Rather than buy a cut tree for the classroom, consider purchasing a
living tree, such as a Norfolk pine, which can then be enjoyed year round. (Lightweight ornaments should be used on a Norfolk pine to avoid weighing down and damaging the branches.)
Balsam fir has a symmetrical shape, and its needles remain green even when dry. Its needles
stay firmly attached, as they are arranged spirally on twigs and have no joints or bracts at their
bases. Its cones stand erect on the boughs, giving a candlelike effect. White spruce, while living,
retains its bluish-green needles for 7 to 10 years! Once cut, it begins to shed. Cedar has short,
scalelike needles. Long-needled pines are sometimes also used at Christmas.

How to keep your Christmas tree from drying out: Use a tree stand that will hold water
and use the following solution: 1 qt. of very warm water, ½ cup Karo syrup, and 1 to 2 Tbs.
Plant Gro, or some good plant food. Mix well. With a temperature of 68°F in the home and a
6-foot tree, this amount of liquid will be used up in approximately a day and a half.

To fireproof your tree, mix well 2 quarts of water, 7 ounces of Borax, and 3 ounces boric
acid powder. Spray the tree, using this solution in a plant mister, and let dry before decorating.

Having a living tree for your classroom is a lovely, as well as ecologically responsible,
endeavor. During vacation, the tree may grace the teacher's or a student's home, and then in
early January, it can be planted by the children on the school grounds. Here are some tips to
help assure that the tree will survive:

1. Be sure to buy a container-grown tree. If the tree was dug up and put in the pot
   without a year's preparation of its roots, it has little chance of surviving.

2. Have your students help dig the hole even before you buy the tree. In northern climates, there is a good chance that the soil will be frozen when you are ready to plant the tree. Dig a hole a bit larger than the container the tree comes in, so that if you have to spread the roots out when you remove it from the container, you will have room. Cover the soil you removed from the hole with black plastic so it will not freeze.

3. Decide on the type of tree that will work best in your school yard. Consider the mature size of the tree as well as its shape and texture now. A dwarf blue spruce has an almost perfect Christmas tree form, if you like a dense tree, and will fit into most yards.

4. Buy your tree a day or two before you want to bring it into the room. If the soil is not moist when you bring the tree from the nursery, water it thoroughly and let the water drain out before bringing it inside.

5. Leave the tree inside for not more than 7 to 10 days, and plant it in your prepared hole immediately once you take it outside. It is better to plant the tree in bad weather than to leave it in the house all winter. (You can put it outside in its container if you put it out of the sun and keep it mulched and watered regularly. Plant it in March or when the ground thaws.) Water it twice right after you plant it, then once every three weeks thereafter.

Helping Birds

This is a fine time for the children to work together on a class project such as a gift for the birds. A lesson like this can induce a quiet, thoughtful working atmosphere and may initiate meaningful ecological discussions. Young children can collect pinecones and then use table knives to stuff the open areas with a mixture of peanut butter and suet. Next cones are rolled in a wild birdseed mixture and hung in a tree near a classroom window so you can all watch to see what happens.

Here's a recipe suggested by the Audubon Society: mix equal parts of melted beef suet and sugar syrup (3 parts water and 1 part sugar, boiled together). Let the mixture cool to a soft, but manageable, consistency and form into balls (about 3″ in diameter). Roll the balls in seeds, nuts, birdseed, bread crumbs, or any combination of these. Chill the balls in waxed paper until they are hard. Tie up the balls with bright string for hanging on a tree or bush, outside a window, or on the fire escape.

Comets and Meteorites

Some historians have suggested that the star of Bethlehem was, indeed, a comet. Older students may enjoy the magazine *Sky & Telescope* and a catalog offered by

Sky Publishing Co.
49 Bay State Rd.
Cambridge, MA 02238

A complimentary copy of the magazine is available.

It's a Fact: Polar bears are born in late December or early January, and each one weighs about as much as three human babies—15 pounds!

A Few Thoughts on Christmas Art and Crafts

Year after year in their school experience, children have a Christmas art curriculum: this year try to develop plans that will present students with fresh opportunities. What symbolic material comes with this season? Choose a symbol and explore its meanings and possibilities for use in the curriculum. What visual elements are especially a part of Christmas? How can these be used in developing one's aesthetic sensitivity?

When choosing gifts- or decoration-making projects for your class, be critical concerning the possibilities each offers for individuality of expression. Ask yourself if the project will give deeper meaning or understanding of old symbols—or is it more likely to perpetuate a cliché?

Teacher's Gifts to Class. Take your class caroling one night (visit a local nursing home), and wind up at your house for hot chocolate and doughnuts. Take several parents along for backup and because they'll enjoy the evening too.

Buy some bulk wild flower seeds. Divide these seeds into as many portions as you have students. Then put the seed mixtures into "baggies" along with a Xeroxed holiday note that tells students how and when to sprinkle the seeds, how you hope these flowers will make people in their families happy, and finally close with your own Merry Christmas wishes!

Present your class with a set of holiday puzzles to be used during free time. Use white glue to completely cover a Christmas picture & transfer it onto tagboard. Press beneath books until dry. Paint the back of each puzzle with a different primary color to help keep the puzzle pieces separate. Then use *sharp* scissors & cut the tagboard into clean pieces; place each puzzle in its own flat box with a lid painted to match the puzzle's identifying color.

CHILD-MADE GIFTS FOR PARENTS

Refrigerator Magnets. Use the craft dough recipe (p. 136) and make up a large batch. Give each child a small lump and ask him or her to make it into a shape that they think their parents will enjoy, such as, a little bird, smiling sun, funny face. Shapes should be 2–2½″ wide & not too thick. Use a toothpick or popsicle stick to press in designs, texture; add a tiny round-headed map tack pressed into dough for an eye. Once dough is dry, firmly glue a piece of rubberized magnet strip (sold in large craft supply stores) to the back of each shape. Finished magnet may be painted and then given a light coat of clear spray. (Do the spraying outdoors.)

Newspaper Logs. If your students have fireplaces or woodburning stoves at home, they can make this unique holiday gift and reuse old newspapers at the same time!

You'll need newspapers, twine, detergent, scissors, a sink, or bucket. Open up a newspaper section and lay it flat. Roll it up leaving a hollow in the middle for air to go through. Add more papers to this log and make the roll tight. When your log is about 5″ in diameter, tie it with twine 3 or 4 times. Now soak each log in a bucket of water in which 1½ cups of detergent has been dissolved. Once log is thoroughly soaked, let it drip for a full minute and then put it in a warm place to dry, which may take up to 4 days. The water compresses the paper, helping the log to burn evenly, while the detergent keeps the paper from molding and unraveling.

A bundle of 6 to 8 logs tied with red yarn and topped with a small pine bough and explanatory note can be a most practical and welcome gift!

Luminarios. (traditional outdoor lights used in winter in the Southwest). You will need smallish brown paper bags; green, white, yellow, or red tissue paper; white glue; scissors; pencil; sand; and votive candles.

Child draws large simple outline design on one side of bag—angel, star, fir tree, and so forth. Child next cuts out this shape being careful not to cut through the backside of the bag. Lay the cut out side of the bag on the appropriate color of tissue paper, and have child trace and cut out the shape from the tissue paper, leaving an inch or more around outside of pattern. Glue the tissue paper cutout carefully over the hole in the bag so that no open space is left anywhere along the cutout edges. Finally, help the child to fold down the top of each sack; do this twice. Add 1½″ of sand to the bag and set the candle in the middle.

Mulled Cider Spices. Each child will need a clean glass (babyfood) jar and lid, orange and lemon rind, ¼ cup crystalized maple syrup, ¼ tsp. ground allspice, 1 tsp. ground cloves, ½ tsp. grated fresh ginger root, 3″ stick of cinnamon, ⅛ tsp. ground nutmeg. You will also need large (plastic) mixing bowls, measuring spoons, scissors, graters, mortars, and pestles.

Have the children collect orange and lemon rinds from home and lunches until you have a good supply. Wash rinds well. Remove the white pithy inside layer and allow rinds to dry. Provide the children with scissors, mortars and pestles, and small handgraters. Then, as a class, enjoy preparing these spices together. Children with scissors can snip the lemon and orange rinds into tiny pieces, others with mortars and pestles can grind each of the spices into powder, while those with graters will grate the peeled ginger.

Place each ingredient, after it has been prepared, into a separate bowl. Have each child measure the ingredients into his or her jar, mix well, and screw on lid. Little self-gummed labels may be printed with this message: Mulled Cider Spice Mix (Simmer with 2 quarts of cider for 20 minutes). Happy Holiday! Love, _____

Christmas Boxes. See Mother's Day Gifts for instructions for making little paper boxes. Have older students choose a holiday picture (piece of gift wrap) and cover it carefully, leaving no air bubbles, with clear self-stick plastic. Next, construct box and fill it with potpourri, Orange Spice Tea (recipe follows), or a series of succeedingly smaller paper boxes with a note suggesting that the boxes can be used for bobby pins, paper clips, stud earrings, rubberbands, and so on.

Orange Spice Tea

1	lb. black tea (can be purchased in bulk for less money)	2	cups dried mint leaves
		1	cup orange peel
½	cup broken up cinnamon sticks	½	cup cloves, bruised in mortar

Coarsely grate orange rinds and dry on paper towels. Break apart any large pieces. Mix all ingredients together. Makes a lovely cup of tea!

Here's an unusual gift for a pet owner or a student's dog or cat—or to be used as a special Holiday Bazaar item!

Biscuits for Dogs and Cats

3½ cups all-purpose flour	2 cups whole wheat flour
1 cup rye flour	1 cup cornmeal
2 cups cracked wheat (bulgur)	½ cup nonfat dry milk
4 tsp. salt	1 pkg. dry yeast (1 Tbs.)
2 cups chicken stock or other liquid	1 beaten egg plus 1 Tbs. milk, to brush on top

Combine all dry ingredients except yeast. In a separate bowl dissolve it in ¼ cup warm water. To this add chicken stock and then add liquid to dry ingredients, mix, and knead for about 3 minutes. The dough will be stiff. If too stiff, add some extra liquid. Roll the dough on a floured board to ¼″ thickness. Cut into biscuits of desired size and shape. Place on an ungreased cookie sheet, brush with the egg and milk, and bake in 300°F oven for 45 minutes. Turn off heat and leave the biscuits overnight in oven to get bone hard.*

Gift-Wrapping Ideas _____

Gift Paper for Very Young Children to Make: Use big sheets of white butcher paper (or red, green, blue mural paper). Have the child paint his or her palm with a thick coat of poster paint. Then have child press hand at random over surface of the paper. Procedure can be repeated with different colors of poster paint. When these gift wraps are dry, they make charming paper which parents will appreciate receiving!

Gift Wrap of Xmas Words: Each child has a styrofoam meat tray and small paper, pencil, pinking shears, poster paint, brush, and white mural or butcher paper. Pressing hard, child prints holiday word (Joy, Noël, Cheers, Love, Peace) with bold lettering on small paper. Then child reverses paper and traces the reverse image onto flat area of meat tray. Leaving 1″ or 2″ border around tracery, child cuts out lettered area of styrofoam. Paint is applied to area all around and up to edge of each reversed word; foam is then laid at random on sheet of mural paper & firmly pressed to apply paint evenly to paper. This process is repeated, using different colors of paint until a fine piece of lettered gift wrap is produced.

Inner-Tube Printed Gift Wrap. See the instructions for making inner tube rubber stamps, page 174. Have children choose holiday subjects for these rubber stamps and print them in lines on butcher paper—or have them share stamps and make each sheet of gift wrap into a unique pattern! They can add glitter while paint/ink is wet for a more glamorous effect!

Santa Sack. Each child will paint the front surface of a new flat brown paper sack using red poster paint. Then each student takes a piece of white posterboard and designs a face which

---

*This recipe first appeared in the *Monterey Peninsula Herald,* Monterey, California.

is glued firmly to the bag. Finally, the gift is put inside the sack and top is tied with heavy green yarn.

Cards

A handmade card is a thoughtful gesture to extend to your room mother and any other person whom the children wish to remember at this time of year.

Standard Greetings: Joy, Peace, Noël, Rejoice, Season's Cheer, Happy Holidays, Glad Tidings, Yuletide Greetings. Children can also be counted on to come up with personalized expressions of good cheer.

Here are some card shape variations:

Fir-Sprig Cards. A fir tree sprig or a piece of holly or mistletoe is dried between sheets of waxed paper under heavy weights. Then it is glued to the cover of a plain folded card. The child can next cut out a shape (snowman, angel, bird, etc.) to hold the sprig or peep out from in back of it. Inside the card, the child may print a simple message such as, "Hello, I just wanted to wish you a great HOLIDAY!"

Flying Angel. Each child cuts out a simple flying angel figure of their own design from a piece of felt. Then they glue figure to a small block of wood and dry under heavy weights. After the figure is completely dry, coat it with poster paint, and press angel image onto a long white folded piece of paper. Once angel print on card is dry, carefully make a tiny slit (with an X-acto™ knife) above and below the angel's hand. Insert stems of dried or straw flowers through the slits.

Christmas Tree Ornaments for Young Children to Make

Glittery Pinecones. These can be made by twisting a thin wire around topmost knob of cone and making a loop for hanging. Child then squeezes lines and spots of glue all over the cone and sprinkles this glue with glitter, tiny mica bits, sequins, or little glass beads. Let glue dry before hanging these flashy ornaments.

Quick 'n' EZ Spirals. For these dandy ornaments, all you will need is a pair of scissors & colored paper. Show the child how to cut a freehand circle* from a 6–8″ square of paper. Next, work from the outside edge & cut a free-form spiral that gradually narrows at each concentric ring. Most students can make these spirals for themselves. Suspended by the center, the spiral hangs naturally of its own weight.

Heavy Aluminum Foil Cutouts. You will need a roll of heavy aluminum foil (used for cooking) or aluminum frozen food containers, scissors, a small-hole paper punch, screwdriver, nail, newspapers, permanent ink markers, and books showing early American tin crafts (if possible).

Each child designs a simple ornament outline, such as a cookie cutter would make. Encourage creative thinking and original ideas.

You might suggest that variations in the aluminum containers (fluted sides, accordian-pleated ridges) be incorporated into the design (wings of angel, girl's skirt). A paper pattern is cut out and lightly traced onto aluminum, and then carefully cut out.

The nail and screwdriver can be used to make a border design by pressing them gently into the aluminum, which is laid on newspaper padding. Use the paper punch to make a hole for

---

*Some youngsters may want to experiment using triangles or squares.

inserting hook or ribbon for hanging. Add bright felt-tipped pen colors, leaving some silver areas to show through.

Snowbirds. These little creatures are quick to make and very sweet to look at, especially when a flock of them appears on your tree. Provide young children with a selection of colored paper tagboard squares (4" × 4"). On the chalkboard, draw a large outline like this:

Ask the children to try & completely fill their paper squares with a bird outline that looks something like the one you've drawn. Then ask them to draw a tiny leaf or sprig of holly in the beak of their bird and add a tiny eye (or glue a glass bead) to their snowbird. Next, the shape is cut out (sometimes it's easier for a small child to cut out the holly sprig separately and later glue this to the bird's beak). Now each child takes a paper cupcake liner in his or her choice of color and cuts out 2 small sections.

2 of these

One of these sections is glued to side of bird to form its wing and the other glued to become the tail.

A threaded needle is drawn through top of bird and a tiny circle is formed and knotted to provide a loop to hang this little snowbird on your tree.

A String of Bells. You will need pencil, scissors, (metallic) paper, glue, (and a ruler & compass). Students will reproduce the figure that follows, either by tracing around master patterns which you have made or by using ruler and compass to draw figures on their papers, copying from a large illustrative one that you have drawn on the chalkboard.

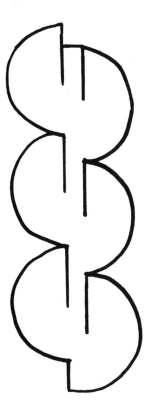

Completed figures are cut out and the six cone-shaped bells formed, with their sides glued into place. These bell strings may be used on a tree or to decorate a gift.

Danish Paper Hearts. Have the child use the half a heart pattern shown on page 136 & cut one from each of two contrasting colors of shiny paper. Then the child weaves the 4 fingers together forming the paper heart ornament.

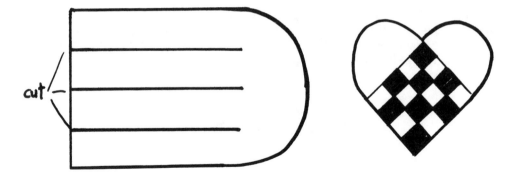

Ornaments Made from Modeling Materials. The Borden Company offers an excellent packet of free craft ideas & recipes for art supplies, including glue paint and glue dough. Free information can be obtained from

Borden Consumer Response Dept.
180 E. Broad St.
Columbus, OH 43215

Glue-Dough® is a nonallergenic and moldable clay made by mixing equal parts of Elmer's® Glue-All or School Glue, flour, and cornstarch. (¼ cup each will give you about a tennis ball amount). Combine in a bowl and knead till well blended. If too dry, add a drop or two of glue. If too moist, add flour & cornstarch. It hardens without baking. The dough will remain moldable if tightly wrapped in plastic wrap. Roll out a section of the dough (on a lightly floured board) to ⅛″ or less thickness. Cut into shapes or mold pieces (e.g., for puppetheads) over plastic foam or balls of foil. Allow 10 to 15 hours for Glue-Dough® to dry (time depends on thickness and humidity). Objects should be turned two or three times while drying.

Cornstarch Dough is made with 1 cup cornstarch, 2 cups baking soda, and 1⅓ cups water. Blend cornstarch & baking soda in pan. Add water and stir until smooth. Over medium heat, bring to boil, stirring constantly. Boil 4 minutes and remove from heat. Stir 2 minutes (for stiffer dough, work it longer). Cover with plastic wrap and cool 30 minutes. Roll out on waxed paper until ¼″ or thinner and cut into shapes. Insert wire hook at top. Let dry 2 days, turning often. Paint with acrylics (& spray with clear matte Verathane).

> It's a Fact: In 1659, the Massachusetts Bay Colony made it illegal (and punishable by a 5 shilling fine) to observe Christmas in any way whatsoever!

A CHRISTMAS TREE GARLAND

Here's how to make a Christmas chain that requires no gluing! Enlist the help of everyone in the class. Have them trace this 3″ × 6″ shape, from tagboard master patterns you have prepared, onto various colors of (metallic) paper. Each figure is cut out (pointed scissors will be needed to cut out center areas) and folded along dotted line:

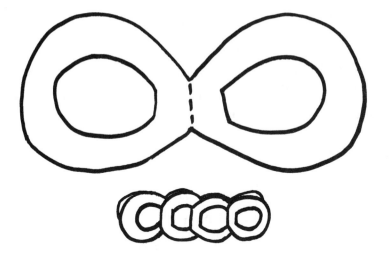

Carefully insert top circle of one figure through bottom circle of second figure. Continue this process until a long garland has been created. Encourage the children to work cooperatively—and quietly—in small groups, coming together finally to combine their efforts into one long chain for your classroom Christmas tree.

Holiday Parties

Avoid any feeling of chaos by being especially well organized for the occasion.

Holiday Party for Young Students. Ask students or the room parents to provide large plain cookies or uniced gingerbread men or cupcakes for the class party. These can be placed on a long table, each on its own paper plate. Also set out dishes of whipped cream, small bowls of icing & knives, shredded coconut, little red-hots, broken walnuts, tiny marshmallows, & chocolate chips. To promote a calming atmosphere, play soft music as several students at a time decorate their cookies or cupcakes. (A supply of wet sponges will aid cleanup. When children finish decorating cookies or cupcakes, each prints his or her name on paper plate rim & places plate on a separate table. Cookies will be consumed once everyone has had a chance to decorate their own—& enjoy them all visually on that table!

(Be certain that there are adequate decorating supplies, as some will—and even should be on such a festive occasion—nibbled along the way; that's part of the Christmas festivities!)

As children are eating, the teacher might come around with a big pillowcase of tiny gift-wrapped presents. Some of these should be humorous to add fun to the party. They may include used paperbacks, markers, small puzzles, and games. Each child reaches in and pulls out his or her own gift.

A Party for Older Students

Entertainment: Hand out to each child a copy of the holly reproducible page. The children make up original pictures, incorporating the holly outline in any way they like. The paper may be used in any direction. The class might enjoy sharing and comparing the variety of results.

Present Relay. Children stand in 2 or more lines. Each child must run to a chair or table on which there is a large gift-wrapped box. The child must untie, unwrap, rewrap, and retie this gift and run back to the line, tagging the second player who repeats the activity.

Refreshments. The students would probably enjoy preparing their own refreshments, such as Russian Kisses, from the reproducible page which follows. This activity could take the place of exchanging gifts, and the money that would have been spent on presents can be contributed to a local homeless shelter or other charity.

December Physical Education

Feel like refreshing your supply of children's games and toys? Send off for these catalogs of very special,—often cooperative,—games, books, and nature materials.

> Animal Town
> P.O. Box 2002
> Santa Barbara, CA 93120

The concept behind cooperative games is simple. . . . People play with one another rather than against one another; they play to overcome challenges, not to overcome people.

—Terry Orlick

The Rein-Deer

Kwanza, Afro-American Celebration [December 25–January 1]*

Kwanza means "first fruits," in Swahili. This holiday was started by Maulana Ron Karenga in 1966. Each day of the week-long celebration emphasizes a different life value:

December 26 *unmoja* (unity)	December 30 *kuumba* (creativity)
December 27 *kujichagulia* (self-determination)	December 31 *nia* (purpose)
December 28 *ujima* (group effort)	January 1 *imani* (faith)
December 29 *ujamaa* (group economics)	

*This holiday (and 364 other special days and creative activities) appear in *The Kid's Diary of 365 Amazing Days*, by Randy Harelson (New York: Workman Publishing, 1979).

RUSSIAN KISSES

(Heat oven to 300°)

1 cup flour
1 cup sugar
1 stick butter
1 tsp. vanilla
1 cup nuts: ground FINE

WASH YOUR HANDS.

Put all the ingredients together in the big bowl. Mix **well**.

Roll dough into balls the size of a quarter.

Place these balls on an UNoiled cooky sheet.

Bake in a 300° oven for 20-25 minutes.
Sift powdered sugar over warm cookies...
........m-m-m..."HARA-SHOW"
↓
which is Russian for **GOOD!**

Each day of Kwanza, a candle is lighted in the *kinara* (candleholder) and the family discusses the importance and meaning of that day's life value. Parents and children find ways to enjoy together each day's special emphasis, idea. On the final day, the family opens *zawadi* (little gifts) which they have made for each other and then they share a *karamu* (feast) together.

Iowa Admitted to the Union (1846) [28]

Iowa is our 29th state.

Etymology: Iowa takes its name from the river that was named for the Ioway Indian tribe. The meaning of the Indian word *Iowa* is uncertain. It has been said to mean "beautiful land" as well as "this is the place," "gray snow," and "sleepy ones."

Texas Admitted to the Union (1845) [29]

Texas is our 28th state.

Etymology: *Texia* was the Indian name for the group of tribes who originally lived in the eastern portion of the state. The Spanish form of this word *Tejas* (tay-haws) means "friends," "allies."

JANUARY

To the Omaha Indians of Nebraska, January is "When the Snow Drifts into the Tents of the Honga." The Iowa tribes call it "Raccoon Month." It is "Little Winter" to Florida's Seminole Indians. The Pawnees, a Plains group, named this time of year that formed their 13th or connective month, "The Entrance Passage to the Earth Lodge." The Northern Alaska Eskimos call January "Sun Returning," "New Sun," and "Great Cold."

Calendar of Important Dates

ʂ Chinese New Year (a movable feast—may occur in December or January).

1 New Year's Day.

First asteroid (an object smaller than our moon that revolves around the sun) Ceres, discovered by Piazzi in 1801.

On this day in 1863, President Lincoln issued the Emancipation Proclamation, freeing the slaves in those areas adhering to the Confederate States of America.

2 Betsy Ross Day commemorates the raising of first U.S. flag by the Continental Army, 1776.

Georgia admitted to the Union as the 4th state (1788).

Isaac Asimov, scientist, sci-fi writer, was born on this day in Petrovichi, Russia, 1920.

Lucretia Mott, American reformer & women's rights proponent was born, 1797.

Alaska became the 49th state to join the Union, 1959.

Terms of newly elected senators and representatives begin today.

4 Sir Isaac Newton, scientist and discoverer of the law of gravity, was born on this day in 1642.

> Quotation of the Day: Nature and nature's laws lay hid in night: God said "Let Newton be!" and all was light.
>
> —Alexander Pope

Jacob Grimm, collector of famous fairy tales, was born in 1785.

Louis Braille, the creator of the Braille alphabet for the blind, was born in France in 1809.

J. R. R. Tolkien, writer, was born in Bloemfontein, South Africa, in 1892.

Utah, 45th state to join the Union, was admitted in 1896.

5 George Washington Carver Day honors the American scientist on the anniversary of his death in 1943 (see entry in July).

First woman governor, Mrs. Nellie Tayloe Ross, took office, 1925.

6 Three Kings Day, Twelfth Night.

On this day in history were born

- Joan of Arc, French martyr of the Inquisition and saint, 1410
- Carl Sandburg, American poet and biographer of Abraham Lincoln, 1878
- Nancy Lopez-Melton, American golfing great, 1957

7 First sighting of a moon of Jupiter, by Galileo in 1609.

First voting under the new U.S. Constitution took place (George Washington was elected president).

Millard Fillmore, 13th U.S. president, was born in a log cabin in Cayuga County, New York, in 1800.

First Tarzan comics distributed, 1929.

8 Elvis Presley, popular idol and singer, was born in Tupelo, Mississippi, 1935.

On this day in 1959, the Cuban Revolution, led by Fidel Castro, was declared successfully ended.

9 On this day in 1493, Christopher Columbus recorded seeing "three mermaids." These were more than likely West Indian manatees, large, gentle sea mammals that are now among the endangered species.

Connecticut became the 5th state to join the Union, 1788.

First American balloon flight, completed by Francois Blanchard, 1793.

Simone de Beauvoir, French feminist writer, was born in 1908.

Richard Milhouse Nixon, 37th U.S. president, was born in Yorba Linda, California, 1913.

> Quotation of the Day: Unlimited power is apt to corrupt the minds of those who possess it. . . . Where law ends, tyranny begins.
>
> —William Pitt, the Elder

10 Thomas Paine published *Common Sense,* 1776.

First aerial photograph taken in San Diego, 1911.

First meeting of the League of Nations, Geneva, 1920. The League was dissolved in 1946, making way for the United Nations.

First meeting of the UN General Assembly, London, 1946.

11 Aldo Leopold, writer and environmentalist, was born in 1887.

First woman to fly solo across the Pacific, Amelia Earhart Putnam, began her 18-hour flight from Honolulu to Oakland on this day in 1935.

First American woman to become a bank president, F. E. Moulton, was born today in Limerick, Maine, 1938.

12 Johann H. Pestalozzi, educator, was born in Zurich, Switzerland, 1746.

First U.S. museum was established in Charleston, South Carolina, 1773.

James Farmer, black leader, was born in Marshall, Texas, 1920.

First woman was elected to the U.S. Senate, Mrs. Hattie W. Caraway (D., Ark.), 1932. (She served until 1945.)

13 Stephen Foster Memorial Day commemorates the death of the composer in 1864. In his pockets at his death were found his worldly goods, consisting of 34 cents and a slip of paper on which he'd written, "Dear friends and gentle hearts."

Woody Guthrie, American folksinger and labor organizer, who chronicled the Depression years and life of the working man in his songs, was born on this date in 1901.

The first black cabinet member, Robert C. Weaver, became secretary of housing and urban development on this date in 1966.

14 Berthe Morisot, artist, was born in Bourges, France, 1841.

Albert Schweitzer, humanitarian and physician (in Africa), was born, 1875.

Julian Bond, black activist and politician, was born in 1940.

15 Human Relations Day commemorates the birth of Dr. Martin Luther King, Jr. (1929–April 4, 1968), winner of the Nobel Peace Prize in 1964.

17 Benjamin Franklin, inventor and statesman, on whose *Poor Richard's Almanack* this present volume is based, was born on Milk Street in Boston, 1706.

First polar bears are exhibited in the United States, in Boston, 1733.

Robert Hutchins, educator, was born in Brooklyn, 1899.

James Earl Jones, great American actor, born, 1931.

18 On this day in 1535, Lima, Peru, was founded by Francisco Pizarro.

A. A. Milne, creator of *Winnie the Pooh* & friends, was born in 1882.

First Chinese to be granted U.S. citizenship, 1944—E. B. Kan.

On this day, these famous people were born:

- Robert E. Lee, Confederate general, in Stratford, Virginia, in 1807
- Edgar Allan Poe, master mystery and horror story writer, in 1809
- Paul Cezanne, French Impressionist painter, in 1839

On this day in 1933, the Soviet government exiled 45,000 Cossacks to Siberia and almost certain death.

20   Inauguration Day, the day on which the American president is sworn into office every four years.

First basketball game was played under the supervision of its inventor, Dr. James Naismith, in Springfield, Massachusetts, 1892.

Joy Adamson, animal expert and author of *Born Free,* was born, 1910.

21   On this day in 604 B.C., Nebuchadnezzar became the sovereign of Babylonia.

22   First American novel published, 1789: *The Power of Sympathy* by "Philomenia."

Red Sunday in St. Petersburg, Russia (1905), when the czar's soldiers fired on 15,000 Russian workers as they marched to beg the czar for better living and working conditions. Hundreds were killed and 5,000 arrested, many being sent to Siberian labor camps.

U Thant, Burmese educator and third secretary general of the United Nations, was born in 1909.

23   First American woman to become a physician, Elizabeth Blackwell, earned her doctor of medicine degree on this day in 1849 in Geneva, New York.

24   On this day in 1922, the Eskimo Pie was patented!

Maria Tallchief, Native American ballet dancer, was born, 1925.

25   Robert Burns Day commemorates the birth of the poet in 1759, Alloway, Scotland.

Shay's Rebellion took place on this day in 1787. Daniel Shay, a captain in the Revolutionary Army, led 2,000 impoverished men in a vain march on the federal arsenal in Springfield, Massachusetts, hoping to overthrow the government. (Soon after, the government did pass relief measures for war veterans.)

Virginia Woolf, writer, was born in England in 1882.

On this day in 1890, Nellie Bly, daring young reporter for the *New York World* returned to New York, completing her amazing trip around the world in the record time of 72 days, 6 hours, 11 minutes.

26   Michigan was admitted to the Union as the 26th state, 1837.

Republic Day in India marks the day when the country became a republic, 1950.

27   Wolfgang Mozart, great German composer, was born in 1756.

Lewis Carroll, author of *Alice in Wonderland,* was born in 1832.

Mikhail Baryshnikov, Russian-born ballet dancer, was born in 1948.

On this day in 1967, three U.S. astronauts (Virgil Grissom, Edward White, and Roger Chaffee) were killed by fire in their *Apollo* spaceship at Cape Kennedy, Florida.

End of the draft was announced by Defense Secretary Laird, 1973.

28   On this day these historic figures were born:

Charlemagne, first great Frankish king and creator of the Holy Roman Empire, 814.

Peter the Great, Russian czar who strove to westernize his vast country, 1775.

Colette, French novelist, 1873.

Jackson Pollack, American abstract painter, 1912.

Claes Oldenburg, Swedish-American painter, 1929.

First appointment of Jew to the U.S. Supreme Court, Louis D. Brandeis, was made on this day in 1916.

First photographs successfully bounced off the moon by United States, 1960.

On this day in 1973, the cease-fire for the war in Vietnam was signed, officially ending the 11-year "limited war."

29　Kansas was admitted to the Union as the 34th state, 1861.

William McKinley, 25th U.S. president, was born in Niles, Ohio, in 1843.

30　Franklin Delano Roosevelt, 32nd U.S. president (and only president to be elected to more than 2 terms of office) was born in Hyde Park, New York, in 1882.

First meeting of antivivisectionist society, in Philadelphia, 1884.

On this day in 1933, the Nazi era in Germany began as Adolf Hitler became the German chancellor.

On this day in 1948, Mohondas (Mahatma) Gandhi, Indian leader and pacifist, was assassinated in New Delhi.

31　On this day in 1709, Alexander Selkirk, a real-life prototype of Robinson Crusoe, was rescued after being marooned for 4 years on Juan Fernando Island in the Pacific Ocean.

Anna Pavlova, referred to as the greatest ballerina in history, was born in Russia, 1885.

Jackie Robinson, the first black major league baseball player, was born in Cairo, Georgia, 1919.

Barbara Walters, television journalist and interviewer, was born in 1920.

First U.S. earth satellite, *Explorer I,* was launched in 1958.

January Quotations

1　The present is the only thing that has no end.

—Erwin Schrodinger

. . . good resolutions are easier made than executed.

—Benjamin Franklin (1770)

Once one has been struck by lightning, there is no point in consulting the I Ching.

—Chinese proverb

Every beginning is a consequence—every beginning ends something.

—Paul Valery

17   Love your enemies for they tell you your faults.
     There's a time to wink as well as to see.
     Do you love life? Then don't waste time, for that's the stuff life is made of.
     Well done is better than well said.
     He who is good for making excuses is seldom good for anything else.
     Don't hide your talents, for use they were made;
     What's a sundial in the shade?

—Ben Franklin

25   The whole world is a work of art; we are parts of the work of art. . . . But there is no
     Shakespeare, there is no Beethoven; certainly and emphatically there is no God; we are
     the words; we are the music, we are the thing, itself. And I see this when I have a shock.

—Virginia Woolf

30   We have learned that we cannot live alone in peace; that our own well-being is de-
     pendent on the well-being of other nations, far away. . . . We have learned to be
     citizens of the world, members of the human community.

—Franklin D. Roosevelt
(Fourth Inaugural Address, 1945)

January

The name comes from the Latin *Januarius,* after Janus the two-faced Roman god who was able to look back into the past and at the same time into the future. Janus also busied himself with the beginnings of all undertakings. The Romans dedicated this month to Janus by offerings of meal, wine, salt, and frankincense, each of which was new. The Anglo-Saxons called January *Wulfmonath* because this was the month in which hunger drove the wolves down into the villages.

January Events

Happy Chinese New Year! ───────────────────────────

This is a movable feast that usually occurs in January. (Find out from your reference librarian where it falls in a particular year.) The festivities continue for several days and may include fireworks, special decorations, and a parade led by a huge dragon.

Many people of Chinese descent celebrate this holiday by serving Chinese fortune cookies. Consider making some of these cookies for a little creative writing self-starter: each middle or upper grade student chooses a cookie and ponders the epigram found inside. Then they may

1. restate the proverb in their own words and explain the lesson that it teaches.

2. make up a very short fable that has this proverb as its outcome or moral.

3. think of another proverb that teaches the same lesson and/or make up one that advocates the opposite position, for example, "Everything comes to he who waits," "Strike while the iron is hot," or "He who hesitates is lost."

CHINESE FORTUNE COOKIES

Making fortune cookies can be very rewarding. You should give over an entire afternoon (or some Saturday) to the process so that you can enjoy creating them without feeling rushed for time. You will need fine-pointed black marker, scissors (or single-edged razor blade), ruler with metal edge, white typing paper, pencil, lightweight white cotton gloves, a wooden spoon, an egg carton, a regular spoon, and a spatula. Cut the typing paper into $7/8'' \times 2\frac{1}{2}''$ strips and carefully print a proverb on each strip. Fold the fortunes in half lengthwise and set aside.

Baking and Forming the Cookies

$3/4$ cup sugar	$1/2$	cup melted butter
3 egg whites	$1/2$	cup flour
$1/8$ tsp. salt	$1/2$	cup *finely* ground blanched almonds
1 tsp. instant tea powder and 2 Tbs. water	$1/4$	tsp. vanilla

Mix the first 4 ingredients together until sugar is dissolved. Add the remaining 4 ingredients one at a time, beating well after each addition. Chill the batter for 30 minutes. Preheat oven to 350°F.

Drop round teaspoonful of chilled batter onto oiled cookie sheet. Use the back of the spoon to smooth out dough to form a 3" circle. Repeat this process with each rounded teaspoonful of dough. Bake just two cookies at a time, until you have mastered the entire procedure. Bake 3 to 9 minutes, until edges of cookies are delicately browned.

Put on cotton gloves. Use spatula to lift up one cookie & place it over wooden spoon handle. Gently mold cookie to fold down. Insert fortune and double cookie carefully in half again.* Store in egg carton until cookie is cool and permanently shaped.

Thirty Proverbs for Classroom Fortune Cookies

Let one blind man lead another and they'll both fall in the river.	Chinese
Have patience and shuffle the cards.	Spanish
Sometimes you catch the bear, sometimes the bear catches you.	Gypsy
You can't learn to swim in a field.	Spanish
Everybody keeps one black pig.	Chinese
When you are an anvil, be patient; when a hammer, strike.	Arab
Be as the tree that drops blossoms on the hand that shakes it.	Japanese
Little by little and often: fills the purse.	German
Help your brother's boat across and lo! your own has reached the shore.	Hindu
It is said that Death and deaf mutes always have the last word.	Chinese
Don't overlook a weak enemy or a small wound.	German
All sunshine makes a desert.	Arab
John has one customer and Jack another.	Russian
Don't see all you see and don't hear all you hear.	Irish
Make yourself a sheep and the wolf is ready.	Russian
Every great feast has its last course.	Chinese
If you would eat the nut, you must break the shell.	Thai
One man cannot breathe through another man's nose.	Thai
Patience and the mulberry leaf become a silk robe.	Japanese
If you don't throw the dice you'll never land six.	Chinese
While we think about when to begin, it becomes too late.	Latin
When one door shuts, another opens.	Spanish

---

*Some cooks hold cookie by either end & place the middle of the folded edge over the outside rim of the egg carton & bend the ends down to form finished cookie. Try your luck.

Measure your cloth ten times, you can only cut it once.   Russian

The sky is the same color wherever you go.   Persian

No snowflake ever falls in the wrong place.   Zen

One step too few is enough to miss the ferry.   Chinese

The more one knows, the more one forgives.   Anonymous

What you do is what you become.   Spanish

A small hole can sink a big ship.   Russian

New Year's Day

In ancient Rome this day was spent honoring Janus, the god of gates and doors and beginnings and endings, for whom January is named. Janus had two faces, one on the back of his head and the other on the front, allowing him to look forward into the future and back into the past.

Etymology: Threshold literally means "thrash-wood." It comes from the Anglo-Saxon words *therscan,* "to thrash," and *wald,* "wood." When the early Britons entered their huts, they stamped their feet on a piece of wood at the door, the thrash-wood.

Ancient Romans spent New Year's Day considering what the past year had meant to them and making plans for the coming year. January 1 became generally recognized as New Year's Day in the sixteenth century, when the Gregorian calendar was introduced.

Etymology: "Calendar" is a more complicated word than most people think. Meaning "a chart of the year," it comes from the Latin *calendarium,* which was an account book kept by money lenders to keep track of debts due to them on the *calends* or the first of each month. This word itself came from *calare,* "to call," which was what the usurers did to proclaim the due date!

New Year's Creative Writing

Have each child design a Janus and then write stories in the first person telling what Janus might say about the past year and the year to come. Display the pictures with the stories (in cartoon balloons above each Janus) for an interesting first-of-the-year bulletin board display.

Ask the students to write about the past year, telling how and why they changed in some way during that time.

NEW YEAR'S READING

CALENDAR PLAYING CARDS

Calendar Playing Cards is a game that helps young children familiarize themselves with the calendar and measurements of the year. Have the students help make these cards. (A master answer sheet can show correct responses to each of the following games.)

1. Print names, one on each card, of the days, the seasons, and the months. Children are to put the cards in correct sequence and then match the months to the seasons.
2. Print names of the days and the months on a set of cards. Print abbreviations of these words on another set of cards. Children match words with the correct abbreviations.
3. Print names of the months and the seasons on a set of cards. Paste (child-drawn) pictures showing different types of weather on a second set of cards; students match each picture card with the month or season typified by that particular type of weather.
4. Print names of the months on one set of cards. Write the number 29 on one card, 30 on four cards, and 31 on seven cards. Children match each month card with a card that has its correct number of days.

More New Year's Activities
Featuring Math, Geography, & Outdoor Games! _____

Marking a new year is the marking of time. Here are some time-oriented activities:

What I'm Doing When It's _____ *O'Clock:* Use this reproducible page with your students to give them practice in telling time and interpreting it personally.

Roman Numerals. Have very young children show the Roman numerals (on an old clock face) by gluing toothpicks to a piece of colored paper. Ask them to show 1 through 10. A few may want to go to 20±!

What Time Is It? This is an outdoor game in which 1 player is the fox and the others are sheep. A designated area is "the fold" (which probably teaches them a new use for an old word!). The sheep must approach the fox and ask him what time it is. The fox may catch sheep only at

Name _____

Fill in the blanks below with the right times.
Draw a clock by each blank to SHOW the time on a clock too!
Here's how: one o'clock = 1:00 = 🕐 HAVE FUN!

What I'm doing when it's ___ o'clock:

I get up at ___

I leave for school at ___

I get to school about ___

My favorite thing in school is . . . . and
we have it at about ___

LUNCH time! It is ___

After noon recess is at ___

Time to go home! It's ___

After school I often do this: . . . .
I do this from about ___ to ___ .

We eat dinner around ___ .

I watch T.V. for about ___ hours a day.

When I go to bed the clock says ___

I sleep about ___ hours every night.

midnight, so if he answers 8 o'clock or 1:30, the sheep are safe. When the fox says, "Midnight," or "12 A.M.," all the sheep must run to the fold. When the fox tags a sheep, they change roles and the game continues.

> It's a Fact: Long ago in China they told time with water clocks! A man put a bowl with a tiny hole in it into a pool of water. It took one hour for the bowl to sink to the bottom of the pool; at that moment, the man would hit a gong to announce that one hour had passed. The bowl would then be emptied and the process started all over again. Quite a life occupation. . . .

CLOCK AND WATCH-MAKER.

Georgia Admitted to the Union (1788) [2]

Georgia is our 4th state.

Etymology: Georgia was named in 1732 for King George II of England by James Oglethorpe, its colonial administrator.

Alaska Admitted to the Union (1959) [3]

Alaska is our 49th state.

Etymology: Alaska is the Russian pronunciation of the Aleutian (Eskimo) word *Alakshak,* which means "peninsula," "great lands," or "land that is not an island."

Birth of Sir Isaac Newton [4]

In the seventeenth century, Kepler, Galileo, and Isaac Newton discovered the laws which govern the movements of the earth. They showed that these laws apply to the other planets, and we have since learned that they apply equally to the sun itself and to most of the stars. Newton did not call the earth a gyroscope because the name had not been invented in his time, but the rules by which gyroscopic instruments are designed today are based on the laws expounded by Isaac Newton.

A magnificent collage time line, featuring Newton and titled "Men of Modern Mathematics, 100–1950," is available free from

> IBM
> Old Orchard Road
> Armonk, New York 10504

The collage (designed by Charles Eames) is very detailed, and older students can make up "treasure hunt" clues to help one another become familiar with its details.

Some students may want to develop a parallel chart, such as "Women in Modern Science" (using the help of, e.g., "Women in America" from the reference room of your library). Students can use magazine cutouts or drawings as illustrations for their chart.

Many of Newton's mathematical discoveries were made, in part or completely, while he slept. He was not unique in this sense. Elias Howe perfected the sewing machine in a dream. Chemist Friedrich Kekule also had a vivid dream about snakes which he knew to be atoms, making rings by taking the tails of one another in their mouths. This dream led to Kekule's revolutionary closed chain theory of the benzene molecule.

Otto Loewi had a dream which explained how the nerves control the muscles, but on awakening, he could not remember some important parts of the explanation. Sometime later, Loewi had the very same dream, and this time he wrote it all down. He tested his ideas and this work led to a Nobel Prize in medicine!

DAYDREAMING SOLUTIONS

You can ask very young students to close their eyes, be still for a bit, and have a "daydream." Then, ask anyone who is willing to share his or her dream with the class. A classroom *Book of Dreams* could be the outcome with Language Experience charts obtained by printing the stories on large sheets of paper as the children dictate them to you.

Ask students "to daydream" a solution or an invention suited to address some social or ecological problem.

Talk about the function of dreams: problem solving, wish fulfillment, affording practice in facing dangerous situations, and so on.

Utah Admitted to the Union (1896) [4]

Utah is our 45th state.

Etymology: "Utah" comes from a Navajo word meaning "upper," as applied to the Shoshone tribe called Utes, the English form of which is Utah. The original name proposed for this state was *Deseret*, "Land of the Honey Bees," from the Book of Mormon. This name was rejected by Congress.

George Washington Carver Day [5]

(For information and activity suggestions see July.)

Three King's Day, Twelfth Night [6]

Since medieval times, France has celebrated Twelfth Night with a *Fête de la Feve*, the Festival of the Bean, featuring a galette du rois (King's Cake) in which a bean is hidden. Whoever finds this bean becomes king of the bean, and everyone must follow his or her commands. This custom of using a bean in this way originated with the Romans who, during their Saturnalian banquets, chose a king of the feast by an election in which beans were used to cast votes.

Twelfth Day Cake (recipe by Rose Mary Provost)*

Group (1)		Group (2)		Group (3)	
1	cup butter	1	tsp. vanilla	4	Tbs. citron
¾	cup sugar	½	tsp. lemon extract	4	Tbs. orange peel
3	eggs	3	cups flour	4	Tbs. slivered almonds
¼	cup milk	¾	cup currants	1	tsp. cinnamon
¼	tsp. salt	¾	cup sultanas	¼	tsp. allspice
		(1	LIMA BEAN!)		

Have the children work in groups to make this special cake. Three groups of 2 children each will set out the correct amounts of ingredients as shown above. Three new groups, of 4 children each, will prepare the ingredients. Group 1 creams the butter & sugar and adds the eggs, one at a time, beating after each addition. Milk & salt are then added. Group 2 mixes a little flour with the raisins & then folds the flour into the batter made by the first group. The flavorings, raisins & bean are then folded in also.

Group 3 sprinkles the spices, orange, & bean over the batter & gently folds them in. Other children can be chosen to oil a bread loaf pan and line it with waxed paper. Then the batter is poured into the pan and baked in a 250°F oven for 2 hours.

The student who finds the bean might be treated as the Bean King—or Queen—for the last half hour of this Three Kings Day!

New Mexico Admitted to the Union (1912) [6]

New Mexico is our 47th state.

Etymology: This state was named *Nuevo Méjico* by Fray Jacinto de San Francisco in about 1561. At that time, the name was applied to lands north and west of the Rio Grande River. *Méjico* comes from *Mexita* and means "the place of the Aztec god of war."

---

*As found in *The Portly Padre, A Church Calendar Cookbook*, edited by Dorothy Taugher (1980).

Connecticut Admitted to the Union (1788) [9]

Connecticut is our 5th state.

Etymology: This is an Algonquin word of the Mohican tribe and means "long river place."

It's a Fact: On January 13, 1932, bright pink snow fell in Durango, Colorado.

Birth of Berthe Morisot (1841) [14]

The great-granddaughter of the French master painter Fragonard, Morisot grew up to marry Eugene Manet, brother of the French painter Edouard Manet. Morisot exhibited with the Impressionists and always signed her work with her maiden name. Her paintings are famous for their beautiful color and sense of light. Her body of work includes 100 canvasses and 300 watercolors, and they stand as concrete proof of her artistic mastery.

Martin Luther King Day [the third Monday in January]

Born in Atlanta, Georgia, on January 15, 1929, Martin Luther King, Jr., was the son and grandson of Baptist ministers. Martin did well in school; he skipped the 9th and 12th grades & entered college at age 15. In 1953, he married Coretta Scott King, a music student. He continued his studies until 1955, when he received a Ph.D. in theology from Boston University. Dr. King's civil rights activities began that same year when Rosa Parks, a black woman (see p. 103), was arrested for refusing to give up her bus seat to a white man. The black leaders of Montgomery, Alabama, urged all blacks to boycott the city buses. Dr. King was asked to head up the boycott. In his first speech as leader of the protest, Dr. King said: "First and foremost, we are American citizens . . . we are not here advocating violence. . . . The only weapon that we have . . . is the weapon of protest. . . . The great glory of American democracy is the right to protest for right."

The boycott was successful and the U.S. Supreme Court ordered integrated seating on all public buses.

Over the next 13 years, King led marches for the poor and hungry; founded the Southern Christian Leadership Conference, an organization dedicated to improving the lot of the poor and minorities; and led blacks and whites in many nonviolent protests against discrimination throughout the country. For his efforts, he was beaten and jailed, but his belief in equality under the law and nonviolent protest eventually won out.

In 1963, Dr. King led a massive march on Washington to highlight black unemployment and urge passage of the Civil Rights Act. Over 200,000 Americans, black and white, marched that day, and Dr. King gave his now-famous speech, "I Have a Dream." In 1964, this minister won the Nobel Peace Prize.

Four years later, while he was in the midst of organizing a campaign to bring to national attention the plight of the poor and homeless, Martin Luther King was shot and killed, in Memphis, Tennessee. James Earl Ray, a white drifter, pleaded guilty to the crime and was sentenced to 99 years in prison.

In 1983, the U.S. Congress passed a law making the third Monday in January a federal holiday in honor of Dr. King.

MLK Day Activities ⎯⎯⎯⎯⎯⎯⎯⎯⎯⎯⎯⎯⎯⎯

This can be a time to encourage discussion among your students about the necessity for sticking up for what you believe, the many great historical figures who faced persecution in their own day, including the founder of one of the world's great religions. The children can be encouraged to make up a list of *Unpopular Heroes,* such as Susan B. Anthony and other feminist leaders, Mahatma Ghandi, Socrates, and so on. Are there unpopular heroes living today? (Archbishop Tutu?)

Birth of Benjamin Franklin (1707) [17] ⎯⎯⎯⎯⎯⎯⎯⎯⎯⎯⎯⎯

Benjamin Franklin was a fireman, an inventor, a printer, a writer, a diplomat, a statesman, and America's first postmaster!

Although he wrote many epigrams praising the wisdom of carefully managing one's money (*and* his birthday always begins National Thrift Week), Franklin seems to have had some problems, himself, with money: when the records of the Bank of North America were turned over to the Historical Society of Pennsylvania, it was discovered that Franklin had been overdrawn on his account an average of three days a week for years.

Franklin wrote his own epitaph, leaving the date of death blank. (His birthdate is based on the Julian calendar, in use at that time; in modern times his birthdate is based on the Gregorian calendar.)

> The body of
> B. Franklin,
> Printer,
> Like the cover of an old book
> its contents torn out
> and stripped of its lettering and gilding,
> lies here, food for worms.
> But the work shall not be wholly lost;
> for it will, as he believed, appear once more,
> in a new and more perfect edition,
> corrected and amended
> by the Author.
> He was born Jan., 6, 1706
> Died ⎯⎯⎯⎯⎯, 17⎯⎯

Inauguration Day [20]

Etymology: In the ancient Roman republic, election to public office was the highest honor that could come to a man. Elaborate ceremonies accompanied the oath of office rites. Seers watched flights of birds in order to determine the most auspicious time for official ceremonies to take place. This practice of taking omens (augeries) influenced the English language of later centuries when the verb "to inaugurate" came to indicate the act of induction into public office.

First American Novel Published (1789) [22]

The first American novel, *The Power of Sympathy,* was published in Boston. It was written by "Philomenia," a pseudonym for Mrs. Sarah Wentworth Morton, who wrote in a time when "no true lady would admit to writing anything for the purposes of publication." Its plot involved scandal, suicide, and illicit love affairs; needless to say, the book sold well!

Stimulating Children to Read More—the Bookworm (or Classroom Dragon). This ever-growing creature will wrap itself around your room and stimulate your students to work together to earn rewards for the whole classroom. Everytime any student finishes a book, the creature grows a little more.

Each child chooses a book geared to his or her own level of reading and reads it through. Young students may read their book silently first and then aloud to a teacher or aide who follows their progress word for word. (If more than four words are missed on a page, the book is probably too difficult for the child, and an easier one should be selected for next time.) Older students should be asked different things after their books, for example, to read to a friend their favorite chapter, or page, to tell the class (or you) about a scary or surprising occurrence in the story, or you might ask them what they think the author's reason for writing the book may have been. Older students should not get in the habit of expecting a rote set of questions at the end of every book reading experience, but should be encouraged to read for the pleasure of it.

Once a book has been read and spoken about in a personal way, the child gets to tape a body segment (a big circle of colored paper, 3″ to 5″ in diameter) to the end of the worm. The name of the book and the name of the child who read it are printed by the child on the circle.

Bookworm is positioned at the top of your classroom wall. As it grows, it should have certain destinations marked off every 3 to 4 feet around the wall in the form of big, bright, clearly printed signs that offer the children special enticements, such as "When Bookworm arrives HERE, the class will see a video about wolves!" This adds real fervor to the students' reading and everyone benefits collectively from the activity. The rewards picked out on reaching the final goal (a treasure hunt or Saturday matinee?) will bring you and the class closer together. Have the reward signs escalate in value, with the last 2 or 3 describing really special activities, such as a roller-skating party or a classroom breakfast!*

Classroom Breakfast. This can be organized so that it is really pleasant and not chaotic or filled with minicrises. Have the children suggest the menu and keep it simple, for example, waffles with real maple syrup, orange wedges, and hot cocoa or granola that the kids make themselves. Sometimes parents are open to contributing ingredients, or cooking materials (e.g., hot plates), or money. Perhaps your PTA could help financially. Do consider any allergies that your students may have and collect the ingredients and paper cups, plates, napkins, plastic forks well in advance. Divide the class into groups so that everyone who wants to cook may have the opportunity. Have 2 or 3 parents come in early and help oversee the operation. One group of students can mix the ingredients for each of the dishes; then they go outside and another "shift" does the cooking. A third group can be responsible for setting up the areas for eating. Try and prepare enough so that each child will have his or her fill. Children can also arrange flowers or other types of centerpieces for the tables. Go over the schedule and general ground rules the afternoon before the breakfast so that everyone knows what is expected of him or her. When the moment for breakfast arrives, the children should come in quietly and be seated before their waitperson (teacher or other adult) comes to take their orders. Good manners and responsible cleanup (by each diner or a cleanup crew) should help ensure a lovely class breakfast. Two small additions: Don't rush during the meal itself. If a child finishes before the others, he or she should be instructed to help serve or read a book quietly. (Remember to remind them the day before to skip breakfast at home!)

Back to the WORM. . . . Once it has wound itself completely around the room, with many a twist and turn on the way, the final reward is achieved and a big sign noting the total

---

*Other classroom rewards might include cinnamon drops for all, a winter picnic, we each get a turn at our grab bag, a nature walk, or a trip to an interesting establishment such as a fire station or a large-machine production plant.

number of books read by the class since the birth of the Bookworm should be posted. If this occurs at the end of the school year, the Bookworm can be dissembled and the segments returned to their owners. The kids will love going through their colored circles and realizing how many books they have read this year. Students with the most circles can be acknowledged, although there shouldn't be an emphasis on quantity. Rather, have fun reminiscing about the different reward signs and activities generated by the Bookworm! Ask the students to recall their reading activities—which stories stick in their minds, and why?

Michigan Admitted to the Union (1837) [26]

Michigan is our 26th state.

Etymology: Michigan comes from the Chipewa words *mici gama,* meaning "great water" after the lake which borders this state.

Kansas Admitted to the Union (1861) [29]

Kansas is our 34th state.

Etymology: This state was named for the Kansas tribe of Siouan Indians who originally lived in what is today northeastern Kansas and other lands beyond.

January Activities

"My Feelings"

Now is the time of year to take stock of your relations with your students. You know each student quite well by now, but it's very enlightening sometimes to listen to children talk about themselves.

Use the "My Feelings" reproducible page to make copies and distribute these to older students, asking them to fill in the sheets. Emphasize the confidentiality of their responses. Or make copies and use one for each young student as you interview him or her (by noting their responses on the paper). If you wish to use the information obtained by these interviews for parent conferences, do so *only* if you have the individual child's permission!

January Language Arts ────────────────────────────

As long as there has been language, there have been riddles. In the Middle Ages, riddles were told as an evening's entertainment and so many riddles were long and complicated. It wasn't until the sixteenth century that riddles grew shorter with a form similar to what is in vogue today. The following riddles are from the year 1511 when they were referred to as Joyous Demands. (Older students may be interested in reading these.)

Demand: What bare the best burden that ever was borne?

Response: The ass that carried our Lady, when she fled with our Lord to Egypt.

Demand: What became of that ass?

Response: Adam's mother ate her.

Demand: Who was Adam's mother?

Response: The earth.

Demand: How many calves' tails would it take to reach from the earth to the sky?

Response: No more than one, if it be long enough.

Demand: What is the distance from the surface of the sea to the deepest part thereof?

Response: Only a stone's throw.

Demand: What is it that never was and never will be?

Response: A mouse's nest in a cat's ear.

Demand: How may a man discern a cow in a flock of sheep?

Response: By his eyesight.

Demand: Why doth a cow lie down?

Response: Because it cannot sit.

Demand: What is it that never freezeth?

Response: Boiling water.

Demand: Which was first, the hen or the egg?

Response: The hen, at the creation.

Demand: How many straws go to a goose's nest?

Response: Not one, for straws not having feet cannot go anywhere.

Demand: Who killed the fourth part of all the people in all the world?

Response: Cain, when he killed Abel.

Demand: What is it that is a builder, and yet not a man, doeth what no man can do, and yet serveth both God and man?

Response: A bee.

Demand: Why doth a dog turn around three times before he lieth down?

Response: Because he knoweth not his bed's head from the foot.

Name _____

MY FEELINGS

Fill in the sentences to tell about **1** time when you felt <u>VERY</u>

EXCITED _____
_____
_____

2. LOVED _____
_____
_____

3 JEALOUS _____
_____
_____

4. LONELY _____
_____
_____

5 SCARED _____
_____
_____

6 very very HAPPY _____
_____
_____

Often, older students will enjoy attempting to solve riddles from other ages. Here are some very old riddles, the first two of which appeared in *The Book of Merrie Riddles*, published in 1629.*

1. Two legs sat upon three legs and had one leg in hand; then in came foure legs and bare away one leg; then up start two legs and threw three legs at foure legs and brought againe one leg. What had happened?

   (A woman with two legs sat on a stoole with three legs and held a leg of lamb in her hand; then all at once in came a dog that hath foure legs and bare away the leg of mutton; so up started the woman and threw the three-legged stoole at the dog with foure legs and picked up the leg of lamb again.)

2. He went to the wood and caught it;

   He sate him downe and sought it;

   Because he could not find it;

   Home with him he brought it. What is it?

   (A thorne. A man went into the woods, caught a thorne in his foot and then he sate himself down and sought to pull it out. Because he could not find it out he must needs bring it home.)

3. We travel much, yet prisoners are,
   And close confined to boot.
   We with the swiftest horse keep pace,
   Yet always go on foot. What are we?

   (Spurs.)

4. Down in the dale there sits and stands eight legs, two hands, livers, lights (organs), and lives three. I count him wise who tells this to me.

   (A man on horseback with a hunting hawk on his arm.)

5. What is it that goes through the woods and toucheth never a twig?

   (The blast of a hunting horn.)

   What is it that goes all about the wood but can't get in?

   (The bark of a tree.)

6. I have legs, but I don't walk. I backbite everyone but I don't talk. I like to hide in small places and you may feed me though you hate me. Who am I?

   (A flea.)

7. I can go where force and strength cannot. Many would be left out in the cold, if I weren't a friend to them. What am I?

   (A door key.)

8. My body is thin and I've nothing within. I have no head or face. But I have a long tail and I fly without wings! What am I?

   (A kite.)

---

*Some of these riddles or very similar ones appear in *The Chapbook Riddles*, ed. Peter Stockham (New York: Dover, 1974), and Charles C. Bombaugh, *Oddities and Curiosities of Words and Literature*, ed. Martin Gardner (New York: Dover, 1961).

The finding out of good riddles
gives quickness of thought and
facility of turning about a
problem every way and viewing
it in every possible light.

                    —Mrs. Barbauld

Roodles of Riddles: One of the myriad uses of riddles in the classroom: they are especially good for filling in those 5-minute pockets of time before dismissal. Riddles may also be a godsend for the substitute teacher! Print them in large letters on 8″ × 24″ pieces of sturdy paper. Children read silently as you hold each card up (answers appear on back). Only raised hands are recognized for the guessing of answers.

Many riddles involve puns or plays on words. There is also a kind of riddle which requires drawing logical conclusions. Riddles offer very young children a fine opportunity to practice listening and speaking.

Another kind of riddle is the analogy: Shoes are to feet as mittens are to _____? Cat is to meow as cow is to _____? Blue is to sky as _____ is to pumpkin?

Try to make up riddles which begin with ambiguous items and gradually reduce the possibilities. "I am big. I can be white or gray. I can bring rain. What am I?"

Social Studies

Another form of riddle develops social concepts: "What kind of worker would you be if you . . . ?" (Give description of different aspects of a job in terms of the work they do—farmer, doctor, nurse, mason.)

EASY RIDDLES

1. I never ask you anything, but you have to answer me all the time. Who am I? (An echo)

2. I have a lot of teeth, but I never use them for eating. Who am I? (A comb, a saw)

3. I can't think. I can't write. I don't even talk. But I tell the truth to everyone. Who am I? (A clock)

4. What 3 letters mean "stiff water"? (Ice)

5. What has 96 legs and cannot walk? (48 pairs of pants!)

6. What do you call a bull when he falls asleep? (A bull-dozer)

7. What driver can never run a red light? (A screwdriver)

8. What did the jack say to the car? (Want a lift?)

9. What kind of bank needs no money? (A river bank)

10. Where does Friday come before Thursday? (In the dictionary!)

11. I ride a horse but I'm not a man. What am I? (A horsefly)

12. Who builds his house with his mouth? (A robin)

13. When is a boy most like a grizzly? (When he's barefooted)

14. What's above the ground, not in a tree? I've told you the answer, now you tell me. (Knot in a tree)

15. Why are wolves like playing cards? (They both come in packs.)

16. What has lots of sharp teeth, but no mouth? (A saw)

17. What runs around the whole backyard and never moves? (A fence)

18. I've a head, a tail, a date, a little worth. What am I? (A penny)

19. Can you spell "dried grass" with just three letters? (H-A-Y)

20. What letter cannot be found in the alphabet? (The one you put in the mailbox)

21. What has no feet or hands but can climb to the ceiling? (Smoke)

22. What is that which the more you take from it the larger it grows? (A hole)

23. Why is an old alarm clock like a river? (It doesn't run long without winding.)

24. Spell "red thief" in three letters. (F-O-X)

25. Spell "blackbird" in four letters. (C-R-O-W)

26. If you carry me, I'll carry you. What am I? (Shoes)

27. What little prisoner is always singing? (A canary)

28. "Little chases big out of the room." What is happening? (A lamp is lit and chases darkness away.)

29. What runs and has no feet, roars, and has no mouth? (The sea)

30. What can go through the bars of a jail and never be seen? (The wind)

31. Spell "black water" in three letters. (I-N-K)

32. What tongue never tells a lie? (A shoe's)

33. What runs but never gets tired? (Water from a tap, or a river)

34. What is the shortest month? (May, it only has three letters)

35. What can open gates without using hands or arms? (The wind)

36. What's the strongest animal? (The tortoise. He carries his house on his back.)

37. What runs round and round a tree and never gets tired or dizzy? (The bark)

38. What's smaller than a mouse yet fills a whole house? (A snail)

39. What can imitate every creature? (A mirror, or an echo)

40. The more you pull its tail, the farther away it goes. What is it? (A ball of yarn)

41. Can you jump higher than a thirty-foot wall? (Sure, walls can't jump.)

42. Why do you expect fish to be well-educated? (Because they're usually found in schools)

43. What's worse than a giraffe with a sore throat? (A centipede with corns)

44. What has five eyes and cannot see? (The Mississippi River)

45. What did the garden say when the farmer made it laugh? (Hoe-hoe-hoe)

46. What's the reddest side of an apple? (The *out* side)

47. How long will a nine-day clock run without winding? (It won't run at all.)

48. Why is the letter "G" like 12 P.M.? (Because it's the middle of "night")

49. What's alive though it has only one foot? (Your leg)

50. A little slave runs all along the ridge cutting down the undergrowth. What is he? (A razor)

51. What runs fast with a thousand people in it? (A train)

52. It helps you understand, but you can't see it. You can grab it, but you can't carry it off. What is it? (Your ear)

53. You throw it into the air and it falls on the ground. You throw it onto the ground and it flies up in the air. What is it? (A rubber ball)

54. What has four legs and feathers? (A feather bed)

55. What does everyone in the world do at the same time? (Grow older)

56. What can cross a lake without stirring up waves? (A shout)

57. What is empty in the daytime and full at night? (A bed)

58. What's the surest way to keep water from coming into your house? (Don't pay your water bill!)

59. What can you hold in your left hand that you can never hold in your right? (Your right elbow)

60. How can you travel very fast and yet not go far from the first place you passed? (Swing on a swing)

61. Can you name the three states that were named after presidents of the U.S.A.? (No, because only one is: Washington.)

62. Why is a penny like a rooster on the fence? (Its head is on one side, tail on the other.)

63. What is it that by losing an eye has nothing left but a nose? (Noise)

64. What has a trunk and a tail and walks? (A mouse going on vacation)

65. What travels but never moves? (A road)

66. When must a man keep his word? (When nobody else will take it)

67. Why is an empty purse always the same? (Because there's never any change in it)

68. Which animal took the most luggage onto Noah's ark and which one had the least? (The elephant had the most for he took his trunk; the rooster had the least for he only took his comb.)

69. How can you make a fire with just three sticks? (Be sure one is a match!)

70. What do we all need and want, but always forget about when it comes? (Sleep)

HARD RIDDLES

1. Why is a hen immortal? (Because her son never sets)

2. What can you eat that you can't plant or plow? It's the son of water but if water touches it, it dies. (Salt)

3. What dead tree stands up and moves? (A ship's mast)

4. What made the pretty tree fall for the handsome woodcutter? (He just axed it!)

5. If you have exactly 100 male deer and 100 female pigs, what have you got? (One hundred sows n' bucks! ($100,000!))

6. What kind of flower would you get if you planted an angry black bird? (Crow-cusses)

7. What vowel is the most contented? ("i"—it's always in the middle of happiness.)

8. Name 3 things that can outrun a horse and cross a stream without getting wet. (Sunlight, the wind, and a shout)

9. I went to the lumberyard and bought some wood. I didn't bring long boards. I didn't bring back short boards. What did I bring back? (Sawdust)

10. Name two things that only have two sides. (A balloon:—inside and outside—and an argument:—his side and your side)

11. Where can you always find love, money, and health? (In the dictionary)

12. Why are the 15th and 14th letters of the alphabet more important than all the others? (Because we could never get on without them)

13. What is worse than raining cats and dogs? (Hailing taxis)

14. What can be an honest judge even though it's not alive? (A scale)

15. I can speak German, English, Spanish, and French, although I never went to school. Who am I? (An echo or a tape)

16. Who can take 85 men to town in one car? (Anyone who is willing to make enough trips!)

17. A woman had five children and half of them were boys. How is that possible? (The other half were also boys.)

18. There is something to eat, something to drink, something to pickle, something to plant, and something to feed the farmer's pig—yet this is just one thing. What is it? (A watermelon)

19. If a dog lost its tail, where would it get a new one? (At Sears, where everything is retailed!)

20. We have 2 legs but can go nowhere without a man, and he can go nowhere without us. Who are we? (Trousers)

21. The more I'm used the fresher I get, but if you don't use me, I get stale fast. Who am I? (Knowledge)

22. Why is an onion like a ringing churchbell? (Peel (peal) follows peel (peal).)

23. What words can be pronounced quicker and shorter by adding a syllable to them? (Quick and short)

24. Why is a burglar upstairs probably an honest man? (Because he is above doing something dishonest)

25. When can a man fall off a 40-foot ladder and not be hurt? (When he falls off the bottom rung)

26. What is it that each of us, no matter how careful he is, always overlooks? (His nose)

27. When were there only two vowels? (In the days of No-A (Noah), before U and I were born.)

28. Why is a loaf of bread four weeks old like a mouse running into its hole? (Because you'll probably see its stale—its tail!)

29. What runs all over town during the day and stays under the bed at night with its tongue hanging out? (A shoe)

30. What gets wetter the more it dries? (A towel)
31. What is it that someone else has to take before you can have it? (Your photograph)
32. Why is a lumberjack's job one of opposites? (First he cuts a tree down; then he cuts it up.)
33. Prove that your baby sister or brother is not worth two cents. (Well, a baby is a crier. A crier is a messenger. A messenger is one sent. One sent is not worth two cents. So, a baby brother or sister is not worth two cents!)
34. What has no hands or feet, but climbs high? (The sun and the mercury in a thermometer on a hot day)
35. What walks all over the pasture by day and sits in the refrigerator at night? (Milk)

36. What drink tells us what the patient has and the doctor gets? (Cof-fee)
37. What is the difference between a bad pianist and 16 ounces of butter? (One pounds away, the other weighs a pound.)
38. What can you break with a whisper more easily than with a hammer? (A confidence)
39. What is the easiest-going bird in the world? (A crow: it never complains without cause—caws.)
40. What common term could you use to describe a man who didn't have all of his fingers on one of his hands? (Normal—normal people have half their fingers on each hand.)
41. What are the hardest things in the world to deal with? (An old deck of cards)
42. What is the difference between a cat and a comma? (One has its claws at the end of its paws, the other its pause at the end of its clause.)
43. Why is very fresh milk like something that never happened? (Because it hasn't a-curd)
44. What is the difference between a thief and a church bell? (One steals from the people; the other peels from the steeple.)
45. When did the greatest drought in English history take place? (1837–1901: there was only one reign in those 64 years.)
46. Why don't jokes last as long as church bells? (Because after they've been tolled a few times, they get worn out.)
47. What do you call a son who is always wiring for money? (An electrician)
48. What is always in fashion, and yet always out of date. (The letter F)
49. Why is a cold like a great humiliation? (It brings the proudest man to his—sneeze.)
50. What's the difference between a crown prince and the water in a fountain? (One is heir to the throne, the other thrown in the air.)
51. Why is a yuppie like a fellow with a short memory? (Both are always for-getting.)

52. What's the difference between a Xerox machine and the measles? (One makes facsimiles, the other sick families.)

53. Why is Westminster Abbey like a fireplace? (It contains the ashes of the grate.)

54. Why is a wise man like a straight pin? (He comes right to a point and his head keeps him from going too far!)

55. Treat me right and I look like everybody, but scratch my back and I look like nobody. Who am I? (A mirror)

56. Why is a former boxer like a beehive? (An ex-boxer is an ex-pounder, and an expounder is a commentator, a common "tater" is an Irish "tater" and an Irish "tater" is a specked "tater," a spectator is a beholder and a bee-holder is a hive.)

The mind ought sometimes to be amused, that it may the better return to thought and to itself.

—Phaedrus (5th century BC)

RIDDLES ABOUT RIDDLES

1. Why is a bad riddle like a broken pencil? (Because it has no point.)

2. Do you know the riddle about the three holes in the ground? (Well, well, well)

3. Do you know the riddle about the red-hot poker? (Don't worry. You couldn't grasp it.)

4. Do you know the riddle about the sky? (Don't bother. It's way over your head.)

5. Why is a riddle like a peanut? (Because it's not much good until you crack it)

6. Why is this riddle like a dirty window? (Because you can't see through it)

7. What should you do when you split your sides laughing at the answer to a good riddle? (Run fast until you get a stitch in your sides.)

8. Why doesn't a riddle last as long as a church bell? (Because after you've told [tolled] it a few times, it's all worn out.)

9. Why is a person reading these riddles like a man in front of a firing squad? (Because he's pretty sure to be riddled to death. . . .)

January Science ───────────────────────

Children can learn a good deal by watching the day-to-day growth of plants in their classroom: plants grow from different beginnings—seeds, cuttings, tubers, bulbs, but plants follow a definite pattern of growth. Baby plants will grow to be like the adult plants. Plants have different temperatures and require various amounts of water, sunshine, warmth, and soil. You can stock your classroom nursery with a variety of plants at no expense: 28 suggestions follow.

Etymology: The root of the word "nature" is found in the Latin *natura,* which comes from *natus* meaning "produced." The latter is the past participle of *nasci,* a verb meaning "to be born."

Apple seeds. Seeds are not ready to be planted directly from the fruit. Put the seeds in a jar with damp moss. Refrigerate for 6 weeks (mark the removal date on your classroom calendar). Turn them over periodically until they begin to sprout. Then fill a small pot with potting compost. Plant seed ½″ down in compost. Keep in light, warm room. Keep moist.

Avocado pit. Place pit, round end down, in a small jar. Fill jar with water so that round end only is submerged. Then wait (for perhaps as long as 2 to 3 months), keeping the round end submerged. When pit looks slimy and even moldy, do not despair; roots should appear any time. When root is ½″ long, plant the pit in a medium-sized pot. Water it well when it is dry and feed it from time to time.

Beet. Cut to within 1″ of its top, retaining leaves. Trim foliage back. Plant beet top in sandy soil. Keep moist, not wet.

Broadbeans. Soak 2 to 3 hours until they swell. Cut and roll a piece of blotting paper and line a 1–2 lb. jam jar up to the mouth with the paper. Place bean about ½ way down between jar and paper. Pour 1″ of water into jar. See that blotter remains quite wet. Place jar in dark cupboard until beans germinate; then bring jar into the light. (If you use 2 jars, placing one in cupboard and leaving one in the light, children will see which grows faster. (Why?) Lay sprouting beans on soil. Keep it moist.

Carrot. Cut, retaining 1″ of foliage and 1″ of root; set in a shallow dish filled with ½″ of water. Add tiny pieces of charcoal to keep water sweet, or trim foliage; cut root 2″ from top and hollow out center; hang upside down like a basket. Keep filled with water.

Corn. As a child in Illinois, my mother was taught to plant corn in this fashion: "When sowing corn, plant 5 grains—1 for the blackbird, 1 for the crow, 1 for the meal worm, and 1 won't grow."

Date Pits (from unprocessed dates). These need lots of room. Plant pit in sandy soil. When roots outgrow pot, break out bottom of pot and plant in a bigger pot.

Grapes. Dry seeds. Put ½″ of clean pebbles in the bottom of a pot. Mix one part humus, two parts potting soil, and a handful of vermiculite. Put in pot. Water, allowing soil to settle. Plant 12 seeds ½″ deep. Keep soil damp. Place pot where it will get just 1–2 hours of direct sun each day until vine is around 7″ tall. Put a reinforcing stick beside vine for it to climb.

Grapefruit seeds. These do best if planted in February. You can use the grapefruit shell filled with potting soil and sand as the seed's initial holder. Soak seed overnight before planting. Sink soil down close about seed. Later transfer young plant to a sturdier container. The plant may grow for years. Keep earth moist by spraying with water every day. Also water twice a week.

Kumquats. See lemon seeds.

Lemon seeds. Cover with ½″ of sand and potting soil, after soaking seeds overnight. Keep earth moist (as described for grapefruit).

Lentils. Spread in single layer in a saucer. Moisten, but don't float lentils. Keep moist and in the sun. In 10 days they sprout and can be planted like beans.

Mango seeds. These are difficult to start as they, like the avocado, are slow in sprouting. Press seed into soil flat side down. Keep soil moist.

Mold. Mold is a plant; different molds will grow on various food surfaces; including cheddar cheese, cooked rice, and bread each of which will produce a different color of mold. Lay a slice of bread on a pie pan. Coat different areas of bread with a little jam, jelly, and grated orange peel. (Use nothing that contains preservatives.) Lightly spray with water and lightly cover with foil. Place in the dark. Occasionally respray with water to keep surface moist. Use a magnifying glass to enjoy these plants! Caution: Students with allergies to mold should not be exposed to these.

Oats. Can be started in the following way: Line the bottom of a pie tin with small stones. Add a layer of rich earth, then lay oats on top. Cover with layer of fine soil. Cover entire top of pan with cheese cloth and set in sunny window. Sprinkle the cloth with water each day. Oats should sprout on the third day. Remove the cloth at this time and continue to keep soil moist.

Onion. Place pointed end up in a small-mouthed jar. Cover half of onion with water. Add small amounts of charcoal to water.

Orange pits. See apple seeds.

Peach pits. See apple seeds.

Pepper seeds. These seeds, from tiny red peppers in pickling spice, are spread out to dry on a paper towel. Punch small holes for drainage in the bottom of a cottage cheese container and then fill the container with soil. Barely cover the seeds and keep moist.

Pineapple. Cut off 1–1½″ from top of plant. Retain spiky foliage. Allow pineapple to dry for three days; then place in sandy soil. Water lightly and keep as warm as possible. In about 2 weeks (if roots have grown), repot plant in good sterilized soil. Keep the soil damp and warm and near light. Your plant won't bear, but it will be attractive.

Potato Porcupine. Slice off the top of an Irish potato. Carve out a hole, leaving plenty of meat on the walls. Insert 4 toothpicks as legs. Make eyes by attaching two small white paper circles with black thumb tacks. Fill cavity with earth (or moist cotton) sprinkled with grass seed. Keep watered for 10 days until Porky's spines sprout.

Plum. See apple seeds.

Pumpkin. See pepper seeds.

Sweet potato. Some are heat-dried and won't grow, so ask grocer for a fresh one. If possible, choose one with a few whiskers. Cut potato in half and insert toothpicks around potato below cut surface. Place potato, tapered end down, in a jar, suspended from the toothpicks. Fill the jar with water and put it in a closet until roots sprout. Then bring it into the light. The plant will sustain itself on water for quite a while, or you may plant it in soil, allowing green sprouts to remain above the earth.

Squash. Follow directions for pepper seeds, except press squash seeds down ¾″ in soil.

Watermelon seeds. Plant directly in soil. Sprinkle lightly and often with water. Seeds sprout quickly and plant has abundant foliage. Continue watering.

White potato. Cut into sections, each section containing an eye or two. Plant in rich earth and keep moistened. Let it have lots of sun.

Yam. Choose one that has purple eyes. Then follow directions for sweet potato.

Charting your Seeds' Progress. Help the children keep a large classroom chart that will show how long each seed took to (1) sprout, (2) leaf, (3) bud, (4) flower, and (5) seed. (Put a plastic sandwich bag over different kinds of growing leaves in your classroom to see the water loss of an hour or an afternoon.)

January Art

Printmaking. The most basic types of prints are made by applying water-based ink (or paint) to a flat nonporous surface (e.g., an apple sliced down the middle) & then pulling a print. Children can compile print samplers, experimenting with unusual surfaces.

Melted Crayon Prints. This is a sure winner with kids! You will need a warming tray (extension cord & masking tape) with a heat control knob, heavy aluminum foil, crayon odds and ends, including some metallic-colored crayons, construction paper of different colors cut to fit inside the top surface of the warming tray, mittens or old socks to protect sensitive hands, and plenty of (low-key) adult supervision. Wrap a piece of aluminum foil over the top of the warming tray and extend it down over the sides. Use a strip of masking tape to divide the tray's surface in half down the middle making two printing areas so that two children at a time may work. Turn the warming tray to low, and supply children with socks on their hands as added protection, although the tray should never get hot to the touch. With a stick crayon, child draws on the foil while the tray is turned on. The image quickly turns liquid. Next he or she presses a piece of paper onto the foil and transfers the impression. Several impressions can be taken to compare lines and techniques.

Variation: A tiny sprinkle of glitter added to the melted crayon on the paper can create a lovely design.

Variation: Try melting white & silver crayon in a design or picture and laying black or dark purple paper on top for making the print.

Cardboard Printing. You will need tracing paper, hard & soft lead pencils, 2 pieces of cardboard (one 3″ × 3″ and one 3″ × 4½″), a heavy piece of cardboard or pad of newspapers for use as a cutting surface, scrap paper (newsprint), mat knife, white glue, tempera paint, colored paper (6″ × 9″), masking tape, and a (no. 8) watercolor brush.

First the student should draw a bold 3″ × 3″ design and trace it. Next, on the back of the tracing paper, the soft lead pencil is used to go over the pattern lines. This tracing paper is placed right side up in the center of the 3″ × 4½″ cardboard & is taped in place. The hard lead pencil is used to go over the pattern outline. The tracing paper is removed to reveal a dark outline pattern on the cardboard. Darken any faint lines. Now the student darkens the back of the tracing paper again, using the soft lead pencil. Repeat the transfer process onto the 3″ × 3″ piece of cardboard and then put this cardboard square on top of the cutting surface. Use the mat knife to cut out the design and glue on top of the larger piece of cardboard which will serve as a base. Allow glue to dry thoroughly.

Encourage students to make test prints to learn the best amount of pressure and paint to apply when taking a print. Paint should be applied to all raised surfaces of the cardboard printing block. Areas between the design should be kept, as much as possible, free from paint. Student quickly presses printing block onto scrap paper, then lifts up block to check the results. Fresh paint should be applied before each print is made. When good, clear images have been achieved, the student is ready to print on the 6″ × 9″ colored paper, which can be folded in half to form a greeting card. Be sure to line up the design with the top and bottom edges of the card. The card may be printed a second time on the opposite half of the folded paper, if desired.

If paint accumulates on the block after a while, rinse it off quickly by just passing it under running water & then gently clean off paint with brush or fingers. Dry block with paper towel before using again.

Variation: When designing a cardboard block pattern, include a few line areas that are achieved by gluing short lengths of heavy string in place atop cardboard printing block surface.

Fingerprint Prints. The children use their fingertips (thumbs & entire fingers) to make cartoonlike pictures or little flipbook illustrations. Thumb is pressed onto inkpad & then pressed onto paper. Marker lines can also be added. Make the thumbprint into a tiny mouse, the petals of a daisy, a person's face. Several fingerprints can be combined to form an airplane, a dinosaur, or a long, segmented snake.

Handmade Stamps. Cut simple shapes from thin foam or felt (or inner tube). Glue shapes to the flat side of a small piece of wood (or, for very small shapes, the end of a cork). Apply pressure to adhered area until glue is dry. Then press stamp onto inkpad and next onto the paper to be printed.

Negative Prints. Collect a variety of small objects with varied shapes such as a leaf, comb, piece of string, pebble, button, seashell, and so on. Take a large piece of paper and submerge it into water; sponge off excess. Arrange objects artistically on paper and sprinkle pinches of one or more tempera powder colors around them. Then use a soda straw to blow puffs onto the powder. When paint is nearly dry, carefully lift off the objects.

Styrofoam Meat Tray Prints. Here's a terrific way to reuse styrofoam picnic plates or meat trays! Wash used containers with warm soapy water to remove any oily residue. Use a ballpoint pen or a pencil to draw a picture or design directly onto styrofoam surface. (Remember: If words are incorporated into the design, they must be printed backward!)

Squeeze some water-based printing ink onto a small pane of glass. Roll a brayer (available at art supply stores) back & forth through ink. Then roll brayer over etched area of meat tray. Lower a piece of paper onto the inked area & gently but firmly rub one hand over paper's surface while other hand holds tray and paper stable. Carefully lift off print and analyze how to improve upon it with your next print.

Variation: Apply 2 colors of ink to glass pane, for example, red at side & blue along opposite side of glass. Roll the brayer through the 2 inks to achieve a vivid red/purple/blue coating. Striking prints (greeting cards) will result from such an ink coating.

January Games and Outdoor Activities

Indoor Games—Who am I?*

This game helps players to feel close to nature and to gain deeper insight into one another. Participants quietly decide what nature object they would most like to be, and then take turns telling the others their decision and reasons for it. This activity is repeated: in the next round, children choose the wild living creature they would most like to be & pantomime its actions for others to try to identify.

Variation: Children first describe reasons for choosing the object or creature and let the rest of the class try to guess their choice!

Heavy, Heavy Hangs over Your Head

This game comes from the days of Queen Victoria. All the children are seated. A small common object is held over a child's head so that he or she cannot see it but everyone else can. The child holding the object says, "Heavy, heavy hangs over your head." Then one by one the other children give a word describing or suggesting the object without naming it or any part of it. After each clue the "It" tries to guess the object. When the object is correctly guessed, the child selects a new object (from a box of things provided by teacher) and holds this (unseen) over the head of the new "It."

I'm Thinking of Someone

This is a way to gently spotlight individual children in the class. Young students especially enjoy the game. "It" looks around the room and privately chooses someone. The rest of the class ask questions to determine who this "someone" is. (The "someone" must be present in the room.) All questions must, of course, be respectful and must be able to be answered by "yes" or "no." The student who finally guesses the person becomes the new "It."

Snowy Weather Fun

Ice Windows. Line the inside edge of an aluminum pie pan with a long section of yarn; leave the end of it hanging out of the pie pan. Place holly berries, leaves, small, flat fir twigs,

---

*This (and loads of other original game ideas) come from *Bag of Tricks: 180 Great Games (and 3 More with Real Potential)* by Jane Seanborn. Available through Search Publications, 2000 Old Stage Road, Florissant, CO 80816.

dried flowers, or potpourri in the pan. Then put the pan on a flat surface outdoors in cold weather. Carefully fill it with water, using a chopstick or twig to settle down anything that may float. When the water has frozen, remove the ice from the pan. If you have any trouble doing this, just set pie pan in shallow pan of warm water for a minute or two. Have the children make lots of these ice windows in different shapes and sizes, using frozen meat pie and TV dinner trays. Hang your ice windows by the free ends of the yarn so you can all enjoy looking at the light coming through them! (Try adding a drop or two of food coloring for special effects.)

Frozen Bubbles. It must be very cold outside for these to work. Plan to bring along a towel to dry off wet fingers and plenty of tissues to wipe off soapy lips. Make a solution of Dawn dishwashing liquid & water: experiment using quite a lot of soap in proportion to the water until you have a good bubble-making solution. Each child will need a small (or large) wooden spool & a dime-sized piece of modeling clay. Dip the end of the spool into the soapy solution and gently blow through the other end to form a bubble. It's fun on a snowy day simply to blow the bubbles and watch them as they float away.

To make a frozen bubble, blow a small bubble, put your finger over the spool's blow hole and cover this hole with clay. Gently stand the spool upright on a flat surface where it is very cold but not windy. With patience, luck, and a low enough temperature, you will see the bubble becoming opaque. Encourage the children to experiment with a frozen bubble and watch what happens if you move your warm hand slowly toward it, you carry it inside, you leave it outside in the cold. How does the frozen bubble behave when it develops a hole? You'd best do this during a science period because a recess will never be long enough! Fascinating fun.

FEBRUARY

The Yuma Indians of the Southwest call this month "Xavatac" meaning "Corn." The Seminoles call February "Wind Moon," and the Eskimos call it "Drying Skins; Snow Is Melting." To the Pawnees, February, like January, is a month that foretells the future: if it thundered to the North as they returned from their travels, they believed cold weather would last late into spring, so they called this month "Thunder" or "Snow-It-Is-White" for the expected snowfall.

Calendar of Important Dates

§ Black History Month.

§ National Children's Dental Health Week, begins with the first Sunday in the month.

§ National Wildlife Week begins the third Sunday in February.

§ National Brotherhood Week always includes Washington's birthday.

§ Leap year occurs only in years in which the last two digits are evenly divisible by the number 4. This extra day comes every four years because it takes the earth 365¼ days to revolve around the sun. Those four ¼ days make a whole day every four years.

1 National Freedom Day commemorates President Lincoln's 1865 proposal of the anti-slavery amendment (13th) to the Constitution.

Discovery of X rays by Roentgen, 1896.

Langston Hughes, black American writer, was born in Joplin, Missouri, in 1902.

First Woolworth lunch counter sit-ins by blacks in Greensboro, North Carolina, protesting the no-service-to-blacks policy, 1960.

2   Groundhog Day

On this day in 1848, the Treaty of Guadalupe Hidalgo was signed, in which Mexico agreed to cede Texas, New Mexico, California, and parts of Arizona to the U.S. in return for $15,000,000.

On this day in 1882, the great Irish writer James Joyce was born.

Yascha Heifitz, superb violinist, was born in 1901.

3   First American paper money was issued by Massachusetts to pay soldiers fighting in the war of Quebec, 1690.

Elizabeth Blackwell, first woman doctor, was born in 1821.

Gertrude Stein, writer and conceptual poet, was born in Allegheny, Pennsylvania, in 1874.

On this day in 1959, Buddy Holly, Richie Valens, & The Big Bopper, popular music stars, were killed in a plane crash.

4   On this day in 1789, the Electoral College named George Washington the nation's first president.

Hank Aaron, baseball great, was born in Mobile, Alabama, in 1934.

5   On this day in 1936, The National Wildlife Federation was founded.

6   Queen Anne of England was born, 1665.

Massachusetts became the 6th state to be admitted to the Union, 1788.

Ronald Reagan, 40th U.S. president, was born in 1911.

On this day in 1952, King George VI of Great Britain died and was succeeded by his daughter, Queen Elizabeth II.

7   On this day, these fine writers were born:

• Charles Dickens, English author, in 1812

• Laura Ingalls Wilder, American chronicler of family life on the frontier, 1867

• Sinclair Lewis, the first American to win the Nobel Prize for Literature, in Sauk Center, Minnesota, in 1885

8   On this day in 1587, Mary Queen of Scots, accused of plotting the murder of Britain's Queen Elizabeth I, was beheaded at Fotheringhay Castle, England.

9   William Henry Harrison, 9th U.S. president, was born in Berkeley, Virginia, 1773.

On this day in 1825, the House of Representatives elected John Quincy Adams president, following the national election in which none of the candidates received an electoral majority.

10   Boris Pasternak, Russian novelist and poet, was born in Moscow, 1890.

First singing telegram was delivered, in New York City, 1933.

On this day in 1936, the Nazi Gestapo were authorized to imprison Germans without trial, making Hitler's dictatorship in Germany absolute.

11   National Science Youth Day is observed on the birthday of Thomas A. Edison as part of National Electricity Week.

Edison was born in Milan, Ohio, on this day in 1847. During his 84-year lifespan, he is credited with 1,097 inventions!

12 Cotton Mather, American Congregational minister and the most celebrated of the Puritans, was born in 1663.

First puppet show was given in America, 1738.

Abigail Adams, writer and wife and mother of U.S. presidents (married to John, the 2nd president and mother to John Quincy, the 6th) was born in 1663.

Charles Darwin, contributor to the theory of evolution, was born in 1809.

Birthdate of our beloved 16th president, Abraham Lincoln, in a log cabin in Hardin (now Larue) County, Kentucky, in 1809.

On this day in 1870, all the women in the territory of Utah were granted full suffrage.

First patent for a baseball catcher's mask, 1878.

Buckminster Fuller, inventor and visionary, was born in 1895.

On this day in 1912, China became a republic as the Manchu Dynasty was overthrown in a rebellion led by Dr. Sun Yat-sen.

On this day in 1960, the Soviet Union launched its Venus probe.

13 First public school opened in America, the Boston Latin School, 1635.

On this day in 1669, William and Mary were proclaimed king and queen of England by Parliament.

First magazine was published in America—*The American Magazine*—in Philadelphia, 1747.

Grant Wood, American painter, was born in 1892.

In 1974, Alexander Solzhenitsyn, Russian writer, dissident, and winner of the Nobel Prize for Literature, was deported to West Germany.

14 Valentine's Day.

Frederick Douglass, black leader, was born in Tuckahoe, Maryland, in 1817.

Oregon became the 33rd state to be admitted to the Union, 1859.

On this day in 1876, Alexander Bell patented the telephone.

Arizona became the 48th state to join the Union in 1912.

Carl Bernstein, American journalist who with fellow *Washington Post* reporter John Woodward uncovered the Watergate scandal that eventually led to President Nixon's resignation, was born in 1944.

15 Galileo Galilei, Italian scientist, was born in 1564.

Susan B. Anthony, pioneer crusader for women's rights, was born in Adams, Massachusetts, in 1820.

On this day in 1879, President Rutherford B. Hayes signed into law a bill admitting women to practice law before the U.S. Supreme Court.

17 On this day in 1801, Thomas Jefferson was elected president by members of the House of Representatives on their 36th ballot.

In 1897, the National Congress of Parents and Teachers—the PTA—was founded in Washington, DC.

Modern art was introduced to the public of the United States at the Armory Show in New York City, 1913.

Chaim Potok, Jewish writer, was born in 1929.

18 First antislavery protest was held in the United States, in Germantown, Pennsylvania, 1688.

Sholom Aleichem, Yiddish classical author, was born in 1859.

On this day in 1861, Jefferson Davis was inaugurated president of the Confederate States of America.

19 Nicolaus Copernicus, Polish astronomer who revolutionized planetary astronomy, was born, 1473.

In 1884, the U.S. Patent Office granted a patent for the phonograph.

20 John Glenn Day commemorates the U.S. astronaut's orbiting of the earth in 1962. Launched from Cape Canaveral, Florida, he circled the earth three times in his space capsule and then landed safely in the Atlantic Ocean.

On this day in 1965, the *Ranger 8* spacecraft crashed into its target area on the moon after relaying back to earth some 7,000 pictures of the lunar surface.

On this day in 1972, President Nixon began his week-long official visit to the Republic of China for talks with Mao Tse-Tung.

21 First woman dentist to be graduated, Lucy B. Hobbs, took her degree from Ohio College of Dental Surgery in Cincinnati, 1866.

Also sharing this date are

• Anaïs Nin, French poet and diarist, born in 1903.

• W. H. Auden, visionary poet, born in 1907.

• Barbara Jordan, black politician and teacher, born in 1936.

22 On this day in 1630, the English colonists were introduced to popcorn by the Native Americans!

George Washington, first U.S. president, was born on his parents' plantation near Fredericksburg, Virginia, in 1732.*

---

*His birthday is now observed as a holiday on the third Monday in February.

Frederic Chopin, composer, was born on this date in 1810.

In 1819 on this date, Florida was ceded to the U.S. by Spain.

First Woolworth Store was opened in 1879 by F. W. Woolworth in Utica, New York.

Edward Gorey, American illustrator, cartoonist, was born in 1923.

As was Edward M. Kennedy, American liberal politician, in 1932.

23   Samuel Pepys, author of the most famous diary in the world, was born in Cambridge, England, in 1633. Pepys had no idea that after his death, millions would read this diary to learn about the society and culture of his time. He wrote his diary in a shorthand that was not deciphered until long after his death.

George F. Handel, English Baroque composer *(The Messiah),* was born in 1635.

W. E. B. Du Bois, black scholar, was born in Great Barrington, Massachusetts, in 1868.

On this date in 1495, Columbus sent the first boatload of slaves from the New World to Spain.

24   Wilhelm Grimm, who, with brother Jacob, collected and edited a book of German fairy tales, was born in 1786.

Winslow Homer, American painter, was born in 1836.

On this day in 1868, the only impeachment proceedings ever instituted against a U.S. president were begun in the House of Representatives when it voted to impeach President Andrew Johnson for "high crimes and misdemeanors." The president had dismissed Secretary of War Stanton and was accused of declaring several laws unconstitutional. On May 28, 1868 he was acquitted by a one-vote margin.

25   First black member of the U.S. Senate, Hiram H. Revels of Mississippi, won his seat in Congress, 1870.

On this day in 1820, Congressman Felix Walker of North Carolina, whose district included Buncombe County, refused to let the House vote on the Missouri Bill until he made another of his long-winded speeches about his beloved Buncombe County—one speech too many—from which we get our word "bunk" meaning "nonsense" or "hot air."

26   On this day in 1848, the French Republic was proclaimed.

Fats Domino, rock 'n roller of the 1950s, was born in 1928.

Johnny Cash, American country singer, was born in 1932.

27   John Steinbeck, noted American writer, was born in Salinas, California, in 1902.

Ralph Nader, American consumer advocate, was born in 1934.

N. Scott Momaday, noted American Indian writer, was born in Lawton, Oklahoma, in 1934.

On this day in 1973, members of the American Indian Movement (AIM) occupied the trading post and church at Wounded Knee, South Dakota (site of a 1890 massacre of Sioux Indians by the U.S. Army), to draw attention to grievances of contemporary American Indians.

28   The Republican political party was created at Ripon, Wisconsin, in 1845.

Yellowstone became America's first national park in 1871.

Linus Pauling, chemist and 2-time winner of the Nobel Peace Prize (1954 & 1962), was born in Portland, Oregon, in 1901.

29 Ann Lee, Mother Ann, who brought the Shaker religion from England to the American colonies, was born on this day in 1736.

February

Named for the Latin word *februare*, which means "to purify" as this was the month in which the Romans purified themselves in preparation for the festivals at the start of their new year.

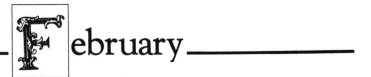

February Quotations

11 We do not know one millionth of one percent about anything.

—Thomas Edison

12 He has the right to criticize who has the heart to help.
Folks are generally as happy as they make up their minds to be.
The ballot is stronger than the bullet.

—Abraham Lincoln

14 May you live all the days of your life.

—Jonathan Swift

We cannot tell the precise moment when friendship is formed. As in filling a vessel drop by drop, there is at last a drop which makes it run over, so in a series of kindnesses there is at last one which makes the heart run over.

—James Boswell, from *The Life of Dr. Johnson, Everyman*

A man should keep his friendships in constant repair.

—Samuel Johnson

Let us see what love can do.

—William Penn

No one has ever loved anyone the way anyone wants to be loved.

—Mignon McLaughlin

15 It is surely harmful to souls to make it a heresy to believe what is proved.

—Galileo Galilei (after having been forced
to recant the doctrine that the earth moves around the sun)

(On being asked to censor the works of Teilhard de Chardin, Pope Pius XII (1876–1858) is said to have answered: "One Galileo in two thousand years is enough.")

22 Labor to keep alive in your breast that little spark of celestial fire called conscience.

—George Washington

I often say of George Washington that he was one of the few in the whole history of the world who was not carried away by power.

—Robert Frost

February Events

Black History Month

February is a month in which we honor the singular accomplishments and strengths of black America. The reference list of historically important black people that follows is simply a beginning point for research projects, book reports, and so on. You and your students will undoubtedly have additional names to add to this list. Note them on this page as they occur to you, and in this way, your reference list can be expanded year by year.

A THANK YOU LIST OF BLACK PEOPLE
WHO HELPED MAKE THIS A BETTER WORLD

Hank Aaron
Kareem Abdul-Jabbar
Marion Anderson
Maya Angelon
Muhammed Ali
Louis Armstrong
Crispus Attucks
James Baldwin
Benjamin Banneker
Mary McCleod Bethune
Guy Blufford, Jr.
Julian Bond
Tom Bradley
Edward Brooke
Jim Brown
Blanche Bruce
George Washington Carver

Tracy Chapman
Ray Charles
Shirley Chisholm
Marva Collins
Bill Cosby
Frederick Daveson
Miles Davis
Frederick Douglass
Cherles Drew
W. E. B. Du Bois
Paul Lawrence Dunbar
Duke Ellington
James Gardiner
Althea Gibson
Dizzy Gillespie
Whoopi Goldberg
Alex Halley

W. C. Handy
Lorraine Hansberry
Patricia Harris
Matthew Henson
Earl "Fatha" Hines
Gregory Hines
Lena Horne
Langston Hughes
Charlene Hunter-Gault
Jesse Jackson
Michael Jackson
Bo Jangles
Jack Johnson
James Weldon Johnson
James Earl Jones
Barbara Jordan
Florence Joyner
Martin Luther King, Jr.
Eartha Kitt
Elizabeth D. Koonce
Sarah Lawrence-Lightfoot
Leadbelly
Nelson Mandela
Wynton Marsalis
Thurgood Marshall
Jan Matzeliger
James Miles
Dorie Miller
Barrett Morgan

Pedro Alonzo Niña
Jesse Owens
Charlie Byrd Parker
Rosa Parks
Pele
Sidney Poitier
Salem Poor
General Clayton Powell
Leontine Price
Otis Redding
Paul Robeson
Jackie Robinson
Diana Ross
Peter Salem
William Thompson
Zora Neale Thurston
Sojourner Truth
Harriet Tubman
Nat Turner
Desmond Tutu
Madame C. D. Walker
Alice Walker
Booker T. Washington
Phyllis Wheatley
Daniel Hale Williams
Carter G. Woodson
Stevie Wonder
Richard Wright
Andrew Young

It's a Fact: Benjamin Banneker was probably the best known black person in early U.S. history. He was a surveyor, a mathematician, a farmer, and an astronomer. In 1753 he completed a clock which he had built entirely of wood! Every gear was carved by hand, and the only models he had to go by were a pocket watch & an old picture of a clock. Benjamin Banneker's wooden clock kept nearly perfect time for 50 years!

A large, high-quality poster featuring exceptional black scientists is available free of charge (no. 16 in a series), from

CIBA-GEIGY Corporation
444 Sawmill River Rd.
Ardsley, NY 10502

(Inquire as to other educational materials they may have to offer.)

WOODCHUCK (20 in. long)

Groundhog Day

The woodchuck, or groundhog, is a small, blackish-gray North American rodent. It was given his name by the Pilgrims when they arrived in America, because it lived in the woods and reminded them of hedgehogs back in England. They also gave the groundhog the responsibility of the hedgehog on February 2—that of predicting the date of spring. Tradition dictates that on the morning of February 2, the groundhog comes up out of his hole and looks about. If the day is cold and cloudy, he decides that spring will be here soon and he emerges from his hole. If, however, it is a bright clear day with the sun causing his shadow to be cast, one look at his shadow sends the groundhog back down his hole to continue his hibernation for six more weeks.

Discuss with your class how do traditions like this get started? What are some probable reasons for the creation of such a tradition?

It's a Fact: Does the groundhog really come out on February 2? Research done at Pennsylvania State University over a period of five years and involving 4,000 groundhogs showed that a great number of them were seen out of their burrows on January 31 and February 1, 2, and 3. Other scientists state that February 2 is the middle of winter for a groundhog, and his hibernation should be at the deepest point. If he is seen above ground, it must be accidental, or he may have awakened to relieve himself. Scientists agree that more research on hibernation is needed.

First American Paper Money [3]

Etymology: Our word "money" comes from the Latin word for "mint," *moneta*. A *moneta* was a place where money was coined or minted, and it, in turn, got its name from Moneta, the surname of Juno, in whose temple all Roman money was minted!

Classroom Math Money: Use a Xerox machine to duplicate several denominations of U.S. bills and coins. Have the children color these with pale water colors; when these are dry, cover pages with clear Contac paper and carefully cut out all the bills and coin. Each child may keep his or her stash in a large envelope. Use this money to practice making change, to add and subtract (large) sums of money & to figure out a week's household expenses for a family. (This money can also be used to stimulate observation of small physical details: have the children make up "mystery questions" concerning tiny details to be found on U.S. coins and bills.)

Birth of Gertrude Stein (1874) [3] ———————————————

After 1903 Gertrude Stein lived primarily in Paris. Her circle of friends included the most avant-garde writers, composers, and painters—Matisse, Picasso, and Cocteau among them. In 1926, she published *The Making of Americans,* which evoked heated literary controversy. She wrote a dozen more books. Some critics found her writing dull, silly, and trivial, while it was hailed by others as unique, innovative, and the work of a genius.

Your students may be interested in reading Stein's work for themselves. Try duplicating copies of some of her poetry and have your class read it silently. Don't give any personal opinions—wait to hear their comments. Some students may even be interested in trying to use words in a way similar to Stein's.

Massachusetts Admitted to the Union (1788) [6] ———————————————

Massachusetts is our 6th state.

Etymology: Named for the Indian tribe, Massachusetts means "large hill place," the exact location of which was identified by Captain John Smith as being near Milton.

William Henry Harrison [9] ———————————————

Harrison, our 9th president, rose to fame as a soldier in the War of 1812, leading the U.S. forces against the Indians at Tippecanoe; since his vice presidential running mate was John Tyler, their campaign slogan was "Tippecanoe and Tyler, too!"

Harrison was honest and sincere. He took his duties as manager of the White House very seriously, even insisting on doing the early morning marketing himself. One chilly March day, he went shopping without his coat. He caught cold and it developed into pneumonia, and Harrison gained the dubious distinction of being the first American president to die in office. He served the shortest term in U.S. history as well—just 30 days.

Birth of Thomas A. Edison [11] ———————————————

Thomas Alva Edison was an inventor. He worked in his workshop. He worked in his laboratory. He worked in his mind. When he got an idea, he looked at it from all sides. He never said, "It can't be done." When he was searching for the right material to burn in a lightbulb, he tried 6,000 different things before he found the one he wanted! In addition to the electric lightbulb, he invented the phonograph and motion pictures. Thomas Edison was truly a person who changed the world!

Etymology: Phonograph is a Greek derivative meaning "sound writing."

("Phonograph: n. A vibrating toy that restores life to dead noises." Ambrose Bierce, from his *Devil's Dictionary*)

It's a Fact: Edison had many visitors at his summer home in West Orange, New Jersey. He would always show them the gardens, and then, when they returned to the house, they found they had to go through a gate with an extremely stiff turnstile. Finally, one day a friend asked why it was there and why an inventor like Edison had not perfected the turnstile so that it wasn't so difficult to turn. "Ah, but it is perfected," he said with a smile. "Each time you pass through this turnstile, you pump 8 gallons of water into the tank on my roof!"

Birth of Abraham Lincoln [12]

> Lincoln, six feet one in his stocking feet,
> The lank man, knotty and tough as a hickory rail,
> Whose hands were always too big for white-kid gloves,
> Whose wit was a coonskin sack of dry, tall tales.
> Whose weathered face was homely as a plowed field.
>
> —Stephen Vincent Benet

Abraham Lincoln (1809–1865) was the 16th president of the United States. A self-educated frontiersman, Lincoln was a towering figure—6'4" tall. He was an outstanding orator and an honest man of great compassion. His administration was marked by the Civil War, the bloodiest conflict in American history, during which, through his efforts, the slaves were freed. When during the war some suggested that a new man in the presidency might be a good idea, Lincoln responded with this story:

> I have not permitted myself, gentlemen, to conclude that I am the best man in the country, but I am reminded in this connection of a story of an old Dutch farmer who remarked to a companion once that it was best not to swap horses while crossing a stream.

Lincoln was assassinated a few days after General Lee's surrender.

Etymology: Ancient Roman law prescribed a ceremony for the purchase of slaves: the new master laid his hand upon the slave's head. This was to fulfill the law of *manicipium:* "possession by the hand." Since *e* in Latin means "away" and *capio* means "taken," our word emancipation means "the master takes his hand off the now emancipated slave."

"Freedom" comes from Old English and is related to a Norse word for "love and peace."

The word "score," meaning "twenty" comes from two sources. As a unit of measurement, it is certainly pre-biblical, and probably developed as a name for one full count of the human fingers and toes. The English word "score" comes from the Anglo-Saxon *sceran,* meaning "to cut," used when people referred to the cut made on a tally stick when a unit of 20 was noted in a business deal. Until the 18th century, such tally sticks were the most common contracts between a creditor and his debtor.

A Lincoln's Birthday Bulletin Board ────────────

Many photographs of Lincoln exist, each showing a slightly different face. See if you can locate a copy of *Mr. Lincoln's Camera Man, Matthew B. Brady* Roy Meredith, ed., (New York: Dover 1974). Many books on the Civil War and Matthew Brady also feature various photos of Lincoln as do several back issues of *Life* magazine and *The National Geographic.* Check second-hand bookstores.

Arrange a selection of Lincoln photos on a bulletin board space; back some photos with red or blue paper for contrast. Then clearly print several signs that state the following:

The Camera Never Lies—but it can tell different stories. Look closely at these photos. Would you know that they are all of the same man? What parts of the face seem to stay the same in each photo? Do you understand why Lincoln thought he was not handsome? Get a paper and pencil and try making a Lincoln portrait.

After a day or two, discuss this display with the entire class. If only 2 or 3 photos are available, show them on an overhead projector. Ask the students to paint, draw, or make a collage of their impression of each image you project. Allow sufficient time for everyone to complete at least one interpretive artwork. Display these so that you can all enjoy seeing the different ways in which one face may inspire many different interpretations.

> It's a Fact: Lincoln was not the only U.S. president to be born in a log cabin. Six others at least claimed to have been born in similar situations (Buchanan, Garfield, Jefferson, Jackson, Fillmore, and Arthur).

Lincoln's Birthday Creative Writing ────────────

Ask the students to decide whether they believe that (1) your personality, the kinds of person you are, shows on your face or that (2) your face does not necessarily reveal your nature and your character. Let the students explain their ideas in writing. Does the age of the person in question make a difference? Ask them to include actual (historic) examples as evidence.

Valentine's Day [14]

Valentine's Day has been celebrated for more than 1,700 years. It commemorates the festival of two saints of this name who were martyred by the Roman Emperor Claudius on February 14, A.D. 269.

It is generally thought that the principal saint for whom this day is named was a priest imprisoned by Claudius for having helped Christian martyrs. While in prison, Valentine spoke so eloquently that his jailer, Asterius, was converted and baptized. This infuriated Claudius who had Valentine beaten with clubs and beheaded.

There is no apparent connection between the early Christian martyrs and modern-day Valentine's Day customs. The early church adapted many pagan customs rather than abolishing them; the Festival of Lupercalia, dedicated to Pan and Juno, was given the name St. Valentine's Day. It was the custom on this festival to place the names of young women in a box from which they were drawn at random & then honored by the one who drew the name. Our exchanging of valentines probably springs from this custom. It is from Roman mythology that we have little Dan Cupid with his arrows dipped in love potion.

Etymology: Cupid is from the Latin *cupido* (desire, passion). Our words "friend" and "free" probably both stem from one Indo-European base which means "to be fond of, hold dear," as the basic sense of "free" is probably "dear to (i.e., akin to) the chief," meaning, not enslaved! The word "flirt" dates back to the 16th century. The early Frisian word for a giddy girl was *flirtje*. It is also strongly influenced by the French word *fleureter*, which means "to touch lightly, to move from flower to flower"!

Valentines

For younger students, hand out a stamp and envelope to each student. (Perhaps each child might bring a stamp from home.) Ask the children to address the envelopes to themselves carefully and then stick on the stamps. Emphasize how important it is that they clearly print these addresses and spell each word correctly. Collect the envelopes and say no more. After school put a valentine into each envelope and drop the cards in the mail. If the children have followed directions carefully, they will each receive a valentine from you!

Handmade Valentines

Traditionally, valentines had a lacy, almost fragile look. Instead of using the commercially made white or gold paper doilies, which are expensive, have the children cut handmade doilies in the following ways:

1. Fold square paper on the dotted lines. Cut shapes out of the folded square and open to form a doily.

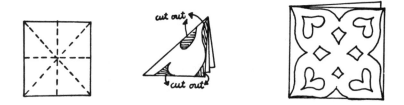

Paste this doily onto card of a sharply contrasting color. Children may want to slip tiny pieces of foil or colored tissue beneath cutout areas before the doily is glued into place. This gives a more collagelike look to the valentine.

2. Fold a rectangular piece of paper in half lengthwise and cut it in half crosswise. Cut as shown. Then fold diagonally and cut again.

3. Fold rectangular paper as described in step 2. Cut as shown. Then open out and fold over each corner and cut as shown below.

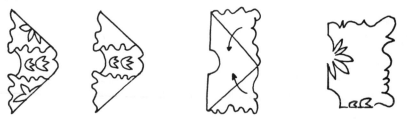

Doilies are opened out flat and carefully glued on top of a folded card. The oval area in the centers of steps 2 and 3 provides a perfect frame for a snapshot of the child, or for a tiny heart that opens, revealing a secret or as a space in which to print a message.

Provide white glue; scissors; colored papers (slick colored pages from magazines); sequins; glitter; remnants of silk, satin, velvet, lace; tiny ribbons; flowered fabric; paper doilies; and silver and gold foil. Let the children design and create their own valentines—the more elaborate the better!

BEAUTY
OUTLOOKING
TOWARD
HOPE'S LAND
OF
PROMISE.

Young children will love making and working with the following unusual (and nonedible) material:

*Plastic Jello.** You will need a hot plate, deep pan, wooden spoon, potholder, and, for each child, a plastic lid from a coffee can, 3 Tbs. water, an envelope of unflavored gelatin, & few drops of red food coloring.

In pairs, children can measure out 3 Tbs. water, a few drops of red coloring, and the contents of the envelope of gelatin into the pan and carefully place it on a warm hot plate. (An adult should unobtrusively watch the children as they use the hot plate.) Children take turns stirring the mixture in the pan until the gelatin is dissolved. Then, using hotpad, they remove pan from heat and carefully pour mixture into coffee can lid. If bubbles appear, these should be gently pushed to the edges of the mixture.

After one or two days, the mixture should be dry, the edges hard and sharp. Your Plastic Jello is now ready for use in valentines!

With sharp scissors or pinking shears, cut small hearts from the Plastic Jello. These can then be taped to white heart-shaped doilies, or needle and thread can be used to string several in a line, making a valentine necklace to be worn or strung in a window as a pretty holiday decoration.

Keepsake Valentines[†]

You will need heavy, flexible clear plastic (sold by the foot at hardware stores), scissors (pinking shears), small-hole paper punch, yarn or thin ribbon, clear plastic thread or fishing line, small pressed ferns and flowers, potpourri (glitter, tiny metallic hearts & stars, bright-colored acetate, colored paper, tiny feathers), a sewing machine or needles and thread, & tagboard.

Have several students help you trace, cut out, and punch holes in tagboard or heavy paper patterns so that each child will have one to use.

Each student uses a paper pattern as a guide to cut out from plastic 2 identical hearts. The pattern is then held atop one of these hearts and used as a guide when punching out

---

*This basic recipe appears in *Mudworks: Creative Clay, Dough & Modeling Experiences* by Mary Ann Kohl, published by Bright Ring Publishing Co., Box 5768, Bellingham, WA 98227.
[†]First created by Gail Rieke, master teacher.

the 20 holes in each heart. Now lay the 2 plastic hearts atop one another & punch out matching holes in second heart with holes matching. Thread a long length of ribbon or yarn through the top center hole, leaving a long length behind, and continue to thread in and out of the holes.

When the 14th hole is reached the yarn should be pulled up through the hole and the heart half-filled at this point with tiny pressed flowers or potpourri (or any combination of the materials listed). Do not overfill these hearts: the idea is to be able to enjoy seeing through them and appreciating their delicate contents. Continue threading the yarn or ribbon through the remaining holes until you return to the center hole where the two ends of the yarn are tied into a small, perfect bow. To make a hanging loop use a needle threaded with clear plastic thread & knotted at end: pull the thread through the heart at the center margin above the holes. Tie a loop in the thread & then thumbtack it to a windowsill so that the sunlight comes through this lovely valentine for all seasons.

Variation: Cut out 2 very small identical heart shapes and, using a sewing machine with a medium stitch, sew an inner heart outline. Start stitching at the top indentation of the heart; insert pretty contents and continue stitching until you once again reach the top indentation point. (Sign your valentine with a fine-pointed permanent marker.) Slip this sweet remembrance into an envelope; address and deliver.

Rebus Valentines. Encourage each of your students to make up a valentine message in the form of a rebus. You might announce this project by writing the following on the blackboard:

("Today I want you to think of a way to write a Valentine with rebus symbols. Can you do it? Try!")

Hand out copies of the rebus symbols reproducible page to help the class get started. As the students come up with their own original rebus formulations, why not have them add their creations to a large classroom rebus chart?

Valentine Envelopes. The simplest valentine card will become quite special when it is enclosed in an envelope made like this one. Enlist the help of several students to trace the pattern. Trace onto tagboard and carefully cut out 8 to 10 of the shapes. Next, have 8 to 10 children trace these shapes onto pink or red construction paper. When you have accumulated 30 to 40 such tracings, have everyone in the class carefully cut out several from rather heavy paper and fold them as shown on page 196.

REBUS SYMBOLS

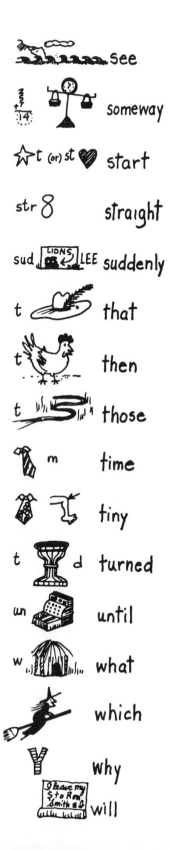

ab [EXIT] →	about	
4/15 mire	admire	
ap	appear	
R	are	
th	bath	
4	before	
b	beg	
b	bring	
d	build	
	can	
	country	
d	dark	
	dear	
D	delight	
ever E	everyday	
4	for	

ing	going
8	great
h	had
I	
I	learn
I k	like
m	my
n	nice
O'c	o'clock
OFF 10	often
	or
	pair
choor	picture
T	safety
	salesman
	saw

	see
3+7/14	someway
t (or) st	start
str 8	straight
sud LIONS LEE	suddenly
t	that
t	then
t	those
m	time
	tiny
t d	turned
un	until
w	what
	which
Y	why
	will

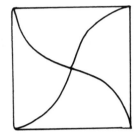

Tiny little valentines can be inserted into these envelopes. Address the front of the envelope using a (silver) felt-tipped pen.

(See Mother's Day cards section for other unusual card format suggestions.)

Personal Valentine Cooky Cutters. You will need a yard of metal flashing (sold at hardware or building supply stores), large metal cutters, a straight-edge ruler, black permanent ink marker, Mystic tape (or a very adhesive cloth tape), string, strapping tape, needle-nosed pliers, scissors, pencil, and paper.

Once you have purchased a yard of 4″ wide flashing, measure it off into four 1″ wide strips. Use the ink marker to draw the three long lines down the flashing and the metal cutters to cut along the lines to make four yard-long strips. Cover the cut edges of the flashing with tape, pressing it flush across the cut edge and firmly down on either side. This will protect the cooks' fingers when little cookies are being cut out.

Now, each child gets to draw an outline on his or her paper of a heart shape (older students might try more complex shapes such as arrows, a flower, a dove). Measure the length of flashing needed for each cookie cutter by tracing along outline with a length of string & then forming a 1″ strip of flashing to exactly correspond to the child's drawing. Use the pliers to help you make right angle and abrupt curve cuts. Leave 1″ to 1½″ overlap at each end of the flashing and bind these with the strapping tape. Your custom-made Valentine's Day cutter is ready to use!

Of course, this idea can be used for any holiday design cookies. Kids will love making and trading their personal cutters.

Valentine's Day Language Arts

Use the "Valentine Crossword Puzzle" worksheet to make copies for the children in the class.

A Valentine's Day Interview

Use the accompanying reproducible page to make copies of the sheet, one for each student in your class. Have the children try to fill it in on their own and use them to conduct their interviews. Each blank should be filled in with the response of the interviewee—a parent, older

VALENTINE ENVELOPE PATTERN

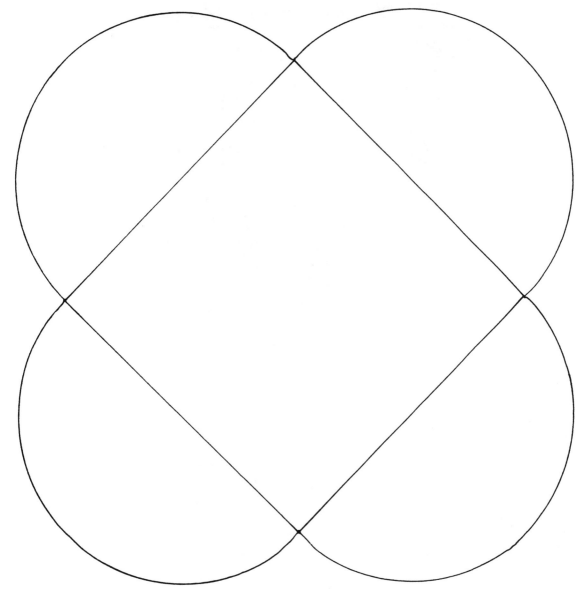

VALENTINE CROSSWORD PUZZLE

Across		Down	
3.	It covers a bottle or a pen	1.	A real friend, a good buddy
5.	I *am,* he *is,* we _____	2.	3: like in a 3-cornered hat
7.	The kind of card we send today	3.	A sweet treat
9.	A book, _____ apple	4.	You write with it
10.	This is how you say 'yes' in German	5.	He *did eat,* or he _____
11.	The opposite of DON'T	6.	To really like something
13.	To move along	7.	Virginia (abbr.)
14.	Beavers do this to a stream	8.	Each (abbr.)
16.	The opposite of STAY	12.	Fourth note in musical scale
17.	Not down	14.	It makes a good pet
18.	You chew this	15.	To keep quiet
		19.	You and me (or the country we live in: abbr.)

Name _____

A Valentine's Day Interview

What is your name?
Where did you grow up?

How did you celebrate Valentine's Day when you were a kid?

Did you ever make your own valentines?
What were your valentines like?

Describe any special valentine that you have ever been given.

Describe what you think would be a really great valentine to get on February 14th.

Thank you for your help. I've really enjoyed interviewing you........and
HAPPY VALENTINE'S DAY !!

friend or relative, librarian, neighbor, babysitter, and so on. The answers written should be as close to the actual responses of the person being interviewed as possible!

For extra credit, you may want to suggest that a child makes a picture or takes a Polaroid photo of his or her interview target. Together with the sheets, they can form a fascinating bulletin board display.

Valentine's Day Language Arts Bulletin Board

Older students may enjoy making a serious or comic valentine for a famous person. Ask each child to design a very special valentine greeting for one of the following: a famous historical person, a storybook character they remember fondly, a mythical hero or heroine, a favorite sports star or TV personality, a rock singer or other musician, or someone the student doesn't really know but would like to get to know. Encourage the students to use a wide variety of materials and to create original heartfelt poems or expressions of their sentiments.

You may find that some older students are not particularly interested in a traditional exchange of valentines. The spirit of the day can be served, and a meaningful experience shared, if the class decides to forgo the trivial and work together for an important mutual goal. Students can pool the money that might have gone toward a party and use it for a more meaningful purpose. Have a student representative call the local homeless shelter or a nursing home, or social services office to learn how the students' desire to help can best be channeled. Handmade cards, poems and notes can be made and included with their donation.

Not always is a valentine
Composed of fancy paper
With buds and birds and clever words
And cupids all a caper.
Oh, birds and darts and sugar hearts
Are very gay and fine
But often just a friendly word
Will make a valentine.

—Unknown

To refresh your spirit, read through the pages of *Love Letters, An Illustrated Anthology,* edited by Antonia Fraser (Contemporary Books, 180 N. Michigan Ave., Chicago, IL 60601, 1989).

It's a Fact: On November 29, 1904 President Theodore Roosevelt wrote to a distant cousin: "Dear Franklin, We are greatly rejoiced over the good news. I am fond of Eleanor as if she were my daughter; and I like you and trust you and believe in you. . . . You and Eleanor are true and brave and I believe you love each other unselfishly. . . . Golden years open before you."

Dear Valentine,

Here's a real challenge for you today! Cut out the pieces & try to mend this broken heart!

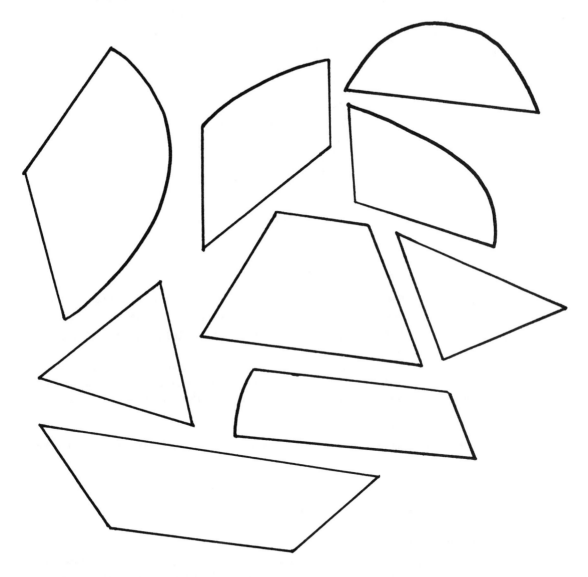

Take your time! (This Kind of Math is called working with spatial relationships!!)

Have fun!

A Valentine's Day Puzzle

The page could be duplicated on small sheets of red construction paper and delivered to each third- to fifth-grade student as a little valentine from you to each of them.

VALENTINE RIDDLES

1. What does the valentine envelope say where you lick it? (Nothing. It just shuts right up.)
2. What did the girl rodent say to the boy rodent? (Wow, I really gopher you!)
3. What kind of fall does make you unconscious, but it's still good for you? (Falling in love, falling asleep)
4. "You'll find me from two to six feet above the ground. I'm not vegetable, mineral, or animal. I'm not male or female. I can't be weighed or measured. I'm mentioned in the Bible, and you can see me in the movies. I am used as a sign of love, *or* as a sign of death. What am I?" (A kiss)

(Note: Make sure that students understand how each part of this last riddle relates to the answer.)

Oregon Admitted to the Union (1859) [14]

Oregon is our 33rd state.

Etymology: The origin of the word Oregon is unknown, but one theory suggests that it may have come from the Wisconsin River shown on a French map of 1715 as the *Ouaricon-sint*.

Arizona Admitted to the Union (1912) [14]

Arizona is our 48th state.

Etymology: The name Arizona comes either from the Aztec word *arizuma* meaning "silver-bearing" or from the Spanish version of a Pima Indian word for "little spring place"—*arizonac*.

Birth of George Washington (honored on the third Monday in February) [22]

George Washington (1732–1799), first president of the United States, is described "first in war, first in peace, and first in the hearts of his countrymen." We learn from his biographers that Washington was a Virginia gentleman who wore dentures made of wood, wire, and elks' teeth. He kept detailed records of the money he spent, was known occasionally to swear, and was not known for his sense of humor. But it isn't for these personality quirks that he is called the Father of Our Country. He was an honest and personally unambitious man, a devout patriot, and a fearless soldier.

On June 14, 1775, the second Continental Congress voted to create a new Continental Army. For commander-in-chief, they chose a gentleman tobacco planter from Virginia—a man who candidly confessed that he did not feel "equal to the command."

George Washington proved to be mistaken in that regard. He had had limited experience with infantry, little with artillery, and none with cavalry. The Congress had no authority to draft men into his army nor money to pay them. Under these circumstances, Washington did well just to keep an Army together. His was the strength, leadership, and perseverance that enabled the Army to keep fighting, even through the darkest months of the Revolution. Without his leadership during the formative years of our country, America might never have survived, much less prospered as a fledgling democracy.

Historically accurate learning skills material can be obtained from

Washington National Insurance Co.
Public Relations Dept.
1630 Chicago Ave.
Chicago, IL 60201

(Consider "George Washington: The Life & the Legend," appropriate for grades 5 through 9, and a similar low-level vocabulary kit for use in grades 1 through 4.)

It's a Fact: The painting by Emanuel Leutze of *Washington Crossing the Delaware Christmas Eve* has at least four inaccuracies, probably made in the name of composition and drama. Can you identify them?

(The flag shown was not adopted by the Continental Congress until 1777, Washington's troops used Durkam boats which were 40–60 feet long, Washington would never have stood up while in such a small boat as the one shown, and his soldiers would have known not to hold their muskets barrel-up in a sleet storm!)

Presidents' Day Creative Writing

George Washington was radically different from Abraham Lincoln, yet each became a great president. Compare the two men in regard to any of the following: parentage and financial status, education, talents, temperament, appearance, marriages, shortcomings, accomplishments, offspring, or final months of life.

Leap Year Day [29]

Of unknown origin is the custom that in leap years, women may take the initiative and propose marriage. In 1288, an act of Scottish Parliament permitted a woman during leap year to propose to a man and if the woman was rejected the man had to pay her 100 pounds (unless he could prove that he was already engaged). In a few years, a similar law was passed in France; in the 15th century, the tradition was legalized in Italy. By 1600, the custom was a part of the common law of England.

RIDDLES

1. How many months have 28 days? (ALL of them!)
2. What month has the fewest beautiful sunsets? (February—because it has the fewest sunsets—period!)

February Activities

Language Arts

A Letter to My Teacher. Set aside a time during which the children will each write you a letter. Ask them to carefully plan the things they would like to ask or tell you. Explain that these letters are strictly personal and will not be read aloud or shared with other students in the class. You might wish to answer each of their letters with a personal one of your own, or post an open letter to all the class in reply to their missives.

Purim is a Jewish holiday and movable feast,
usually occurring in late February or early March.

Etymology: In Persian, *pur* means "the casting of lots" and the origin of Purim, The Feast of Lots, is described in the Book of Esther in the Old Testament.

This celebration marks the salvation of the Jews of the Persian Empire from their destruction as planned by Haman, an advisor to the king. It was through the influence of Queen Esther and her uncle Mordecai that the Jews were saved.

Hamantaschen are delicious, filled pastries that are part of the celebration of Purim.

Etymology: *Hamantaschen* is a German word meaning "the pocket or purse of Haman."

Here's how they're made.

Hamantaschen*

4	eggs	2	tsp. vanilla
1	cup oil	3	tsp. baking powder
1¼	cups sugar	½	tsp. salt
5½	cups flour (approx.)		

Beat eggs, beat in oil, sugar, vanilla, baking powder, salt. Add flour gradually; mix thoroughly. Knead dough until it is smooth enough to roll out on a floured board. Roll out. Cut dough into 3″ to 4″ rounds. Place desired filling on each round. Pinch together sides of lower half of circles to form triangles.

Place Hamantaschen on a lightly greased baking sheet and bake at 350° F for 30 minutes, or until golden brown.

Fillings: The fillings are usually cooked prunes or mohn (a sweetened poppyseed paste). The prune filling may be made from 2 cups cooked dried prunes with ½ cup ground nuts and 1 Tbs. grated orange rind added. Prepared puréed prune baby food may also be used, or use the mashed prune filling called lekvár.

(Thanks again, Janie Stein Romero)

---

*Haman's hat pastries are made in a tricornered hat shape. This recipe is from *Guide for the Jewish Homemaker* by Shonie Levi and Sylvia R. Kaplan (National Women's League of the United Synagogue of America, New York 1964).

Codes & How to Crack Them

Many children love the challenge of breaking a code, and it gives them practice in thinking logically, as well as learning concentration and perseverance!

Introduce only one code at a time. Have fun with it for a while before you go on to a new one. You can use a bulletin board area to announce "This Week's Code to Crack!" or send a daily message or riddle to your class and have them try to decipher it. Encourage the kids to invent their own codes. Here are a dozen good ones:

1. L—v- —t th- v-w-ls -nd sh-w th—r p-s-t—ns. (Indicate vowels with hyphen.)
2. Jst lv t ll th vwls n th sntnc. (Omit vowels.)
3. Siht ekil sdrawkcab egassem eht etirw. (Message is backward.)
4. Divi deth emes sage upin togr oups offo urle tter seac hand spac eitl iket his! (Divide the . . . .)
5. Reverse the position of the letters in the alphabet: a = z, b = y, c = x.
6. A number corresponds to letter's position in the alphabet: a = 1, b = 2, c = 3. (9-20-19 5-1-19-25!)
7. Reverse the position of the letters and number accordingly: a = 26, b = 25, c = 24. (19-26-5-22 21-6-13!)
8. Assign a symbol to each vowel:

   a = ◆
   e = □
   i = ♥
   o = ☾
   u = △
   y = ●

9. Letters are moved down one letter in the alphabet: a = b, b = c, c = d.
10. Secalpd dota edi vid & sdrawk cabsd roweh ttup. (Read the message backward from the end of the sentence & divide into new units.)
11. A B C D E F G H I J K L M N O P Q R S T U V W X Y Z
    Z Y X W V U T S R Q P O N M L K J I H G F E D C B A
12. And, finally, a code that requires intuition & logic and stick-to-itive-ness; *older* students may enjoy trying to unlock this:

    Abgj fzb pbmf pyyom weamf, ya lyq vgl syf zgdb g kzgskb fy abgj fzbv gf grr. Fzyabgq

February Math Fun

Without using a ruler, try to guess the size of each of these common objects. Then write the decimal (or metric) measurement you estimate in the blank.

1. The length of your first finger: _____.

2. The width of your foot: _____.

3. The width of your desktop: _____.

4. The length of your math book: _____.

5. The diameter of a quarter, a nickel, a penny: _____, _____, _____.

6. The length and width of the most commonly used postage stamp: _____.

7. The height of your desk from the floor: _____.

8. The length of your pencil (pen), a ruler, a yardstick: _____, _____, _____.

9. The diameter of a kickball (basketball): _____.

10. The length of the bridge of your nose: _____.

Now take a (metric) ruler and measure each of the things listed above. How did you do? What did this show you about the way you think about measurements?

(Note: Make sure you have quarters, nickels, pennies, string, rulers, and postage stamps ready for checking answers on these sheets.)

February Science

At this time of year, most birds, insects, and wild animals are not in evidence in many parts of the country.

Many (older) students will be interested in animals that are disappearing permanently and in learning what, if anything, can be done to help endangered species. A reference librarian can give you the current list of endangered species, here and around the world.

Have each student choose one of the vanishing mammals and write about it from the animal's perspective. These stories can be written as appeals, complaints, reminiscences, hopes, or dreams, and they can take the form of letters, diaries, or biographies. A fine classroom or library bulletin board can result; have interested students organize this display themselves, with illustrations from nature and environmental magazines such as *Ranger Rick, Natural History,* or *National Geographic.*

February Physical Education

Looking in the Mirror. Divide the children (fourth grade and up) into groups of two. Within each group, one child leads the action while the second child follows, doing exactly as the first child, but in reverse—a mirror image. Encourage children to include many details in each activity and to move in a deliberate manner. Each activity should last about 3 minutes and roles may be reversed occasionally. Some suggested activities to mime: driving a car from home to school, brushing your teeth, washing windows, getting up in the morning or going to bed at night, shaving, sweeping the floor, making a snowman, or trying on clothes in a store.

Snakeskins. (Participants should be wearing jeans or slacks.) Divide the class into groups of 8 or 9, each made up of only one sex. Players line up and each places one hand through their legs which is held by the next person in line. The last person in line lies down while the player in front backs over him. The backer lies down while the player in front of him now backs over the two students lying down and so on until everyone on the team is lying down, that is, the snake has shed his skin! At this point, the process is reversed. Still holding hands, the last player who went down, jumps up and walks backward over the prone members of his or her group. This pulls up the rest of the snake behind and once the entire action is completed, you should have a snake with skin intact and lots of laughing children.

Quick Paintstick Hand Puppets

You will need paint-mixing sticks, tongue depressors, a hot glue gun (or white glue), markers, poster paint, yarn, fake fur pieces, cloth, trim, scissors, needles, and thread.

Adhere the tongue depressor to the back of the paintstick to form a basic body.

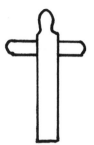

Paint on skin tones; add yarn or fur hair. Finally sew or glue fabric clothing and attach to the paintstick puppet.

MARCH

To the Omahas, this is "Little Frog Month." To the Pawnees, "Clearing." To the Seminoles, "Big Wind Moon." To the Crow Indians, "When the Ice Breaks." The Alaskan Eskimos call March "Sun Gets High, Snow Is Melting."

Calendar of Important Dates

§ Red Cross Month.

§ Pesach or Passover is a movable Jewish feast day, occurring in the spring.

§ Youth Art Month.

1   First Crusade announced by Pope Gregory in 1074.

   On this day in 1781, the American colonies adopted the Articles of Confederation, paving the way for a federal union.

   Ohio became the 17th state admitted to the Union, 1803.

   Nebraska became the 37th state in 1867.

   Ralph Ellison, black American author *(The Invisible Man)* was born in 1914.

   First H-bomb testing at Bikini Atoll, 1954.

   The U.S. Peace Corp was created by President Kennedy in 1961.

2   On this day in 1877, Rutherford B. Hayes was declared president by a special electoral commission in the disputed election with Samuel Tilden.

In 1962, Wilt Chamberlain scored 100 points in a basketball game against the Knicks.

In 1972, a U.S. spacecraft was sent to the planet Jupiter.

3   Dolls Day in Japan.

Florida became the 27th state to enter the Union, 1845.

Alexander Graham Bell, chief inventor of the telephone, was born in Edinburgh, Scotland, in 1847.

The Star Spangled Banner became the United States' official national anthem in 1931.

4   Antonio Vivaldi, great Italian composer, was born in 1678.

On this day in 1789, the U.S. Constitution went into effect.

Vermont became the 14th state to join the Union in 1791.

Theodor Geisel (Dr. Seuss) was born in Springfield, Massachusetts, 1904.

Miriam Makeba, remarkable South African singer, was born in 1932.

5   Gerard Mercator, greatest of the Renaissance geographers, was born in 1512.

In 1770 on this day the Boston Massacre occurred. British troops fired into a crowd of unruly Bostonians, killing five men (including a black, Crispus Attucks) in this prelude to the Revolutionary War.

> Quotation of the Day: Not the Battle of Lexington, nor the surrender of Burgoyne or Cornwallis, were more important events in American history than the Battle of King Street on March 5, 1770.
>
> —John Adams, 46 years later

6   On this day were born

- Michelangelo, most famous sculptor since the Classical Greeks and monumental painter, in 1475.

- Cryano de Bergerac, French playwright, author, soldier (famous for his large nose), the hero of a poetic drama by the same name, in 1619.

- Elizabeth Barrett Browning, Romantic poet and wife of poet Robert Browning, in 1806.

Alamo Day commemorates the end of the Battle of the Alamo. For 13 days, a tiny courageous band of Texans tried to defend their compound in San Antonio against a large Mexican Army. On this day in 1836, Davy Crockett was killed as well as the 186 other Americans who had fought alongside him.

7   Burbank Day honors the birth of horticulturist Luther Burbank in Lancaster, Massachusetts, in 1849.

First telephone patented by Alexander Graham Bell in 1876.

8   International Women's Day originated in the Soviet Union; now it is recognized throughout the world.

On this day in 1917, riots and strikes in St. Petersburg marked the beginning of the Russian Revolution.

9   Amerigo Vespucci, Italian navigator whose family name was given to the continent of America, was born in 1451.

Yuri Gagarin, Soviet cosmonaut, was born in Smolensk, Russia, in 1934.

10　On this day in 1775, Daniel Boone and a group of frontiersmen were hired by the Transylvania Company to cut a road through the wilderness to the Kentucky River.

　　The first U.S. paper money was issued for general circulation in 1862.

　　Harriet Tubman, antislavery activist and black spokesperson for her race, died on this day in 1913. During her lifetime, she led more than 300 slaves to freedom along a route called the Underground Railroad.

11　On this day in 1810, the Emperor Napoleon was married by proxy to 18-year-old Princess Marie Louise of Austria.

13　Standard time was established in the United States on this date in 1884.

　　On this date in 1971, the *Explorer 43* satellite was launched.

14　On this day in 479 B.C., an eclipse of the sun thoroughly frightened Xerxes's army.

　　First letter from Columbus about his discoveries made its way to the queen of Spain on this day in 1493.

　　First town meeting, which became famous as a New England political institution, was held at Faneuil Hall, Boston, in 1743.

　　Maxim Gorky, Russian novelist, was born on this day in 1868.

　　Albert Einstein, physicist and originator of the theory of relativity, was born in Ulm, Germany, in 1879.

15　On this day in 44 B.C., Julius Caesar was assassinated.

　　In 1493, Columbus reached Spain on his return from his first voyage to the New World.

　　Andrew Jackson, 7th U.S. president, was born in Waxhaw, South Carolina, in 1767.

　　Maine became the 23rd state to be admitted to the Union, 1820.

　　On this day every year the turkey vultures make their annual return to Hinckley, Ohio, from their winter roosts in the Great Smoky Mountains.

16　James Madison, 4th U.S. president, was born in Port Conway, Virginia, 1751.

　　First liquid fuel rocket was fired by Robert Goddard, at his Aunt Effie's farm in Auburn, Massachusetts. This rocket went less than 12 feet in the air, but it was the forerunner of the space age.

First docking of one space craft with another took place on this day in 1966 when U.S. astronauts Neil Armstrong and David Scott succeeded in linking up in space.

On this day, the long-billed curlews return to Umatilla National Wildlife Refuge in Oregon to nest and raise their young.

17 St. Patrick's Day honors the patron saint of Ireland, who died about 461 A.D. in Eire.

Kate Greenaway, artist-illustrator, was born in London in 1846.

The first national baseball league—the National Association of Baseball Players—was established in 1871.

18 First magician's advertisement in the *New World,* in New York City in 1734.

Grover Cleveland, 22nd and 24th U.S. president, was born in Caldwell, New Jersey, in 1837.

Nicholas Rimsky-Korsakov, composer, was born in Novgorod, Russia, in 1844.

First person to walk in space, USSR cosmonaut Aleksei Lenov remained outside his spacecraft for 20 minutes, secured only by a long lifeline.

19 Nikolai Gogol, Russian writer *(The Overcoat)* was born in 1809.

Traditionally, this is the day on which the cliff swallows return to their summer nesting grounds at San Juan Capistrano, California.

Spring begins either on March 20 or 21 (spring equinox).

National Wildlife Week (Write to the National Wildlife Federation for their catalog of slides, filmstrips, posters, and units: *Challenger II Kit* and, *U.S.S.R., Land of the Russian Bear.*)

20 Henrik Ibsen, dramatist, was born in Skien, Norway, in 1828.

21 On this day in 1556, the Archbishop of Canterbury was burned at the stake by Queen Mary.

J. S. Bach, great German composer of late Baroque period, was born in 1685.

22 On this day in 1775, Patrick Henry spoke out in favor of arming Virginia in case of war against England.

> Quotation of the Day: Is life so dear, or peace so sweet, as to be purchased at the price of chains and slavery? . . . I know not what course others may take, but as for me, give me liberty or give me death!
>
> —Patrick Henry

On this day in 1943, the Danes bravely defied the Germans who were occupying their nations by going to the polls to vote for or against democracy. Of the ballots cast, 99% were for democracy and only 1% favored the New Order of Germany.

On this day in 1972, the Equal Rights Amendment was approved by the U.S. Senate, 84–8.

Anniversary of oil spill with Exxon Tanker *Valdez,* 1989.

23 Fannie Farmer, cookery expert who standardized measurements in recipes, was born in 1857.

24   Harry Houdini, famous American magician, was born in 1874.

On this day in 1965, the Reverend Martin Luther King, Jr., led 25,000 blacks and white sympathizers in a march on the Capitol of Alabama, culminating a five-day, 54-mile march from Selma in protest of the state's denial of equal voting rights to blacks.

> Quotation of the Day: Walk together, children. Don't you get weary, and it will lead to the promised land. And Alabama will be a new Alabama and America will be a new America.
>
> —Martin Luther King, Jr., speaking to
> the marchers as they left Selma, March 21

25   Flannery O'Connor, writer, was born in Savannah, Georgia, in 1925.

26   Robert Frost, American poet, was born on this day in 1874.

On this day in 1953, Jonas Salk made his new polio vaccine available for public use.

27   Edward Steichen, master photographer, was born on this date in 1879.

28   Nuclear accident at Three Mile Island power plant near Harrisburg, Pennsylvania, 1979.

29   John Tyler, 10th U.S. president, was born in 1790 in Charles City County, Virginia. He was the first vice president to succeed to the chief executive's office because of the death of an incumbent (William Henry Harrison).

30   Moses Maimonides, Jewish philosopher & physician to the sultan, was born in 1135 in Cordova, Spain.

Vincent van Gogh, world-renowned painter, was born in 1853.

Anna Sewell was born in 1820; she wrote *Black Beauty,* the children's classic.

First pencil with an eraser attached to it was patented by Hyman L. Lipman of Philadelphia in 1858.

On this day in 1867, Secretary of State William Seward and the Russian minister to the United States reached an agreement on the purchase of Alaska by the United States for $7,200,000 in gold (2¢ an acre). Seward was bitterly criticized for buying Alaska, which was called "Seward's Folly" and "Seward's Ice Box."

31   Franz Joseph Hayden, one of the world's greatest composers and creator of the string quartet form, was born in 1732.

On this day in 1776, Abigail Adams wrote her husband, John, a member of the Continental Congress: "In the new code of laws, which I suppose it will be necessary for you to make, I desire you would remember the ladies and be more generous and favorable to them than your ancestors."

On this day in 1889, the Eiffel Tower was officially opened in Paris despite vigorous protests by 100 writers, artists, and composers.

First use in America of Daylight Savings Time, 1918.

Caesar Chavez, Hispanic labor leader and advocate for migrant workers, was born in 1927.

First black was selected for the astronaut training program—Edward Dwight, Jr., of California, 1963.

MARCH

In the Roman calendar, March was the first month of the year. This was the season for the waging of war and so the Romans named this month after Mars, the god of war. In 45 B.C., Caesar reformed the calendar, and March became the third month. The expression "mad as a March hare" evolved since "March is the mating season for hares and during this month they are supposedly 'full of whimsy.'"

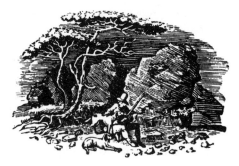

March Quotations

§ Youth Art Month

Art flourishes where there is a sense of adventure.

—Alfred North Whitehead

When I sit down to make a sketch from nature, the first thing I try to do is to forget that I have ever seen a picture.

—John Constable

Only the birds are able to throw off their shadow. The shadow stays behind on earth. Our imagination flies. We are its shadow on the earth.

—Vladimir Nabokov

While I work I leave my body outside the door, the way Moslems take off their shoes before entering the mosque.

—Pablo Picasso

If Heaven had only granted me five more years, I could have become a real painter.

—Katsushika Hokusai (at age 89)

4   I expect to pass through life but once. If, therefore, there be any kindness I can show, or any good thing I can do to any fellow being, let me do it now, and not deter or neglect it, as I shall not pass this way again.

—William Penn

14   Imagination is more important than knowledge.
Everything should be as simple as it is, but not simpler.

—Albert Einstein

15   Our Federal Union! It must and shall be preserved!

—Andrew Jackson (toast at Jefferson's birthday banquet, 1830)

17   For the great Gaels of Ireland
Are the men that God made mad,
For all their wars are merry,
And all their songs are sad.

—G. K. Chesterton

20–21   No wind in Spring means no rain in Summer.

—Chinese proverb

Make your plans for the year in Spring; make your plans for the day at dawn.

—Chinese proverb

March Events

March Is Youth Art Month

Collage is a French word meaning "a pasting, a paper hanging." A collage is a kind of surrealist picture made of such flat materials as cloth, cardboard, paper, or pressed natural materials. Pablo Picasso and George Braque are thought of as the fathers of modern collage. Many Victorian women made intricate paper collages years before either of these artists created theirs in the early 1900s.

Have the students collect textures, colors, fragments of flat (pressed) objects, photographs, and imaginative pictures to represent thoughts and sentiments that are important to them. Then have them cut, tear and arrange, overlap, and glue these materials to lightweight cardboard to make their own, personalized collages. Next ask the students to create a biographical collage of a parent or best friend (or a teacher? . . .). Eventually they can be encouraged to make collages of seasonal interest or of subjects that they select on their own.

Collages based on letters can be inventive and often humorous. Have each student choose a word which interests or involves them, for example, love, soccer, Texas, peace. Next each student hunts through magazines to collect many examples of the letters contained in his or her word. The letters should be of different sizes, styles, and colors. They can be combined to create designs of animals, people, objects, or scenes that relate directly to the word selected by the student. Colored paper pieces may also be included as part of the composition, for example, clouds, grass, clothing. The final compositions should be carefully glued into place on colored paper backgrounds.

Drawing suggestions: Giant in a Box helps children to draw BIG. Bring a very large cardboard box to class. The young students imagine themselves as giants. Then each one actually gets into the box, where they are encouraged to be aware of where and how different parts of the giant's body (their body!) fits—the head, toes, arms, and hands. Then give each child a big sheet of newsprint and challenge them to think of the paper as the inside wall of a box. How big a giant can fit inside this paper? Very original—and sometimes silly—solutions will be created!

Rubbing Pictures. Each student gets 2 to 3 large pieces of construction paper of one color *only.* One sheet will be the background on which the picture pieces will be glued. Now the child chooses an animal, cuts out its body shape, and glues it firmly to the background paper. Next, paper details (eyes, tongue, stripes, mane, hair, wagging tail) are cut out and glued firmly on top of the body shape. Additional smaller details (eyelashes, toenails, fine hairs, inner stripes, eye details) are glued on top of the layered papers. Landscaping or room interiors are cut, glued, and layered in the same way.

When the original is completely dry, lay a sheet of thin paper (typing or tracing paper) over it. Have a second child hold these two papers together firmly on the table while the first child makes the rubbing. The full length of a wax crayon is used. First, rub evenly all over the top paper to get an all-over feeling of the picture. Next decide which parts of the picture you want to make really important. Follow the shape of these parts as you rub over them again and again until you have the intensity you want.

Variations: Place the original on a wood-grained board or table to get an unusual background effect, or use pinking shears for some of the edges of the paper pieces you glue in layers, or try using different weights and textures of paper. Try creasing, folding, or cutting and slightly pulling apart the papers before you glue them to the background sheet. Encourage the children to come up with variations of their own.

Painting Suggestions. It's really quite simple. You need high-quality brushes and good paper and paints—these and sufficient time so as not to feel rushed. The students will need time to experiment with wetting the cakes of paint before using them, with dampening certain areas of their paper before applying paint, with using pointed or straight-cut brushes. Once they have each come to personal conclusions about the mechanics of painting, they are ready to consider some subjects. Here are a few ideas:

Things we see—in the sky, in the sea, in the country, in winter, in a movie theatre, during spring break, on a video, only at night, in a pleasant daydream, in a nightmare. Things we see only when we're kids—people's feet and legs, ants and bugs in grass, underneath tables, chairs, and so on.

Ohio Admitted to the Union (1803) [1]

Ohio is our 17th state.

Etymology: It's name probably means "great river" from the Iroquoian word *o-he-yo*.

Nebraska Admitted to the Union (1867) [1]

Nebraska is our 37th state.

Etymology: Nebraska is an Omaha Indian word meaning "flat (or broad) river" and describes the Platte River.

Florida Admitted to the Union (1845) [3]

Florida is our 27th state.

Etymology: Ponce de Leon first landed in this region during the feast of flowers (Pascua, Florida) in the spring of 1513. Florida is a Spanish word meaning "flowery."

Vermont Admitted to the Union (1791) [4]

Vermont is our 14th state.

Etymology: Vermont comes from the French *vert* meaning "green" and *mont* meaning "mountain." The Green Mountains were said to have been named by Samuel de Champlain. In 1777, Dr. Thomas Young suggested combining *vert* and *mont* into Vermont.

A Singular Day in U.S. History (1849) [4]

> It's a Fact: The one man who was president of the United States for ONE day was named David Atkinson, and he was our president from noon on Sunday, March 4, 1849 until a little after noon on Monday. This happened because Mr. Atkinson was president pro tem of the Senate and so he served as acting president from the expiration of James Polk's term on Sunday until the new president, Zachary Taylor, was sworn in on Monday. A piece of U.S. history!

Luther Burbank Day [7]

Born in 1849 & educated in the public schools, Burbank as a boy worked for the Ames Plow Company in Worcester, Massachusetts. There he showed remarkable inventive abilities and soon began some small seed-raising experiments. By 1873, he had developed the Burbank potato. Two years later, he moved to Santa Rosa, California, and began his lifelong work of creating and improving fruits, vegetables, grains, and grasses.

Burbank had a special affinity for plants. This, coupled with 50 years of practical daily plant study, allowed him to make connections and visualize growth outcomes in a truly unique way, making Luther Burbank the most famous plant originator in the world.

> It's a Fact: Special hormones (auxims) in a plant cause the stem to grow up and the roots to grow down. If they did not have such hormones, plants would be growing every which way and it would be impossible to have agriculture!

Some Classroom Plants

A hanging garden. Use a needle and thread to suspend a sponge from the ceiling. Children wet the sponge and sprinkle parsley seeds on it. The sponge is then hung in a sunny window and kept moist by daily sprays from an atomizer.

Green *unprocessed* coffee beans, fig seeds, & grape seeds can all be sprouted indoors.

Ginger root (fresh) grows a lovely green foliage with delicately scented white blossoms. Place root horizontally in a shallow dish with water over two-thirds of the root. Change the water to keep it fresh. Eyes of the root will sprout, and green leaves, vinelike growths develop, but it takes time.

A pineapple top should be cut off just under the green growth. Place it in water by a sunny window. Roots will develop after several weeks. Keep the water fresh. Plant in soil and water once a week when roots are well established. This can develop into a big plant.

PLANT RIDDLES

1. What herb cures all ills? (Thyme)
2. What berry is red when it's green? (Blackberry)
3. What berry is a bird? (Gooseberry)
4. What berry is not happy? (Blueberry)
5. What berry is the oldest in the world? (Elderberry)
6. Why is the gardener the most special person in the world? (The gardener has more business on earth than any other person; sets his or her own thyme when he or she works; is the absolute master of the local mint; takes more boughs than the most famous actor; and, best of all, can raise his or her own celery [salary] whenever he or she wants!)

International Women's Day [8]

This special day was first celebrated in the Soviet Union to honor women workers. Today it is recognized in many countries around the world.

Following is a list of historically important women.* It is by no means conclusive and should be viewed as a "starter list" for students in their research into the contributions of women. From it, the class can develop its own personal list of "Women Who Made a Difference" and research and report on their lives.

SOME IMPORTANT WOMEN IN HISTORY

Bella Abzug	Jane Byrne
Abigail Adams	Mary Cassatt
Louisa May Alcott	Catherine of Russia
Jane Austen	Chi'iu Chin
Gertrude Bell	Shirley Chisholm
Mary McCleod Bethune	Agatha Christie
Catherine Booth	Camille Claudel
The Brontë Sisters	Marie Curie

*There are many references in this book to singular women and their contributions to the world. Use the index to find specific names and their historic references. Also check the lists of important blacks and Hispanics for additional women who have contributed to their cultures.

Bernadette Devlin	Golda Meir
Emily Dickinson	Maria Montessori
Babe Didrickson	L. M. Montgomery
Isadora Duncan	Toni Morrison
Eleanor of Aquitaine	Mother Teresa
Queen Elizabeth II of England	Florence Nightingale
Betty Ford	Sandra Day O'Connor
Anne Frank	Georgia O'Keeffe
Indira Gandhi	Eva Peron
Emma Goldman	Pocahantas
Jane Goodall	Eleanor Roosevelt
Sara and Angelina Grinke	Wilma Rudolph
Queen Isabella of Spain	Sacajawea
Mary Harris Jones	Mary Slessor
Barbara Jordan	Samantha Smith
Coretta Scott King	Margaret Thatcher
Dorothea Lange	Marie Tussaud
Clare Boothe Luce	Queen Victoria of England
Mary, Queen of Scots	Alice Walker
Margaret Mead	Laura Ingalls Wilder
Margaret Mee	Jane Yolen

Suggestions for Using This List: Select one of these women to investigate. Try to choose someone you know very little about. First, compare two encyclopedia entries on your woman. (Do they differ? How?) What exciting or unusual part of her life do you want to know more about? Next find a library book that highlights or includes the person you've chosen to study and read it, keeping the previous questions in mind. Finally, try and locate more information in magazine articles, filmstrips, *Current Biography.* You can ask the librarian for help. Finally, choose one of the following approaches to share the information you have gotten:

1. Write her biography in the form of a Classic Comic or first-person account by her best friend, or as the last person who saw her alive. Be sure to include what obstacles she had to overcome to accomplish what she did, what her major accomplishments were, and details that you think are important to understanding her life, for example, what her family was like, her education, people who influenced her thinking, & so on. Tell how her life made this a better world and how it has affected you.

2. Make a long time line of her life. Show events from all parts of her life and why you think she was important. Display this time line on a bulletin board in your classroom or in the school hallway.

3. Design a mural that uses symbols (magazine photos or drawings) to show your subject's life and important contributions to humanity.

4. Design a TV miniseries based on your subject's life. Be sure to make it suspenseful. Perhaps you will want to use the device of flashbacks for dramatic interest.

Regardless of the way in which each child shares information about their special woman, the presentation should be lively & original and concentrate on the unique qualities of the subject. Discourage rote listing of dates, jobs, residences. These projects should not be dry but rather engaging and spirited! Emphasize this to the students. Final projects should form an outstanding display!

Maine Admitted to the Union (1820) [15]

Maine is our 23rd state.

Etymology: This state gets its name from the ancient French province of Maine. It also is descriptive and refers to the mainland as distinct from the many islands off the coast.

St. Patrick's Day [17]

Born in Britain, Patrick at the age of 16 was kidnapped by Irish pirates and enslaved in Ireland. For six miserable years he tended sheep on the cold hills of Ballymena. He finally escaped aboard a ship to France, which then was known as Gaul. There he studied for the priesthood and in 431 A.D. was named a bishop. The next year he was sent by the pope to teach the gospel to the people of Hibernia—the same wild Irish tribesmen who had kidnapped him as a boy. Patrick spent nearly 30 years trudging up and down the Emerald Isle, teaching Christianity. The Irishmen who knew him when he was alive must have loved him dearly, for they have transmitted their affection for him to their descendants for 1,500 years.

Etymology: In Gaelic *seamrog* is the diminutive of *seamar*, a clover. So *shamrock* is "a little clover." Because of its three leaves, it was used by St. Patrick to illustrate the Trinity, and in this way it became the symbol of Ireland.

The potato is a native of Peru. The Spanish conquistadores discovered it in the Andes Mountains and brought it back to Europe. The potato was introduced to America in 1719 by a group of Irishmen—hence the Irish potato!

"Snake" is an ancient word and comes from the Indo-European base *sneg*, meaning "to creep"; it is also related to the word "snail," which has the same root.

St. Patrick's Day Science

SOME UNUSUAL FACTS ABOUT SNAKES

1. How long do snakes live? We can't know for certain, but snakes in zoos have long lives. One boa constrictor has lived 27 years in a zoo, and a South American anaconda is still going strong after 28 years!

2. How big do snakes get? They can be very tiny or very large, depending on the kind. The ground snake is about 5 inches long while a python can grow to be 30 feet in length and weigh 200 pounds.

3. How often does a snake eat? Snakes eat only when they are hungry. This can be once every 3–4 days or the interval may be even longer—weeks or months. Zoo snakes, because they don't move much, may eat just one or two times a year!

4. Do all snakes lay eggs to reproduce? No, some snakes give birth to tiny living snakes that crawl off and take care of themselves right from the start.

5. What snake is the best mother? No snake mothers her babies the way humans do, but the python mother makes a nest and coils up on her eggs to keep them safe until they hatch.

6. How does a snake keep clean? Its scales are very smooth and fit together so there is no place for dirt to catch on a snakeskin. Also, snakes get brand-new skins every once in a while so they are usually very, very clean.

7. How many kinds of snakes are there? There are about 2,600 different kinds of snakes. Of these, about 400 are poisonous.

8. How many different kinds of snakes live in the U.S.? There are 126 different kinds of snakes in the United States. Only 19 are harmful to people.

9. Why is it true that snakes are good for the world? Snakes are very helpful. The small ones eat harmful bugs and insects. The big ones eat rats, mice, gophers, and animals that destroy crops. Good farmers and gardeners know how helpful most snakes are and are happy to have them around. All snakes except those that threaten people should be kept safe from harm. They are part of the chain of living things—as *we* are!

St. Patrick's Day Reading

St. Patrick's Snake Game uses a gameboard. Make a copy of the snake gameboard. (You might add bright colors to it.) Take a sheet of heavy white paper and rule it off into twenty 1" squares. Into each square clearly print a sightword which your students need to learn or practice.

WIN

START

Name _____

✿ St. PATRICK'S DAY ABCs ✿

Put these St. Pat Day words into the right ABC order. Number each word (1–4 or 5) to show its ABC order.

GOOD LUCK!

© 1991 by The Center for Applied Research in Education

_____ green   _____ shamrock   _____ saint
_____ olive   _____ clover   _____ St. Patrick
_____ emerald   _____ three-leaf   _____ Paddy
_____ Kelly   _____ good luck   _____ St. Pat
_____ color   _____ symbol   _____ Irish

_____ Eire   _____ Ireland   _____ ship
_____ Ireland   _____ Britain   _____ shepherd
_____ Emerald Isle   _____ kidnapped   _____ sheep
_____ island   _____ pirates   _____ snakes

✿ Now write a story about St. Patrick & see how *many* of the words above you can use in it!

Cover the entire sheet with clear Con-Tac plastic and cut the paper into 1″ squares with a paper-cutter. Place each of the squares face down on one of the empty squares on the snake.

The game begins with the first child rolling a die and moving the number of spaces shown on the die. If the player lands on a shaded square, he or she turns up card and reads it aloud. If the player does so correctly, he or she replaces word card face down and stays on the square; if not, card is returned face down to square and player must retreat to nearest shaded square behind space on which he or she landed. The first player to get to WIN, and reads it correctly, does!

St. Patrick's Day A-B-C requires that you make a copy of the worksheet for each child. The page itself has complete instructions.

Answer Key:

3	3	3
5	1	5
2	5	2
4	2	4
1	4	1
1	2	3
3	1	2
2	3	1
4	4	4

Have one or two students correct their classmates' papers. This is good hand-eye coordination practice for them and saves you repetitive rote work too. Once papers are returned to their owners, children should verify corrections by referring to an answer key you put on the blackboard.

Encourage several of the students to read their stories aloud. All the children who succeeded in using the 26 words in a story might be eligible for a small St. Patrick's Day reward!

A riddle for today . . . for older students: Why is Ireland likely to become very rich? (Because its capital is always Dublin!)

A misty winter, a frosty spring,
a varied summer, and a sunny
harvest . . . an ideal year.

—Irish proverb

Birth of Harry Houdini (1874) [24] ─────────────────────────

America's most famous magician, Harry Houdini was born in Budapest, the son of a rabbi. He was renowned for his ability to escape from handcuffs, ropes, strait jackets, and every kind of confined space—from a filled milk can to a coffin. Houdini was able to perform feats of great strength as he was a trained athlete and champion swimmer. Houdini died of a ruptured appendix. He had said he could never be hurt by being hit in the stomach, but a boy struck him a blow there unexpectedly, giving Houdini no time to steel himself to withstand the shock, and it ended by killing him. His death was due to a misunderstanding.

E-Z TO READ MAGIC TRICKS

These little tricks can be printed onto separate sheets of paper and used as incentives or rewards when students complete long or demanding assignments. You may also want to print them on six sheets of typing paper folded in ½″ strips and then assemble the pages into little books. Once the child can read the entire trick aloud to you, give him or her the materials to go and practice the trick on their own. Many kids will love this way of learning (and practicing basic sight words)!

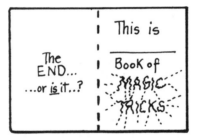

Page 2, left: "The Trick Thread." Tell a friend, "I can make a thread go up in the air without touching it! Then I can make the thread follow me when I call!!" At the bottom of the right-hand page, print the following: "Always try out the whole trick on your own, by yourself, before you show it to a friend."

Page 2, right: How to do it! Hold a bit of thread in one hand. Hold a little plastic comb in the other hand. Run the comb through your hair. Do it again 2 or 3 times. Now hold the comb just above the bit of thread. The thread will go up! Now move the comb a bit to the side as you "call" the thread. The thread will follow your hand when you call it.

Page 3, left: "The Magic Eye." Tell someone, "I can tell you the date on a coin even though you cover it with a piece of paper."

Page 3, right: How to do it! Have someone put a coin face up on the table and then cover the coin with a piece of paper. Say to a friend, "There is a coin under this paper. I haven't seen it, but I can tell you the date on it without removing the paper!" Then rub a pencil back and forth over the paper on top of the coin until you can *read* the date.

Page 4, left: "The Magic Jumping Seed." Say, "I can make an apple seed do what I tell it to do. I can tell the seed to jump and it will, or I can tell it to lay down and it will do that too!"

Page 4, right: Here's how to do it! Put an apple seed into a glass of soda water. First it sinks. Then it comes up as soda bubbles form on it. When it gets to the top of the glass the bubbles will pop and the seed will sink again. More bubbles form on the seed and up it goes again!

Page 5, left: You need to try out this trick so you know just how long it takes for the seed to go up and down. Now take the seed out of the glass. Put some new soda into the glass and have a friend watch. Put the seed into the water and tell the seed to sink (just as it is about to go down) and, just before it is about to rise, tell it to come up.

Page 5, right: "The Magic Thread in the Straw." Tell your friends, "I can put a thread through this straw, cut the straw in two, and then hold up the thread—uncut! How do I do it?"

Page 6, left: In secret, cut a slit about 2″ long in your straw. Cut it in the middle of the straw.

Now hold the straw so the slit is on the underside. Ask your friends to watch as you put the thread through the straw. Next bend the straw in the middle. The thread will fall through the slit. Hold the straw so that the thread is hidden behind your hand and your friends can't see it. Now cut the straw in the middle, and quickly pull out the thread and hold it up so your friends can see it has not been cut. Magic!

Thread

Page 6, right: "The Water Glass That Fills Itself." Show a friend a ½ cup of water in a cup and a clear 5½″ tall water glass. Tell them: "This water glass can fill itself with this water! Want to see how?"

On the bottom of the sheet, upside down write the answer to the trick: Make a ¾″ × 1½″ tall candle stand in the middle of a small dish. Light the candle and pour the water onto the dish. Then lower the glass down over the candle until the glass stands on the dish. See what happens next!

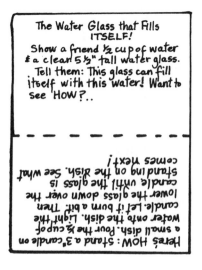

First Day of Spring [21] ———————————————————

On this day there are just 12 hours from sunrise to sunset and 12 hours from sunset to sunrise. This is called the day of the equinox, because that word means "equal." In Greek mythology, Demeter and Zeus had a daughter named Persephone. One day Hades, the ruler of the underworld, kidnapped Persephone and married her. When Persephone left the earth, the flowers died and the wheat withered. Demeter begged the gods to send her daughter back. The gods agreed to let her return for two-thirds of each year. When Persephone returned to earth, life began anew. She corresponds to the Corn Spirit of the American Indians, which dies and is reborn each year.

Note: Children have a tendency to grow restless at this time of year. Plan a class walk to see pollywogs, pussywillows, or other signs of the changing season. If your school is in a city, what signs of spring can be seen and heard? (the beginning of the baseball season!)

Spring Science ———————————————————————

Honeybees. The study of this fascinating insect can involve students of all ages. Write, requesting a current booklist, to

> Dadant & Sons, Inc.
> Hamilton, IL 62341-1399

These publishers offer Bee Coloring Books, honey recipes, and complete honeybee (raising) information at modest prices.

Seeds. Watching seeds sprout and grow (in the classroom, in a cold frame, hothouse, or a school garden plot) gives a child a feeling of purpose and direction. Discuss with your class how they might plant and grow flowers or vegetables and then find a way to do it, if only on a very small scale. Write to

> Stokes Seeds, Inc.
> Box 548
> Buffalo, NY 14240

and request copies of the *Growers' Guide.* The bright photographs are sure to involve some of those future farmers!

It's a Fact: Great horned owl babies hatch this month, while in the northern U.S. maple sugaring, the collecting of the sweet sap of the maple tree, is now taking place.

SPRING RIDDLES

1. What can stay up without any support? (The sky)
2. What weeps without eyes and moves all over the world without feet? (A cloud)
3. In spring I bring you pleasure; in summer I cool you; in fall I feed you; and in winter I warm you. What am I? (A tree)

Pesach or Passover

A movable Jewish feast occurring in the spring. Passover is the celebration of the freeing of the Israelites from Egypt. A traditional dinner, the "seder" is preceded by a reading of the *Haggadah,* which tells the story of the flight from Egypt, the great Exodus.

The seder includes eating of vegetables dipped in vinegar & salt water as was done in early times. Unleavened bread (matzo) is served to remind one of how the Jews had to leave Egypt so quickly that there was no time for bread to rise. It is the custom at a seder to dip bitter herbs in a mixture of crushed fruit and wine before eating them; this is to mingle the bitter taste with the sweet, a symbol of how freedom and spiritual growth were gained only through suffering and sacrifice.

March Activities

If we had no winter, the spring would not be so pleasant: if we did not sometimes taste of adversity, prosperity would not be so welcome.

—Anne Bradstreet

March Language

Newspaper Ads. Here's one way to help your students learn to be concise in what they write. Discuss newspaper ads: what they are designed to do and why they must be concise. Then have each child write a newspaper ad for some inventor who has been discussed during the school year (Edison, da Vinci, Watts, Bell, Carver, Franklin, and so on). These ads may be composed as though the inventor were trying to sell his patent or as if the invention has just been discovered today.

March Math

Make a stiff dough of flour, water, and salt. Ask kids to make little pea-sized balls of dough and use toothpicks stuck in these balls to construct structures, such as a horse corral, a maze, or a windmill. Let them find which structure is the strongest: a triangle? a square? an octagon? a pentagon? What is the tallest structure they can make with 9 dough balls and 13 toothpicks? or 13 dough balls and 9 toothpicks?

March Reading (and Math)

Card games are an excellent way for children to gain practice in word and numbers skills. The following card game formats can be used either for math or reading practice. If you have a hand in the game, you can help equalize playing abilities while the game is being learned—and, of course, you will be so involved with helping the other players that it will be natural for you to keep having losing hands! Sometimes, however, children really prefer to play by themselves. Respect their wishes.

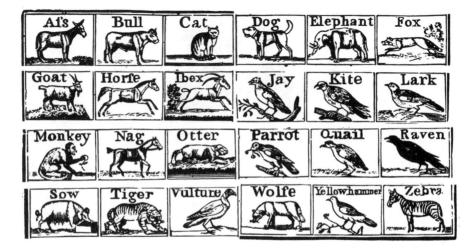

ANIMALS

Purpose: Improvement of number recognition and practice in making quick responses.
Materials: Deck of cards with face cards removed.
Procedure: Three or more players each choose a different animal to be during the game. Animals with long names make it a little harder on opponents. Dealer gives out all the cards face down, making a neat pile in front of each player. The child to the left of the dealer begins by turning up the top card in his or her pile and placing it to the center, forming a throwaway pile. From here on, whenever a card matches the top card on any player's throwaway pile, the 2 players involved quickly try to call out each other's animals name. Whoever is able to say the right name first gets the other player's throwaway pile. Once a hand has been used up, the throwaway pile is reversed to become a new hand, and play continues until one child loses all his or her cards, at which point all the others count their cards and the one with the most becomes the new dealer.

Variation: ANIMALS #2

Before game begins, each child chooses a familiar animal sound instead of the name of an animal and calls out *the sound* during play. Makes for a very light-hearted card game!

GHOST

Purpose: Practice in word or number discrimination and attention to details.

Materials: Oaktag playing cards, as many sets of 4 identical words (numbers) as there are players, for example, 12 cards for 3 players, 16 cards for 4, and so on, & small paper scoresheets, pencils.

Procedure: The object of the game is to get all four of any one set of cards in your hand. Dealer shuffles cards and deals them all out face down. Children get to look at their own hands. Then they say together: "Put one down!" at which point each player discards 1 card face down and passes it to his or her left. Then all the players say together: "Pick one up!" Each picks up the card at their right and places it in his or her hand. Play goes on like this with everyone discarding and picking up together, all the while trying to get 4 identical cards. As soon as one child succeeds in this, he or she places a forefinger alongside his or her nose. The moment another player notices, this child also stops playing and puts a finger next to his or her nose. The last player to notice must say "G" and prints a "G" beside his or her name on the scoresheet. Play goes on. When a child is the last to notice for the second time, this player gets an "H" after his or her name, (an "O" the third time, "S" the fourth time, and finally a "T".) When the word is complete, the game is over.

Variation: Busters! (a challenging version of Ghost)

If 4 children are playing, you put 3 corks (or spoons, lima beans, etc.) in the center of the table. Always use 1 less object than players. Once player has 4 matching cards he or she quietly takes 1 object from the middle of the table. As soon as another player sees this movement, he or she reaches for an object too! The player left without an object gets the letter "B," and the first player to spell out "BUSTERS" goes bust and the game is over. Ghost and Busters are two games that kids often enjoy having their teacher play with them!

SLAP JACK

Purpose: Practice in word analysis & word recognition.

Materials: Oaktag cards, each with a word (of a family group) with which your class is having difficulty (e.g., thorough, through, though, tough, thought, trough, taught, rough, those, these). You might keep a running list (on your weekly schedule book) of the most frequently misused, misspelled words). Use one word that gives many students trouble and print it on four cards. This is the Slap Jack card, and every player should be aware of this.

Procedure: The cards are dealt face down to all the players, and left in a pile in front of each. First player turns over a card from his or her pile and places it face up in the center of the table, pronouncing the word printed on it. If he or she pronounces it correctly, the next player lays a card from his or her pile on top of the first and pronounces the word printed on it. Play continues around the table. Should players not pronounce a word correctly, other players correct them, and the card is returned at random to the pile. Game continues until a card with the Slap Jack word is turned up. Then every player tries to be the first to put a hand over the cards in the pool and say "Slap" plus the word on the card which has been designated the Slap-Word, for example, "Slap-bicycle"! The cards in the pool are then added to his pack. When a player's supply of cards becomes exhausted, he or she is automatically out of the game. The person with all the cards at the end of a game is the winner and gets to begin a new game of Slap Jack.

AUTHORS

Purpose: Word discrimination.

Material: Cards of approximately the size of regular playing cards made from tagboard or heavy construction paper. Four cards make up a book, and there can be as many books as desired. A book consists of the four forms of a verb such as play, plays, played, playing. The order of the words on the cards is rotated. The first word on the card is underlined and serves as the name of that card.

Procedure: Three or more may play this game, depending on the number of books in the set. Each player is dealt four cards, and the remainder of the pack is placed in the center of the table face down. Each player in turn asks another player for a particular card (to be used in completing a book in his or her hand). If a card is received, the player may ask again. In this way the player continues to call for cards as long as he or she receives the card requested. When the player fails to receive the card, he or she draws from the top of the deck on the table. If the player draws the card just asked for he or she may continue by asking another player for another card. When four cards of a book have been completed, the book is placed on the table in front of the player. When the books have all been assembled, the player having the most books is the winner. Each player is required to repeat all the words in each book, and if he or she cannot read the words, this book is not counted toward their final score.

CHANGE OVER

Purpose: Word analysis, drill on initial consonants, blends, endings.

Materials: Cards of oaktag $2'' \times 3''$ with words printed on them:

hat	shell	will	all	sing	sand	look
cat	well	spill	tall	wing	band	book
rat	fell	fill	wall	swing	land	brook
sat	tell	bill	ball	bring	hand	shook

Also four cards having these words: "Change Over."

Procedure: Deal out five cards to each player. The child to the left of the dealer begins by playing (laying down) any card and naming it. The next player either plays a card that rhymes or begins with the same letter. For example, if "fill" has been played, "will" rhyming with "fill" (or "fall") having the same initial letter could be played. If a child cannot play, he or she draws from the extra cards until he or she can play or has drawn three cards. If a player has a "Change Over" card, it can be used as a substitute for any other card, that is, a rhyming or alliterative card. First player who makes books of all his or her cards wins and gets to deal the next hand.

CRAZY EIGHTS

Purpose: Practice of initial and final consonants, blends, and the locating of small words in bigger words.

Materials: A deck of 40 cards ($2'' \times 3''$), words containing parts to be emphasized printed clearly near the top of the cards. For example, if "ing," "er," "ew," and "ight" are to be studied, print 10 cards with words containing "ing," 10 with "er," and so on. Make six extra cards upon which the figure 8 has been drawn.

Procedure: Two or more children may play. The object of the game is to get rid of all your cards. Dealer gives 4 cards to each player, and the remainder are placed on the table in a pack, face down. Player at left of the dealer begins by placing any one of his cards face up on the table, reading it aloud. The next player must play a card from his or her hand containing the same word grouping (e.g., if the first person plays "night," the second player must play a card containing "ight." If the player doesn't have a card with the same word grouping and has an "8" card, it can be substituted, at which time the player may be laying down a new card, call for another letter group to be played. Naturally, the player will call for a grouping of which he or she has the most cards. If, however, there is no 8 card in the player's hand & no other card can be played, he or she may draw 3 times from the pack. If the child fails to draw an 8 card (or a word card that can be played), he or she loses this turn and the next player continues. If a player does not read the card correctly, he or she must take the card back and lose this turn. If the next player fails to read a card correctly, he or she also loses this turn.

Variation: CRAZY-EIGHT TOO!

Purpose: Practice of vowels.

Materials: Forty-card deck, 32 cards, each with a word of one vowel sound, including both long & short a-e-i-o-u. Eight cards with a large 8 written on them.

Procedure: The object of the game is to get rid of all your cards. Dealer gives each player 4 cards and places remainder face down on the table. Player to the left of the dealer puts a card face up on table (forming discard pile) and says the word on the card, its vowel, and whether vowel is long or short. Second player must find a card in his or her hand with the same vowel sound. If this isn't possible, player may place an 8 card on top of discard pile and change the vowel sound to any he or she chooses, or, draw from center pile until a needed vowel sound or an 8 card is drawn. Then the play continues with 3rd player putting down matching card, and so on.

March Pop-Up Puppet

For each puppet you will need 12" long wooden dowel; 3–4" of a mailing tube, cotton fabric; one 3" long fingertip of a glove; polyfill, yarn, or fur for hair; buttons (beads or sequins for eyes); string; narrow ribbon; white glue (or hot glue gun or needle & thread) for making puppet's clothes and adhering felt to outside of mailing tube; and felt pieces to exactly cover outside of tube.

Firmly stuff the glove fingertip with polyfill to form head. Put glue on one end of dowel and push it deep into filled head; tie it off by binding bottom of glove finger to the dowel.

Glue on hair (hairbow), eyes, and felt mouth, or use a marker to draw features. You can build up an opaque nose by putting a dot of white glue on glovetip and letting it dry, and then building up nose to desired length with additional applications of glue.

Cut out front and back of puppet's clothes and place face to face to be glued or sewn together.

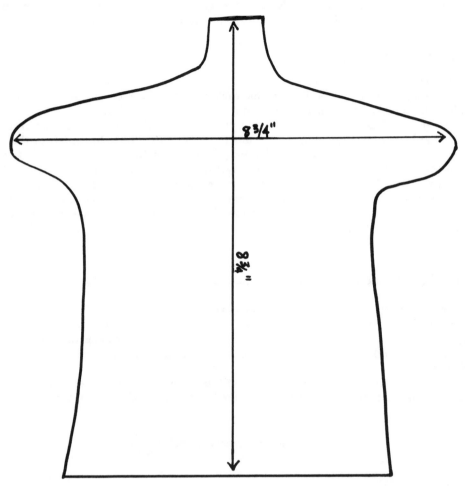

(You may cut out tiny felt hands and insert them at end of each sleeve to be glued or sewn in place.) When glue is completely dry, turn clothes right side out. Felt hands should now stand out away from sleeves.

Run the end of dowel down through neck of clothes, and tucking in top edge of neckline, neatly glue clothes' neck to cover string-tied puppet neck. (A thin ribbon or lace can be glued to outside of clothes' neck to further reinforce juncture.)

Now glue the bottom of puppet's skirt firmly around the outside of the mailing tube. When glue is dry, cut felt to completely cover the tube from top to bottom.

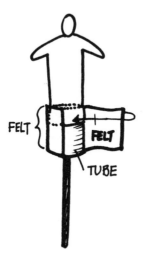

A band of contrasting-colored felt can be glued to top rim of tube for added color if you like.

A bit of practice is needed to learn to manipulate pop-up puppets most effectively. A speedy retreat into tube and a rapid reappearance are best. Then turn figure slowly around and about, holding the tube stationary until the next rapid retreat. Two or three of these puppets conversing together amid appearances and disappearances can be hilarious. A child trying to talk with one may be equally effective. These puppets are wonderful in slapstick routines.

APRIL

To the Omaha Indians, this is "The Moon in Which Nothing Happens." To the Pawnees, April is "Planting," and to the Crow Indians, it is "When the Leaves Sprout." The Alaska Eskimos call April "Little Birds Come, Owls Come."

Calendar of Important Dates

§   National Automobile Month.

> April prepares her green traffic light
> and the world thinks GO.
>
> —Christopher Morley, *John Mistletoe*

§   Good Friday is a movable Christian holy day.

§   Easter, a movable feast.

§   National Library Week begins with the third Sunday of the month. (National Book Committee, 1 Park Ave., New York, New York 10016)

§   Arbor Day, often celebrated on April 22, but this date varies from state to state.

§   Daylight Savings Time, which is 1 hour later than Standard Time, generally used in the summer to give an hour more of daylight at the end of the usual working day.

§   Public Schools Week, dates vary from state to state.

1   [ɹООℲ ꞀIꓤԀⱯ]

In 1972, the *Pioneer* spacecraft drew closer to the planet Jupiter.

2   Charlemagne, king of the Franks (768–814) and holy roman emperor (800–814) was born on this day in either 742 or 743.

International Children's Book Day (The Children's Book Council, 67 Irving Place, New York, New York 10003) marks the birthday of Hans Christian Andersen, 1805.

3   The Pony Express, a route of 1,980 miles between Missouri and California, opened today in 1860.

Jane van Lawick-Goodall, chimpanzee expert & advocate and anthropologist, was born in London, 1934.

4   First American newspaper was founded—*The Boston News-Letter*—in 1704.

On this day in 1968, Dr. Martin Luther King was assassinated.

In 1976, a 52-year-old Japanese, Kazukiko Asaba, succeeded in flying 1,050 kites all at one time!

5   Booker T. Washington, black American educator and reformer, was born in 1856.

Alex Haley, black American writer (*Roots*) was born in 1920.

On this day in 1963, the Soviets & Americans established a 'hotline' linking their two capitals by telephone.

6   On this day in 1909, Matthew Henson, a black explorer and member of Robert Peary's expedition, became the first western man to reach the North Pole.

> Quotation of the Day: My dream and goal for 20 years. Mine at last! I cannot bring myself to realize it. It seems all so simple and commonplace.
>
> —Robert Peary, (diary entry of
> April 6, 1909)

First worldwide commercial communications satellite was launched by the United States in 1965.

8   Flower Festival in Japan celebrates the birth of Buddha.

Juan Ponce de Leon, Spanish explorer, was born in 1460; on his 53rd birthday (in 1513) he discovered Florida.

First Jewish congregation in America, Shaarit Israel, consecrated their synagogue in New York City in 1730. This congregation dates back to 1655 when Sephardic Jews from Portugal settled in what was then New Amsterdam.

First public library in America supported by city taxes was founded by the citizens of Peterborough, New Hampshire, in 1833.

Betty Ford, former first lady (wife of Gerald Ford) and founder of a famous drug treatment clinic, was born on this day in 1918.

In 1974, Hank Aaron hit his 715th home run, breaking Babe Ruth's 47-year-old record.

10   On this day in 1866, the ASPCA was chartered.

Clare Booth Luce, writer and stateswoman, was born in New York in 1903.

11   On this day in 1947, Jackie Robinson broke major league baseball's color barrier by playing for the Brooklyn Dodgers. He helped his club win the pennant 6 times in the next ten years and was voted in the Baseball Hall of Fame in 1962.

12   The Civil War began on this date in 1861 when Confederate soldiers fired on the Union-held Fort Sumter from the harbor of Charleston, South Carolina.

     Imogen Cunningham, who took masterful photographs for 75 years, was born on this day in 1883.

     On this day in 1981, the U.S. space shuttle *Columbia* was launched from Cape Canaveral.

13   Solar New Year.

     Thomas Jefferson, 3rd U.S. president, was born in Shadwell, Virginia, in 1743.

> Quotation of the Day: We hold these Truths to be self-evident, that all Men are created equal, that they are endowed by their Creator with certain unalienable Rights, that among these are Life, Liberty and the Pursuit of Happiness.
>
>   —Thomas Jefferson, The Declaration of Independence

     In 1796, the first elephant arrived in America, in New York City.

     Eudora Welty, American novelist (*Optimist's Daughter,* which won her the Pulitzer Prize in 1972), was born in 1909 in Jackson, Mississippi.

     On this day in 1961 the United Nation General Assembly condemned apartheid in South Africa.

14   First major dictionary by Noah Webster was published on this day in 1828.

     In 1912, 1,517 people died when an iceberg sank the *Titanic* on its maiden voyage across the Atlantic.

     First public demonstration of videotape, in 1956.

15   Leonardo da Vinci, artist-inventor, was born in Italy in 1452.

     On this day in 1865, President Lincoln died of the gunshot wounds he had received at the Ford theater the previous night.

16   On this day in 1862, slavery was abolished in Washington, DC.

     Kareem Abdul-Jabbar, basketball great, was born in 1947.

     U.S. spacecraft *Apollo XVI,* with astronauts John Young, Charles Duke, Jr., and Thomas Mattingly II began an 11-day mission, which included a record 75-hour exploration of the moon, 1972.

17   Isak Dinesen, Scandinavian writer (*Out of Africa*), was born in 1885.

18   On this day in 1906 at 5:15 A.M., San Francisco suffered the worst earthquake ever to hit North America. Huge fires raged for three days following the quake, and half the city was destroyed, leaving 500 dead and over a quarter of a million people homeless.

     First crossword puzzle book was published in America in 1924.

19   Patriot's Day commemorates the battles of Lexington and Concord, which marked the start of the American Revolutionary War in 1775.

Quotation of the Day: If they mean to have a war, let it begin here.

—Captain John Parker, commander of the Minutemen,
April 19, 1775

On this day in 1783, eight years after the Battle of Lexington, Congress announced the end of the Revolutionary War.

First reports of the Holocaust were received in the United States in 1943.

On this day in 1967, *Surveyor III,* U.S. lunar probe vehicle, made a soft landing on the moon and, with its digging apparatus, analyzed the surface.

20   Many famous people in history were born on this day:

- Napoleon III, emperor of France, in 1808
- Marcus Aurelius Antoninus, Roman emperor and philosopher, in 121 A.D.
- Adolf Hitler, 1889
- Joan Miro, painter, in Barcelona, Spain, 1893

21   This is the traditional date of the founding of Rome, in 753 B.C.

Charlotte Brontë, author of *Jane Eyre,* was born in Thornton, England, 1816.

John Muir, writer and naturalist, was born in 1838.

Queen Elizabeth II was born in London, 1926.

Quotation of the Day: Remember, remember always that all of us, and you and I especially, are descended from immigrants and revolutionists.

—Franklin D. Roosevelt, April 21, 1938

22   Earth Day, and the week around it, celebrates the equinoxes and stands for balance and harmony on earth. The first Earth Day celebrations were held in 1967.

23   On this day in 1616, William Shakespeare died, on his 52nd birthday, in Stratford, England.

James Buchanan, 15th U.S. president, was born in Franklin County, Pennsylvania, 1791.

24   First American newspaper to be printed on a regular basis, *The Boston News-Letter* began publication on this day in 1704.

On this day in 1789, the U.S. Supreme Court was established; the following year, the Library of Congress.

Robert Penn Warren, American poet and novelist, was born in 1905.

The launching of the first satellite by the People's Republic of China in 1970 made China the fifth nation to orbit a satellite with its own rocket. The Chinese version broadcast telemetric signals and the song "The East Is Red."

26 First British colonists to establish a permanent settlement in America landed at Cape Henry, Virginia, on this day in 1607.

The Great Plague began in London, 1665.

John James Audubon, artist-naturalist, was born in Les Cayes, Santo Domingo, in 1785.

Ulysses S. Grant, 18th U.S. president, was born in Port Pleasant, Ohio, in 1822.

27 Two U.S. astro events occurred on this date: first telescope put into satellite orbit, in 1961, and the *Apollo 16* astronauts returned safely from their moonwalk, 1972.

28 James Monroe, 5th U.S. president, was born in Westmoreland County, Virginia, 1758.

> Quotation of the Day: Preparation for war is a constant stimulus to suspicion and ill will.
>
> —President James Monroe, April 28, 1818

Maryland became the 7th state to enter the Union, 1788.

On this day in 1947, Thor Heyerdahl set sail from Peru on the raft *Kon Tiki* in an attempt to prove that early man could have sailed from the Americas to the islands of the South Pacific. He made it, but his theory has been generally discredited.

29 First patent for a "separable fastener" (our modern-day zipper) was given to Gideon Sundback of Hoboken, New Jersey, in 1913.

On this day in 1945, the bodies of Benito Mussolini and his companions were hung up and displayed to the citizens of Milan, Italy.

On this day in 1945, Adolf Hitler, Nazi dictator of Germany and instigator of the deaths of 6 million Jews, gypsies, and political dissidents, committed suicide in his bunker, 30 feet beneath the ruins of the Reich's chancellory in Berlin.

30 Walpurgis Nacht (May Eve). Folklorists say this is one of three great festivals the fairies celebrate each year, which also include Midsummer Eve (June 23) and Halloween (October 31). On May Eve, fairies are said to dance and sing to welcome back the warm weather!

Louisiana Admission Day: Louisiana became the 18th state to join the Union in 1812.

Kaspar Hauser (1812?–1833), a German "feral child" around whom grew up one of the most celebrated mysteries of the nineteenth century. It was early alleged that he was the hereditary prince of Baden; this was not proven & he died from a wound inflicted by a stranger.

Alice B. Toklas, superb cook, wit, and companion to Gertrude Stein, was born on this day in 1877.

On this day in 1975, the last 1,000 Americans left South Vietnam, ending more than 25 years of military involvement there. They left 56,555 American dead behind them and 303,654 American wounded. In the last 14 years alone, the war cost America $141 billion.

April

The word probably comes from the Latin *aperire*, "to open," referring to the opening of spring buds and flowers.

April Quotations

I have never been able to school my eyes
Against young April's blue surprise.
                    —Charles Leo O'Donnell, *Wonder*

A little Madness in the Spring
Is wholesome even for the King.
                    —Emily Dickinson

§ For National Library Week,

Why shouldn't truth be stranger than fiction? Fiction, after all, has to make sense.

—Mark Twain

1 Lord, what fools these mortals be!

—Shakespeare, *Midsummer Night's Dream*

13 When asked by Alexander if he lacked anything, Diogenes replied, "Stand a little less between me and the sun."

I'm a great believer in luck, and I find the harder I work the more I have of it.

In questions of power, let no more be heard of confidence in man, but bind him down from mischief by the chains of the Constitution.

—Thomas Jefferson

15 Don't expect anything original from an echo.

—Anonymous

[Said of da Vinci] He might have been a scientist if he had not been so versatile.

—G. Vasari

16 You will give yourself relief if you do every act of your life as if it were the last.

—Marcus Aurelius Antoninus

The people will live on
The learning and blundering people will live on
They will be tricked and sold and again sold
And go back to the nourishing earth for rootholds.

—Carl Sandburg, *The People, Yes*

20 The universe is change; our life is what our thoughts make it.

—Marcus Aurelius Antoninus

22 He plants trees to benefit another generation.

—Caecilius Statuis

There is no doubt in my mind that, should we have been choosing our leaders on the basis of their reading experiences, and not their political programs, there would be much less grief on earth.

—Joseph Brodsky, winner of the 1987
Nobel Prize in Literature

23 All the world's a stage, and all the men and women merely players: they have their exits and their entrances; and one man in his time plays many parts.

—Shakespeare, *As You Like It*, Act II

There is nothing either good or bad, but thinking makes it so.

—Shakespeare, *Hamlet*, Act II

April Events

National Automobile Month ⸻⸻⸻⸻⸻⸻⸻⸻⸻⸻⸻

Etymology: In French, *auto* means "by itself" and *mobile* means "moving," so automobile means "a self-propelled machine."

In ancient Gaul the *carros* was a two-wheeled war chariot. This word came into French as *carre* and later in English became our word "car."

ACTIVITY SUGGESTIONS FOR STUDENTS WHO ARE CAR ENTHUSIASTS

1. Design a crash helmet or a car decoration using fire, or a phoenix, or a skull.
2. Study some modern cars. Then design a fast car with air foils.
3. Write a race car driver's life story in the form of excerpts from a diary.
4. Visit a car showroom with an adult. Get background information and literature from the salesperson. Find a good way to share with the class what you have learned.
5. Do a comparative study of different makes of cars and decide which one(s) are best for the environment. What are the reasons for your choice?
6. Read some articles in car magazines about famous drivers. Choose a driver you admire. Write him or her a letter (in care of the magazine) and ask some good questions. Enclose a stamped self-addressed envelope for the reply.
7. Finish each of these sentences and use them in a paragraph. Cars are a big part of our lives. Because of them we have ＿＿＿＿＿, ＿＿＿＿＿, ＿＿＿＿＿, and ＿＿＿＿＿. Because of cars, people are able to ＿＿＿＿＿, and ＿＿＿＿＿. Because of cars, we have had to build ＿＿＿＿＿, ＿＿＿＿＿, and ＿＿＿＿＿. Cars cause some problems. They ＿＿＿＿＿ and ＿＿＿＿＿. They have made life better in some ways also. They ＿＿＿＿＿ and ＿＿＿＿＿.

It's a Fact: In 1938, there was 1 automobile for every 5 people in the U.S., 1 for every 22 in France and Britain, 1 for every 109 in Italy, and 1 for every 1,284 in Poland. Today, in Communist China, there is 1 car for every 14,500 Chinese.

CAR RIDDLES

1. What should you take when you feel run down? (The license number of the car that hit you.)
2. When is a Ford not a Ford? (When it's turning into a driveway.)
3. How is your front door like a speeding driver? (They both need to be locked up!)

4. How is a loaf of bread related to a sports car? (Bread is the car's mother: bread is a necessity, a car is an invention, and "Necessity is the mother of invention.")

5. What is the difference between a dog's tail and a rich man? (One keeps a 'waggin' and the other keeps a BMW!)

It's (Another) Fact: In 1895, there were two cars registered in the state of Ohio. They collided.

April Fool's Day [1]

Traditionally, on this day Noah sent out the dove from the ark, and it returned, unable to find land. Some sources say that April Fool's Day is descended from an old Celtic festival. In any case, there are eighteenth-century records of April Fool's Day celebrations being held throughout Europe. In Scotland, if you're tricked today, you're a *gowk* (Scottish for "cuckoo"). In France, you become *un poisson d'Avril* (an April fish—in other words, a person who is easily caught). Today, April Fool's Day is observed in Portugal, France, Mexico, India, and the United States.

Some general suggestions. Write the day's date on the chalkboard: "April 1, 1943," asterisk the date, and at the foot of the board, in tiny letters, print "April Fool." Set the clock ahead (or back), and when this is discovered, use the opportunity to emphasize time-telling.

Etymology: The term "giddy" comes from the Anglo-Saxon *guddig,* which meant God-possessed. It was usually not used in a Christian context by the English but rather when referring to a person who was very drunk, one who acted as if the pagan gods had taken over his body and spirit.

The word "dunce" once meant an exceptionally gifted person. The term was taken from the name of Johannes Duns Scotus, a thirteenth-century scholar and professor of theology at Oxford. When a student had performed well academically, he was called a *duns,* which gradually developed into dunce. A hundred years later, however, during a movement of scholarly reform, theologians felt that those who steadfastly followed the orthodox methods of Duns Scotus were obstinate, stupid fellows, and the word "dunce" came to have its present-day meaning of a dull, inflexible person.

> That which seems the height of absurdity in one generation often becomes the height of wisdom in another.
>
> —Adlai Stevenson

The Latin word *follis* from which we get "fool" means "a bag of wind." In the Middle Ages, a "fool" was a dessert made of stewed fruit with whipped cream. Another name for a sweet dessert, still in use today, is "trifle." Trifle also means something unimportant, and so a silly person whose ideas are unimportant is now called a fool!

The court jester and the court fool were entirely different. The fool was a kind of village idiot, who was often physically malformed and was kept because the courtiers found his stupid antics amusing. The court jester was physically normal and had a superior mind. It was his responsibility to entertain the court with his intelligence and sarcastic wit.

"Preposterous" is a curious word. Its roots in Latin mean "before and after," and, in fact, the word is put together to describe the folly of placing something first that ought to be last.

A "paradox" is something which seems to contradict itself. It comes from the Greek *para* meaning "beyond" and *doxa* meaning "opinion."

> It's a Fact: In April you can find *flowers* growing on alder, hazel, and red and silver maple *trees*.

A RIDDLE

Why is an umbrella a paradox? (Because it is best when used up)

April Fool's Day Reading

Use the following reproducible page to make copies for your students. Have them read the directions and fill in the page to discover your personal message to each of them. (Do ask that they keep the message a total secret once they have decoded it.)

Answers: Automatic, Powder, Revise, Igloos, Lawnmower, Flashlight, Oyster, Ounces, Loiter. Message: April Fool.

April Fool Language Arts

Here are some vocabulary enrichment words for today. Give a small prize to everyone who succeeds in defining each one and using them all in a sensible sentence or paragraph: gullible, deceptive, ingenious, guile, dunce, and preposterous.

Here's an April Fool's Day game that promotes concentration.

Each child will need a rubber ring from a canning jar, a plastic drinking straw, a pile of dry pinto beans placed on a table, a timer or clock with minute hand. Children sit at the table, each with a ring, straw, and beans close by. A reserve pile of beans is in the middle of the table. The object of the game is to see how many beans you can transport by straw to the inside of your rubber ring in 2 or 3 minutes. Start them off with a "Go!" at which time each player sucks in on his or her straw to pick up a bean and convey it to the inside of the ring. (The pinto beans are large enough not to go through the straw.) No hands allowed! The first player to get all the beans inside the rubber, within the time period allowed, is the winner.

Name _____

Can you find the
SECRET MESSAGE
that I am sending you?...........
(Fill in the words to the right & then read the message in the 1st letters DOWN.)

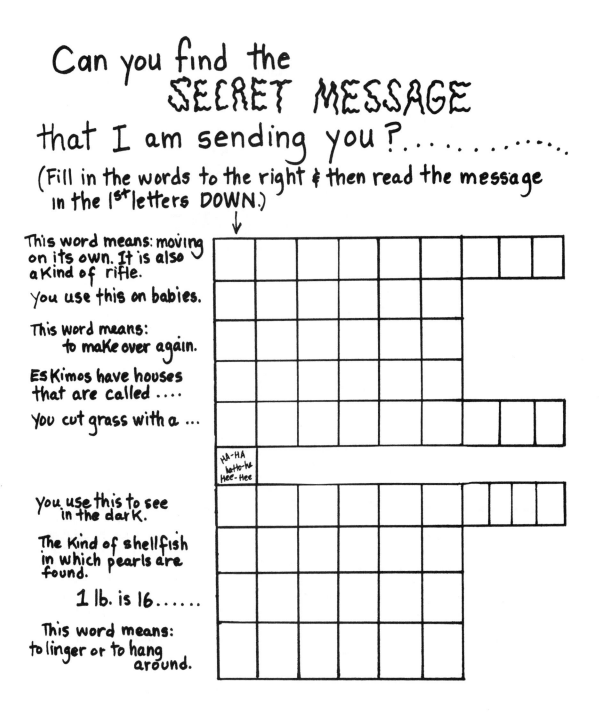

This word means: moving on its own. It is also a Kind of rifle.

You use this on babies.

This word means: to make over again.

EsKimos have houses that are called ....

You cut grass with a ...

HA-HA ha-Ho-he Hee-Hee

You use this to see in the dark.

The Kind of shellfish in which pearls are found.

1 lb. is 16......

This word means: to linger or to hang around.

This game promotes absolute quiet and concentration. It may be continued noncompetitively to see if children can beat their *own* records.

ANOTHER RIDDLE

What's the difference between a loaf of bread and an elephant? (If you don't know, I don't think I'll ever send *you* out to buy bread!)

The first of April, some do say
Is set apart for All Fool's Day:
But why the people call it so
Nor I, nor they, themselves, do know.

Poor Richard's Almanack

International Children's Book Day [2]

Today you will want to have a variety of books from other countries for the children to look at and enjoy. Make it a special celebration by choosing a book you especially like, or perhaps owned as a child, and read it aloud. Perhaps the occasion can be made even more special by serving herb tea in paper cups for the students to sip while they listen to you read. (Be sure to make it clear before you start that seconds on tea will be available *after* the story and not during!) Give a big sponge to one caretaker child who may, if it's necessary, go and wipe up spills.

Young children can be given little books with Xeroxed title pages which they can write in (or you can dictate to them or they can copy your writing from the board):

---

*You may be interested to learn of a resource book that lists children's stories dealing with specific problem areas that children themselves may be experiencing: *The BookFinder*, Vol. 2, *A Guide to Children's Literature About the Needs and Problems of Youth Aged Two to Fifteen* (Circle Pines, MN: American Guidance Service, 1981).

(Title) What is a Home? (pages will have the children's illustrations.)

Page 1: for a baby bird

Page 2: for a goldfish

Page 3: for a cow
Page 4: for ants

Page 5: for an owl

Page 6: for a frog

Page 7: for a whale

Page 8: for bats, and on the back of the book—for ME!

This format can be used to develop a book: What is Food? Fun? Love? and so on. The animals named should be favorites of your class.

The following publisher offers K–6 children's books of a nice variety and selection. Write for a catalog to

> Sundance Publishers
> P.O. Box 1326
> Littleton, MA 01460

World Health Day

Securing world health is the main purpose of WHO, the World Health Organization, an agency of the United Nations. A catalog of resources available from the Institute for Food & Development Policy, can be obtained by writing

> Food First
> 145 Ninth St.
> San Francisco, CA 94104

Birth of Thomas Jefferson (1743) [13]

He was described by his biographer James Parton as "the gentleman of 32 who could calculate an eclipse, survey an estate, tie an artery, plan an edifice, try a cause, break a horse, dance a minuet, and play the violin."

Jefferson himself wrote this epitaph for his grave: "Here was buried Thomas Jefferson, author of the Declaration of American Independence, of the statute of Virginia for religious freedom, and father of the University of Virginia."

First Edition of Noah Webster's Dictionary (1828) [14] ————————————

Very often, Webster's Dictionaries are not written by Webster! There are dozens of "Webster's" dictionaries because the name cannot be copyrighted. Noah Webster named his great reference work *The American Dictionary.*

Birth of Leonardo da Vinci (1452) [15] ————————————

Leonardo da Vinci was a pioneer in modern anatomy, inventor of a parachute and a helicopter, architect, engineer, scientist, and the man who used steam before Watt and who knew before Copernicus that the sun didn't revolve around the earth but stood still. He spent his life imagining, creating—inventing.

Original ideas aren't always that "new." Thomas Edison, as well as Shakespeare, Henry Ford, James Watt, and the Wright Brothers, took known ideas and changed them a little, added or took off a bit—and came up with originals!

To stimulate creativity and original thought among your kids, distribute a copy of "The Inventor's Worksheet" to each student. Tell them that this is one way that "new" things can be invented. Have each child print his or her name in the top left square of the grid and draw a different object in each of the other seven top squares. It can be a plant, an animal, a geometric shape—whatever the child likes. Once this is done, move the paper around so the empty squares on the left-hand side make the top of the page. In the first two squares, the child writes a color; in the next five, he or she should print the name of a material from which different things can be made. (You may want to help them out a bit here with your own illustrations.) Now the child matches the first shape with the first color and fills in the space below the shape; then the first shape with the second color which is filled in the second space below. Go on this way until the grid is filled. Afterward, students can look over their grids to see the strange and often funny combinations. Are there any new inventions? Have students choose one of their squares which has possibilities and think of ways it could be used or places that would be appropriate for it (e.g., a rubber apple, a bathtub toy, a hand exerciser). Who would buy this creation? Why? Now, *you* are an inventor, just as da Vinci was 500 years ago!

You can obtain a fine booklet on the inventions and life of Leonardo da Vinci, which can easily serve as the basis of an excellent bulletin board, by writing to

> IBM Corporation
> External Publications Dept.
> Old Orchard Rd.
> Armonk, NY 10504

Ask for their catalog, which offers materials on Copernicus, Newton, Hiroshige, and Diego Rivera in addition to da Vinci.

The Inventor's Worksheet!

Arbor Day [22, but date varies]

J. Sterling Morton proposed to the Nebraska legislature the establishment of an Arbor Day to be observed on April 10, 1872. The date in many states is fixed at April 22, coinciding with Morton's date of birth.

> **It's a Fact:** How does a sprouting seed, buried in the ground, know which way is up? If a plant stem can sense the warmth of the sun, it will go toward this heat. If water is near, the plant's roots often grow toward this. If the plant cannot sense heat or water, it will develop in response to hormones and gravity.

Etymology: Even in prehistoric times, people were interested in plant life and its cycles. In one of the earliest Anglo-Saxon documents, written over 1,000 years ago, reference was made to a plant's "vital juice" or *saep.*

It most plants, sap abounds while the plant is young and immature, and so it's natural that people began to make jokes about the amount of sap in the head of some inexperienced person. Eventually, any green or unsophisticated person was referred to as a "sap."

ARBOR DAY ACTIVITY SUGGESTIONS

1. Arbor Day is the day to plant a tree. You can get a small sprouting tree at a nursery and ask advice there on how best to plant it and care for it in your community.

2. If you have no room for a tree, you might call the City Parks and Recreation Department and ask if the children could help plant a tree for them.

3. Research the trees in your area. Make plastic-covered labels that tell the (Latin) names of the nearby trees and a little about their history. (Use the *Tree Key,* a 280-page paperback by Herbert Edlin, published by 1978 by Scribner, New York, a really handy reference book.)

Earth Day [22]

First celebrated in 1970 to remind us all to take care of the natural resources of our Mother Earth, this is the perfect day to introduce the following environmental information list to your upper grade students; lower and middle graders might take a week to cover all 4 points—perhaps a section or two at a time.

It is our responsibility as adults to teach students how to live on this earth in a way that is not destructive to the environment. There is an underlying principle which can be taught to children from age 3 up, that is, to be respectful to all living things. When working with very young children, this concept will mean helping them empathize, to understand the feeling of others when they are hurt or made to feel uncomfortable. Help the small child to examine a plant; explain simply about how it makes seeds and thus feeds other creatures and helps make fresh air for us to breathe.

Really look at a tiny insect; examine its eyes and legs and body parts and compare them to the child's. It spends its life working to help others be born and live. Often it provides food for birds or bats. It has a place in this world just as a child does, and it has the same right to exist as we humans do. Very young children may wish to draw and paint and make up stories about Mother Earth and her living parts, how we need to learn to live together in harmony with one another.

Every child needs to be able to do things to help improve the quality of life on his or her planet. Even the youngest can begin forming life-affirming habits which can begin to make a difference!

45 E-Z WAYS KIDS CAN HELP SAVE PLANET EARTH

STOP WASTE! LEARN TO REUSE THINGS

1. Take your lunch bag and lunch wraps home so they can be used again.

2. Collect the throwaway sheets of paper at a Xerox copy store and use the back sides of these for scrap paper at school and at home.

3. Wash out plastic produce bags and take them back to the store to put your produce in again!

4. Clean, fold, and store wax paper and aluminum foil to use over and over.

5. Organize a SWAP DAY at school or in your neighborhood and get together with friends to trade used books, toys, clothing, and so on.

6. Go to thrift stores and garage sales instead of always buying new things.

7. Get some white gummed labels and cover old addresses on big mailing envelopes you've received so they can be used again.

8. In general, try to mend or fix rather than replacing or throwing away things.

LEARN TO RECYCLE

9. Newspapers, and all dull finished paper including used envelopes and brown paper bags. Remember, 120 pounds of recycled paper saves one tree!

10. Glass. Sort it according to clear, green, and brown. Remember the energy saved by recycling 1 glass bottle will light a 100-watt bulb for 4 hours.

11. Aluminum. Crush, bag, or box cans, foil, frozen food trays, and pie pans. Remember: Making aluminum from recycled metal uses 90% less energy than making it from scratch!

12. Set up a paper (& glass & aluminum) recycling system in your home, in your classroom, and in your neighborhood. Help it work!

13. Buy & use rechargeable batteries for your flashlight, calculator, radio, and toys. There are solar-powered battery rechargers (see also suggestion 31).

STOP THE WASTE OF JUNK MAIL!

14. Buy self-stamped postcards and a roll of wide Scotch tape. Put these and a pair of scissors and pen next to the place where you open your mail each day. Then when the mail comes, take out the unwanted catalogs, (and advertising) immediately, cut out their return address, tape it to the front of a postcard, cut out your (computer-generated) address, and tape it to the back of the card. Write on the card: "Please do not send me your catalog" (advertisements, letters, etc.). Sign and mail. With luck and patience, this may reduce the junk mail polluting your house!

CUT DOWN ON THE USE OF PLASTIC WRAP & STYROFOAM

15. Use covered reusable containers to save food in the refrigerator.

16. Reject styrofoam; ask fast-food places to wrap your food in paper, not in styrofoam. Styrofoam uses up the ozone layer!

17. Buy paper, not plastic, and have your purchases put in paper rather than plastic bags. Use a paper or ceramic cup. In general, see if you can cut back on buying manufactured items that you don't truly need.

18. This Christmas (Hanukkah, or the next birthday celebration), make your gifts. It can be lots of fun to do this with a friend or your family. Look in the index of this book under Gifts for lots of unique ideas.

SAVE WATER

Think about how you use water every day. Then,

19. Don't let the water run when you're not actually using it.

20. Turn the water off when you're brushing your teeth.

21. Take short showers instead of long tub baths. Showers use much less water.

22. Don't run the water to get a cold drink; keep a container of cold water in the refrigerator.

23. Don't run the water to rinse dishes: this can use 30 gallons for each meal! Instead, have a pan or sink of boiled water and rinse each dish in it. The dishes will dry faster too.

24. Don't run the water to wash down your driveway, sidewalk, steps, or walkway. Use a broom and some elbow grease!

25. Use a bucket of hot water when you wash the car and only hose it down to rinse it off, saving half the water you once used!

26. Collect rainwater & use it to water your plants.

SAVE OUR AIR

Be careful with chemicals!

27. Before you use a chemical spray* (to kill gnats, flies or get rid of ants, deflea your pet, sweeten the air in your house), see if there is a natural way to achieve the same thing. Here is a recipe for nontoxic all-purpose plant spray

1	cup slightly soapy water	3	big onions, peeled, chopped fine
1	big head of garlic, all cloves peeled	½	cup dried chili pepper

Blend well in an electric blender. Pour into a covered jar and let stand for two days. Strain mixture into a gallon jar and fill with water. (Bury the pulp under a rosebush—it will love it!)

Decant into spray bottle and spray on vegetables and flowers to repel insects.

28. See if your parents will buy pump spray products instead of aerosol cans containing chlorofluorocarbons, for example, CFCs or halcons, which deplete the earth's ozone layer.

29. Encourage others to use woven or stringbags to carry produce home from the market in place of plastic.

30. Next time it is your birthday, ask to be given a tree! When you plant a tree, it helps cool your yard, and it gives off oxygen as it uses up carbon dioxide. A tree can be home for birds and animals and you, and it can grow together all your life long!

---

*The study of chemical pesticides can be fascinating from both pro and con positions. To show upper grade students the other side of the issue, send for these free educational materials: "The Chemical Facts of Life." They include a cassette and filmstrip, wall chart, duplicating skills masters, ten resource booklets, and a teaching guide. This set of materials is subtitled "A Matter of Balance: The History of Chemicals, Their Use, Misuse, Testing Procedures, Benefits, and Risks to Human Beings" and is available from

Monsanto Co.
800 N. Lindbergh Blvd.
St. Louis, MO 63167

SAVE OUR LAND

31. Help start compost piles at home and at school. This will cut down on the amount of garbage you send to the landfill, and it will enrich the soil in your yard or school grounds.

32. Don't throw used household batteries into your garbage. They'll either go to the landfill where they'll corrode and come apart, leaking toxic mercury and cadmium into the soil, or if they are burned at the city dump, the poisonous mercury and cadmium will go into the air. Inquire at the local recycling center to see if your community has a battery recycling program or can tell you how to safely dispose of them.

33. Support the rain forests! Encourage your parents not to buy from companies involved in tropical deforestation. Write The Rain Forest Action Network, 300 Broadway, Suite 29, San Francisco, CA 94113 to learn the current situation.

34. Try to eat less red meat. Cutting down forests to raise beef cattle is not an efficient use of land, water, or energy!

35. You can help the people of the rain forests to earn a living without cutting down their trees. Here's how: Sell Ben & Jerry's Rainforest Crunch Candy—perhaps as part of a class environmental project—it's made with nuts from tropical rain forests. For information, write

> Ben & Jerry's Homemade
> P.O. Box 240
> Waterbury, VT 05676

SAVE OUR WILDLIFE!

36. Each day of your life, be kind to all living things.

37. Help little kids to learn to think this way, too. Explain how an ant, or a butterfly, or a frog has just as much right to live as we do. Get the children to think about what happens when you kill a plant or a ladybug. How will many things be changed by what you did? Can we all live together peacefully in this world of ours?

38. Especially if you live near the ocean, snip with scissors each circle of plastic six-pack holders before you throw them away. These rings often choke marine life when they end up in the ocean.

39. Don't release helium-filled balloons into the air because they too can float out to sea, fall into the water, and kill turtles and sperm whales who swallow them.

40. Set up a birdfeeder in a place that is safe from cats, and keep it well-stocked year round. Birds are often parched for water in the winter if you live where it freezes. See if your parents or school can purchase a heated birdbath. Hundreds of thirsty birds will thank you!

SPREAD THE WORD!

41. Draw a poster for little kids that shows one of these ideas (nos. 1, 15, or 30 on this list). Then display it in your school hallway or library.

42. Set a good example. Pick up litter when you see it. Be part of a group cleanup project at your school or in your community.

43. When somebody gives you good service *thank* them! This way, you will both feel good and you'll be setting an example for the grownups!

44. Write letters expressing your concerns (and have an adult add his or her signature to your own: this may add some punch to your letter).

    a. The Rain Forest Action Network (301 Broadway, Suite A, San Francisco, CA 94133) will send you current names and addresses of people involved in destructive practices in the rain forests.

    b. Local fast-food restaurants may be asked to use paper products for take-out: plastics contain 5 of the 6 chemicals whose production generates the most hazardous waste!

    c. Your elected representative (the reference librarian can give you his or her name and address, or it can be found in the government section of the telephone book), this representative can be told for example that you and your family want a citywide household hazardous waste pickup, the development of safer nontoxic products; federal mandates for recycling programs, laws that give us cleaner water and air.

45. Talk about these 44 ideas with your friends and classmates. This is one way you can spread the word so we can all learn to live lightly on this earth.*

For a quick reference and teaching aid that emphasizes global perspectives and state-of-the-planet awareness, see *Teachable Moments* by Jan Drum and George Otero. These 1-page mind-expanders are mailed to you every few weeks. They are pertinent & original and offer fascinating suggestions that can be implemented in 10 to 15-minute blocks of time. Write

> The Stanley Foundation
> 420 E. Third St.
> Muscatine, IA 52761

---

*Girls, Inc. (formerly Girls Club of America), offers outstanding environmental activity suggestions in the science-oriented information packet. Write to Girls, Inc., 30 East 33rd Street, New York, New York 10016.

Birth of John James Audubon (1785) [26]

Audubon spent his life painstakingly recording, in beautiful watercolors, the wild birds of 19th century America. Many states celebrate Audubon's birthday, and in some places Audubon Day and Arbor Day are celebrated as one.

Have the children observe birds. Help them to learn to discriminate as to size (relative to the robin, starling, and sparrow), color (markings), shape of body and bill, & habits (what they like to eat). With experience, children will learn to make finer discriminations. (How does it fly? Does it run or hop? What kind of nest does it build? What time of year does it come around? What value are these birds ecologically?)

Some Facts About Our National Bird: The Bald Eagle

Today the bald eagle is shown on the Great Seal of the United States, the presidential flag, and on our coins and bills.

Early patriots had wanted a noble American bird as the national emblem. Eventually the choice came down to the wild turkey (indigenous to the United States) and the bald (white-headed) eagle, which early Americans did not realize could be found in other parts of North America as well as here. In 1782, the eagle was chosen as the official emblem. Benjamin Franklin hated the choice and said flatly that the bald eagle ". . . is a bird of bad moral character . . . and he is generally poor and often very lousy."

For 150 years the eagle was widely hunted. Alaska even offered a bounty for eagle feet (50¢ a pair in 1917 and $2 in 1930). Finally, in 1940, the eagle was given legal protection in 48 states. It was almost too late for the bald eagle, though, & it was on the endangered species list for much of the decade of the eighties. Because of careful preservation efforts, his numbers are presently on the rise, making our national bird one of the few preservation success stories of recent years.

When an American Indian medicine man needs eagle feathers for a religious ceremony, he is not allowed to send out scouts to find a bird. Rather, he sends an application to the U.S. Fish & Wildlife Department which collects eagle feathers from downed birds and zoo-raised birds and supplies them to Native Americans for use in sacred ceremonies.

Audubon Materials

The National Audubon Society offers excellent books, charts, videos, tapes, and records covering topics such as seashells, dinosaurs, and exotic plants as well as birds. Write for a catalog to

> The National Audubon Society
> 950 Third Avenue
> New York, NY 10022

If you want to learn how to create a backyard environment especially suited for the birds in your area, write to

> US Department of Agriculture
> Soil Conservation Service
> P.O. Box 2890
> Washington, DC 20013

Or contact your local soil conservation service agent, listed in the telephone directory under U.S. Government, Department of Agriculture.

Three Bird Snacks You Can Make in Class

1. You will need suet (available free of charge at some grocery stores), peanut butter, a thin plastic mesh bag (like orange and grapefruit containers), a measuring cup, a bowl, and a spoon. Chop up the suet into small bits and mix equal parts suet and peanut butter. Spoon this mixture into the mesh bag and hang firmly from a tree branch. Count the different kinds of customers!

2. You will need empty orange, lemon, or grapefruit halves; pointed scissors; yarn; bulk sunflower seeds; cranberries; and bulk raisins. Use the scissors to punch out 3 equidistant holes around the top of a fruit half. Knot the yarn and thread it through the holes to form a hanging basket.

Fill each citrus half with any of the seeds, fruits mentioned. Then hang several of these from a tree branch so that they can be seen outside of the classroom window.

3. You will need pinecones, string, a spoon, bulk cornmeal, peanut butter, & a measuring cup. Tie a string around each pinecone, leaving one long end. Mix one part peanut butter to four parts cornmeal. Use the spoon to smear this mixture onto the pinecone, next hang it from a tree. If you have any of the mixture left over, smear it onto the bark of a tree high off the ground.

Etymology: "Nest" is an ancient word; its probable Indo-European root is *nizdos* (*ni* for "down" and *sed* for "sit"). Incidentally, the correct word for the place where an insect or spider lays her eggs is a "nidus," also derived from the same root.

BIRD RIDDLES

1. What can you throw up in the air and it won't fall back down? (A live bird.)
2. How many steps does a sparrow take in an average day? (None. A sparrow hops.)
3. Why is a lawyer like a crow? (He likes to have his cause—caws—heard.)
4. Why are birds always sad in the morning? (Because their bills are all over dew—overdue.)
5. If a guy is trapped on top of a burning building with a goose in his arms, what is the wisest way for him to get down? (Start plucking that goose, . . . that's how you get "down.")

National Library Week [begins with third Sunday of April] ———————

Have students make a group list of every type of book they can think of. Then show them a list of the Dewey Decimal System for classifying books.*

000–099	General Works (Encyclopedias, Magazines, Bibliographies)
100–199	Philosophy, Psychology, Ethics
200–299	Religion and Myths
300–399	Sociology (Civics, Economics, Education)
400–499	Philology (Languages, Dictionaries, Grammar)
500–599	Science (Math, Chemistry, Biology, and Botany)
600–699	Useful Arts (Medicine, Agriculture, Television)

*Be sure to explain any words with which they are not familiar.

700–799	Fine Arts (Painting, Music, Photography)
800–899	Literature (Novels, Poetry, Plays)
900–999	History, Geography, Biography

Elicit their ideas as to why one type of book is made to precede another. Do the groupings make sense? This should greatly assist them in understanding the logic behind the layout of their library.

This is a time when your school or local library may be especially crowded. Contact the librarian to see if there is a 45-minute period when you might bring your class for a Library Quiz Hunt. Explain to the children before you go that a library is like a huge treasure house full of information. Brainstorm with them and devise a list of the variety of information that is available in different forms of a modern library. Have the students keep 2 running lists on the board as the class offers ideas, one that includes the different subject matter contained in a library, the other listing the formats these subjects may come in, that is, books, periodicals, microfiche, reference books, records, & videotapes. When they have run out of ideas, distribute large file cards and ask each student to write his or her name and to list in a column on one side of the card any subjects which particularly interest them. On the reverse side, instruct them to list any of the ways the information is packaged with which they are not familiar. Explain that each child will have half an hour at the library to explore one or two subjects and find out what is available on them in one or two formats. (This might be less frantic if younger children worked in pairs.) Have each student or twosome prepare 3 mystery questions on their subjects which can be answered by going to the card catalog or a basic reference source (*Encyclopedia Americana, Readers' Guide to Periodicals, Index to National Geographic,* microfiche catalog). Have each child write out the exact source of where the answer to his or her mystery questions can be found, including page numbers or any other identifying information, on the file card. Once the sources for the answers to the mystery questions have all been written down, the file cards should be returned to the teacher, and students can use any remaining time to browse in their favorite magazine.

My Rainbow Reading Wheel

This reproducible page is copied and given to each student. The concentric circles are colored in to record books read; these circles, starting with the outermost ring, should be colored with crayons or fine-pointed markers. The first band is red, the second pink, the third orange, the fourth yellow, fifth gold, and so on through to blue-violet. Writing book titles on the back of the sheet also helps track students' reading. This wheel can motivate a child to enlarge his or her commitment to the written word.

Easter [a movable feast]

The three principal events celebrated by those of Christian faith are the birth, death, and resurrection of Christ. Easter week commemorates the last two.

Easter falls on the first Sunday following the full moon of or after the spring equinox (March 21). Its name and time of celebration indicate that it was originally a festival of ancient times, celebrating the death of winter and the resurrection of the sun. Early Germanic peoples honored "Ostern," the goddess of spring, at this time of year; her name was also related to the East—where the sun comes up.

Easter Eggs. From earliest times, the egg has been the symbol of the universe. It also stands for fertility. Ancient Babylonians exchanged eggs at the beginning of each spring. Colored eggs symbolize rebirth; the Persians, Egyptians, and Chinese dyed eggs for their spring festivals.

Easter Bunny. Our Easter bunny is related to the ancient Egyptian belief that the rabbit is the symbol of spring, the beginning of a new life.

Easter Lily. There is also an original American Easter symbol—the lily. Toward the end of the last century, churches in America began having special Sunday services to help console those who had lost loved ones in the Civil War. The churches were filled with flowers, one being a Bermuda lily that was used in such profusion so as to become associated with the spring and with Easter.

Decorating Easter Eggs in Unusual Ways

Dyes. This is how the pioneers colored their Easter eggs: Select one of the dyeing agents listed below. Put it into a pan, and add enough water to eventually cover the eggs, which go in later. Bring the water to a boil and add a teaspoon of vinegar for every 6 eggs. The vinegar makes the dye penetrate the shells. Gently lower the eggs into the dye water, which should cover them, and just barely simmer for 20 minutes. If any colors are too pale, refrigerate eggs overnight in the dye water to achieve deeper tones. Rub the cooled eggs with a bit of salad oil to give them sheen.

Beets for red
Orange peel for soft yellow-green
Carrot tops for brown on yellow-green
Red cabbage for bright blue
Spinach for light gray-green
Coffee for brown

Let the children suggest other plants to experiment with and try to guess the colors each will produce. Among some they may want to use are chrysanthemum leaves, tea leaves, walnut shells, and fresh herbs like dill, thyme, and oregano.

Wrapped Eggs. Wrap a small flat leaf or flower or paper cutout around the egg. Hold in place with a square of nylon stocking gathered up and fastened tightly by a tied thread or a rubber band. Dip in dye (in natural dyes, simmer for 20 minutes) until egg is dark hue. Remove nylon and allow to dry. Rub dry egg with salad oil to make it shine and to make the design stand out.

My Reading Interest Wheel

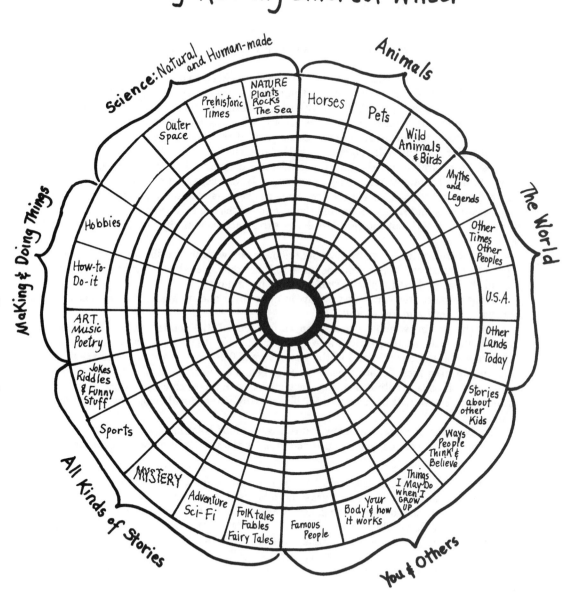

Science: Natural and Human-made

Animals

The World

Making & Doing Things

You & Others

All Kinds of Stories

NATURE Plants Rocks The Sea

Prehistoric Times

Outer Space

Horses

Pets

Wild Animals & Birds

Myths and Legends

Other Times Other Peoples

U.S.A.

Other Lands Today

Stories about other Kids

Ways People Think & Believe

Things I May Do when I GROW UP

Your Body & how it works

Famous People

Folk tales Fables Fairy Tales

Adventure Sci-Fi

MYSTERY

Sports

Jokes Riddles & Funny Stuff

ART. Music Poetry

How-to-Do-it

Hobbies

Photocopy Eggs. Wash an egg carefully with liquid detergent to remove oils from the egg surface and then dry. Cut out small magazine photos and letters. Coat part of the egg with clear acrylic medium. Adhere the photo, face down, to the egg and press firmly. Then peel off. Egg should now have the printed image on it.*

Sugar Molded Diorama Eggs (makes several eggs)

Try making some of these eggs at home over a weekend to be certain that for you, they are worth the effort and classtime to attempt in school. They are quite magical creations!

Combine 2 cups of granulated sugar with 2 tablespoons of ice water (which has been tinted with 2 teaspoons of food coloring) in a glass bowl, using an electric mixer or kneading the mixture by hand until it is of uniform consistency. If the mixture becomes too dry, add a few drops of water and mix well. Then cover with damp cloth.

Use cornstarch to lightly dust the inside of a plastic pull-apart Easter egg. (The plastic L'Eggs hosiery containers make larger view eggs.) Have a square of cardboard ready that is just a bit wider than the open area of the egg. Then use your hand to pack the mixture into each egg half. Pack evenly and firmly all around the interior of the egg to a depth of ¼–½″. Use the back of a spoon to smooth out interior. Level any excess at open end by smoothing it with a knife blade.

Immediately unmold egg by covering the open end with the cardboard square. Gently turn egg inside down so cardboard is on the bottom. Place this on a table and with a light, gentle tap, unmold the egg and lift its plastic shell straight up and off.

If the mixture sticks, it's too wet: mix in more sugar and try again. If it crumbles, add a bit more water to mix and knead well.

For the viewing window, use a sharp knife to cut off the pointed end of the egg while the mixture is still damp. (For L'Eggs-size egg, cut a 1–1¼″ diameter window.) Let the eggs dry completely (for an hour or more) in the sun or in a 200°F oven. While the eggs are drying, the children can plan their decorations. Tiny jelly beans for eggs, green-dyed coconut grass (see below), as well as tiny cutout drawings or pictures of bunnies, chicks, flowers, birds, & lambs can be used. These will be anchored within eggs by using Royal Icing, the recipe for which follows.

To dye coconut grass, add a few drops of green food coloring to a few teaspoons of water. Toss coconut with colored water and if the grass is too pale, add more food coloring and less water and toss again.

Royal Icing. This icing dries very hard so it should be used where you want permanence in design or in an adhesive. If coconut grass is to be used inside a view egg, cement grass to egg with (lightly green tinted) Royal Icing. Use it also to hold other scenic elements in place and to adhere a small circle of colored cellophane to the inside of the viewing hole on diorama egg half. Cement 2 egg halves together by laying a layer of icing along each flat edge. If any icing runs along the egg sides, wipe it off gently with a damp Q-Tip. A pastry decorating tube can be used to cover the seam line with a decorative border cover (or you can tie a pastel ribbon in a bow to cover the seam).

---

*Some magazine photos have a very slick surface and don't reproduce well. Have students experiment with different kinds of photos from funny papers and magazines.

When making the icing, do not get any yolk in the mixture:

1 lb. powder sugar	½ tsp. cream of tartar
4 egg whites	food coloring (add later to part of icing)

Combine ingredients in a bowl and beat at high speed 7 to 10 minutes. Keep the icing in a tightly covered container as it dries out quickly.

The hen is an egg's way of producing another egg.

—Samuel Butler

Easter Baskets (& an exercise in recycling!)

Have your young students collect and bring to class a wide variety of containers: juice, milk, and cream containers; cottage cheese and yogurt cartons; as well as any small sturdy boxes that they think would make cute Easter baskets.

Make 2 to 3 prototypes (perhaps one from a pint carton, one from a ½ gallon carton, and one from a small Velveeta cheese box) and do not decorate the baskets but simply show them to the children so that they can see the possibilities.

Then provide the children with a variety of well-washed containers, scissors, indelible markers (for showing you where to use an X-acto® knife to cut out a basket shape), many colors of posterboard strips (for handles), staplers, glue, colored paper for making little flower decorations, or grass to make a nest with in the basket.

A mixture of poster paint and liquid soap and water can be made up before class for the kids to use to paint the outside of the baskets. This mixture will adhere to the oiled cardboard of the dairy cartons. Pretty little bows or fresh flowers or class-made dyed eggs may decorate and/or fill each basket. Suggest that the children add a small personal note to each basket before they deliver it.

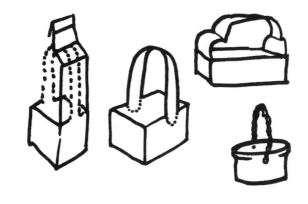

Easter Math

Scrambled Eggs is a review game to help children practice any of the four basic math operations. You will need an empty egg carton with its lid attached; scissors; glue; a marker; a button; and white, yellow, and other brightly-colored papers. Cover the top of the egg carton with a strip of brightly colored paper and glue this firmly in place. With the marker print "Scrambled Eggs" (plus the mathematical symbol of the operation you wish to have practiced as well as the number to be used in the drill).

Write a different number on the inside bottom of each egg holder. On the underside of the carton, write the answer to the problem that appears on the corresponding inside holder.

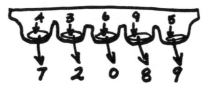

A student puts a button in the carton and shakes it vigorously. When the lid is lifted the child must answer the problem composed of the number in the holder where the button has landed and the number on the lid of the box. After answering, the underside of the carton is checked to make sure that the problem has been solved correctly. Two or more children can play this game.

Nature Cutouts

Provide the children with a variety of large picture books showing closeups of butterflies, birds, standing chickens, and roosters. Have them draw big outline pictures of some of these creatures. Explain that the butterflies should be shown as if you were looking down on them from overhead.

Don't make a drawing on the board showing what you mean—some kids will just copy your drawing and not make their own independent observations. Have children find their own photos (or bring in a mounted butterfly for class study). The birds and flowers should be in a side view.

Provide students with white and pastel-colored paper squares, which you have previously folded in half. Give one to each child and have a quantity of extras for the enthusiasts! Show them a folded paper on which you have drawn half a butterfly and ask them to look at their pictures and make half-drawings of their chosen plant or animal.

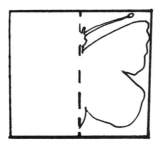

Encourage them to keep these drawings big! Next, have them cut out the outline, and with your help, string them on knotted thread which can be hung from the ceiling and twirl in the breeze.

The birds require a rectangle of thin paper folded twice into 3 to 6 upright rectangles. Ask the students to make a bird with its beak on the top fold, its tail on the cut edge, and the grass in which it stands on the bottom of the paper. Once they have made a complete bird drawing, check each one to make certain that the beak and chest touch the fold. Then have each child cut through all 3 to 6 layers. Emphasize that beaks and chest must not be cut out touching the fold. These long rows of birds, once displayed, will give your room a festive spring feeling.

Have the children punch out additional designs on their birds using a paperpunch if they like. Display white cutouts against bright paper strips, and vice versa.

Easter Egg Art

Provide the children with a variety of precut colored paper eggs, varying from 4" to 15" in height. Ask them to design the prettiest (or most unusual or original) Easter egg they can devise, using colored pencils, pastels, watercolor, or poster paint. Use the finished eggs to border an Easter bulletin board displaying creative writing or Easter riddles from the selection below.

Easter Riddles

These may be presented in the form of three or four Easter rabbit riddle books which children read (or print and illustrate). The correct answer to the riddle should appear on the back of each page. Children will like to read these books during their free time.

1. What does every duck become the first time it learns to swim? (Wet!)
2. A bunny before two bunnies, and a bunny behind two bunnies, and a bunny between two bunnies. How many bunnies does that make? (Just three)
3. How can you buy eggs from a farmer and be sure no babychicks are in them? (Buy duck eggs!)
4. I can throw an egg against the wall, and it will neither break nor fall. How is that possible? (A wall would never break or fall just because an egg hit it!)
5. What did one Easter egg say to the other Easter egg? (Nothing. Easter eggs don't talk.)
6. Why is a promise like an Easter egg? (They both can be broken.)
7. My father and mother were both great singers though neither one of them had any teeth. I am white and completely bald and I have a yellow heart. Who am I? (An egg)

HARDER-TO-CRACK EGG RIDDLES

8. Which came first, the chicken or the egg? . . . Why? (The egg. Reptiles laid eggs for millions of years before chickens were even invented!)
9. Why is Easter like the letter T? (Because it's at the end of Lent.)

Public Schools Week *[date varies from state to state]*

Some suggestions for preparation of your room: Display the children's work by subject matter but don't label groups as "Our Best Work" unless all students have papers exhibited. Every child should have several examples of his or her efforts on display; some papers can be taped to windows if these are at eye level.

You might put together a large book of drawings and stories covering many subjects. Put little signs on classroom plants noting date the seeds were planted. Try emphasizing the foreign language taught, if any, by labeling common objects in the room in that language. Post examples of a child's comparative writing efforts, one from September and one from April! Include one sentence that is the same, if possible, such as, "This is my very best penmanship," and short paragraphs written especially for this display: "What I Love About My Parents," "The Funniest Day in (Fourth) Grade," "Why I Think I Want To _____ When I Grow Up." Display different types of artwork, labeled with the medium used: tempera, collage, silkscreen, rubbings. Have a small group of photographs taken each month, covering as many subject areas as you can. Set out the microscope with slides that the children, themselves, have made.* Have an experiments display on the Science table, composed of a list of the purpose, materials, procedure, results, and conclusion of an experiment with the materials set up in the center.

Reproduce the information which the parents can take home and peruse at their leisure. Such information might include the characteristics of a (fourth) grader—physical, emotional, and intellectual.

Learning projects and students' written work can be enlivened with tape recordings (in a corner of the room labeled "Listening Post") or by having an automatic cartridge of slides shown in one part of the room.

For parents of older students, prepare a sheet of objectives for each subject covered at your grade level. Word these concisely and avoid educational jargon and generalizations. Note areas to be covered, projects, and enrichment work. For example,

> Reading: Continuation of the developmental reading program. In addition to this, a study of vocabulary, root words, and structural and phonetic analysis is emphasized. Recreational reading (reading for fund and profit) is encouraged through the library program. Subject matter reading is stimulated through assignment of projects in

---

*Boxes of unprepared slides (and directions for their preparation) are available through scientific supply houses.

science, social studies, and other academic areas. Your child will be encouraged to develop a lifelong interest in reading.

Maryland Admitted to the Union (1788) [28]

Maryland is our 7th state.

Etymology: Maryland was named for Queen Henrietta Maria, wife of Charles I of England.

> It's a Fact: On March 29, 4166 B.C., according to fundamentalist British biblical historians, Noah's ark came to rest upon Mount Ararat.

Louisiana Admitted to the Union (1812) [30]

Louisiana is our 18th state.

Etymology: This state was part of a region of the country named Louisiana by Sieur de La Salle for the French king Louis XIV.

April Activities

Creative Writing Self-Starters

The following suggestions may stimulate younger students to write short stories, paragraphs, or daily journal entries; many of these ideas can also be used as motivational themes for paintings or other artwork.

1. The World in the Very Beginning.
2. All About Things That Make Me MAD!
3. My Good Friends and Why I Like Them.
4. My Favorite Parts of the School Year.
5. Invent-a-Pet. Create an animal that would make an ideal pet for *you.*
6. Today I feel _____ because _____.
7. Choose an antique object—something used in the world before 1900—and invent a complete history for it. Tell about how it was first invented, who all its owners have been, and all the adventures it has had!
8. Draw a picture of real things and have it include 3 triangles, 4 circles, 2 squares, and a rectangle. Make up a story to explain the picture.
9. Take a trip in your mind: meet a Pegacorn and then tell what you do and say together.
10. What it means to me: my healthy body, my talents, my friends, my teacher.

11. The Differences Between Work and Play.

12. An Afternoon in the Life of a Dog.

13. The Thoughts of a Cat Sneaking Up on a Bird.

14. The Time I Was Caught in a Lightening Storm.

15. How to be Liked, a Complete Guide.

16. If I Could Be Something Else in the Natural World, I Would Be _____.

17. Today you're going to get to create a monster story in detail about a specific kind of monster which you get to choose: a water monster, a flying monster, a vegetable man, a snake woman, an insect monster, or a monster that lives in a bottle. Write (or dictate) a life history of your monster. Include where it lives, what it eats, how it feels about being a monster, what friends (if any!) it has.

18. Discuss together what the word "ache" means and then ask the children to write about "a time when my heart has ached."

19. What kind of things do you like to daydream about? Write down a favorite daydream.

20. Obtain a 5″ × 9″ paper sack for each of your students. Ask them to neatly print a list on both sides of all the things they can think of that their sack can be used for.

WRITING THEMES FOR OLDER STUDENTS

1. Make up an advertisement about yourself in 25 words or less.

2. Write your life story, but do not sign your name. Include lots of details. Use the papers to make a bulletin board display for your classroom.

3. Pretend you are a particular type of weather, such as a hailstorm, sleet, fog, dust-devil, or a rainbow. Describe your life, what you do for fun, why you enjoy being what you are.

4. "Below are cutouts of my favorite cartoon characters cut from different strips. One day they got together and this is what happened to them. . . ."

5. Four or five hundred thousand years ago dangerous animals roamed our planet. There were wild boars, huge rhinos, wolves, mammoths, and saber-toothed tigers. Early man was a scavenger, and like today's jackal, he cleaned up after larger animals had finished with their kills. Use this information as the basis of a science fiction thriller.

6. Make believe that you are looking into a crystal ball that shows your future. Tell about what you see.

7. You are on the 14th floor of a skyscraper. Suddenly a piece of paper blows in the window. There is handwriting on it. What does it say? (Use your imagination on this one!)

8. Complain—at length—about something that particularly bothers you.

9. Tell about one of the happiest days of your life.

10. Pretend you are an animal wronged by a human. Tell what happened and what you do.

11. Should a grown man ever cry? (If no, why not? If yes, why and when and under what circumstances?)

12. When was the last time you cried? What did you cry about? Did you feel better after you cried?

It's a Fact: During the Revolutionary War, Deborah Sampson disguised herself as a man and joined the fourth Massachusetts Regiment. She fought undetected alongside the other members of the regiment. In 1804 she was ill and poor. At the urging of Paul Revere, she was placed on the U.S. veterans' pension rolls, receiving a $4 monthly pension.

13. Imagine that you have found the journal Deborah Sampson kept during her years in the army. Write entries for the day of her enlistment, a day when a battle was fought, and a day in retreat. What problems did she face? Why did she join the army? Think of a situation in which you would need to appear incognito. You are a spy, or kidnapped, or a detective, or . . . ? Write a journal of your own adventure.

14. Choose a letter of the alphabet and give it lots of characteristics that a human might have. Or pick the letter of the alphabet with which you identify and tell why.

15. Make a list of "hot" things (or slippery, whirling, or American things) and then tell how this heat (or other characteristic) is perceived by each of your senses.

16. As shaman, or witch doctor, of your tribe, what are your duties? How do you deal with sickness? an enemy? the threat of a war against your people?

17. Here's the beginning of a scary story. Write a good ending for it: "I had been so clever that I smiled contentedly. It was only then that I heard the lock behind me."

18. Conduct an imaginary interview with a "being" from the center of the earth, or a mummy brought back to life, or a space alien.

19. Look through magazines like *National Geographic* or take a Polaroid photo of some creature or plant in the world that you think is disgusting and ugly. Then see if you can find something likable about this thing. Write a paragraph about it, describing how you found positive aspects to a creature or plant that you originally thought was totally unattractive.* A bulletin board on this theme, "Ugly Things Can Be Beautiful," is also a possibility.

20. You have a supernatural experience. What is it? What do you do?

---

*The teacher may make a collection of ugly things, such as, a spider, picture of industrial smokestacks, train wreck, or a rattlesnake, as stimuli for this writing project.

April Unicorn Hand Puppets ———————————

For each puppet, you will need scissors; small pieces of light blue, dark beige, and pink felt; white felt; white short-haired fake fur fabric; white yarn; metallic gold elastic thread (sold at yardage stores—large quantities come in each package); a small amount of polyester fiber fill; white thread; a sewing machine; white glue; needle; & bamboo chopstick.

Cut out from fur fabric the pattern as shown.

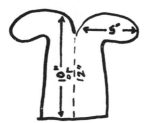

Loop the white yarn 10 to 12 times:

With right sides together and looped yarn near top of head, stitch on machine to form basic head.

Turn right side out. Make 2 small "V" cuts on either side of head.

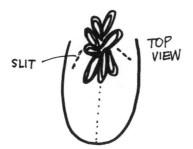

This is where 2 small felt ears will be inserted. Use a small amount of Elmer's glue to attach pink felt inner ear to white felt ear.

Pinch the bottom 2 corners of ear together and insert into one of the ear slits in head. Position facing forward and glue ear firmly to inside of fabric of head. Repeat with second ear.

Take a 2″ × 6″ piece of white felt and stitch it along both long sides, leaving bottom open. Turn this felt horn inside out, using a bamboo chopstick to help. Once turned, horn may need a little polyester stuffing pushed up into its base. When horn is straight and rigid, it is ready to be inserted into a small slit you have made in the high middle of unicorn's forehead.

With needle and thread, tack the horn firmly to forehead. Knot the gold thread and wind it down to unicorn's horn to give it a convoluted look. Anchor gold thread at base of horn with the white thread. With a pencil, lightly mark each nostril and eye area on the head. Use your scissors to trim the fur back to the fabric in these places. Using white glue (don't soak felt as it gets hard) adhere 2 pink felt spots to unicorn's muzzle for his nostrils and 2 felt eyes.

Add a few small pastel ribbons, tiny bells, or flowers to the unicorn's mane and forelock and you are done! A herd of these little creatures with their creators makes a fine photograph!

April Field Trip Suggestions

Because Earth Day falls in April, it is a perfect time to plan a visit to the source of your city's water supply (reservoir, artesian well, lake, etc.) or to the water purification plant. Check and see if there is an employee available to speak with the students about your local water situation and problems.

Or visit a city dump, a recycling site, or auto emissions checkpoint. If you have a paper manufacturing plant nearby, arrange to visit it and ask if the plant uses virgin or recycled materials to produce its paper. What are the reasons behind its decisions?

A trip to a glass manufacturing plant and inquiry into the nature of the materials it uses can also be interesting and fun. How much energy does the plant use to operate? Does it have a recycling program?

Also, consider these destinations: the zoo, an assembly line at a (car) factory, a (small, private) airport, a bird sanctuary or Audubon bird walk, or your local library (for guided tour, especially of the children's section).

Invite to the class a forest ranger, a bird-watcher, a small-animal vet who enjoys telling stories about his or her patients, an environmentalist, or citizen from your community who has traveled to faraway places and enjoys recounting personal adventure stories.

MAY

The Eskimos call May "Rivers Start Running" or "Geese Come, Birds Hatch." The Omaha Indians call it "The Moon in Which the People Plant." The Seminoles of Florida call May "Big Mulberry Moon."

Calendar of Important Dates

- § May is Red Cross Month (American Red Cross National Headquarters, Washington, DC 20006).
- § May is Senior Citizens Month.
- § National Music Week begins the first Sunday in May (National Federation of Music Clubs, 600 S. Michigan, Chicago, IL 60605).
- § Be Kind to Animals Week is also celebrated the first week in May (American Humane Association, P.O. Box 1266, Denver, CO 80201).
- § Mother's Day, the second Sunday in May.
- § Memorial Day, last Monday in the month of May, originally was a day to honor those killed in the Civil War but is now observed in memory of those Americans lost in all wars.

1   May Day—traditionally a spring festival involving flowers and dancing around a Maypole.

First U.S. postal card issued, in 1872.

Scott Carpenter, U.S. astronaut, was born in Boulder, Colorado, in 1925.

> Quotation of the Day: I can see the day coming when none of the great offices of the Republic will be closed to women of talent, not even the office of President—although I hope you will forgive me for hoping that day is still a few years off!
>
> —President Lyndon B. Johnson, 1964

3   Solar Day or Sun Day, first celebrated in 1978, has been established to help make people aware of the many ways in which the sun enriches our lives.

On this day in 1963, thousands of blacks staged protest marches in Birmingham, Alabama, and 2,000 were arrested. Police dogs and water hoses were used against the civil rights marchers.

4   On this day in 1776, Rhode Island declared its independence from Great Britain.

Eugenie Clark, biologist and expert on shark behavior, was born in 1922.

5   Children's Day is celebrated in Japan: Kodomo-no-hi, the Feast of Flags.

Karl Marx, economic philosopher, was born in Treves, Prussia, in 1918.

Nellie Bly, investigative reporter, was born in Cochrane Mills, Pennsylvania, in 1867.

On this day in 1961, Alan Shephard, Jr., was rocketed 115 miles into space, becoming America's first astronaut.

6   Willie Mays, great black baseball player, was born in Fairfield, Alabama, on this day in 1931.

7   First communications satellite, the U.S. *Telestar II,* was launched in 1963.

8   International Red Cross Day, commemorating the birthday of the organization's founder, Jean Henri Dunant.

Harry S. Truman, 33rd U.S. president, was born in Lamar, Missouri, in 1884.

9   On this day in 1502, Christopher Columbus and his 13-year-old son set out from Cadiz, Spain, on Columbus's fourth and last voyage. His crew of 150 mutinied near the easternmost tip of Central America, and Columbus was stranded for a year on the island of Jamaica before being able to return to Europe.

First Nazi book burning: 25,000 books were consumed in fire in Berlin in 1933.

10 First transcontinental railroad completed, with the eastern and western sections meeting in Utah, where a golden spike joined them in 1869.

11 John Chapman, also known as Johnny Appleseed, planter of thousands of apple trees, was born in 1768.

Minnesota became the 32nd state to join the Union in 1858.

12 Florence Nightingale was born in England in 1820.

Dorothy Crawfoot Hodgkin, Nobel Prize winner (for her study of penicillin and vitamin B12), was born in 1910.

13 First permanent English settlement in the New World, Jamestown, was founded near the James River in Virginia, 1607.

First practical printing press, the Washington press, was patented by Samuel Bust in 1821. Its design was so good that this type of press is still in use in some places.

14 On this day in 1804, Captain Meriwether Lewis and William Clark set out from St. Louis for the Pacific Coast, exploring the newly acquired wilderness—the Louisiana Territory—on their way.

15 First copyright law was passed in Massachusetts in 1672.

On this day in 1869, a group of women met in New York to form the National Woman Suffrage Association to campaign for the women's vote. Elizabeth Cady Stanton was the first president.

Artist Jasper Johns was born in Augusta, Georgia, in 1930.

16 On this day in 1868, the Senate failed—by only one vote—to impeach President Andrew Johnson.

17 On this day in 872, the Kingdom of Norway was founded.

In 1792, the New York Stock Exchange came into being.

On this day in 1954, the U.S. Supreme Court declared racial segregation in schools to be unconstitutional.

> Quotation of the Day: Separate educational facilities are inherently unequal.
>
> —Chief Justice Earl Warren, May 17, 1954

18 World Goodwill Day commemorates the anniversary of the first Hague Peace Conference in 1899. Many countries sent representatives to help improve international relations; it was at a later meeting at the Hague that the United Nations was founded.

International Museum Day

First woman to fly faster than the speed of sound, Jacqueline Cochrane, piloted an F-86 Sabre jet fighter plane to Edwards Air Force Base in California at an average speed of over 600 mph, in 1953.

On this day in 1980, Mt. Saint Helens, a volcano in Washington state, erupted, causing floods, fires, mudslides, and the loss of 60 lives. Volcanic ash filled the air throughout the area for many weeks.

19 On this day in 1536, Anne Boleyn (mother of Elizabeth I), who had been married to King Henry VIII of England for three years, was beheaded on the Tower Green in London; the execution was carried out by an expert imported from France by the king.

20 Dolly Madison, one of the most popular American first ladies, was born on this date in 1768.

First public viewing of motion pictures occurred in New York City, projected by the Latham family in 1895.

First solo nonstop flight across the Atlantic. Charles Lindbergh took off from New York in 1927 and landed in Paris 33½ hours later, to be greeted by a crowd of 100,000.*

---

*His plane was stocked with 451 gallons of gas and 20 gallons of oil but had no lights, heat, radio, automatic pilot, or deicing equipment.

21 On this day in 1881, the American Red Cross was founded by Clara Barton.

First test explosion of an airplane-borne hydrogen bomb was conducted over Bikini Island in the Pacific by the United States, 1956.

Robert Creeley, poet, was born in Arlington, Massachusetts, in 1926.

23 Carl von Linne (Linnaeus), botanist, was born in South Rashult, Sweden, in 1707. He is remembered for devising a scientific nomenclature for living things.

South Carolina became the 8th state to enter the Union, in 1788.

Mary Cassatt, American painter of gentle mother & child scenes, was born in Pittsburgh, Pennsylvania, in 1844.

On this day in 1969, five U.S. satellites were launched by one rocket.

24 On this day in 1626, Peter Minuit, director of the Dutch West India Trading Co., bought the island of Manhattan from the Indians for $24 worth of trade beads and then founded the colony of New Amsterdam.

Queen Victoria was born in Kensington, England, in 1819. This day is celebrated as Commonwealth Day in Great Britain and the Commonwealth countries, including Canada.

On this day in 1962, Scott Carpenter became the second American to go into orbit, circling the world three times.

25 Theodore Roethke, poet, was born in Saginaw, Michigan, in 1908.

On this day in 1969, Thor Heyerdahl set sail from Egypt in a reed boat named *Ra* in an attempt to prove that ancient Egyptians could have sailed to the Americas. His expedition was successful.

26 On this day in 1954, the funeral ship of the Egyptian Pharaoh Cheops was unearthed in a limestone chamber near the Great Pyramid in Egypt.

Africa Freedom Day celebrates the founding of the Organization of African Unity (OAU) in 1963. Sporting events, parades, and speeches commemorate the day in African countries.

On this day in 1973, the U.S. spaceship *Skylab* took off on its successful 28-day flight around the earth.

27 Amelia Bloomer, women's rights champion, was born in Homer, New York, in 1818.

Isadora Duncan, pioneer in the modern dance movement, was born on this day in 1878.

Rachel Carson, writer and environmentalist (before there was such a title), was born in Springdale, Pennsylvania, in 1907.

28 In 1892 on this day, the Sierra Club was founded taking as its mission the conservation of the earth's natural resources and wildlife.

On this day in 1959, two monkeys (Able and Baker) survived a 300-mile space trip in the nose of a rocket and were picked up uninjured.

In 1967, Sir Francis Chichester sailed back into Plymouth, England, after completing a round-the-world solo voyage.

29 On this day in 1453, Constantinople, the capital of the Byzantine Empire, was captured by the Turks, signifying the end of the Middle Ages.

Rhode Island was admitted to the Union as our 13th state in 1790.

Wisconsin was admitted as the 30th state in 1848.

First successful climb to the summit of Mt. Everest was completed on this day in 1953 by Edmund P. Hillary of New Zealand and Tensing Norkay of Nepal.

John Fitzgerald Kennedy, 37th U.S. president, was born in Brookline, Massachusetts, in 1917.

30 Czar Peter the Great was born in Moscow in 1672.

31 Walt Whitman, American romantic poet, was born on this day in 1819.

The first taxis came to New York City, imported from Paris, in 1907.

On this day in 1964, the longest double-header in major league history as played in New York by the Mets and the San Francisco Giants. The Giants finally won both games after a total playing time of 10 hours and 22 minutes!

On this day in 1971, U.S. *Mariner 9* satellite was launched to explore the planet Mars.

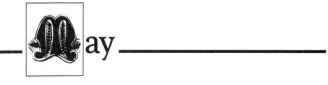

This month was probably named for the Roman goddess, Maia, goddess of growth.

May Quotations

Money will buy a pretty good dog, but it won't buy the wag of his tail.

—Josh Billings

4   Be ashamed to die until you have won some victory for humanity.

—Horace Mann

7   What has destroyed every previous civilization has been the tendency to the unequal distribution of wealth and power.

—Henry George

Life shouldn't be printed on dollar bills.

—Clifford Odets

12 [Of Florence Nightingale] She held that the universe—including human communities—was evolving in accordance with a divine plan; that it was (our) business to endeavor to understand this plan and guide (our) actions in sympathy with it. But to understand God's thoughts, she held, we must study statistics, for these are the measure of His purpose. Thus the study of statistics was, for her, a religious study.

—Karl Pearson

Too kind—too kind [when she was handed on her deathbed, the insignia of the Order of Merit].

—Florence Nightingale

18 There never was a good war or a bad peace.

—Benjamin Franklin

The secret of happiness is this: let your interests be as wide as possible, and let your reactions to the things and persons that interest you be as far as possible friendly rather than hostile.

—Bertrand Russell

There is one thing stronger than all the armies in the world, and that is an idea whose time has come.

—Victor Hugo

You can't say civilization don't advance, for in every war they kill you in a new way.

—Will Rogers

27 For all at last returns to the sea—the beginning and the end.

—Rachel Carson

31 We have frequently printed the word democracy. Yet I cannot too often repeat that it is a word the real gist of which still sleeps, quite unawakened, notwithstanding the resonance and the many angry tempests out of which its syllables have come, from pen or tongue. It is a great word, whose history, I suppose, remains unwritten, because that history has yet to be enacted. It is, in some sort, younger brother of another great and often-used word, Nature, whose history also waits unwritten.

—Walt Whitman

MAY

May be chill, may be mild,
May pour, may snow,
May be still, may be wild,
May glower, may glow,
May freeze, may burn,
May be gold, may be gray,
May do all these in turn—
May May.

—Justin Richardson, *"The Countryman"*

May Events

Be Kind to Animals Month

Animals are such agreeable friends; they ask no questions, pass no criticisms.

—George Eliot

One reason people choose to be kind to animals is that we should be able to empathize with weaker creatures. Empathy is "a feeling into-ness"—the ability to sense how another is feeling. Help children learn to be more empathetic; here are some ideas:

Ask each student to pretend that he or she is a pet. Then have them describe the things that make them happy and comfortable and how they are treated by their master or mistresses. Tell what makes them feel surprised, anxious, or lonely.

Have the kids write stories in the first person, pretending that they are animals living in places like a game refuge, zoo, farmyard, or jungle. Have them anthropomorphize these animals:

For example, a golden eagle in a game reserve waits to experience the sights and sounds of people away from their natural habitat of noisy, dirty, smelly cities. He's anxious for the younger birds to observe how unfortunate the human species is not to have wings. He expects to show them the shell-like metal objects people crawl into to get around, often jostling one another and honking like geese. He wants his youngsters to also observe the strange eating and drinking habits of people. He tells them how humans seldom eat mice or grasshoppers, but instead consume strange mixtures out of cans and paper sacks! He plans to spend most of the afternoon feeding in the fields and creeping as close as possible to watch the people without frightening them off.

Ask each student to write about how his or her own pet may see him or her: in what way is the child a good owner and how might he or she improve? Or let students talk about being kind to animals, why kindness is important, why we care, and how each of us can honestly help make this a better world for our pets.

Older students may be interested in receiving information from

The Animal Protection Institute of America
2831 Fruitridge Rd.
P. O. Box 22505
Sacramento, CA 95822

In Defense of Animals
816 W. San Francisco Blvd.
San Rafael, CA 94901

The Spotted Opossum of New South Wales   The Tendrac

The Long-Eared Bat

Here are some *Gee-Whiz Facts* about animals. You may find them useful in developing learning centers, bulletin boards, individualized readers, game cards, and so on. They are written with a low vocabulary.

RECORD BREAKERS

We keep track of the biggest and smallest things in the world. We keep track of the fastest and tallest and oldest things. When we hear of something that is even BIGGER or even smaller,

TALLER or *FASTER* we say "It breaks the record!"

What is the fastest animal in the world? Well, the cheetah can *RUN* the fastest. This cat with the small head can run as fast as 70 miles an hour! But the *VERY fastest* animal in the world is the Peregrine falcon, which can fly *over* 215 miles an hour when in a 45° dive.

What animal can live the longest? Some animals can live 50 years! The crocodile, the rhino, the parrot, the swan, and the eagle can all live 50 years. The elephant may live more than 70 years. But the animal that can live the longest? It's the big land turtle! He lives longer than people! He can live more than 125 years! *He's a real* record-breaker!

What bird can fly the highest? The condor. It can fly *4 miles up* into the sky! A kangaroo can jump quite high—25 feet up—and it can *only* jump because the kangaroo is an animal that cannot walk! Its front legs are the size of a dog's, and its back legs are the size of a mule's.

If you made a list of *really odd* animals, what would you put on it? Any one on this list is very *unusual.* Look them up in an animal picture book and you will see what I mean . . . .

the walking leaf	the frog fish	the sloth
the sea elephant	the roadrunner (a bird that can store solar energy)	

The Sloth

Some of the animals that hold the record for being the worst killers are the king cobra, killer bees, the piranha, the great white shark and the spider crab. But the number 1 champion in this category is . . . . (guess!).*

Fossils (the bones, shells, and tracks of very very old plants and animals which have over the years been turned to stone!) were found by the Greek people in 600 B.C. They thought they were art done by very early men and women. Today there are some living fossils—kinds of animals that can be seen alive today and which also lived many thousands of years ago on the earth—*long* before human beings were here in the world! Some of these living fossils are

the giant crab	the lobster
the sea mouse	the octopus

Let's see which animals are record-breakers because of the way they look? Here is a list of the *ugliest* animals in the world (at least, they seem ugly to most humans!):

The three-toed tamandua, which has a tongue like a drooping whip

The great anteater, which is 4 feet long with a 3 foot tail, has a long snout, and weighs 100 pounds

The komodo dragon, the gila monster, the sungazer lizard, & the marine iguana, which are all very ugly-looking to *us,* are probably not unsightly to other lizards

The star-nosed mole, which has huge claws, no eyes you can see, creepy-looking feet, and a sickening nose with 22 feelers all around it and its mouth

---

*The malarial mosquito! If we don't count wars and accidents, this mosquito has been responsible for 50 percent of all deaths since the Stone Age!

Maybe you can find some of these record-breakers in a book. Then you can draw them and make a chart to show the other kids the "Animal Record-Breakers" *you* like the best!

Etymology: The word "walrus" comes from Iceland by way of Scandanavia. In Icelandic, this animal is called a *hross-hvair,* meaning a "horse whale" because of its horselike neighing. In Scandanavia, the name became "whale horse" and our English word "walrus" comes from this.

The word "kangaroo" has an unlikely origin. In the 18th century, Captain James Cook landed in Australia where he became intrigued by the animal we know as the kangaroo. Cook asked the aborigines what this animal was called. The native people did not understand what he was asking and replied, *Kangaroo,* which meant in their language, "What did you say?"

THE HORSE

Certainly one of the most popular animals among children, the horse is a fascinating subject for research. Colorful and informative materials are available free of charge from the following sources:

> Appaloosa Horse Club, Inc.
> P. O. Box 8403
> 5070 Highway 8 West
> Moscow, ID 83843
>
> Tennessee Walking Horse
> Breeders' & Exhibitors Assoc.
> P. O. Box 286
> Lewisburg, TN 37091

Request "For You, An American Quarter Horse" from the American Quarterhorse Association (P.O. Box 200, Amarillo, TX 79168), and "Esquine Careers" from the American Horse Council (1700 K. St., NW, Suite 300, Washington, DC 20006).

Here is a horse activity sheet which you can reproduce for your equine enthusiasts!

Name _____

The Horse

You already know the names of many parts of a horse: the mane, tail, ears. Here is a list of some other parts of this fine animal. Print in the right names on the drawing above.

1. poll: the top of the head

2. crest: arch of the neck

3. dock: top of tail

4. flank: side of hip

5. barrel: round middle sides

6. gaskin: back upper leg

7. hock: 'the knee' of back legs

8. muzzle: upper lip & mouth area

9. fetlock: it juts out right below the ankle

10. forelock: right above the forehead

11. pastern: it is between the fetlock & the hoof

12. cannon: it is between the hock & the postern

13. withers: the highest part of the back; between the shoulders

14. chestnut: a hard spot on the inner side of a horse's leg

Nine parts of the horse have names like parts of *our* bodies. Print these names in too: chest, cheek, forearm, knee, shoulder, rump, abdomen, back, forehead & . . . . . hoof!

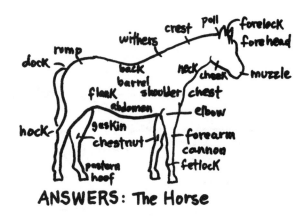

ANSWERS: The Horse

HORSE RIDDLE

How many legs does a horse have? (Six: A horse's forelegs are in front and it has two legs behind.)

DOG RIDDLES

1. Is a dog dressed warmer in the summer or in the winter? (In the summer, because in winter, he just wears a fur coat, while in the summer he wears a coat and pants!)

2. When is a dog's tail *not* a tail? (When it's a waggin'—a wagon.)

3. When is a red puppy not likely to enter a house? (When the door is closed *or* when the puppy is asleep.)

National Music Week

Children need weekly—if not daily—opportunities to make and listen to music, to enjoy a wide variety of musical experiences. You can build up a repertoire of songs you all sing together (even during 5-minute breaks): encourage the children to teach you their favorites and invite parents to stop by and teach you songs from their childhood. Here's a dear old favorite of mine:

Waltzing with Bears

Chorus:
He goes wa-wa-wa-wa-wa waltzing, waltzing with bears
Raggy bears, baggy bears, shaggy bears too
And there's nothing on earth Uncle Walter won't do
So he can go waltzing, wa-wa-wa-waltzing
He can go waltzing, go waltzing with bears

I went to his room in the middle of the night
I tiptoed inside and turned on the light
But to my dismay, he was nowhere in sight
'Cause my Uncle Walter goes waltzing at night

We bought Uncle Walter a new coat to wear
But when he comes home, it's all covered with hair
And lately I've noticed several new tears
I'm sure Uncle Walter's been waltzing with bears

We told Uncle Walter that he should be good
And do all the things we say that he should
But we know he'd rather be off in the woods
We're afraid that we'll lose Uncle Walter for good.

We begged and we pleaded, "Oh please won't you stay?"
And managed to keep him at home for a day
But the bears all barged in and took him away
Now he's dancing with pandas
and we don't understand it
But the bears all demand at least one waltz a day.

Students need to be exposed to different types and styles of music—African singing, sitar-playing from India, Gregorian chants, Caribbean songs. One source of fine tapes is The Mind's Eye, which offers fine jazz, medieval, chamber, & ballet (story and music) as well as an outstanding selection of literature and poetry for children. Ask for their catalog: The Mind's Eye, Box 6727, San Francisco, CA 94101.

The Aristoplay Game Co. (P.O. Box 7529, Ann Arbor, MI 48107) offers award-winning educational games for all ages, including Music Maestro II, a game of musical instruments, and The Game of the Great Composers. Write, requesting a current catalog.

Music-related materials are also available free of charge from the Selmer Company (P.O. Box 310, Elkhart, IN 46515-0310). Their offerings include color booklets on flutes & piccolos, clarinets, oboes and bassoons, and saxophones and Bach brass.

Mother's Day [second Sunday in May]

President Woodrow Wilson proclaimed this day as a national observance on May 9, 1914, but it has its roots far back in history. In pre-Christian times, the people of Asia Minor worshipped Rhea, the great mother of the gods as she was called. When Christianity gradually spread throughout the region, the Virgin Mary became "the Mother of the Roman Catholic Faith," and the idea of the Mother Church was born. During the Middle Ages in England, this mid-Lent Sunday was called "Mothering Sunday." It was the custom for each person to return to the place of his birth and attend his mother church. As all the people were already in their hometowns, after church services, everyone would go & visit their parents, bringing cakes and gifts to their mothers.

Mother's Day Language Arts

Have middle and upper graders write descriptive paragraphs on any of the following themes:

What it takes to be a good mother

What my mom means to me

One time that my mom really came through for me

Such papers, when corrected and recopied in the students' best penmanship, may become the basis of a fine bulletin board or go home with the students to be shared with their mothers.

Have the younger children as a group dictate sentences (which you record) based on their ideas and feelings about "Mothers." The teacher can organize these and print them up in large letters on a piece of butcher paper for the bulletin board. Then make a colorful border and have the class choose a title for the composition.

This is also an appropriate time to remember your room mother by sending her a small gift or note saying thank you for her year-long efforts and thoughtfulness.

Mother's Day Cards

Pop-up Card. Fold a piece of 8″ × 10″ paper in half lengthwise and cut out a 3″ × 3″ notch as shown. The portion that is left jutting out from the card is folded inside and pops up when the card is opened. Children can modify pop-up shape (oval, heart) or draw a face, a bouquet, or a jack-in-the-box on it. The cover of the card should be designed so as to accommodate the cutoff top left-hand corner.

Have each student compile a long list of *Reasons I Love My Mom*. Each item should be in the form of a complete sentence. Check for grammar and spelling. Children can recopy their lists, fold and put into envelopes or roll them as scrolls, and tie each with ribbons. They should make very pleasurable reading for lots of mothers!

Science: Find My Mother

To encourage growth in the concept of development, provide young children with two sets of pictures, one of baby animals and one of their adult counterparts. Ask the children to match babies with adults. This can be set up as a desktop game or manipulative bulletin board.

Mother's Day Gift Suggestions

Here are a few gift suggestions. Be sure to also check the index for other ideas.
Grow a plant in class from a seed or carrot top.
Bath scent is easy to make. Each child will need a pretty, clean, glass bottle with a cork or screw-on lid. Have the class as a group collect the ingredients:

BATH SCENT

½	lb. rose petals		½	cup rosemary*
½	lb. lemon peel		1	cup lavender*
½	lb. assorted flowers		½	cup pennyroyal, if available
6	bay leaves*		3	oz. table salt

Put all the ingredients into a large square of cheesecloth. Tie closed. Suspend the bag in a very big pot filled with 2 gallons of water. Bring the water to a slow boil and simmer for 30 minutes. Allow to cool and then strain.

Use a funnel to fill sterilized glass bottles. This recipe should make enough bath scent for 30 portions, depending on the size of the bottles.

Each child should design a label, letter it, and glue it to his bottle. It might read: "Bath Scent. Just add some of this to your bathwater. It is made from flowers, herbs, and lemon peel. Happy Mother's Day!"

Little Paper Boxes: These may be made in graduated sizes to hold little treasures, or a colorful magazine photo can have clear self-stick vinyl adhered to it so that resultant boxes can hold heavier objects such as hair clips, bobby pins, or rings.

To make a paper box with a lid, you will need 2 squares of paper, 1 slightly larger than the other, scissors, clear tape, and a ruler. Directions:

---

*Rosemary and bay leaves are sold in the spice section of any grocery store and may often be purchased in bulk at co-ops and natural food stores. If lavender isn't grown by a parent, it can also be found at nursery or herb store.

1. Use a ruler to draw an "X" on the inside middle of the paper.

2. Fold a point to the center.

3. Take the outside fold and bring it to the center line; press firmly and unfold; repeat on all other sides. The crease lines should be apparent.

4. Cut on the dotted lines.

5. Fold as shown in this illustration.

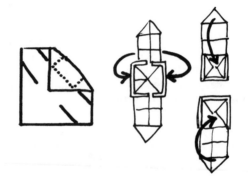

6. Repeat with all other sides and you have a pretty little box. Now do this again with the larger paper for its lid!

TOP VIEW

Bouquets Garnis (little bundles of herbs used in cooking). Each child will need dried thyme, bay leaves, marjoram, parsley, sweet basil (summer savory), 5–6 peppercorns, 4″ squares of cheesecloth, heavy white thread (string), and a small lidded jar.

Herbs plus a single bay leaf and peppercorns are placed in the middle of the cheesecloth square; then the corners are gathered and tied together using thread or string. Every young child could give 1–3 of these bouquets garnis tied together with a red bow as a gift while older students could make 10 or more and put them into a small jar with a note saying something like: "Bouquets Garnis—Put one of these little herb bundles into soup or homemade stock as it cooks to give it a natural, rich flavor."

A Sprouting Jar. For this healthful gift, each child will need a glass jar, a square of cheesecloth, a rubber band or screw-on jar ring, and a very fine no-rust aluminum screening mesh circle that fits inside the metal jar ring. Available from a health food or seed store are mung bean, radish, fenugreek, or alfalfa seeds (3 tablespoons for each student) and tiny plastic bags.

Have the students soak a few tablespoons of seeds overnight in water and pour this off in the morning. Rinse the seeds and drain using cheesecloth. Put the jars of seeds in a warm dark place, for example, a classroom cupboard. Tilt each jar a bit so that the moisture drains out and the air can circulate through. Rinse the seeds twice a day for alfalfa and radish, 3 times daily for mung and fenugreek. After 3 days, bring the jars out and set them along a sunny window area. Once the tiny leaves turn bright green they are ready to use in salads or sandwiches. Rinse out the jars, tie red bows around the tops and attach notes that say: "Fresh Sprouts. Drain and store in a plastic bag if they are not eaten at once. Then use these little bags of seeds to grow your own fresh sprouts!

The Completion of the U.S. Transcontinental Railroad [10] ——————

On this day in 1869, near Promontory, Utah, the golden spike was driven in to complete the laying of the U.S. transcontinental railroad. If any of your students are particularly interested in railroads, have them write

> Association of American Railroads
> 50 F St., NW
> Washington, DC 20001-1564

They will receive general materials on the history of American railroading, including a photograph taken at the golden spike ceremony.

"An Introduction to Scale Model Railroading" is available from

> Kalmbach Pub. Co.
> 21027 Crossroads Circle
> P.O. Box 1612
> Wallkesha, WI 53187

Minnesota Admitted to the Union (1858) [11]

Minnesota is our 32nd state.

Etymology: Minnesota comes from the Dakota Indian words meaning "sky-tinted waters."

Birth of Florence Nightingale (1820) [12] ——————

Florence Nightingale is regarded as the founder of modern nursing. After completing her medical studies in France and Germany, she returned to England and volunteered her services to the British wounded in the Crimean War. She was put in charge of 33 nurses and sent to the Crimea in southern Russia in November 1854. Sanitation was so bad when they arrived that almost half of the British wounded were dying of infections. Under Nightingale's direction, care of the wounded improved until less than two in every hundred wounded became a fatality.

In 1856, she contracted Crimean fever and was bedridden for 11 days but she refused to return to England. She remained in the Crimea until the summer of 1856, when peace was made and the hospitals were closed. As a consequence of her experience there, her health was broken, and she was never able to practice active nursing again. Florence Nightingale spent the next 64 years writing about nursing, hospital administration, and women's suffrage. She was the first woman to receive the British Order of Merit.

Founding of the New York Stock Exchange (1792) [17] ——————

On this day in 1792, 24 New York brokers met under a buttonwood tree on the present site of 68 Wall Street and signed an agreement to fix uniform rates of commission for the sale of stocks and bonds. Thereafter, they went into a Broad St. coffee shop when the weather was poor. This was the real beginning of the New York Stock Exchange.

Etymology: A "tycoon," meaning a very wealthy person, is one of the few words in English that is derived from the Japanese language. *Taikun*, the Japanese word from which our term comes, arrived in America courtesy of Commodore Perry's voyages of the 1850s. It in turn comes from 2 Chinese words, *ta* meaning "great" and *kiun* meaning "prince." Our spelling is the way Perry anglicized the word when he first heard it.

The word "fee" comes from the Anglo-Saxon word for cattle, *fech*. Livestock was a principal form of exchange throughout early Europe, and *fech* was often collected in payment for services rendered.

If you have upper grade students who are interested in the workings of the New York Stock Exchange, send for their pamphlet describing available educational materials:

> New York Stock Exchange
> Educational Products
> P.O. Box 4191
> Syosset, NY 11791-4191

Elementary Economics is a bibliography for teachers of grades K–6. The free and/or inexpensive materials listed include booklets, newsletters, teaching units, audiovisuals, microcomputer disks, posters, and educational games. The materials have been examined by an advisory committee and evaluated by classroom teachers. All items are indexed by grade level. Write for a free copy to

> Public Information Centres
> Dept. 1M
> Federal Reserve Bank of Chicago
> P.O. Box 834
> Chicago, IL 60690

South Carolina Admitted to the Union (1788) [23]

South Carolina is our 8th state.

Etymology: This territory was called Carolina in the Charter of 1628 in honor of Charles I.

Birth of Rachel Carson (1907) [27]

Rachel Carson foresaw our polluted future and tried to warn us about ecological dangers in an industrialized world. In 1955, she wrote a book about the time that might come if we did not become more conscious of the ecological consequences of living "as if there were no tomorrow." She called her book *The Silent Spring*. It foresaw many of our present-day environmental disasters.

Preserving the creatures of the sea continues to be an idea that engages many children. If your students (K–6) share this concern, the book *Gentle Giants of the Sea* (Whale Museum, P.O. Box 945, Friday Harbor, WA 98250, is highly recommended. It includes teaching activities and many, many reproducible pages.

FISH RIDDLE

What are 3 very strange places that you can always find a fish?

(In a bird cage, a perch; on the bottom of your shoe, a sole; and in a sporting good store, a skate!)

Wisconsin Admitted to the Union (1848) [29]

Wisconsin is our 30th state.

Etymology: First spelled *Miskonsing*, it comes from the Native American name for the main river in the region and meant "gathering of the waters."

Rhode Island Admitted to the Union (1790) [29]

Rhode Island is our 13th state.

Etymology: Opinions differ on the origin of this state's name. Some say Giovanni de Verrazano gave the area this name in 1521 because it reminded him in size of Rhodes in the Mediterranean Sea. Others believe the state was named by Adriaen Block, a Dutch explorer, who called it Roode Eylandt, referring to its red clay.

Memorial Day [last Monday in May]

Originally called Decoration Day, the first observance was on May 30, 1868. In the South after the Civil War, mourning friends and relatives of slain soldiers put flowers on the graves of both Union and Confederate dead. The news of this gesture traveled north, and soon most of the states honored their war dead on this day. Over the years American families have expanded the meaning of the holiday to honor memories of dead relatives and friends and a time to visit cemeteries. Since 1950, at the request of Congress, the presidential Memorial Day proclamation has included an appeal for permanent peace.

Etymology: "Memory" comes from the Latin *memor,* meaning "to be thinking of" or "remembering." "Memorabilia" also has a Latin root in *memorabilis,* which means "worth remembering" and "remember" uses the Latin *re* meaning "again" plus *memorare* to equal "to bring to your mind again."

Language Arts. Ask older students to discuss orally, or in writing, one of these topics:

What does it mean to give your life for your country?

Or, to give your life for an ideal?

What principles or ideals—if any—do you think are worth giving your life for?

What principles or ideas are worth *living* your life for?

May Events

May Science

Etymology: "Entomology" is the study of insects. This word comes from the Greek *entomos,* which means "cut up." Insects have segmented or cut-up bodies. Our word "insect" comes from the Latin *insectum,* which means "cut up."

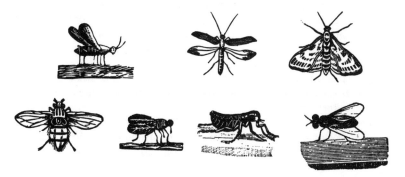

Grasshoppers can be raised in a gallon jar with the bottom lined with 2″ sod or grass. This should be watered from time to time and provides food and an egg depository place for grasshoppers.

(Caterpillars) Larvae are raised in a wooden crate that has its bottom knocked out and its sides covered with screening. Box should be stood on end and potted "feedplant"* with larvae on it placed inside, or line the bottom of an aquarium with 2″ of moist soil into which are planted "feed plants" (or jars of water with stalks of feed plants placed in tank). Put the larvae on the feed plant and cover the top of the aquarium with plastic wrap. The more airtight the larvae's cage, the longer the food supply will remain fresh and edible. There's little chance of suffocating the larvae as they need a minimum of air.

Praying mantises are carnivorous and eat live insects. Give a baby mantis aphids to eat; an adult will eat houseflies and roaches. If not fed enough, the mantis will turn cannibalistic. Spear a tiny piece of liver on a toothpick if no live insect food is available. Egg cases must be collected in the fall or winter, brought indoors, and placed in a jar (as described for roaches). Babies emerge in 2 to 4 weeks.

(Cocoons) Larvae will molt several times and then stop eating. They may go beneath the soil in a jar to pupate. Don't bother them. Keep pupae to watch the adult emerge (or children may collect cocoons and bring them and branches of the food plant to class). Put 1″ of soil in the bottom of a large jar; stick branches in the soil, and with a few drops of glue, attach cocoons to sticks. Cover the mouth of the jar with screening. Once a week, spray the soil and pupae with water to keep the air in the jar humid (but never to the point of producing mildew or mold). If kept in a warm room, cocoons will produce adults in a few months; these will die if their host plants are not in leaf and available. If you wish to raise eggs and larvae from the adults, you must prevent their emergence until the spring when food is available. To do this, place the jar between a regular window and a storm window on the north side of the school building. To make certain that you get fertile eggs, you'll need both sexes of moth from pupae. A newly emerged female attracts males, so just put her in a cheesecloth covered jar and set this outside in the evening—males should arrive in great, great numbers.

Let the children study photographs to learn how bees (and other insects) are physically constructed. Then let the children make big insect constructions using colored paper, fuzzy pipe cleaners, and plastic† for wings.

Or let students plan and execute professional filmstrips or slides about insects. Educational supply houses offer clear-mounted slide blanks, filmstrips, and specially treated slides that have surfaces on which students can draw, write, and erase for reuse.

---

*The real secret to successful rearing of larvae is to keep them well supplied with their food plant. Each adult female lays her eggs on a specific plant which provides the food for the emerging larvae. These eggs will usually not consume any other plant, and so most captive larvae in the classroom starve to death amid heaps of grass and green leaves. It is essential to identify the particular food plant preferred by each type of insect. Use Frank Lutz's book *Field Book of Insects of U.S. and Canada* (New York: G. P. Putnam, 1948) as a guide.

†The clear plastic used in dry-cleaning bags is suitable.

It's a Fact: Guess how many kinds of plants are dependent upon bees for the preservation of their species? Honeybees are responsible for the fertilization of at least 100,000 different kinds of plants!

INSECT RIDDLES

1. What does this mean? hiBve? (A big bee is in a little hive.)
2. Why is a bee in a house like a house on fire? (The sooner it's put out, the better!)

May Social Studies

The following activities* may be used as the culmination of a unit, as a book report, or as a personal student assessment.

A Letter to Dear Abby: Think of some problem your historical figure faced and then compose a letter in the "Dear Abby" style. Have students read and become familiar with the newspaper column style prior to initiating their own efforts. Their letters should include a statement of the problem, what led up to it, solutions that were tried & that did not work, as well as a request for advice. Historical details & proper and place names should be included. The teacher may wish to compose snappy answers of his or her own to these letters, again using historical fact as a basis for each.

---

*The basic ideas for these activities come from Jill Fenton, Jasper School, District #3063, Alberta, Canada. Thank you, Jill!

Go Ahead, Ask Me About . . . (a culmination activity)

With the help of a few students, make some large star badges on which are printed: GO AHEAD, ASK ME ABOUT. Use colorful posterboard and attach safety pins to the back. Give out to students when they complete a unit or a research project with the blank filled in according to their completed area of study. Children get to wear their badges for an entire day, and anyone may question them about their subject of expertise. This encourages each child to know a subject well and review it carefully before his or her turn comes to wear a star!

A Chance of a Lifetime Meeting. Let's say that you get the chance to meet any famous person in history for just 10 minutes. Who would you like to meet and what would you ask him or her? Take turns with a friend acting out both parts. Have fun!

Telestories. Students work in pairs on this project, after finishing a short reading or listening to a short historical selection. They compose a telegram (using as few words as possible at 50¢ a word) that includes the important points covered in the reading. A good challenge!

Six Things I Never Knew. At the end of a unit or research project, have each student write six endings to this phrase: Before this (study unit or project) I never knew that . . . .

A Muddled Matching Bulletin Board. Go back over the social studies and current events that have been brought up in class this year. Find pictures from magazines (or Xeroxes from social studies texts) to illustrate the people, places, and events you have discussed. Prepare 5 large rectangles from 5 different colors of posterboard and print at the top of each card one of the following: TIME, PLACE, PEOPLE, EVENT, OUTCOME. Select four events you want to cover, and for each, print or glue a picture on a 3″ × 5″ card giving the time, place, person(s) involved, plus one line on the outcome of the event.

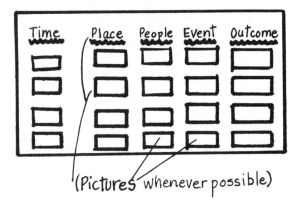

(Pictures whenever possible)

Then post the cards, all mixed up on the appropriate rectangles. Once the children have finished their day's work, they get to sort out the cards and put them in the correct order. Once a child has correctly identified all the cards for one event (time, place, people, event, outcome), mix them up again for another child to try. Encourage the class to create new lines of cards and incorporate these with whole fresh groups of 20 every week or so. This is a great device for easy reviewing of material taught during the school year.

May Language Skills

This is a good time of year to return the focus of attention to the children, themselves, through student-centered activities.

What Our Names Mean. This chart will be a hit no matter what time of year it is introduced. Use a dictionary that lists given names and their derivations (or an etymological reference book from the library) and look up the given names of all your students. You might wish to list them alphabetically, like this:

Aaron is a Hebrew name. It means mountain and light. In the Bible, Aaron was the brother of Moses.

Amy comes from the French word *aimee* and means beloved.

Kate is short for Katherine which is Greek for "pure." It's a name of saints, queens, and heroines.

Yasha is a Russian nickname for Jacob.

Be sure to include your own first name on this list. The study of surnames is a natural follow-up to this chart and can be investigated and documented by the fifth and sixth graders themselves.

Two poems to enjoy with your students, just because its May!

Bee! I'm Expecting You!

Bee! I'm expecting you!
Was saying Yesterday
To Somebody you know
That you were due—

The Frogs got Home last week—
Are settled, and at work—
Birds, mostly back—
The Clover warm and thick—

You'll get my Letter by
The seventeenth; Reply
Or better, be with me—
Yours, Fly.

—Emily Dickinson, (1830-1886)

Sonnet

Guido, I wish that you and Lapo and I
Were carried off by magic
And put in a boat, which, every time there was wind,
Would sail on the ocean exactly where we wanted.

In this way storms and other dangerous weather
Wouldn't be able to harm us—
And I wish that, since we all were of one mind,
We would want more and more to be together.

And I wish that Vanna and Lagia too
And the girl whose name on the list is number thirty
Were put in the boat by the magician too

And that we all did nothing but talk about love
And I wish that they were just as glad to be there
As I believe the three of us would be.

—Dante Alighieri, (1265-1321)

May is a month that often is accompanied by severe attacks of spring fever. Here are some invigorating games that you may find helpful in staving it off.

Wind & Flowers. Divide the children into 2 groups and have them stand facing each other on parallel lines about 60 feet apart. Spread the groups out so that there are 4 foot gaps between them. One group chooses in secret the name of a flower and slowly advances on the line of the other group, which plays the Wind. One at a time going down the line, the Wind players shout out the name of a flower until the one chosen is identified. All this time, the Flower line is slowly advancing. When the right flower *is* called, all the Flower group turns and races back to their line with the Wind players chasing them. Any flower caught by the Wind returns to the Wind line and the remaining flowers choose a new name and start up again until they have all been captured. If the Flowers should all succeed in crossing over the Wind's line, they become the Wind and the game continues.

Minotaurs-in-a-Maze. Construct a maze outdoors using rope, chairs and big metal drums, trees, wooden boxes, or logs. Divide the class into groups of 6 to 8 players. Blindfold the players of one team and spin each around in a circle so as to disorient them. Have the players hold hands and make a long line as they begin to try to find their way out of the maze. Time each team and when they repeat this activity, see if they can beat their own time.

An Outdoor Scavenger Hunt for Young Readers. Explain to the children what a scavenger is and emphasize the positive meaning: a person who picks up litter or cleans the streets.

Etymology: "Scavenger" is an ancient word coming from the Old Norman word *easuwer* meaning "to see."

The Scavenger Hunt. Divide the children into groups of 4 to 6. Each team receives a list of seven things to be found outside. (See the reproducible.) Team members are to work together to try and find something that fits each description. For example, one item might be described as "I am bright yellow & part of me will fly. What might I be?" (A dandelion . . . or a Juicy Fruit gum wrapper!) The children will no doubt come up with "answers" to the riddles that would

The <u>Hunt</u>!

Work with the kids on your team to find each of these:

① Once I was alive, but I'm not anymore. Now I can be used to help people!

② I am smooth and black. I am pretty.

③ I smell good, but don't try to eat me!

④ Watch out for me!! I am long and thin and I can be bad luck!

⑤ Once I flew, but I don't anymore ......

⑥ You cannot live without me!

⑦ I am `bright`- in color. I can make people ———→ SAD <u>OR</u> HAPPY ......

⑧ Once I was VERY BIG, but now I am small. People use me, but NOT for food.

· GOOD LUCK ·

never have crossed *your* mind! Each team that finishes the hunt, and can rationalize each of their items, gets a prize. (Remind children not to be destructive in their quests.)

Make certain that all the words found on the lists are familiar to the children before you pass the lists out.

Prize ideas: popcorn balls, peanuts in the shell, little magnets for each team member. Try to discourage teams from seeing the scavenger hunt as a competition; encourage them to view it as a cooperative effort: "Let's help the whole class finish the hunt!"

May Puppets Made from Gloves

Check at Goodwill and other secondhand stores to see if they will donate 2 to 3 dozen unmatched gloves for use in your class. Often they will agree to save them for you throughout the year. (Long black cotton socks would also be useful as noted shortly.)

Provide your students with scissors, needles, thread, sequins, buttons, beads, felt scraps, yarn, thin ribbons, lace, and an assortment of gloves plus the time to experiment and invent their own finger puppets. Challenge them to think imaginatively of what they want to make—sea creatures, perhaps, or take-offs on popular cartoon characters, animals that lived long ago, and so on. After their initial flurry of personal creation has worn off, you might suggest the following:

A finger from a brown seamless glove can become a sweet mouse.

A white glove, with thumb & middle 2 fingers stitched down can be made into a bunny.

A colored glove with the thumb and 2 fingers sewn down can become the head of a caterpillar, Loch Ness monster, or dragon.

A high-topped sock of a matching color worn over the arm will extend the bodies of these clever little glove puppets.

May Field Trip Suggestions

This is a fine month to go on a hike. Bring along watercolors and pads to document a spring day. Or take a nature walk retracing a route taken in the fall to note the many changes. This is also an appropriate month to arrange a visit to the local hospital, railroad yard, or stock exchange. See if school tours are available at any of these sites. Finally, a class trip to see a play together can be an experience your students will treasure.

JUNE

To the Omaha Indians, June is "The Month When Buffalo Bulls Hunt the Cows." Eskimos call this month "Ice Breaks; Birds Fledged," and the Yuman Indian tribes named this time of year *Kumaz,* which means "When Giant Cactus Fruits Are Gathered." The Pawnee Indian calendar has 13 months: June 19–July 18 is named "Standing Alone" because this is the time when tribe members left on their summer hunts.

Calendar of Important Dates

§ Dairy Month.

§ Father's Day is the third Sunday in June.

§ Midsummer's Eve.

1 First earthquake recorded in America at Plymouth, Massachusetts, 1638.
   Kentucky, 15th U.S. state, entered the Union in 1792.
   Tennessee, 16th U.S. state, entered the Union in 1796.

2 Martha Washington, first first lady, was born in 1732.
   On this day in 1924, Congress conferred citizenship upon all American Indians.
   Charles Conrad, Jr., U.S. astronaut, was born in Philadelphia in 1930.

3 Jefferson Davis, president of the Confederate States of America, was born in Fairview, Kentucky, in 1808.

Josephine Baker, black American vocalist, known in the 1920s as "The Toast of Paris," was born in 1906.

4   King George III was born in London in 1738.

First documented eating of tomatoes—heretofore thought deadly—in the United States, 1834.

5   World Environment Day.

Federico Garcia Lorca, Spanish poet and playwright, was born in Fuente Vaqueros, Spain, in 1889.

6   On this day in 346 A.D., an eclipse was recorded at Nisibus.

Nathan Hale, U.S. patriot, was born in Coventry, Connecticut, 1755.

In 1966 on this date, James Meredith, a young black man, was shot from ambush as he marched with others for voting rights.

Children's Day.

7   Freedom of the Press Day.

8   First paper money in America was issued, New York City, 1709.

Frank Lloyd Wright, American architect-visionary, was born in 1869.

It's a Fact: The architect Frank Lloyd Wright once urged that the city of Boston be evacuated and preserved as a museum piece and that the city of Pittsburgh simply be abandoned.

---

9   Peter the Great, Russian czar and modernizer of his country, was born in 1672.

10   On this day in 1692, several "witches" were hanged at Salem, Massachusetts.

Maurice Sendak, American artist & writer of children's books (*In the Night Kitchen, Where the Wild Things Are),* was born in 1928.

11   King Kamehameha, unifier of the Hawaiian Islands, was born in 1758.

First woman member of Congress, Jeannette Rankin, was born on this day in Missoula, Montana, in 1880.

Jacques Cousteau, French oceanographer, author, and environmentalist, was born in 1910.

12   Anne Frank, young author of *The Diary of a Young Girl,* who died in a Nazi concentration camp, was born in 1929.

13   On this day in 323 B.C., Alexander the Great died in Babylon.

The missile age was born as German flying bombs, V-1 & V-2 rockets, hit England in World War II, 1944.

14 Flag Day commemorates the adoption of our flag by the Continental Congress in 1777 & Flag Week includes this day.

In 1834 two U.S. patents were granted, one for the first diving suit (Leonard Norcross of Dixfield, Maine) and one for sandpaper (Isaac Fischer, Springfield, Vermont).

Margaret Bourke-White, adventurous journalistic photographer, was born, 1906, in New York City.

15 On this day in 1215, King John of England, under pressure from his barons, set his seal on the Magna Carta, basic document of Anglo-Saxon law, "the cornerstone of American liberty," at Runnymede, England.

Arkansas, 26th U.S. state, was admitted to the Union, 1836.

Saul Steinberg, intellectual cartoonist, was born in 1914.

16 Joyce Carol Oates, prolific American writer (*Them*), was born in Lockport, New York, in 1938.

On this day in 1940, Russia appropriated Latvia, Estonia, & Lithuania.

Anniversary of the first flight by a woman in outer space. Valentina V. Tereshkova manually piloted the USSR's *Vostock-6* through 48 orbits of the earth, in 1963.

On this day in 1939, showers of hundreds of little frogs fell on Trowbridge, England.

17 Iceland's Republic Day marks its independence from Denmark, 1944.

On this day in 1972, five men were caught trying to wiretap the Democratic National Committee Headquarters in the Watergate Building in Washington, DC. The subsequent political scandal—Watergate—would continue to fester until President Richard Nixon resigned, on August 9, 1974.

18 On this day in 1812, Congress declared war on Great Britain, for the second time in American history.

In 1815, Napoleon was defeated at the Battle of Waterloo by British and Prussian troops. Waterloo was Napoleon's final effort to conquer Europe. Four days later, Napoleon wrote his act of abdication.

On this day in 1873 in Rochester, New York, Susan B. Anthony was arrested for voting.

Paul McCartney of the Beatles, composer & singer, was born in 1942.

First American woman in space, Sally Ride, flew aboard the spacecraft *Challenger,* 1983.

19 West Virginia was admitted to the Union as the 35th state on this day in 1836.

Lou Gehrig, baseball great, was born in New York City, 1903.

20 In 1782, Congress adopted the bald eagle as the official symbol of the United States. It appears on the Great Seal on every dollar bill.

21 Summer solstice is either today or tomorrow.

> Quotation of the Day: It ever was, and is, and shall be ever-living Fire, in measures being kindled and in measures going out.
>
> —Heraclitus

New Hampshire, 9th state to join the Union, put the U.S. Constitution into effect, 1788.

22 In 1191, a total solar eclipse was recorded in England.

Karl von Humboldt, German naturalist & traveler, for whom the ocean current off South America was named, was born in 1767.

On this day in 1772, slavery was abolished in Great Britain—nearly 100 years before the United States did so.

23   On this day in 1603, William Penn signed a treaty with the Indians promising eternal peace.

First balloon flight in America, 1784.

24   Midsummer's Day.

First suffragette in American history, Mistress Margaret Bent, a niece of Lord Baltimore, appeared before the all-male Maryland Assembly and demanded both voice and vote for herself in that body, in 1647. The Assembly was shocked.

Ambrose Bierce, writer, was born in 1842 in Horse Cave Creek, Ohio.

First reports of flying saucers came from the area of Mount Ranier, Washington, 1947.

25   First color TV broadcast, 1951 (first demonstration of color TV had been in New York City in 1927).

26   Virginia, 10th state to join the Union, was admitted, 1788.

First bicycle patented in United States, 1819.

On this day in 1947, Oregonian Ken Arnold started a UFO scare with his announcement of having sighted skyborne objects traveling at 12,000 mph.

27   Helen Keller, blind and deaf author and lecturer, was born on this day in Tuscumbia, Alabama, 1880.

> Quotation of the Day: Literature is my Utopia. Here I am not disenfranchised. No barrier of the senses shuts me out from the sweet, gracious discourse of my book-friends. They talk to me without embarrassment or awkwardness.
>
> —Helen Keller, *The Story of My Life*

28   King Henry VIII was born in Greenwich, England, in 1491.

Henry VIII

On this day in 1778, Mary Ludwig Hays McCauley, better known as Molly Pitcher, took her fallen husband's place at a cannon at the Battle of Monmouth (New Jersey). In recognition of her heroism, the valiant woman was granted an annual $40 pension by an act of the Pennsylvania Assembly in 1822. She died 10 years later.

29   Antoine de St.-Exupéry, French aviator & author (*The Little Prince*), was born in 1900.

30   First Japanese, Joseph Heco, to take U.S. citizenship, 1858.

The Federal Pure Food & Drug Act became law in 1906.

The U.S. constitutional amendment providing for the 18-year-old vote was ratified on this date in 1971.

June

June may have been named for the great goddess Juno, protectress of women, although some Romans felt that its name came from the Latin *juniores,* in which case June would be a month dedicated to the young.

June Quotations

3   All we ask is to be let alone.

> —Jefferson Davis, Inaugural Address as president
> of the Confederate States of America

5   We are the echo of the future.

> —W. S. Merton

Remove a tree and you remove its shade.

> —Chinese proverb

People who develop the habit of thinking of themselves as world citizens are fulfilling the first requirement of sanity in our time.

> —Norman Cousins

What is the use of a house if you haven't got a tolerable planet to put it on?

—Henry David Thoreau

Modern education is competitive, nationalistic, and separative. It has trained the child to regard material values as of major importance, to believe that his nation is also of major importance and superior to other nations and peoples. The general level of world information is high but usually biased, influenced by national prejudices, serving to make us citizens of our nation but not of the world.

—Albert Einstein

Nobody made a greater mistake than he who did nothing because he could only do a little.

—Edmund Burke

7   It is completely unimportant. That is why it is so interesting.

—Agatha Christie

12   There is a saying that "paper is more patient than man"; it came back to me on one of my slightly melancholy days . . . . Yes, there is no doubt that paper is patient.

—Anne Frank

21   Summer approaches like Mother; Winter comes like the enemy.

—Chinese proverb

24   Barometer, *n.* An ingenious instrument which indicates what kind of weather we're having.

—Ambrose Bierce, *The Devil's Dictionary*

27   Science may have found a cure for most evils, but it has found no remedy for the worst of them all—the apathy of human beings.

—Helen Keller

29   Grownups never understand anything by themselves, and it is tiresome for children to be always and forever explaining things to them.

—Antoine de St.-Exupéry

Of a good leader when his task is finished, his goal achieved, they will say: We did this ourselves.

—Lao-tzu

June Events

A few words about June. Try to plan these last weeks of school so that the inevitable restlessness of the children will not be compounded. Let the children work with the encyclopedia, tracking down answers to questions the class raises as a group. Bring in a large, sturdy puzzle of the United States or the world. Bring to class a set of wildlife books for free-time reading. Construction paper scraps need to be used up, so encourage the making of collages, torn paper compositions, or a scrapbook of magazine and student-made pictures for a hospital children's ward.

The classroom will have to be cleaned on the last day of school. This can be facilitated by dividing older children into four groups, each assigned the responsibility of thoroughly cleaning one area side of the classroom. Make sure that all things to be accomplished in each area are clearly noted, such as where to put old papers and so on, before you announce the beginning of house cleaning. The first group finished can be rewarded in some small way. This may mean 5 to 10 minutes of noise, but at the end of that time your room should sparkle!

The First Commercial U.S. Oil Refinery (1860) ────────────────

This was erected near Oil Creek Valley, Pennsylvania, in June 1860. The only product saved was the kerosene. The small amount of gasoline produced was disposed of in nearby Oil Creek. The kerosene was sold in competition with whale oil to be used in lamps.

In energy-conscious times, oil and its location and refinement are of special interest. Have older students write to the oil companies listed here, requesting the latest information about this natural resource and what the industry is doing to help cut down on pollution.

Atlantic Richfield
515 S. Flower St.
Los Angeles, CA 90071

Chevron
225 Bush St.
San Francisco, CA 94104

Exxon Corp.
1251 Avenue of the Americas
New York, NY 10020-1198

Shell Oil Co.
1 Shell Plaza
P.O. Box 2463
Houston, TX 77252

Kentucky Admitted to the Union (1792) [1]

Kentucky is our 15th state.

Etymology: Kentucky is either Iroquois or Cherokee in origin and has been said to mean: "dark and bloody ground," "prairie," "meadowland," and "land of tomorrow."

Tennessee Admitted to the Union (1796) [1]

Tennessee is our 16th state.

Etymology: Tennessee is of Greek derivation, *Tanase*, with the meaning of "old or beloved town." First a place, then a river name, it finally became the name of a large region.

World Environment Day [5]

Discuss with your class the implications of this day. Students may want to write to

> National Wildlife Federation
> 1400 16th St., NW
> Washington, DC 20036-2266

The Wildlife Federation offers fine 15-minute filmstrips, slides, and tapes on the following environmental concerns: "Water, We Can't Live Without It"; "Soil, We Can't Grow Without It"; "Let's Clear the Air"; "This Is Your Land." (Write for current price list.)

You may also want to contact

> Bethlehem Steel Corporation
> Bethlehem, PA 18016-7699

which offers a free 40-page book of dramatic photographs concerning air pollution and its many causes: "Steelmaking and the Environment." Middle and upper graders could use this and the photos would make an excellent basic air pollution explanation display or bulletin board exhibit.

The U.S. Environmental Protection Agency (EPA) offers free materials, including the publications "Ozone, the Invisible Problem," "Acid Rain," "Earth Trek . . . Explore Your Environment."

> EPA
> Office of Public Affairs
> Washington, DC 20460

Eco-News, an environmental newsletter for young people, is published by the Environmental Action Coalition (156 Fifth Ave., New York, New York 10010).

Students wanting to learn more about the current state of rain forests can write to

> Rain Forest Alliance
> 295 Madison Ave., Suite 1804
> New York City, NY 10017

The Rain Forest Alliance publishes *The Canopy,* which is filled with information on international developments, new publications, and so on. Write requesting a review copy. (Membership in Rain Forest Alliance & receipt of 4 issues of *The Canopy* cost $20.)

Older students will find fascinating reading in the comparative charts of *Shopping for a Better World.** The policies and programs of companies influence your world—and *you*. Some makers of products dump toxic waste, make parts for nuclear weapons, or lobby against sound environmental policies. Other companies recycle waste, use biodegradable materials in their packaging, and rely more on alternative energy sources. This handy guide, which is published annually, rates U.S. companies on 11 issues, including animal testing, the environment & the advancement of minorities & women.

Children's Day [7]

Each second we live is a new and unique moment of the universe, a moment that never was before and never will be again. And what do we teach our children in school? That we think 2 and 2 makes 4 and that Paris is the capital of France. What will we also teach them what they are? We should say to each of them: Do you know who you are? You are a marvel. You are unique. In all the world there is no other child exactly like you. In the millions of years that have passed, there has never been a child like you. And look at your body—what a wonder it is! Your legs, your arms, your cunning fingers, the way you move! You may become a Shakespeare, a Michelangelo, a Beethoven. You have the capacity for anything. Yes, you are a marvel. And when you grow up you harm another who is, like you, a marvel? You must cherish one another. You must work—we must all work—to make this world worthy of its children.

—Pablo Casals

Build Your Own Learning Machines: A Children's Day Activity

"Teachers spend too much time making things for kids. The kids should make the things. Why? Because by the time a kid has figured out how to make and how to use a learning device, he doesn't need it. He has already learned all that it is designed to teach."[†]

Here is a do-it-themselves learning device that is appropriate to any subject, any child, at any level—and it can be done today without special materials, supplies, or preparation.

Step 1: Talk over with the class and work together to define the term "learning machine" or "learning device"; that is, it asks a question, or gives you a problem, while keeping back the answer for a certain amount of time while you are coming to your own conclusion. Then it gives you the correct answer so you can see if you were right. Have the children list several types of learning devices. (Yes, flash cards and teachers both qualify.)

Step 2: Have the students each decide about some specific material that they want to cover, for instance, "I need to learn my Roman numerals"; "I always forget the way to spell 'dictionary'"; "I want to know the state capitals."

Step 3: Provide a selection of heavy card stock—index cards, posterboard, tagboard, corrugated cardboard,—and sharp scissors. Now tell the students that they are to pose (write or illustrate) a question on the left-hand side of their card and write or illustrate the answer on

---

*Written by Ben Corson et al. and published annually by the Council on Economic Priorities, 30 Irving Place, New York, New York 10003.
[†]Bill Page, *Dela Rosa Tribune*, Highland, California, July 3, 1974. This quote and the learning machine idea appeared in "The Rasperry Report Card."

the right-hand side. Next, the 2 sides are to be separated by cutting them apart in (jigsaw) puzzle fashion.

Step 4: Help the children see for themselves that they need a number of options for each question if their learning devices are to be really valuable; they will need to make several answers from which to choose.

By creating these learning devices, the students will learn a great deal more than the correct answer to the question posed. "The skill required to compose a good worksheet correctly phrased and written is infinitely more valuable than merely answering questions on an adult-prepared worksheet."

Finally, encourage variations in materials used, jigsaw cuts, types of illustrations used, and ways in which to store and share their very special creative learning devices!

Here's an opportunity for the children to really "show off" their personal hobbies, collections, enthusiasms. Encourage them to think about something they have or do or collect which they could share with the rest of the class.*

If it is something they make or do for fun in their free time, ask them to plan a way to show the class, step by step, how you could do it too. This might be in the form of a chart, a written description, or an actual demonstration (which is documented via Polaroid to become part of the bulletin board display).

How to share hobbies and actual collections without anything getting broken or turning up missing. Brainstorm together to discover creative ways to display their personal objects, for example, invert an aquarium over a collection and neatly duct-tape it permanently to table top, or tape sheet of clear acetate (available at art stores) or flexible plastic (from hardware stores) to cover a collection of coins or stamps, while on display.

Finally, ask for volunteer artists & copywriters to create a bulletin board titles and small descriptive labels for each student collection or contribution to their Children's Day bulletin board.

Mirror Magic

To celebrate this special day, buy 3 large mirror squares (e.g., 8″ × 8″ × 8″). These are sold at glass and mirror stores. Use reinforced strapping tape to firmly tape their backs together to form this shape.

---

*Without informing the children, you can arrange to demonstrate your own hobby or examples of things you now collect or collected as a child. They'll be happy to see *you* have fun on Children's Day too!

Cut a cardboard box to exactly fit this shape & insert the mirror construction into this box corner for reinforcement. Provide tangram geometric figures, cutout geometric paper shapes, or colored plywood pieces and scissors, magazines, paper, and markers. Encourage the children to place the tangram figures on the table top up into the corner of the mirror construct.

See what happens! Now elaborate by adding other tangram or geometric pieces placed flush against the first. Encourage extensive personal experimentation with their hands, coins, buttons, cutout magazine pictures, (parts of) drawings *they* make.* Keep a collection (in a folder next to the mirrors) of the most successful magazine or child-drawn pictures and add some of your own. Always encourage remarks concerning the humor, or oddness, of the reflections and the reason these pictures work well.

This construct can provide long periods of pleasure and concentration for your students, "a perfect reflection" of your respect for those we honor this day!

The First Mirror, a Listening and Creative Writing/Art Self-starter _____

Explain to the children that you want them to imagine themselves living in a primitive world, a world of so long ago that mirrors had not been invented. Then read aloud (or have a student who reads well and has practiced this piece, perhaps as last night's homework assignment, read) the following to the class:

The First Mirror

In the beginning I was just a lump of copper. SHE found me on the rock by the dead fire. I had melted out of a rock when the fire was blazing in the night. SHE picked me up and rubbed me with her hand. Then SHE rubbed me with a piece of soft leather. I got hotter and hotter and I got shinier too. I heard her make a sound like, "Ohhh!" SHE kept rubbing me, faster and faster! First SHE put her hand in front of me and I showed her a picture of it. Then SHE put me up in front of her face. This time I showed her long brown hair, her brown eyes, and her thick eyebrows. SHE looked and looked. At last SHE smiled at me and then SHE took me out of the cave into the bright sunlight.

Elicit their reactions to the story. Encourage them to respond to the story by writing their own ideas of how the first mirror came to be. Provide poster paints, watercolors (or markers), and large areas for them to make pictures to illustrate this story or their own mirror tales.

A striking bulletin board that displays The First Mirror, printed out on a big sheet of paper and surrounded by student illustrations, can be easily constructed by the children themselves.

---

*Rows of color, dots, strange outerspace creatures, "new" dinosaurs, parts of a pie or cake, the "full" moon—all have interesting possibilities!

Freedom of the Press Day [7] ———————————————

Here are some unusual ways to use up any stacks of newspapers you may have.

1. Make a collage using different styles of type and photographs to build up "a tabloid image."

2. Twist and roll a newspaper and tie it to form a rough shape that stands. Use strips of cheese cloth soaked in delayed-setting plaster to cover the form which may be abstract or representational. Wrap and work in any additional plaster needed. Sculpture can be painted when dry.

3. Once the class has discussed and studied different famous people, have each child pick one that he or she especially admires. Then each child prepares an article in the form of a newspaper report written as though the student had known (or knows) the famous person. Each report should include main idea (headline), identification of main points, conciseness in wording.

4. Ask the students to see in which part of the newspaper they would most likely find: reports of important events, personal opinions about the news, entertainment announcements, and legal notices.

5. Have them compare writing styles of editorials and news stories.

6. Give each student a page from a newspaper. Have each child skim the page for a 1- to 5-minute time period. Then, papers are put away, and each student makes a list of as many ideas as he or she can remember having read on the page.

7. Have each child skim a newspaper story to answer who? what? when? where? why?

8. Headliner. Divide students into groups of six. Cut the words from some newspaper headlines, mix them up in a sack, and have one child from each team choose 3 to 5 words. These words are taken back to the teams, and the children try to arrange them in an order that forms some kind of plot, around which they can develop a 3- to 8-minute play or pantomime. An announcer gives the introduction to each presentation and the other children try to guess the 3 to 5 words involved.

First Paper Money Issued in America [8] ———————————————

Children are often fascinated by money, its relative value, foreign coins, & numismatic information. For some of the latter, you may write to the following address and ask for "The

Story of Money" and "The Story of Checks and Electric Payments" (both in small, comic book format) and the catalog of public information materials from

> The Federal Reserve Bank of New York
> Public Information Dept.
> 33 Liberty St.
> New York, NY 10045

Birth of Jeannette Rankin (1880) [11]

America's first congresswoman, Jeannette Rankin, was elected in Montana and was the only representative to vote against the United States' entry into World Wars I and II, protesting that "we have to get it into our heads once and for all that we cannot settle disputes by eliminating human beings."

She cosponsored the amendment to give women the vote & lobbied effectively as a private citizen for maternity measures, child labor laws, and, always, peace. She led the Jeannette Rankin Brigade through the streets of Washington in 1968 to protest the war in Vietnam.

Jeannette Rankin was an active feminist right up until her death at age 92 in 1973. One of her last wishes was to see a female in Congress from every district. "Maybe we wouldn't do any better than the men," she liked to say, "but we certainly couldn't do any worse."

Ask the students to write about "The Strongest Woman I Ever Met," or "Why I Don't (Do) Believe in War," or "Women Who Have Influenced My Life," or, for girls only, "The Woman I Hope to be Ten (or Twenty) Years from Now."

Flag Day

When he taught in Wisconsin in the early years of this century, Dr. Bernard J. Cigrand, each June 14 (in honor of the anniversary of the day in 1777 when the U.S. flag was adopted), would fly the American flag over his school. In 1916, President Wilson officially designated June 14 as Flag Day.

History. Each day, as the children salute the flag, they should understand the true meaning of the words they speak. Why not (with the assistance of the children and their dictionaries) paraphrase the salute to the flag:

> I promise (myself) that I'll be loyal to the American flag & what it means and to the United States, whose power belongs to the voters, a country which, believing in God, cannot be divided and offers liberty and justice to everyone.

(See Independence Day entry for addresses you may contact for free U.S. flag materials.)

Arkansas Admitted to the Union (1836) [15]

Arkansas is our 25th state.

Etymology: Arkansas comes from a Siouan Indian tribe, the *Uga Khpa*, meaning "downstream people." Through the years it was pronounced and spelled in various ways, but in 1881, the present spelling and pronunciation were legalized.

Father's Day [the third Sunday in June] ————————————

Mrs. John B. Dodd and her five brothers and sisters had been raised by their father after their mother's death. One spring day in 1919, while listening to the Mother's Day sermon, Mrs. Dodd had an idea. She thought how she would like to honor her father and other men like him, and she shared her idea with her minister after the sermon. He agreed with Mrs. Dodd and drew up a resolution for her, proposing that June 10, 1919 be set aside as Father's Day. Three years later, on the third Sunday of June, America celebrated its first national Father's Day.

Although Father's Day often falls after the closing of school, a small gift made in advance would undoubtedly be welcomed. (See December Christmas gifts in the index for gifts and recipe suggestions.)

Ask the children to finish "My Daddy is ——————" and illustrate their sentiments.

West Virginia Admitted to the Union (1836) [19]

West Virginia is our 35th state.

Etymology: West Virginia was named for the Virgin Queen Elizabeth I of England. Virginia comes from the Old French *virgine*, which comes from the Latin *virgo*, a maiden, and may be derived from *virga*, a slender branch, twig, or shoot.

Summer Solstice [21] ————————————

In the northern hemisphere, the sun appears at its highest point in the sky on June 21 or June 22. On this day, the sun's rays shine directly on the Tropic of Cancer, an imaginary line north of the equator, which encircles the globe. This line goes through Havana, Cuba; Calcutta, India; and Hong Kong, China. People living in these three cities see the sun directly overhead on June 21 or 22.

Etymology: "Summer" can be traced back to Sanskrit: *sama,* meaning "half a year" or "a season." The word "vacation" is from Latin and means "to empty out" or "to make vacant"!

"Heat" and "hot" (and "hoarse") are related to the Gothic word *heito* meaning "fever."

New Hampshire Admitted to the Union (1788) [21]

New Hampshire is our 9th state.

Etymology: It was named for Hampshire, England, in a grant in 1629 to Captain John Mason of Hampshire.

Virginia Admitted to the Union (1788) [26]

Virginia is our 10th state.

Etymology: Virginia, like West Virginia, was named for Queen Elizabeth I of England (1558–1603), called The Virgin Queen because she never married.

First bicycle patented in United States (1819) [26]

Etymology: June is a fine month to learn more about the bicycle, which derives its name from Latin *bis* (twice) and the Greek *kyklos* (wheel). Have interested students research the invention, history, and evolution of this nonpolluting form of transportation and ask one to write to the following address, requesting a free pamphlet, "Bicycle Safety," which includes a quiz as well as maintenance and safety tips:

> Aetna Life & Casualty
> 151 Farmington Ave.
> Hartford, CT 06156

Birth of Helen Keller (1880) [27]

Free information concerning the extraordinary life and achievements of this great American is offered by

> American Foundation for the Blind, Inc.
> 15 West Sixteenth St.
> New York, NY 10011

June Reading

On finishing a reader, ask the children to think back over the stories they have read and choose one, giving it a different ending (or beginning). Ask how each character might have behaved differently in this case.

Variation: Go through the reader and choose sentences at random from different stories. On slips of tagboard print 2 or 3 sentences that might begin or end a story. These slips are drawn from a box by children. Each child thinks for a few moments and then tells his original story, based on these sentences, to his group. Children might enjoy trying to identify the story in the reader from which sentences were actually taken.

June Language Arts

At the end of the school year, have the children write a class letter thanking the school custodian, secretary, principal, or room mother. Each child designs and cuts out of colored paper a tiny bird, flower, butterfly, heart, or angel, and these are pasted around the letter in its margins. The letter is rolled up and tied with a pretty ribbon. Be sure these letters mention specific ways in which each of these people have helped the children to have a really good school year!

June Math

By this time of year, math work may seem routine and unstimulating. For a welcome change of pace, give this math assignment: ask the students to each create a series of math problems based on information found in any of their other textbooks; for example, social studies books give dates & number of years a war lasted, monarch reigned, & so on as well as population, rainfall elevation, commercial statistics. Health books list number of foods in food groups, bones or teeth in a human, average weight statistics, calorie intakes, & so forth. Science texts may have information on astronomical distances, or weight and measurement numbers. Have the children create math problems that require a variety of math processes: this may be done as a homework assignment if you like.

When you check their papers, watch for erroneous use of any math process, and note on paper; select the most clever, humorous problems, & transfer these (with identifying initials of the originator) to a master sheet, which you then reproduce, one for each student. This math page should be an entertaining departure from the usual end-of-the-year math review work! The student who created each math problem used on this sheet could then be asked to act as "the expert" if anyone should have difficulty in solving their particular problem.

The reproducible page, "A Tale of Math Marvels" is another math activity that is unexpected in format—and should be fun for the kids to complete.

MATH RIDDLES

1. What's the difference between 1 yard and 2 yards? (A fence, or a property line)
2. A nickel and a dime were crossing a high bridge. The nickel jumped off; the dime didn't. Why? (It had more cents than the nickel!)

June Science

Tadpoles are often plentiful in June. If you catch some of these tiny creatures and care for them, you can watch their transformation and then release the frogs or toads where you found the tadpoles. You can keep tadpoles in a fishbowl. Clean the container once a week.

When they develop four legs, keep only 1" of water in the bowl and add rocks onto which they can climb. Cover the bowl with screening so they they don't hop out. The tadpoles can eat little bits of boiled egg yolks, cooked oatmeal, fish food, cooked lettuce, and sausage. The grown frogs and toads eat only moving insects. If you can't provide live insects, release your frogs or toads right away.

Name _____

© 1991 by The Center for Applied Research in Education

A Tale of Math Marvels! *

for Roman
Numerals

_____
_____
_____
_____
_____
_____
_____
_____
_____
_____
_____
_____
_____
_____
_____
_____
_____
_____

One day I invited fifty-two ____ people for lunch, but all I had to cook was BEANS ... so I put three thousand seventy-six ____ beans in a pot. I added forty-eight ____ gallons of water and cooked it all for nineteen ____ hours and twenty-three ____ minutes.

When my friends arrived, they brought me candy— six hundred nine ____ pieces of chocolate.. and flowers: one hundred four ____ daisies: it took seventeen ____ vases to hold them all!

Lunch was fun! We laughed four hundred nine ____ times! For dessert I served cherry pie: there were just eight hundred twelve ____ cherries in that pie .... and two thousand ninety-six ____ grains of sugar! By then we all felt very full, so after thirteen ____ minutes we took eighty-nine ____ spoons of antacid.......... After fifteen ____ hours of sleep we were all refreshed and we went outside to play a nineteen ____ hour game of baseball ... what a great day!!

* Fill in each blank with the written number for the printed words: fourteen→14 or seventy→70 and so on. (If you know Roman Numerals you can try writing each number as a Roman Numeral at the left of this page!)

Grasses and cacti. Grasses are among the most useful of all plants. They flower in summer but do not ripen until late July, August, or September. Wild grasses include timothy, rye, meadow foxtail, cock's foot, and common quaking grass. Cultivated grasses include wheat, barley, and oats. The flower head of grass is called the "ear" or *panicle.* The flowers that develop are called *spikelets.*

Classroom cacti may flower in June. Give them a bit of water once a week if the weather is dry.

(See July Science for other summer science suggestions.)

June Field Trip Suggestions

If you are lucky enough to live in an area that has fossil beds, plan a fossil-hunting field trip: it's a special kind of treasure hunt for most young kids.

June is a good month to visit a flag factory if your city has one. Another June field trip would be to arrange an hour with one child's Dad (Mom) at his or her place of work—this could be a fascinating time—and a way to give this one child (and the parent) a real place in the spotlight for those 60 minutes!

A Little Shadow Theater and Movable Figures

As a variation on the time-worn diorama, this small gem can be used for unique book reports, science & social studies displays—and it's lots of fun!

You will need: 4 pieces of Bristolboard (or plywood in sizes of one 10″ × 10″, two 7″ × 15″, and one 10″ × 15″; and X-acto™ knife (jigsaw); cloth tape; hot glue gun (or heavy stapler, or hammer & finishing nails); a piece of very fine nylon cloth (or white tissue paper); white glue (optional); bamboo shish kabob skewers (inexpensive & sold at cookware or grocery stores); scissors; posterboard; markers; magazine illustrations (optional); a table; and reading lamp.

Use the X-acto™ knife or jigsaw to cut the 10″ × 10″ piece of board and the two 7″ × 15″ boards to the shapes shown here:

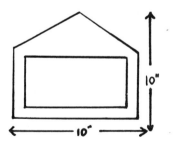

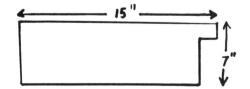

Then glue (staple or nail) the boards together to make the following shape:

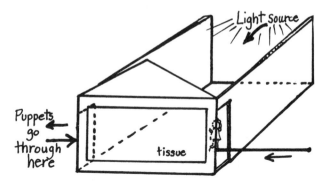

Tape the thin fabric (tissue) stretched tight to the inside of the front opening. Place the theater on a table.

Movable figures can be made by gluing a drawn (or magazine) picture to a piece of poster-board and this, in turn, to the end of a bamboo stick.

The bamboo stick is then inserted through the opening behind the fabric (tissue) screen and moved about. Place the reading lamp behind the theater and turn it on. The figures may be inserted through either side of the theater, and their sharp outlines will be cast upon the screen.

Encourage interested students to create movable backdrops or scenery from colored tissue paper or lightweight fabric (into which they cut tiny holes to outline trees, hills, buildings). Let them come up with creative solutions to this challenge!

End-of-the-School-Year Activities

For young students. One afternoon, ask the children to help you make a long list of everything they remember doing, learning, having happened during the past school year. Print each suggestion by one or two key words on a long sheet of newsprint. (This group recollecting should be done without the help of referring back to student journals.) See how many things they can list: every memory counts & 100 is quite good recall! This activity can be great fun; it gives practice in recall and emphasizes the many shared experiences of the past school year.

For middle graders: Explain to the students that for you to improve as a teacher you want to learn what they think worked especially well this school year & what they would suggest for improving things for the fall. Hand out copies of the "Looking Back" reproducible page.

Do not rush them as they complete these sheets. Allow them all the time they need to answer the page in full. Tell them that you are filling out one of these sheets as well & do it while they complete theirs. The next day, post a composite list in class for everyone to read.

Interested students may be put in charge of creating/producing this list. Be sure to emphasize how much you appreciate their help.

The results of this questionnaire will in some ways be *your* report card for the year, but more important, they can be an invaluable guide to you as you prepare for that new upcoming class of the fall.

END-OF-SCHOOL RIDDLES

1. What 3 letters mean "You've done very well!"? (UX-L)
2. What should you do this summer if you can't find any shorts to wear? (Race around and around your room until you're left in short pants!)

Name _____

Looking Back
at my
year..... Fill in the blank spaces below....

1) This year we did a lot of things.
   Here are some things I got done:

2) These are some things I NOW know & understand that
   I didn't know last fall.

3) When I look back over this school year the best part
   for ME was   because

4) The best videos (or movies) we saw:

5) If I were the teacher, I'd change these things for
   the kids NEXT year:

6) Here is what I'd teach them:

7) The most important thing(s) I learned this year:

JULY

A day of leisure is a day of immortality.

—Chinese proverb

Calendar of Important Dates

1   On this day in 1190, Richard the Lionhearted began the Third Crusade.

First smallpox vaccine delivered by Jenner, 1796.

George Sand (assumed name of Baroness Didevant), French writer (*History of My Life*), born in 1804.

On this day in 1863, the Battle of Gettysburg was fought.

2   Amelia Earhart, U.S. aviator, was last heard from on this day in 1937.

3   Dog Days (the period between July 3 and August 15), so-called by early Egyptians, Greeks, and Romans, as they all noted how Sirius the Dog Star now rose just about at sunrise and seemed to add its heat to the sun's, giving us the hottest three weeks of the year!

Idaho Statehood Day (the 43rd state to join the Union, 1890).

First solo circumnavigation completed by J. Slocum in Fairhaven, Massachusetts, 1893.

4   On this day in the year 1054, Chinese astronomers first noticed the explosion of a star which became Crab Nebula.

In 1636, on this day Roger Williams founded Providence, Rhode Island.

Since 1776, AMERICAN INDEPENDENCE DAY!!

Calvin Coolidge, 30th U.S. president, was born in 1872.

Also born on this day were

- Rube Goldberg, creator of inventions extraordinaire, 1883
- Louis Armstrong, jazz great, in 1900
- Ann Landers & Abigail Van Buren, twins who both write advice columns in our daily papers, 1918

5   Etienne de Silhouette, French finance minister who cut out shadow portraits as a hobby, was born, 1709.

6   On this day in Ripon, Wisconsin, the modern-day Republican party was founded in 1854.

Beatrix Potter, beloved creator of Peter Rabbit, Mrs. Tiggy Winkle, and many other animal story characters, was born in 1886.

On this day in 1918, the czar of Russia & his entire family were executed at Ekaterinburg by the revolutionaries.

7   Russian Jewish artist Marc Chagall was born in 1887.

Satchel Paige, American baseball great, was born in Mobile, Alabama, 1906.

On this day in 1917, Emma Goldman was sentenced to 2 years in prison for interfering with U.S. Army registration.

Ringo Starr, drummer-singer with the Beatles, was born, 1940.

On this day in 1972, NASA announced plans to collect solar energy to be used as a power source on earth.

8   In 1835, on this day the Liberty Bell cracked as it tolled the death of U.S. Chief Justice Marshall.

9   On this day, President James Garfield was shot in Washington, DC. He died 2 months later on September 19, 1881.

The donut cutter was patented by J. F. Blondel of Thomaston, Maine, in 1872.

10   Wyoming was admitted to the Union as the 44th state, 1890.

11   John Quincy Adams, 6th U.S. president, was born in 1767.

On this day in 1804, Aaron Burr killed Alexander Hamilton in a duel.

E. B. White, author of *Charlotte's Web,* was born in 1899.

12 On this day in 100 B.C., Julius Caesar was born.

Henry David Thoreau, writer-naturalist, was born, 1817.

George Washington Carver, black botanist, soil conservationist, was born on this day in 1864.

Buckminster Fuller, an architect, designer, inventor, and visionary, was born in 1895.

Pablo Neruda, Chilean Nobel Prize–winning poet, was born in 1904.

Jesse Owens, great black athlete, was born near Danville, Alabama 1918.

14 Bastille Day, the French Independence Day, celebrates the French Revolution, which began on this day in 1789 when Parisians stormed the Bastille, a prison, and freed its inmates, many of whom were political prisoners.

Isaac Bashevis Singer, master Jewish storyteller and novelist, was born in 1904.

Ingmar Berman, Swedish filmmaker, was born in 1918.

15 St. Swithin's Day.

On this day in 1099, Jerusalem was taken on the First Crusade and its population massacred.

Rembrandt van Ryn, world-acclaimed Dutch painter, was born in 1607.

On this day in 1965, *Mariner IV* sent back close-up photos of Mars; in 1968, the first Moscow–New York air link was put into regular service.

16 First world atlas published in 1482, composed of maps drawn by Ptolemy around 150 A.D.!

In 1790, the District of Columbia was carved out of Virginia and Maryland to become the nation's capital.

Mary Baker Eddy, founder of the Christian Science Church, was born, 1821.

First A-bomb was tested in Alamogordo, New Mexico, in 1945.

17 In 1975, the U.S. *Apollo* & the Soviet *Soyuz* spaceships linked up in outer space.

18 In the year 64, Rome began to burn. This fire lasted 8 days with Nero blaming the inferno on the Christians.

On this date in 1203, Constantinople (today's Istanbul, in Turkey) was conquered in the Fourth Crusade.

John Glenn, U.S. astronaut, was born on this date in Cambridge, Ohio, 1921.

Yevgeny Yevtushenko, Russian poet, was born in Zimar, USSR, in 1933.

19 First Women's Rights Convention in America was held in Seneca Falls, New York, in 1848. It was organized by Lucretia Mott, Elizabeth Cady Stanton, and others.

Rosalyn Yalow, Nobel Prize–winning scientist, famous for her study of hormones, was born on this date in 1921.

20 In 1969, *Apollo II* landed on the moon!

In 1976, *Viking I* landed on mars!

21 Ernest Hemingway, American writer (*For Whom the Bell Tolls, The Sun Also Rises,* etc.), was born in 1899.

22   In 1376, the Pied Piper led the plague of rats away from Hamlin, Germany. When the city government refused to pay him as they had contracted to do, he whistled away all the town's children.

Emma Lazarus, Jewish-American poet whose sonnet appears on the base of the Statue of Liberty, was born, 1849.

Alexander Calder, father of the mobile, was born in 1898.

First solo air circumnavigation completed by U.S. pilot Wiley Post in 1933; his flight took 7 days, 18 hours, and 45 minutes.

23   On this day in 1972, the United States put the ERTS satellite into orbit in order to study the earth's environment.

24   Simon Bolivar, explorer and liberator, was born in Caracas, Venezuela, in 1783.

Amelia Earhart, first woman to pilot a plane across the Atlantic, was born in 1898.

Bella Abzug, feminist and New York congresswoman, was born in New York City in 1920.

25   First U.S. Commonwealth created—Puerto Rico—in 1952.

26   New York Statehood Day, the 11th state to join the Union (1788).

Carl Jung, psychoanalytic visionary, was born on this day in 1875.

Pearl S. Buck, American author (*The Good Earth*) was born, 1892.

Mick Jagger, lead singer of the British rock group the Rolling Stones, was born, 1944.

28   In 1868, the 14th Amendment to the Constitution was ratified.

World War I began in 1914 when Austria declared war on Serbia.

Jacqueline Kennedy Onassis was born on this day in 1929.

29   Don Marquis, American newspaper columnist and ironic writer (*the lives and times of archy and mehitabal*) was born, 1878.

Marcel Duchamp, French-American artist, was born, Blainville, France, 1887.

On this day in 1890, a lonely, desperate Vincent van Gogh killed himself beside a wheatfield 20 miles north of Paris.

Dag Hammerskjold, Swedish economist and first secretary general of the United Nations, was born, 1905.

In 1958, NASA was authorized.

30   First U.S. patent was issued in 1790.

Emily Brontë, genius of the three writing Brontës (*Wuthering Heights*), was born in England, 1818.

Henry Ford, American auto inventor, was born in Dearborn, Michigan, in 1863.

Henry Moore, sculptor, was born in 1898.

On this day in history, U.S. astronauts drove the LRV (lunar roving vehicle) across the surface of the moon, 1969.

31   In 1964, the U.S. spacecraft *Ranger 7* crash landed on the moon.

July

The Alaskan Eskimos call this month "Birds Lay Eggs" and "Molting." The Omaha Indians call July "When the Buffalo Are Ripe." To the Pawnees, July is "Cultivating." This month is *X A mitute* (mesquite) to Yuman tribes, during which time they gather mesquite because it is gone by the end of July. (The month of July was named for the Roman leader, Julius Caesar.)

July Quotations

4 Civilization and profits go hand in hand.

—Calvin Coolidge

7 When I am finishing a picture, I hold some God-made object up to it—a rock, a flower, the branch of a tree, or my hand—as a kind of final test. If the painting stands up beside a thing man cannot make, the painting is authentic. If there's a clash between the two, it is bad art.

—Marc Chagall

12 When a dog runs at you, whistle for him.

—Henry David Thoreau

Thinking: freeing birds, erasing images, burying lamps.

—Pablo Neruda

26 One does not dream; one is dreamed. We undergo the dream, we are the objects. Freedom of will is to do gladly that which I must do.

—Carl Jung

29 God should not be judged on the basis of this world—it is just one of His rough sketches.

—Vincent Van Gogh

A throw of the dice will never abolish chance.
Do unto others as they wish, but with imagination.

—Marcel Duchamp

30 If I can stop one heart from breaking, I will not have lived in vain.

—Emily Brontë

Failure is only the opportunity to begin again, more intelligently.

—Henry Ford

July Events

Dog Days (the hot uncomfortable days of July and August) [3] ——————

So called because during this period the Dog Star rises and sets with the sun.

Drying Fruits ——————

These are perfect days for drying fruits for eating fun now or in the fall. Have the children help construct the following drying rack.

Easy Drying Racks: You will need large sturdy cardboard sheets (the sides of appliance boxes), utility knife, cheesecloth, staplegun, a nail, and some heavy cord. Cut 2 sheets of cardboard to the same size. Cut the middle from each sheet leaving a 4″ border of cardboard. Stretch the cheesecloth across this opening. Staple the stretched cheesecloth to the bottom sheet and then lay second cardboard sheet on top. Along the outside edge of cardboard, staple the 2 sheets together. Use the nail to make a hole well inside each corner of double-layered cardboard. Through each hole at one end of sheet, run a long cord & knot firmly; repeat with the 2 holes at opposite side of cardboard.

Now have the children wash their hands & use blunt-ended knives to make ¼″ slices or wedges of banana, pear, apple, apricot, peach, and/or plums. Hang the dryer rack outdoors during sunny days in semishade. (Apricots dried in direct sun become bitter.) Lay the cut fruit on the cheesecloth so fruit doesn't overlap, and turn the fruit daily until it is dried. Cover the fruit with a layer of large piece of cheesecloth to keep off any insects. Try not to overload the rack with too much fruit.

Idaho Admitted to the Union (1890) [3]

Idaho is our 29th state.

Etymology: The derivation of the word Idaho is unclear. It may be a coined name with an invented "Indian" meaning "gem of the mountains." First proposed for what is now the state of Colorado, it was next applied to the new mining territory of the Pacific Northwest. Another theory suggests that "Idaho" is a Kiowa Indian word for the Comanche people.

Independence Day [4]

This is the day in 1776 when the Declaration of Independence was adopted by the Continental Congress. Have the children each volunteer a reason why they are happy to be Americans and make a list of these 4th of July thoughts.

Etymology: The word "independence" has an unusual derivation: while *in* means "not" in Latin & *ence* means "the state of," "depend" comes from *de*, meaning "down," and *pendere*, meaning "to hang"—so to be independent means to not be hanging from or, more to the point, relying on someone else for support.

"Fireworks" and "firecracker" both come from the ancient Middle English word *fyre*, which is related to the Greek *pyra*, meaning "fire," from which our words (funeral) "pyre" and "pyrotechnic" come. *Wor* is a descendant of the ancient Anglo Saxon *werc* and is related to the Greek *ergon* from which we get "organ," "tol," "instrument"—all mechanisms that *work*! "Crack" comes from the Anglo-Saxon *cracian*, meaning "to cry hoarsely" (as does the crane) & is related to the Sanskrit *garjate*—"it roars or snarls."

For older students, ask them to tell you everything they (think they) know about fireworks. Then go to the *World Book Encyclopedia* & assign a different paragraph to each student to read, restate in his or her own words & finally report back to the class.

4th of July Math

A reproducible 4th of July follow-the-dots puzzle is provided for your students' pleasure!

Name _____

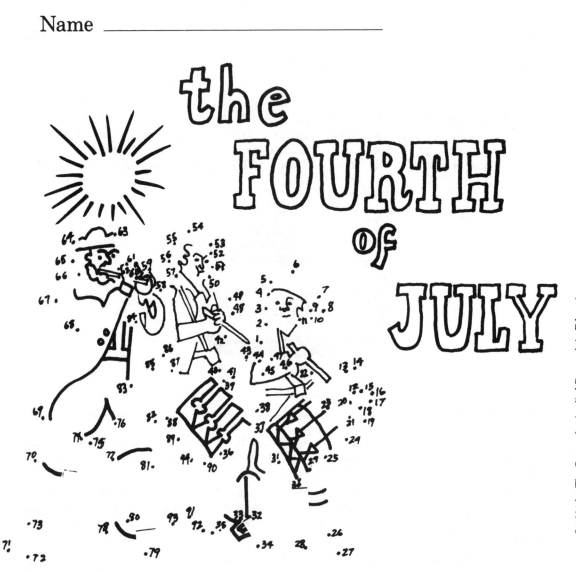

Draw a line from 1–94.

Then color the picture.

Use **blue** to color in all the vowels in the words above: the 4th of July.

Use red to color in any letters that are in your first name.

Make yellow stripes on all the other letters.

Birth of Etienne de Silhouette (1709) [5]

Etymology: The silhouette is an outline (especially a profile portrait) filled in with a solid color. Usually silhouettes are cut from black paper & adhered to a light background. This artistic form is named after Etienne de Silhouette, a French finance minister who lived in the mid 18th century and who was famous for being a pinch-penny. His hobby was cutting out paper portraits; the phrase "à la Silhouette" originally meant "on the cheap."

The first silhouettes were made by the paleolithic peoples whose paintings and drawings in the limestone caves of France & Spain show remarkably realistic animals and people in profile. The Egyptians, Greeks, and Etruscans decorated tombs, relief sculpture, and pottery using the silhouette.

Classroom silhouettes are quickly made if you have a slide projector to use to cast a sharp shadow. Tape a large piece of colored paper on the wall directly behind the head of a seated child. Use a (white-colored) pencil to carefully trace an outline of the shadow onto (black) paper. Traditionally, teachers have done this drawing, but upper and middle grade students can easily make the tracings of one another or themselves, and then cut them out. They enjoy it and it reinforces hand-eye coordination and concentration while offering successful, even magical, results! So encourage interested students to execute your classroom silhouettes this year.

Wyoming Admitted to the Union (1890) [10]

Wyoming is our 44th state.

Etymology: The name Wyoming originally was used to refer to the Wyoming Valley in Pennsylvania and is a corruption of a word of the Delaware Indians meaning "upon the great plain."

Birth of George Washington Carver (1864) [12]

This is the reputed birthdate of the great American chemist-researcher who was born of slave parents in Missouri. Carver was hungry for an education and worked his way through school, receiving his M.S. degree from Iowa State College in 1896. Then he went to Alabama where he worked hard to persuade farmers to plant soil-enriching peanuts and sweet potatoes instead of the soil-exhausting cotton crops. The farmers responded, leading Carver on a quest

to discover new uses for the now overabundant crops. This he did with gusto, fabricating a kind of rubber, molasses, and vinegar from the sweet potato. He experimented with peanuts and discovered how to make flour, coffee, milk, cheese, ink, dyes, wood stain, insulation, soap—over 300 different products in all!

In 1940, three years before his death, he gave his life savings to establish the Carver Foundation, which carries on his research for the betterment of the South and its people.

Birth of Buckminster Fuller (1895) [12]

R. Buckminster Fuller is well known as the inventor of the geodesic dome, but he created hundreds of other inventions as well. Unhappily, some of his inventions are sensible and inexpensive, but they would threaten their commercially produced counterparts and so they have not been made available on the American market.

For example, there was the *Dymaxion Car,* a streamlined three-wheeled car that could carry 10 adults & turn in its own length; had front-wheel drive, shatterproof glass & above-spring suspension, an aluminum body, and aircraft steel frame; it was powered by three small (10- to 15-hp) engines mounted in the rear; and could cruise at 70 mph. while getting 40-plus miles to the gallon.

Unfortunately, the Dymaxion was developed at the wrong time—in the middle of the Depression when U.S. automakers could not afford to retool to produce a superior car; it didn't make economic sense to them to make cars that would last 4 times as long as the current models and for the same price! And so the Dymaxion automobile died away as America prepared to go to war.

St. Swithin's Day [15]

St. Swithin was the bishop of Winchester, England, from 852 to 862. Although it was the custom for all important people, such as bishops, to be buried inside the church in those days, St. Swithin expressly requested that he be buried outside where the nurturing rains of heaven could fall on his grave. So at his death in 862, St. Swithin was buried outside.

A hundred years passed & the bones of St. Swithin were moved inside the church. Many people believed that this displeased the saint's soul and soon a weather-forecasting rhyme sprang up:

> St. Swithin's Day if thou dost rain,
> For 40 days it will remain.
> St. Swithin's Day if thou be fair,
> for 40 days 'twill rain nae mair.

Talk together with the children about weather forecasting & other ways they have for telling when the weather will change. Why was correct weather forecasting important 100 years ago? What does it affect today?

ST. SWITHIN'S DAY COOKING

Here is a recipe from the Middle Ages; it is traditionally prepared and savored in England on this day—as has been done for 500 years!

Swithin Cream (for 25 or more children)

3 big lemons	1/8 tsp. salt
15 dandelion flowers	3/4 cup sugar
3 cups whipping cream	1/2 tsp. vanilla
12 (Granny Smith) apples	

Peel the yellow rind from the lemons. Finely grind rind & set aside. Wash the dandelion flowers and carefully pluck the petals from each blossom. Chop petals finely. Gently mix petals & lemon rind. Wash & cut the apples into wedges. Core each wedge.

Whip the cream, adding salt, sugar, & vanilla until cream forms peaks. Sprinkle petals & lemon rind over cream & gently fold together. Serve 3 or 4 apple wedges & a dollop of Swithin Cream to each child. Wedge is dipped into cream & then eaten. Close your eyes as you eat an apple wedge & imagine you are in the 14th century!

First World Atlas (published, 1482; maps drawn by Ptolemy in c.150 A.D.) [16]

Etymology: An atlas is a book of maps, often on the front page of which is a picture of the giant, Atlas, who in Greek legend is compelled to support the heavens on his shoulders.

Classroom Atlas: Here's an opportunity to let the children play with an idea! Introduce the concept of an atlas and briefly look through a World Atlas and a U.S. road atlas. Then encourage the children to think of completely personal and fantastic ideas for creating a unique set of atlases, for example, an atlas of maps of famous fairy tales, maps of the children's rooms, houses, hide-outs, walks to school, maps of the first house a child remembers living in, & maps of the travels of famous (fictional) people. (The teacher should join in with personal maps, too!) The children can break into small groups, each of which will produce its own personal atlas, composed of maps of whatever subject the children decide on. Encourage the use of humor, originality, and neatness. Make world atlases available to the groups so that the children can learn how to structure their own books. Have a deadline for finishing this project, and then allow ample time for each group to present their atlas to the rest of the class (and perhaps to another class as well).

A free road atlas and travel guide are available from

> Best Western International, Inc.
> Marketing Services
> P.O. Box 10203
> Pheonix, AZ 85064-0203

First A-bomb Tested (1945) [16] ———————————————

Etymology: "Atomic" (coming from the French *atome* & Latin *atomus*) derives from the Greek *atomos,* meaning "uncut" (*a* = not, *tomos* = cutable) and "indivisible."

The U.S. Department of Energy offers free materials on nuclear energy, including "Atoms to Electricity" (DOE/NE-0085); "Radio Isotopes" (DOE/NE 0089); "Answers to Questions" (DOE/NE-0088); and "The History of Nuclear Energy" (DOE/NE 0068). Write to

> U.S. Department of Energy
> P.O. Box 62
> Oak Ridge, TN 37830

The photographs in these booklets can be used as the basis of several fascinating bulletin board displays, the first which you construct and the following ones student made, using your example as a guide. Cover board with large areas of brightly colored paper, cut out 6 to 10 interesting photographs from one of these booklets and pin these at random on the board, adding a rectangle of contrasting colored paper behind 3 of the photos.

Next paraphrase the captions in the booklet, using low-level vocabulary words and 2 or 3 different colors of markers for the captions. Intersperse 3 or 4 provocative questions that have no one, simple answer to help in eliciting discussion. Finally, run a long banner across the top of the board and have it read: "Want to Learn Something About Nuclear Energy? Just Read Below!"

The subjects of nuclear weapons, nuclear testing, and nuclear energy are emotionally charged. Help your students investigate their individual attitudes and apprehensions. Then help them locate materials to broaden their ideas and address their anxieties.

You may be interested in contacting the Educators for Social Responsibility, requesting a list of current teaching aids and materials:

> E.S.R.
> 23 Garden St.
> Cambridge, MA 02138

First Earthlings Land on the Moon (1969) [20] ———————————————

U.S. astronauts Neil Armstrong and Edwin Aldrin, Jr., were the first people to walk on the surface of the moon. When they returned to earth on July 24, they brought back photographs, "soil" samples, and moon rocks!

Our word "moon" is related to "month" (the period between one new moon and the next); its Indo-European root is probably *me*—which means "to measure" or "that which measures time."

"Rocket" is an Italian word coming from *rocchetta,* a "spool" or "bobbin," being the diminutive of *rocca,* meaning "distaff" and referring to the cone shape which both the rocket and filled distaff share.

NASA offers extraordinary (and free!) outerspace materials. Write, requesting a catalog of their educational publications, to

Superintendent of Documents
U.S. Government Printing Office
Washington, DC 20402

Birth of Amelia Earhart (1898) [24]

The first woman to pilot a plane across the Atlantic, Amelia Earhart set many aerial records before her still mysterious disappearance somewhere over the Pacific Ocean in the last part of World War II.

Why not order a cassette tape of her life story—one of 24 famous "Groundbreakers," "Worldshakers," and "Great Americans" (3 series) offered by The Mind's Eye (Box 6727, San Francisco, CA 94101).

Learn about Earhart, Sacajawea, Deborah Gannet, Elizabeth Blackwell, and Felisa Rincon de Gautier among many. Tapes are reasonably priced.

New York Admitted to the Union (1788) [26]

New York is our 11th state.

In 1664, the British took from the Dutch and renamed New Netherlands as New York, in honor of the Duke of York who later became King James II of England.

Birth of Don Marquis (1878) [29] ───────────────────────

Don Marquis, Chicago newspaperman, came up with the idea that one night he left a sheet of paper in his typewriter & the following morning, he returned to his office to find that a cockroach—a poetic cockroach—had left him a missive typed out in all lowercase letters, of course!

Many middle and upper grade students will love having you read aloud to them *the lives and times of archy and mehitabel* (New York: Doubleday, 1950). Give it a try!

Birth of Marcel Duchamp (1887) [29] ───────────────────

Marcel Duchamp was a French-American artist famous for his painting and an important contributor to modern sculpture with his "ready-mades," which included a wine bottle rack, a white porcelain toilet, & cubes of sugar in a cage, titled *Why Not Sneeze?* Duchamp ridiculed accepted aesthetic values by exhibiting as works of art mass-produced articles. In 1915, he moved to New York and became a U.S. citizen in 1955. In 1923, he gave up painting and spent his time mainly from then on in playing chess.

Duchamp had a final joke on the world; when he died in 1968, it was found that he had been working on an entire room or artistic design which could be viewed only through a slit in a brick wall at the back of his New York apartment. Since his death, the Philadelphia Museum of Art has obtained this very special artistic achievement and moved it to their grounds so that many interested viewers may look through the slit in the brick wall!

Dadaism* was an international literary and artistic movement which lasted from 1915 to 1922. In reaction to World War I, it was dedicated to the demolition of existing ethical and artistic standards. Marcel Duchamp was a leading American Dadaist. He and Francis Picabra and Alfred Stieglitz used their work to force people to see "art" through fresh eyes.

─────────────────

*"Dada," according to Richard Hulsenbeck, was accidentally discovered by Hugo Ball and himself in a German-French dictionary. "It is French for 'wooden horse' and is impressive for its brevity & suggestiveness." Tristan Tzara, the Romanian poet, said that he discovered the word "Dada" at 6:00 P.M. one evening at the Terrace Cafe in Zurich!

The Dadaists invented a game which they called "The Exquisite Cadaver." Duchamp and his artist friends often played it. You can too. Make a long strip of opaque white paper 6″ wide and long enough so that each student player has 6″ on which to work. Lightly mark off the 6″ intervals down the length of the paper. The first player makes the head, in good detail, of a man, woman, child, bird, alien, or animal and indicates with 2 small lines at the bottom of the space where the neck is to be added. This first space is now folded under the strip so that the next player can't see it. The second player draws an extraordinary neck of his or her own concoction and then indicates with a line where the torso is to begin. This (neck) contribution is folded over and the game continues with players adding torso, arms (wings) to waist, the fourth space is for hips to knees, the fifth for just below knees to ankles, and the final space for the feet (paws, high heels, claws, ballet shoes?).

Open out these delicious Exquisite Cadavers and display a group of them (with the historic background) on a fine July bulletin board!

Etymology: "Exquisite Cadaver," the Dadaist drawing game, has an interesting etymology. "Exquisite" originally meant "carefully sought out" or "choice" and comes from the Latin *exquistus,* "to search out" (*ex* = out + *quaerere* = to ask). "Cadaver" comes from the Latin verb *cadere,* meaning "to fall" as a deceased body would . . . .

July Puppet: A Prancing Pony* ———————————————————

You will need an X-acto™ knife (fret saw), compass (awl), Bristolboard (plywood), carpet thread, needle, white glue, poster paints, verathane, ½″ dowel cut to 5″, tiny beads, and a big bead.

Draw enlargements of the patterns below onto Bristolboard.

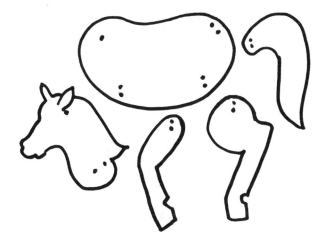

Carefully cut them out. Have a child paint the pieces (on both sides if you like) and then varnish them. Allow the pieces to dry. Drill holes using compass point (awl or drill) at the

---

*With slight variation in shapes, this puppet can be a horse, zebra, unicorn, camel—any quadraped!

places indicated; make them just large enough to allow carpet thread to pass through. Study this diagram.

Then assemble puppet accordingly. Dotted lines indicate that one piece is beneath another piece. Make the 4 hinges as indicated. Thread needle with carpet thread and insert it through the 2 coinciding holes, leaving a long thread end. Put needle through a small bead, back through the same 2 holes and through another small bead. Tie off thread and cut ends.

To make the action thread connections, thread a loop through the A holes and tie loop. Repeat with B holes. Now tie a connecting thread to bottom of loop A and run this thread down and around the bottom of loop B and extend thread (to bottom of legs) through a big bead and tie off with a small bead.

Tie the pony to the holding bar; drill 2 holes in the dowel. Use knotted carpet thread to go through dowel hole and down through pony's head; knot thread at back of head. Repeat procedure with second dowel hole and the hole at rear of the puppet. Finally, squeeze a bit of white glue on all knots to prevent them from working loose.

A Scavenger Hunt for July

Here's an activity that will promote cooperation & emphasize the importance of reading carefully. Give students plastic produce bags in which to collect objects & an area to display the final collection. Use the reproducible Scavenger Hunt page to make copies of the list of things each team will attempt to collect. Important: *Emphasize the importance of not damaging natural*

Let's work TO GETHER to finish this
<u>Scavenger Hunt</u> !

We need to collect:

1 thing that can make you laugh

2 things that S-T-R-E-T-C-H...

3 things that can be eaten.

4 things that can be read.

5 green things.

6 round things.

<u>7 man-made objects</u>

<u>8 things</u> that were <u>once</u> <u>alive</u>

9 pretty objects

10 pieces of litter

NOW: line these up on a big piece
of news paper & have your teacher
check them. Hurray: <u>You're</u> WINNERS!

elements in the area or private property! Teams are made up of four to six students each, & every team that finishes wins.

July Field Trip Suggestions

Why not arrange to take your class to visit a foundry that specializes in casting artists' work? The kids can learn a great deal from such a trip, especially when they have specific questions prepared.

Older students would benefit from coming in contact with a conceptual artist or one who does surrealistic work. Such an artist can help students learn brand-new ways of thinking—and seeing!

An ice cream factory is a favorite field trip for all ages and welcome at anytime of the year, but particularly in the warm months of summer!

Solar energy businesses will often be happy to provide a speaker for your class, and such a visitor can explain solar collectors as well as solar energy itself to your students.

Planning Ahead

Are you already thinking about September and the NEW school year? Here is a list that you may want to begin using right now in preparation for the fall.

SOURCE LIST OF FREE (or very inexpensive) LEARNING MATERIALS

- Appliance repair shop may be willing to donate unclaimed (nonworking) appliances, parts for children to dissemble and use for creating robots, sculpture, Rube Goldberg inventions.
- Appliance stores will save huge cardboard refrigerator boxes (use for display screens).
- Architects are a source of used blueprints which make interesting collage material, can be bookcovers, or wrapping paper.
- Bakeries often use ingredients such as flour that is sold in large, sturdy reusable buckets with lids. You're bound to find these handy sometime during the school year!
- Butchers—ask your butcher to save you some large, unusual (uncut) bones. Boil to remove meat fibers; bleach in summer sun. Kids love examining, comparing, drawing, and identifying such bones.

- Cleaners and laundries may donate *unclaimed sheets:* (tepees, banners, ghosts, room dividers, book covers, or clothes for dress-up).

- Computer store or large business must dispose of large quantities of readout sheets. The backs are blank & are perfect for scratch paper. Arrange with the manager to pick up some on a weekly or monthly basis.

- Contractors—ask them to save their scraps for your class; this could include aluminum sheets, wire, foam rubber, tile, linoleum, pipes, plastic—all great construction materials.

- Department stores—contact the display department manager & request their discarded crates & damaged or outmoded display units. The interior design department may donate wallpaper, rugs, & curtain sample books.

- Dentists regularly throw out old dental tools which students can use for etching, carving, crayon-resist.

- Fabric store—put in a special request for any odds & ends they may accumulate, including, odd buttons, fasteners, ribbon, fabric remnants, spools, yarn.

- Feed store—ask them to save any burlap bags which are great for stitchery, tapestries.

- Florists regularly throw away old roses & rose buds which your class can use for potpourri or making valentines. They may also come in handy for Mother's Day.

- Framers are a fine source of mat board and foamcore scraps!

- Garment factories and outlet stores may be able to provide buttons, trim, fabric, sequins, polyester fill, & spools (for counters) that can be used for crafts, scrolls, & puppets.

- Hardware, paint, and interior design stores can be sources of wallpaper sample books, tile charts (counters), linoleum (printmaking), & paint sample charts (sequencing light to dark).

- Highway Department—if you live in or near your state capital, go and visit this department. See if they will donate a nonoperative traffic light (for playground and safety practice) or old stop or road signs. You may be surprised at what they consider useless.

- Hospital and doctors' offices—worn bed sheets & plastic pill bottles, containers (for hand puppets, construction), surgical gowns (dress-up), used X rays are fascinating to all ages of students.

- Ice cream stores dispose of their round 3-gallon containers (with lids), which can be used for storage, spacemen or knights' masks, or attractive wastebaskets coverings (for Father's Day or a birthday gift).

- Junkyards offer endless possibilities, including, fittings, hinges, handles, old steering wheels. Take a student or two with you to help discover the possibilities!

- Libraries often receive donations of back issue magazines (*National Geographic, Natural History, Ranger Rick*) which they will share with schools.

- Lumberyards have wood scraps, shavings, odd nails.

- Magazine & paperback book distributors (see your Yellow Pages) return the covers of recalled magazines and paperback books to their publishers for reimbursement. The publications themselves are then destroyed. Some distributors, if contacted personally, will pass these on to a teacher.

- Metal fabrication companies or foundries often discard interesting scrap pieces which young inventors and sculptors will appreciate.

- Overseas shipping companies—if you live in a large city, you might contact such a company and ask them if you could have any huge (slightly damaged) packing crates or fiberboard drums they are discarding (for classroom private spaces or playground use).

- Paper companies are often open to giving a class paper samples, ends of rolls (for murals), and cardboard rolls.

- Photography supply houses may donate scrap photographic paper, film canisters, and spools.

- Plumbers may have tile, wire, linoleum, and pipe scraps.

- Post offices can be contacted and asked to save worn mail-carrier bags or an out-of-date storage unit for use in your classroom.

- Poultry farm—ask if you might collect chicken and turkey feathers for use in crafts—or taped to a long strip of colored paper they become an Indian headdress for a youngster!

- Printshop—establish a personal relationship with a printshop so that you can collect their scrap paper on a permanent basis. This paper is often high quality, brightly colored—perfect for little storybooks.

- Professional portrait photographer—ask for used backdrop paper: it's huge & great for murals, time lines, bulletin boards.

- Restaurants may, if asked, save large tomato cans, giant mayonnaise jars, large plastic cheese tubs for you. Use the jars for terrariums, fishbowls, & shell/rock collections, and the cans—with drainage holes punched in the bottoms—make fine flower pots.

- Rug companies and carpet outlets may donate remnant end pieces from rug rolls & sample rug swatches which when pieced together with double-sided carpet tape can become a sturdy comfortable floor covering for a quiet reading area.

- Supermarkets are a source of display materials, such as, banners, posters, decorations, & cardboard display racks (book shelves for class).

- Surplus supply warehouses—again, if you live in or near your state capital, you may have access to such a surplus supplies clearing department. (Call your state Department of Education and ask for information.) These departments have a variety of damaged or outdated supplies, including, typewriters, maps, globes, books, chairs, aquariums, desks, and these items are often free to teachers or inexpensive in price. Go personally and rummage through their inventory. This warehouse can turn out to be a treasure house.

- Telephone company—source of thin colored wire and child-size wooden spools (for student tables).

- Thrift stores have limitless possibilities. Nonworking appliances such as TVs, radios, and phonographs are often available for free to teachers.

- Tobacco shops will often save their cigar boxes for you, and these sturdy containers are great fun to use, decorate, cover, stack.

- Travel agencies may donate outdated travel posters and colorful brochures.

- Tree-trimmers—see if you can arrange to pick up some large, flat-bottomed tree trunks (for use as stools, table bases, flower stands) or 6″ wide slabs of trunks for tree-ring studies in science.

- Video stores may contribute movie posters, collages, and display units.

- Weavers—a commercial weaver could donate spools or yarn from the ends of rolls.

- Wedding shops that do alterations may save silk & veil remnants, odd sequins, seed pearls, & lace bits for you.

- Wineries throw away used corks which children can glue together to make trivets: glue 28 corks to one another or use for printmaking.

It's wonderful to know that you are saving money and showing the children how practical and how much fun it is to reuse & give new life to discarded objects!

AUGUST

To the Quinault, August was "Time of Summer." The Pawnee Indians called it "Cultivating." To the Alaskan Eskimos, August was "Geese Lack Feathers, Geese Cannot Fly." The Omahas referred to August as "When the Elk Bellow."

Calendar of Important Dates

1 On this day in 1493, Columbus discovered the continent of South America.

First U.S. census begun in 1790.

Colorado Statehood Day, 1876, when Colorado became the 38th state to join the Union.

On this day in 1893, shredded wheat was patented.

First solar-heated commercial building was completed in Albuquerque, New Mexico, in 1957.

2 Friendship Day, suggested by Joyce C. Hall (who founded Hallmark Cards) and decreed by Congress in 1935.

3 Columbus set sail from Spain in search of a new route to India on this day in 1492.

5 On this day in 1884, the cornerstone of the Statue of Liberty was set in place.

First electric traffic lights installed, Cleveland, Ohio, in 1914.

Neil Armstrong, U.S. astronaut, was born in 1930.

6 On this day in 1945, the United States dropped the atomic bomb on Hiroshima, Japan.

7 Ralph Bunche, black American educator, UN statesman, and Nobel Peace Prize recipient (1950) was born in 1904.

8   Marjorie Rawlings, author of *The Yearling,* was born in 1896.

In 1974, Richard Nixon resigned as president of the United States.

9   Jean Piaget, renowned child behaviorist, was born in 1896.

10   Missouri Statehood Day: in 1821, Missouri became the 24th state to join the Union.

On this day in 1846, the Smithsonian Institute was created in Washington, DC.

Herbert Hoover, 31st president, was born in 1874.

On this day in 1972, the only meteorite known to have entered the earth's atmosphere and to have left it flew in over Utah and departed the atmosphere over Alberta, Canada.

11   Alex Haley, black author of *Roots,* was born in 1921.

On this day in 1934, Beebe descended ½ mile down into the ocean in his bathysphere.

On this date in 1961, Warren Spahn won his 300th baseball game.

Last of the U.S. troops were ordered from Vietnam on this day in 1972.

12   First U.S. police force was formed in New Amsterdam, New York, on this day in 1658.

Lucy Stone, American suffragist, was born in 1818.

Mary Roberts Rinehart, American writer, was born in 1876.

13   This is the birthdate of

- William Caxton, 1422, the first English printer.
- Annie Oakley, 1860, American rifle expert whose targets resembled small, punched tickets.
- Alfred Hitchcock, 1899, renowned maker of mystery films.

14   On this day in 1040, Duncan was slain by Macbeth.

15   On this day in 309 B.C., an eclipse was recorded in Greece.

In 1057, Macbeth was slain by Malcolm.

First American hurricane recorded, in Plymouth, Massachusetts, in 1635.

17   Davy Crockett, American explorer-frontiersman, was born, 1786.

18   First English child to be born in North America: Virginia Dare, 1587.

On this day in 1972, the United States and the Soviet Union agreed on nuclear arms limitations.

19   Ogden Nash, American humorist and poet, was born in 1902.

National Aviation Day.

20   Benjamin Harrison, 23rd U.S. president, was born in 1833.

On this day in 1940, the Russian revolutionary thinker Trotsky was assassinated in Mexico City by a Stalinist agent.

21   Hawaii was proclaimed the 50th state of the Union in 1959.

Ozma, princess of the Emerald City, celebrates today as her day of birth.

22   First Jew arrived in America, Jacob Barsimson, in 1654.

On this day in 1865, liquid soap was patented.

Dorothy Parker, American writer & humorist, was born in New York, 1893.

24 On this day in 79 A.D., Mt. Vesuvius erupted, burying the city of Pompeii.

Jorge Luis Borges, Argentine author and one of the outstanding figures in all of literature, was born in 1889.

25 UFO Day.

26 First U.S. kindergarten established, 1873.

On this day in 1883, Krakatoa, an uninhabited Indonesian volcanic island, exploded, creating tidal waves that killed 36,000 people in faraway Java and Sumatra.

Women's suffrage, provided for in the 19th Amendment, became effective on this day in 1920.

27 Confucius, Chinese philosopher and founder of Chinese literature, was born in 551 B.C.

Lyndon Johnson, 36th U.S. president, was born in 1908.

On this day in 1916, Congress established the National Park Service.

In 1966, Francis Chichester began his solo circumnavigation of the world in his sailboat, *The Gypsy Moth IV.*

28 Johann Goethe, German poet, was born on this day in 1749.

Leo Tolstoy, Russian novelist and author of *War and Peace* and *Anna Karenina,* was born in 1828.

On this day in 1957, Senator Strom Thurmond set the filibuster record in that body by speaking for 24 hours and 18 minutes.

In 1963 Martin Luther King, Jr., delivered his famous "I Have a Dream" speech at the Lincoln Memorial.

On this date in 1968, British scientists, using sonar, detected several huge objects speeding through the water of Loch Ness in Scotland.

29 John Locke, English philosopher and educational theorist, was born in 1632.

First state Indian reservation was established in New Jersey in 1758.

30 On this day in 30 B.C., Cleopatra committed suicide.

In 1637, Anne Hutchinson (one of the founders of Rhode Island), spoke out against the legalism of the Massachusetts Puritans & was banished from Plymouth Colony. She settled on Long Island Sound & was killed by Indians in 1643, an event regarded in Massachusetts as an act of divine providence.

Mary Wollstonecraft Shelley, author of *Frankenstein,* was born in 1797 in London. She married the English poet Shelley.

Maria Montessori, educator, founder of schools for workers' children, was born in 1870 in Italy.

On this day in 1963, the Washington-Moscow hotline—an emergency communication link—was established. It is still in operation.

31 Caligula, infamous Roman emperor, was born on this day in 12 A.D.

R. Crumb, eccentric American cartoonist, was born in 1943.

William Saroyan, Armenian-American author, was born in 1908.

ugust

August receives its name from the Latin Augustus, as it is named for Augustus Caesar.

August Quotations

1 All sunshine makes a desert.

—Arabic proverb

2 Love is the reward of love.

—Johann Christoph Friedrich von Schiller

Help thy brother's boat across and lo! thine own has reached the shore.

—Hindu proverb

This delusion (experiencing separateness) is a kind of a prison for us, restricting us to our personal desires and to affection for a few persons nearest to us. Our task must be to free ourselves from this prison by widening our circle of compassion to embrace all living creatures and the whole of nature in its beauty.

—Albert Einstein

4 Liberty is the only thing you cannot have unless you give it away.

—William White

Freedom exists only when the people take care of the government.

—Woodrow Wilson

8 We Americans have no commission from God to police the world.

—Benjamin Harrison

10 Peace is not made in documents, but in the hearts of men.

—Herbert Hoover

15 When the hurricane passes, the whole ground is strewn with pears.

—Chinese proverb

20 I know what I meant.

—Richard Nixon

27 Now, therefore, the superior teacher leads his (her) students and does not pull them along. S/he urges them to go forward and does not suppress them. He opens the way to them, but does not take them to the place.

Leading without pulling makes the process of learning gentle. Urging without suppressing makes the process of learning easy and opening the way to the students without taking them to the place makes them think for themselves.

Now if the process of education is made gentle and easy and if the students are taught to think for themselves, we may call the (person) a good teacher.

—Confucius

August Events

Colorado Admitted to the Union (1876) [1]

Colorado is our 38th state.

Etymology: Colorado, which is Spanish for "colored, rusty red" was named after the great river of that name which arises in this state.

Shredded Wheat Patented (1893) [1]

Henry Perky of Denver, Colorado, turned wheat berries into threads by drawing the heat-softened grain through rollers. Eventually his airy wheat pillows were sold as shredded wheat to early morning tourists at Niagara Falls. Soon their fame spread throughout America.

Two cereals your students can make and sample:

Amish Cereal (3 cups)

3	cups whole wheat flour	1	tsp. salt
2	tsp. baking soda		buttermilk, as needed
1	cup brown sugar	1	tsp. vanilla

Bind dry ingredients with buttermilk. Add vanilla. Put mixture into cake pan. Bake at 300°F until golden brown. Cool & crumble. Store when dry in tightly sealed container.

Homemade Granola (12 + cups)

½ cup honey	1 cup wheat germ
⅓ cup brown sugar	½ cup vegetable oil
½ cup instant dry milk	½ tsp. salt
4½ cups oats	(1½ cups chopped nuts)

1   pkg. dried fruits, cut up into small pieces
½   cup peanut butter (with no preservatives)

Heat honey, sugar, peanut butter, and oil to a simmer. Combine the remaining ingredients and add honey mixture to dry ingredients. Mix well and spoon onto cookie sheet. Bake 1 hour at 300°F, stirring every 20 minutes or so. Remove from oven and transfer granola to cake pans. Pack down by placing weight (heavy skillet) on top of cereal and cool. (Thanks again, Dixie.)

First Solar-Heated Commercial Building (1957) [1]

Children need many opportunities to perform real actions on objects in contrast to just reading or hearing what others did. Facilitate these experiences with the following suggestions:

Solar-Heat Experiment for Young Children: Lay a sheet of white paper and a sheet of black paper side by side in the sun. Fill 2 Ziploc™ plastic bags with an equal number of ice cubes. Place 1 bag on the white paper and 1 bag on the black paper. Now what do you imagine will happen?

Check back on the bags in 10 minutes. What is happening? (Is it what you guessed would happen?) Finally, keep track of the 2 bags until 1 is filled with water. Is it the one you expected to melt first? Can you explain what happened, and why?

Solar Fun for Older Students: The first practical solar cells (photovoltaics) were developed in the mid-1950s, and the first application was to power satellites and far-off weather equipment. Today, solar cells are being used to pump water and heat buildings, for generating power to run watches, calculators, radios, battery chargers, electric fences, and street lights! Older students will be fascinated by the information and project suggestions found in the inexpensive solar cell manual: *Using Solar Cells for Fun, Education, Hobbies and Crafts.* It, as well as *Ranger Rick Solar Cells and Motors,* can be purchased from

Mr. Sun, Inc.
2504 Aga Dr.
Alexandria, MN 56308

Write, requesting their current supply and price list.

Friendship Day [2]

Etymology: The word "friend" comes from the Anglo-Saxon word *freond,* meaning "one who is loved." It is related to our word "free" (which comes from the Indo-European *prei,* to hold dear, and in Sanskrit *priya,* "dear, desired"). The basic sense of "free" is probably "dear to the chief" and therefore "not enslaved."

Here is a suggestion for a unique way in which to express international friendship.

Working Classroom Storytellers is a student-to-student cultural exchange. It involves the writing and sharing of life stories with people in Nicaragua. The stories appear in Spanish and/or English and are sent in booklet form to students in central America.

For more information, write to

> Working Classroom Storytellers
> 218A Gold SW
> Albuquerque, NM 87102

Missouri Admitted to the Union (1821) [10]

Missouri is our 24th state.

Etymology: The word Missouri comes from a Native American (Illinois tribe) word *Emissourita,* which means "the people who dwell on the Big Muddy," which was their name for the Missouri River.

Birth of Herbert Hoover (1874) [10]

Herbert Clark Hoover, the 34th U.S. president, was in office from 1929 to 1933—exactly the time of the Great Depression in America. In fact, he once said, "It is my dubious honor to have been given sole credit for the Great Depression."

If you want extensive materials on this president, write to

> Herbert Hoover Library
> West Branch, IA 52358

Birth of Alex Haley (1921) [11]

This black writer helped create a new interest in genealogy in America with his novel *Roots,* which traces people from Africa who were kidnapped and brought to the American South as slaves and who struggled through the years to find their freedom and dignity in America.

Classroom Family Trees

Note: This activity is not appropriate for all classrooms. If you have students who will be made uncomfortable—for any reason—tracing his or her genealogy, please do not include this activity in your lesson plans.

Family trees can be a lot of fun for whole families to work on together. Following are various formats for family trees, but often the students or their parents will develop their own thoroughly personal creations.

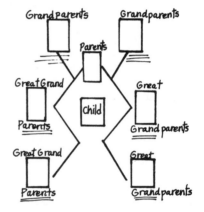

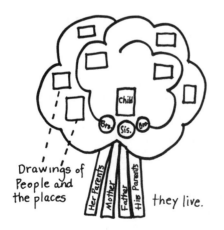

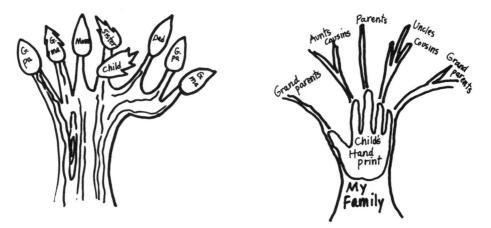

Etymology: "Genealogy" comes from the Greek *genos,* meaning "family" or "race," and *logos,* meaning "a discourse" or "a long treatment of a subject."

Language Arts: Talk with your students about the idea of family trees. When do they imagine these were first made? Why were they important to kings and queens? Are they important today? Why? And why not?

Encourage them to look up the genealogy of an English queen or king and to make up imaginary family trees for famous storybook characters.

First U.S. Hurricane Recorded (1635) [15]

Etymology: The word "hurricane" comes from the Spanish. The first written mention of this word appeared in 1555 by the Spanish explorers of the New World:

These tempestes . . . which the Grecians caule Tiphones they caule (here) furocanes: violénte and furious . . . that which plucked uppe great trees.

You can receive information on hurricanes and other natural hazards such as tornadoes and lightning, as well as *Oakie Skywarn's Weather Book* and NOAA Weather Radio, by writing

> NOAA
> National Logistics Supply Ctr.
> 510 E. Bannister Rd.
> Kansas City, MO 64131

National Aviation Day

Etymology: The word "aviation" comes directly from the Latin *avis* which means "bird."

An aviation time line can be researched and executed with three-dimensional paper plane models. Students might include the ornithopter designed by da Vinci (c. 1550), Stringfellow and Hensen's idea of steam-powered flight (1840), Langley's unfortunate aerodome (December 8, 1903), the Wright brothers at Kitty Hawk, North Carolina (December 17, 1903), Curtiss's June Bug (1908), Farmsman's biplane (1909), the first crossing of the English Channel, military planes, Lindbergh, Earhart, & Rickenbaker.

Transworld Airlines offers "Flight," a brochure that explains how a plane flies, and "A History of TWA Aircraft," a very interesting black and white fold-out which compares the 18 airplanes which TWA has flown over the last 60-plus years.

> TWA
> P.O. Box 20007
> Kansas City, MO 64195

Birth of Benjamin Harrison (1833) [20]

His presidency (1889–1893) was marked by new ventures in foreign policy and by a deteriorating domestic situation. Harrison carried out his duties as president conscientiously and with dignity and ability, but he failed to provide strong leadership.

He lost out in his bid for reelection in 1892 and after leaving Washington returned to his law practice in Indianapolis. He had 3 children by 2 marriages and died in 1901.

Hawaii Admitted to the Union (1959) [21]

Hawaii is our 50th state.

Etymology: Hawaii is a Hawaiian word related to the Marquesan *Havaike,* the name of the traditional homeland of the Polynesians.

Liquid Soap Patented (1865) [22]

Bubble-blowing is a great summer science experience! Choose a calm, sunny day for this activity, and cover tables & floor with plastic drop cloths—as the bubbles may stain some surfaces. You may want each child to put on a big T-shirt over his or her own clothes to help protect them.

Young children will use plastic straws, clear tubing, meat basters, and empty spools. Each group of four children is given a flat pan of this mixture:

8 Tbs. liquid dishwashing soap
1 qt. warm water
1 Tbs. glycerine (sold in pharmacies, it strengthens bubble surface)

Then turn the children loose. Encourage their experimentation and speculation.

Bubble-Making for Older Students. Bigger bubble-blowers can be made from big tin cans with both ends removed or wire (coathangers) bent into circles with wire handle sticking out. Another bubble producer can be created by threading 3 feet of kite string through 2 halves of a plastic drinking straw. Tie ends of string together & tuck this knot inside one of the straws. Wet hands with the first batch of soapy mixture given; then grasp one straw in either hand and lower string into bubble solution. Pull outward on string to form a rectangle. Lift this slowly out of the solution while maintaining the rectangle. A film will cover the rectangle. Hold this out from your body, parallel to the ground. Gently but firmly pull rectangle upward. A huge bubble should form. Bring the 2 straws together to close off the bubble and set it free. A surefire winner!

The big tin cans and wire circles can also produce fine results. Dip the can or wire into soap mixture to form a film over opening. Take a deep breath and blow gently and steadily (through the open end of can) near the film to form bubble. Sharply twist can or wire to disengage bubble. Try your own techniques!

Bubble Art* Put ½" of water in a large flat pan. Add ¼ cup of liquid detergent and 1 tablespoon of blue food coloring. Use 1 hand to tilt the pan toward you, raising the water level at end of pan nearest you. Use a plastic drinking straw to blow lots of bubbles in the water until they cover the surface. Lay pan flat again and quickly lay a sheet of white paper the same size as the pan on top of the bubbles without allowing the paper to sink into water. Carefully remove paper and let dry. If color is too light, add more blue food coloring. Once the paper is dry, use crayons, markers, or watercolors to make a picture that incorporates the bubble background. This could be a picture of skindiving, outer space, or the inside of an aquarium.

Variations: Use crayons to color deep sea creatures or the Loch Ness monster or sunken ships before you apply the bubble effect. Then dip the paper in the bubbles, dry. Add yellow mixture in pan and redip the edges of your paper to form a frame for the picture.

UFO Day [25]

People have been reporting unidentified flying objects for the past 40 years. Children are often fascinated by the idea of UFOs.

On this day in 1951, two Texans saw a flash of light outside of Lubbock and then an enormous spaceship with blue lights along its sides silently passed overhead! The Texans quickly phoned the police. Twenty minutes later, four scientists from Texas Technical Institute

---

*This idea comes from the Oregon Museum of Science & Technology in Portland, Oregon.

sighted strange blue lights in the sky. They took photographs to show the authorities. No one has ever been able to explain these incidents.

UFO Creative Writing. The subject of unknown aliens and outerspace visitors can encourage several creative writing activities. Students can create stories and blank verse poems based on these themes: *Life on Earth* (as seen by a creature from another galaxy), *A Secret Friend* (how you discovered an alien and what you did together), *Taken up into Space* (how you were captured by outer space robots, what you did up in their ship and how and why you returned to earth), *I Am Really a Space Alien* (imaginary diary entries by [you as] a celestial visitor, with details about your entry into earth's atmosphere and how things are going—what you are thinking/feeling about your stay on this planet!).

A Spaceman Reading Tachistoscope. This encourages children to review the specific phonetic elements they need to practice.

Each student will require 2 sheets of colored tagboard, scissors, markers, and 2 long (2" × 20") strips of white paper. Discuss with the children how spacemen might look (robotlike heads, several eyes, or antennae). Then ask them to each design an alien's head—the stranger the better. Give each a piece of tagboard (their choice of color) and have them fill the tagboard with their head design. If they can use scissors well, have them cut out their head designs, or you may do this. Each head will need mouth holes which can be quickly cut by the teacher using a sharp X-acto™ knife and laying spaceman head on several thick newspapers. A second head for each child is made by tracing around first head on second sheet of tagboard. Once both heads are cut out, they are stapled on either side.

Learn what initial digraphs and blends each child needs to practice, such as th, wh, sh, ch. On the first strip of paper, using markers, the student will (in a long line down the strip) print the blend he or she needs to practice. Each time the student prints the blend, he or she may use a different color of pen.

On the second strip of paper, going straight down, the student will print these word endings, according to the blend which is to be practiced:

th (-an, -at, -aw, -in, -ick, -is, -e, -em, -en, -ere, -ese, -ey, -ose, -ud, -ug); sh (-ack, -ag, -in, -ip, -ell, -ed, -els, -op, -ock, -ot, -ow, -uck, -ut); ch (-at, -ar, -ip, -in, -ick, -ill, -eck, -op, -ug, -uck, -um); wh (-ack, -am, -ap, -ee, -eel, -eat, -ip, -iz, -im, -op)

Once strips are printed & checked by teacher for errors, for example, reversals, child inserts blend strip in left opening & ending strip in right opening. Strips are then systematically moved from topmost letters down & word that appears in combined opening is read by student to the teacher or to a child who has already mastered this initial digraph.

Paper-clip strips to spaceman head & use to periodically review blends and endings.

Birth of Mary Wollstonecraft Godwin Shelley (1797) [30]

At age 17, Mary eloped to Europe with the English poet Percy Shelley, accompanied by Mary's stepsister Claire. During the summer of 1816, Mary, Claire, Shelley, and the romantic poet Byron spent time together, writing by day and sharing their works of an evening. It was in this circumstance that Mary wrote the most widely known of science fiction novels, *Frankenstein.*

When Shelley's first wife died, Mary and he were married. They had four children, three of whom died young. Shelley himself was drowned in a storm off Tuscany in 1822 at the age of 32. Mary spent the rest of her life (until 1851) raising their only surviving child, Percy, and caring for her aged father until his death in 1836.

Mary wrote numerous historical novels, essays, and travel books. *Frankenstein* remains the best known of her work.

An Outdoor Game for August

Camouflage and Seek! is a game to be played out in nature, which helps youngsters understand the concept of camouflage. You will need scarves for blindfolds. One child, the predator, is blindfolded & stands in the middle of the play area. All the others are prey: to survive, they must blend in with their surroundings so that the predator cannot see them!

At a signal, the prey run and hide as carefully as they can. They must each be able to still see the predator. Once the prey are all hidden, the predator removes the blindfold. Without moving from that very spot, the predator tries to sight any of the prey. Once he or she describes loudly the hiding place of a child, that player comes out and joins the predator in the center of the play area. When the predator can spot no one else, he or she and all the captive prey are blindfolded. A circle is drawn on the ground around these kids, & they are not to go over this line.

Any remaining prey change their hiding places and find new ones, where again, they can see the predator. Then the blindfolds are removed, and, staying within their circle, the predators try to sight the remaining prey.

In this way, the game continues until only 1 prey player is left. This child should share any camouflage tricks and techniques with the rest of the players. Whenever you play this game again, the remaining prey gets to be the first predator to start off Camouflage & Seek!

August Field Trip Suggestions

If you live near an air force base, contact the public information officer & arrange a visit which might include learning about air traffic control systems & radar equipment by speaking with pilots and navigators.

Other field trip ideas include the kitchen of a large Chinese restaurant at a very slow "prep" period of the day, a walk that involves filling large garbage bags with litter from the roadsides or empty lots in your neighborhood, or a gold-panning trip to a small river or brook (take extra adults and dry clothes along for this one).

August Paper Rod Puppets

These puppets have exceptionally smooth movements because their limbs are joined together with small metal rivets used in leather work.

For each puppet, you will need a piece of 9″ × 16″ tagboard, 6 rivets (available from leather craftstores), hammer, pencil, ruler, scissors, paper punch, 2 thumbtacks, 2 thin wooden dowels ¼″ in diameter by 20″ long, and markers or poster paints. Some special effects may require feathers, lace, sequins, fur, & yarn, but this is up to each child's personal artistic vision.

Show the class a sample pattern you have drawn on a piece of 9″ × 16″ tagboard. (Emphasize that this is just to give them the idea of possible puppet parts needed to make a rod puppet.)

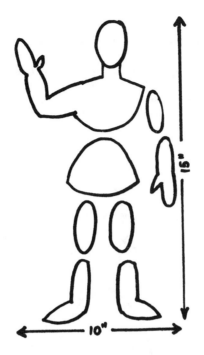

Encourage them to come up with a variation on this pattern which they draw on scrap paper. Also encourage them to share ideas with one another. Animals and birds can also be designed. Next, each student transfers his or her drawing to scale onto the tagboard.

The puppets are carefully cut out and holes are punched where parts are to be joined.

Puppets are colored or painted & extra details glued onto tagboard if child wishes.

Place parts that are to be joined with holes matching. Fit top & bottom sections of rivet through holes. Place puppet parts on top of a piece of scrap wood which will take the impact of the hammering. Use hammer to gently tap & set the rivet. Don't pound rivet pieces together or puppet joints will be stiff.

(If possible, cut & sand one end of each dowel at a 45°angle: this is not essential, but it will improve puppet manipulation possibilities.) Now attach the cut end of one dowel to the back of puppet head by using a hot glue gun to adhere dowel to head or by pushing a thumbtack through front of puppet head into the dowel. Attach second dowel via thumbtack at cut off end to back of the hand on the joined arm. The children can move these puppets by taking one dowel in each hand & setting the puppet's feet on a hard surface like a desktop or puppet stage. By moving the rods, the puppets can be made to bow, dance, jump, do the splits, run, kick—whatever the script demands.

Getting Off to a Glorious Start! _____

Here are some ways you can prepare for your upcoming school year, ahead of time!

BIRTHDAY CROWNS

This is for very young children. Using a pencil, ruler, & the accompanying illustration, make a posterboard master pattern for the birthday crown. Then trace this onto a variety of colors of posterboard (not construction paper—it's too thin and band will tear). Trace one crown for each child in your upcoming class. Cut out each crown & carefully glue sequins, flat-backed jewels from odd earrings (these can be found sometimes at Goodwill), and lines & triangles of glitter to the front & sides of each crown. Once dry, these birthday crowns are put in a safe place in your room and can be whipped out to add glamor to each child's birthday celebration.

LITTLE BLANK BOOKS

Use good-quality scrap paper from a printer to cut and assemble little (hand-sized) blank books, 3 or 4 for each of your students. These books will have colorful covers (construction paper or wallpaper) and can be cut in a variety of simple geometric shapes. Staple the cover to the blank paper (4 to 10 sheets in each book). Keep these little books at the ready for almost daily use in the early grades! If you feel ambitious, this is a fine time to make up a collection of scroll and accordion fold-out books too!

RHYMING-NAME READERS

If you can secure a class list of the children who will be in your room in the fall, try creating a little beginning reader based on words that rhyme with each of their first names, for example, A Book for Bob (or Rob). At the bottom of each blank page a word is printed job, mob, rob, sob, Bob (cob, knob, gob are other possibilities). The child draws a simple picture above each word and then can rapidly read & reread his personal reader.* Eventually, you can use short adventure stories based on each child's name. Here's one about a boy and a shark. Again, children should illustrate each page.

Thin Quinn

Thin Quinn goes in. Thin Quinn goes in up to his shin.
Thin Quinn goes in up to his chin.
Oh, no! See the thin fin, Quinn! The fin is after Quinn.
But Quinn has a pin. Quinn sticks the pin into the fin!
Thin Quinn, YOU win! No more thin fin!
Thin Quinn has a big grin!!

LARGE-SIZED GEOMETRIC PUZZLES

These help to develop children's mental and manual skills, giving them practice in discerning size, shape, parts of a whole, & area relationships. Cut each puzzle from heavy cardboard, chipboard, or plywood, and (spray) paint each puzzle a different color for easy differentiation. Solutions for each puzzle can be shown on a color-coded chart, but students should first try to make each geometric shape by themselves before referring to the answer chart.

---

*When children's names are too complex (e.g., Juanita, Alexander) you may offer the child a little ME book. The pages of these books would read me, bee, he, see, we (tree, three, she, sea, tea, key, knee can be introduced later).

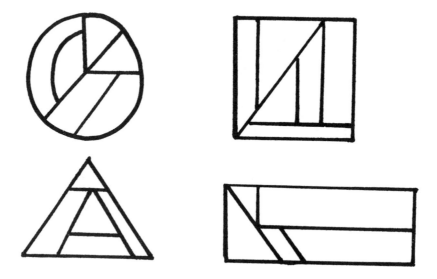

A Collapsible Puppet Theater

You can make one in an afternoon, using only a mat knife and a hot glue gun. The theater, whose construction is shown on the next two pages, folds flat for easy storage.

A Sounds Tape

To help improve your students' listening skills, this can be easily made in the summer. Tape record a short introduction that describes how the tape of sounds can help them to really hear details & then tape a familiar sound for 10–15 seconds, leave a blank spot & repeat process until you have 15–20 Sounds of our Town, or Sounds of Summer, or ask the children for some topic suggestions.

Things to Collect

For very young children, collect examples of "things we already can read," for example, the skull & crossbones picture on a dangerous liquids bottle, an example of the crossed-out cigarette sign meaning "No Smoking," a picture (drawing) of a Stop sign or Watch Out for Children sign, an undulating dark shape in the grass = SNAKE, a picture of a steaming kettle = HOT, photographs depicting different facial expressions, and so on. Youngsters love to show how they already can read—a change in the weather, the time of day, the season. Encourage them to bring in additions to this class collection.

Little objects can be used by children to demonstrate comparative size, weight, length, height, color, smoothness, and math sets and subsets, for example, "The keys, buttons, and pennies are a set because people use them, but the keys and pennies are a subset because they are made of metal." Any plausible reasoning is acceptable! You'll want to save large nuts & bolts,

PATTERN FOR COLLAPSIBLE PUPPET THEATER

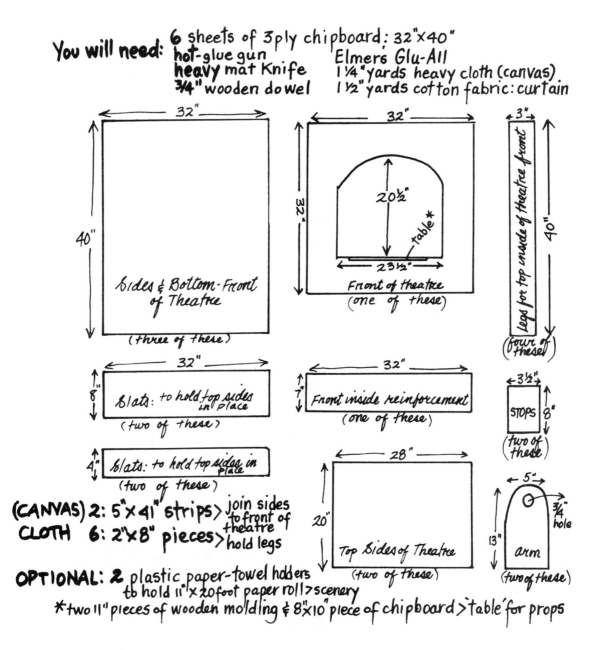

You will need: 6 sheets of 3ply chipboard: 32"x40"
hot-glue gun   Elmers Glu-All
heavy mat knife   1¼" yards heavy cloth (canvas)
¾" wooden dowel   1½" yards cotton fabric: curtain

40" × 32" — Sides & Bottom-Front of Theatre (three of these)

32" × 32" — Front of theatre (one of these) — 20½", 23½", table *

3" × 40" — Legs for top inside of theatre front (four of these)

8" × 32" — Slats: to hold top sides in place (two of these)

7" × 32" — Front inside reinforcement (one of these)

3½" × 8" — STOPS (two of these)

4" × Slats: to hold top sides in place (two of these)

20" × 28" — Top Sides of Theatre (two of these)

5" — arm — 13", ¾" hole (two of these)

(CANVAS) 2: 5"x 41" strips > join sides to front of theatre
CLOTH   6: 2"x 8" pieces > hold legs

OPTIONAL: 2 plastic paper-towel holders to hold 11"x 20 foot paper roll > scenery
* two 11" pieces of wooden molding & 8"x10" piece of chipboard > table for props

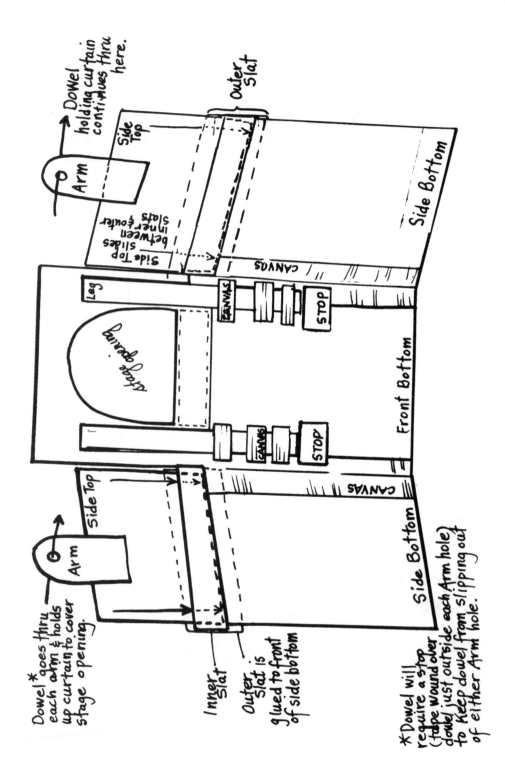

Dowel
holding curtain
continues thru
here.

Outer
Slat

Side
Top

Arm

Side Top slides
between
inner & outer
slats

CANVAS

Side Bottom

Leg

stage opening

CANVAS

STOP

Front Bottom

STOP

CANVAS

Side Top

Arm

Side Bottom

Inner Slat

Outer
Slat is
glued to front
of side bottom

Dowel * goes thru
each arm & holds
up curtain to cover
stage opening.

*Dowel will
require a stop
(tape wound over
dowel just outside each Arm hole)
to keep dowel from slipping out
of either Arm hole.

keys and foreign coins of all kinds, bottle caps, big bright buttons, large glass jewels (from a costume or theatrical supply house). These little objects can be wrapped separately in colored tissue, tied with gold metalic thread, & put in a Birthday Grab Bag from which each student gets to draw a surprise gift on or near his or her birthday. Always a big hit!

an afterword

I hope you will drop me a line (in care of the publisher) and share your teaching experiences with me. I always enjoy hearing about projects that have gone well, or suggestions on how the 'Almanack' might be modified or expanded.

If you send the description of a learning activity or teaching idea, I'll reciprocate with a small southwestern-token-of-appreciation! ... (be sure to include the grade level of your class this year...)

THANK YOU Gene and Alba for the affection and support you gave me during the months it took to complete this manuscript!

¡Un mil gracias, Kathleen! for the million keys you pressed in typing it all up — and for the gems of wisdom you included with each month's pages!

Looking forward to hearing from you, dear reader,

Warm regards,
Dana

INDEX OF ACTIVITIES